The Epidemiology of Cocaine Use and Abuse

Editors:

Susan Schober, Ph.D.
Division of Epidemiology and Prevention Research
National Institute on Drug Abuse

Charles Schade, M.D., M.P.H.
Division of Epidemiology and Prevention Research
National Institute on Drug Abuse

Research Monograph 110
1991

U.S. DEPARTMENT OF HEALTH AND HUMAN SERVICES
Public Health Service
Alcohol, Drug Abuse, and Mental Health Administration

National Institute on Drug Abuse
5600 Fishers Lane
Rockville, MD 20857

For sale by the U.S. Government Printing Office
Superintendent of Documents, Mail Stop: SSOP, Washington, DC 20402-9328
ISBN 0-16-035854-X

ACKNOWLEDGMENT

This monograph is based on the papers from a technical review on "The Epidemiology of Cocaine Use and Abuse" held on May 3–4, 1988, in Rockville, MD. The review meeting was sponsored by the Division of Epidemiology and Prevention Research of the National Institute on Drug Abuse.

DHHS publication number (ADM) 91–1787
Printed 1991

NIDA Research Monographs are indexed in the *Index Medicus*. They are selectively included in the coverage of *American Statistics Index, BioSciences Information Service, Chemical Abstracts, Current Contents, Psychological Abstracts*, and *Psychopharmacology Abstracts*.

Contents

Page

Introduction

Susan E. Schober and Charles P. Schade

A technical review meeting entitled "The Epidemiology of Cocaine Use and Abuse" was held in Rockville, Maryland, on May 3–4, 1988. The purpose of the meeting, sponsored by the Division of Epidemiology and Prevention Research of the National Institute on Drug Abuse, was to discuss current research since the last technical review meeting on this topic in 1984 and to define research needs. Four areas of research were covered—trends in cocaine use, health and social consequences related to cocaine use and abuse, the natural history of cocaine abuse and predisposing factors for cocaine use, and the economics and distribution of cocaine. The proceedings of this meeting are presented in the following chapters.

Surveys describing trends in cocaine use in general population groups are presented by Rouse, O'Malley and Johnson, and Smart. Rouse reports on trends in cocaine use among U.S. household residents aged 12 and older based on the National Household Survey on Drug Abuse for 1972 through 1985. She describes demographic characteristics of the cocaine users and makes important observations on the association of cocaine use and its perceived availability. The ongoing series of surveys of American high school seniors entitled Monitoring the Future is described by O'Malley and Johnson. These surveys show declining rates of cocaine use with later ages of onset. Smart presents data from general population surveys of illicit drug use in Canada. Overall, rates of use in Canada are much lower than in the United States.

In contrast to these general population groups, cocaine use among high-risk populations is much more common. Wish presents data on arrestees from the Drug Use Forecasting survey, sponsored by the National Institute of Justice. Among arrestees who voluntarily participated, about half of the urine samples screened for illicit drugs tested positive for cocaine. Of those who tested positive for cocaine, an alarming 20 to 40 percent preferred to inject.

Health and social consequences related to cocaine use described in this monograph include psychiatric disorders, overdose deaths, violence, and criminal activity. Anthony and Petronis present longitudinal data from the Epidemiologic Catchment Area (ECA) study that demonstrate that cocaine use is associated with an increased risk of panic attacks, persistent depression, mania, and self-reported symptoms of delusions and hallucinations. The study of medical examiner records presented by Ruttenber and others indicates that severe atherosclerosis increases the risk of dying from a cocaine overdose. Goldstein et al. describe the association of violence and cocaine use as determined by ethnographic research in New York City's lower east side. The authors present a conceptual framework for studying violence that underscores the complex relationship with cocaine use. Hunt describes a similarly complex association. The interaction between cocaine use and crime appears to be influenced by a common set of characteristics among criminals and heavy drug users: the drug lifestyle, low income, and a prior history of delinquency.

Studies of risk factors of cocaine use and abuse and studies describing the clinical presentation of cocaine dependence are presented next. Kandel's analysis of drug use among a nationally representative sample of youth aged 19 through 26 validates the "gateway" theory of drug use and progression. Cocaine users almost always precede this habit with use of tobacco, alcohol, and marijuana. Ritter and Anthony present a longitudinal analysis of the ECA study showing that depression is associated with initiating cocaine use. This finding supports the self-medication hypothesis presented by Khantzian. Through clinical observations of users, he suggests that heavy use requiring treatment is associated with feeling-state dysfunction and that users may be attempting to treat their own underlying depression or lack of self-esteem. Rounsaville and Carroll also found psychological illness among heavy cocaine users seeking treatment. In their study, major depression was often associated with heavy cocaine use, and alcoholism was a frequent concomitant diagnosis. Adams and Gfroerer report on the prevalence of cocaine dependence and abuse among the U.S. household population and examine risk factors for cocaine dependence. Inciardi presents results of ethnographic research on crack and other cocaine use among youth in Miami.

The last chapters are concerned with the economics and distribution of cocaine. Characteristics of international cocaine trafficking are discussed by Montagne. He describes the sources of the supply of cocaine, historical changes in international distribution patterns, and social phenomena of trafficking networks and their implications for controlling cocaine trafficking. Rinfret presents data on the price and purity of cocaine in the illicit market. These figures indicate the increasing availability of cocaine during the 1980s. For example, import prices of cocaine hydrochloride fell from a range of $47,000–$70,000 per kilogram in 1982 to $10,000–$38,000 in 1988. Street purity increased during that time to more than 70 percent. The wide availability of cocaine in this country is also examined by Shreckengost. He presents a dynamic simulation model that estimates cocaine imports into the United States. These apparently increased from approximately 25 metric tons in 1975 to 180 metric tons in 1984.

Two issues stood out in the discussion of these scientific presentations. The first was methodologic: the need for clear and consistent definitions of abuse, dependence, and use of cocaine so that researchers and policymakers can compare data from different sources without misinterpretation. The second was observational. Population-based estimates of cocaine use show a decline in the number of users in the United States and less new use among teenagers and young adults. Simultaneously, measures of consequences related to cocaine abuse are increasing. These include gang-related violence, crime, overdoses requiring medical treatment, and death. These divergent observations can be explained by several factors. Specifically, the increased incidence of consequences may result from more intensive use by current cocaine users, including greater frequency, higher doses, and more intensive routes of administration. In addition, some consequences may reflect chronic effects from long-term cocaine use. The reduced price and increased purity of cocaine may also explain some of the increases. A final explanation of the divergence in prevalence of use and consequences is that surveys measuring prevalence may not capture groups who have the highest prevalence of use and who are most likely to use cocaine intensively.

Additional research is needed on the association of cocaine with violence, especially crack cocaine and homicide. Mechanisms of death from cocaine overdose need further elucidation. The teratologic effects of cocaine are not well described in humans, and this area is worthy of more study. Further psychopharmacologic observations may provide more insight into the relationship between cocaine use and psychiatric disturbances and reinforce or refute the self-medication hypothesis. Such studies may also yield more effective treatment for cocaine addicts. Further epidemiologic research is needed to describe physiologic and psychiatric consequences related to cocaine use. Studies are needed to describe both acute and chronic effects and to relate consequences to frequency, duration, and intensity of use. Finally, future survey research will be important in establishing whether the present downturn in number of cocaine users is merely a pause in a relentless, malignant social process, or the beginning of the end of the most recent cocaine epidemic.

AUTHORS

Susan E. Schober, Ph.D.
Division of Epidemiology and
Prevention Research
National Institute on Drug Abuse
5600 Fishers Lane
Rockville, MD 20857

Charles P. Schade, M.D., M.P.H.
Office of Professional Affairs
American Public Health Association
1015 15th Street, NW
Washington, DC 20005

Trends in Cocaine Use in the General Population

Beatrice A. Rouse

As a Schedule II drug under the Controlled Substances Act of 1970, cocaine is classified as a substance with accepted medical use and a high potential for abuse that may lead to severe physical or psychological dependence. Other Schedule II drugs include morphine and other opiates and amphetamines and other stimulants. Cocaine hydrochloride is used medically to anesthetize mucous membranes of the oral, laryngeal, and nasal cavities. Its use as a topical anesthetic in ophthalmology has been reduced because of its corneal toxicity (American Hospital Formulary Service 1988). Although technically a legal drug, the amount of cocaine used illegally in this country has now surpassed its use for medical purposes.

HISTORICAL BACKGROUND

During the 19th century, cocaine was available in the United States as an ingredient in patent medicines and was prescribed by physicians for a variety of physical and mental ailments. However, cocaine was not regulated until the Harrison Narcotic Act in 1914. Thereafter, all producers and distributors of cocaine were required to maintain records and register with the Federal Government. Cocaine was first defined as a narcotic in 1922, and the importation of cocaine and coca leaves was prohibited except for controlled pharmaceutic purposes (Amendment to Narcotic Drugs and Export Act 1922).

In the early 1930s, amphetamines became available; with their similar effects and longer duration, amphetamines delayed the widespread nonmedical use of cocaine for the next 30 years. Indeed, in a controlled clinical study at the University of Chicago, subjects found the immediate effects of intravenous cocaine and of amphetamines indistinguishable (Van Dyke and Byck 1982). Amphetamines, along with hallucinogens and other nonnarcotic drugs used nonmedically, were labeled "dangerous drugs" under the Drug Abuse Control Amendments of 1965. This widening of the concept of drug abuse or nonmedical drug use resulted from the public concern about the growing acceptance among youth and young adults of using marijuana, hallucinogens, amphetamines, and other drugs for "recreation."

Early in the 1970s, the National Commission on Marihuana and Drug Abuse evaluated the various dangerous drugs in terms of their (1) risk to health, (2) risk of drug-induced behavior, and (3) dependence liability. The Commission stated that "Cocaine, like heroin, is a drug with high dependence liability and appeals to the same vulnerable populations attracted to heroin use and intravenous amphetamine use" (1973, p. 218). In addition, they recommended that the American Medical Association (AMA) determine whether cocaine had any "unique therapeutic use" and, if not, they recommended that the manufacture of cocaine be prohibited. What, if any, action was taken by the AMA is unknown; however, subsequent to this Commission report, the manufacture of cocaine was not prohibited.

The dependency-producing property of cocaine was recognized not only by the Commission but also by the general population. In 1971, a National Household Survey sponsored by the Commission asked respondents whether a variety of drugs including cocaine, alcohol, and tobacco were addictive. An addictive drug was defined as one that "anyone who uses it regularly becomes physically and/or psychologically dependent on it and can't get along without it" (p. 128). Among the adults aged 18 and older, only heroin was considered addictive by more people than was cocaine (88 versus 75 percent). Among the youth aged 12 to 17 years, however, cocaine was considered less addictive than several other drugs. The proportions of youth who considered heroin, barbiturates, and alcohol to be addictive were 88, 72, and 71 percent, respectively, compared with 66 percent who considered cocaine to be addictive. Over 50 percent of both adults and youth considered marijuana addictive with regular use, but it was seen as the least addictive of the several drugs presented.

In recent years, a variety of sources has indicated an accelerated increase in self-perceived cocaine dependency as well as increased cocaine-related medical problems. These include physician contacts (Weinstein et al. 1986), a study of a Veterans Administration psychiatric population (Brower et al. 1986), the 800-Cocaine Hotline (Washton and Gold 1987), and the Drug Abuse Warning Network's cocaine-related emergency room episodes and medical examiners' cases (NIDA 1988*b*). These studies of treatment populations and medical emergency episodes provide important information on the casualties of drug abuse.

Most illicit drug use increased after 1972, reached its highest level in 1979, and then declined more or less steadily. Illicit cocaine use, in contrast, did not reach its peak until the mid 1980s. This difference in trend line and rate of increase for cocaine compared with marijuana and most other drugs during the last decade was found in several nontreatment population studies in addition to the National Household Survey on Drug Abuse (NIDA 1988*a*). For example, Johnston et al. (1988) found these trends in both high school seniors and college students for lifetime and past year use. Dezelsky, Toohey, and Shaw (1985), who studied college students at five universities from 1970 to 1984, also found cocaine use vastly increased during this time. While the lifetime rate of marijuana use among the college students doubled, cocaine use increased tenfold from 2.7 percent in 1970 to 30 percent in 1984.

METHOD

This chapter examines the trends in nonmedical cocaine use in household residents aged 12 and older living in the coterminous United States. Data are provided from the National Institute on Drug Abuse (NIDA)-sponsored series of National Household Surveys on Drug Abuse conducted since 1972 (NIDA 1988*a*). For each survey in the series, the same methodology was used. A national area multistage probability sample of households was drawn; Alaska and Hawaii were not included. Because drug use is more prevalent in younger people, those aged 25 and under were oversampled to provide more stable estimates for these ages.

In the analyses, data were weighted to adjust for different probabilities of selection so that each survey reflected the actual distribution of the age groups in the population. The response rate for each of the surveys was at least 80 percent. Respondents participated in a structured personal interview in which the interviewer recorded information on cigarette use and demographic characteristics. The respondents filled in answer sheets on their use of marijuana, cocaine, hallucinogens, inhalants, heroin, alcohol, and the nonmedical use of prescription-type sedatives, stimulants, tranquilizers, and analgesics.

Estimates of drug use from these surveys may be considered conservative for several reasons. First, these surveys did not include the homeless or persons living in military installations, dormitories, other group quarters, and institutions such as hospitals and jails where more drug abusers may be found. Second, the estimates of drug use are based on self-reports. While self-reported drug use rates may be conservative, methodological studies indicate that reliable data can be obtained from self-reports (Rouse et al. 1985). Finally, while the rates for any household survey may be a conservative estimate of the illicit drug use at that time, the trends over time may be considered a reliable estimate of the general direction of drug use rates in the noninstitutionalized population.

COCAINE PREVALENCE RATES (1972–85)

Trends in the rates of cocaine use in the general population as measured by NIDA's National Household Survey are shown in table 1 for adults aged 18 years and older. In general, prevalence increased steadily from 1972 to 1985.

TABLE 1. *Trends in percentage of adults aged 18 years and older reporting lifetime and past month use of cocaine, U.S. household population, selected years 1972–85*

	1972	1974	1976	1979	1982	1985
Lifetime	3.2%	3.4%	4.1%	9.0%	14.8%	12.5%
Past month	0.9	0.7	0.7	2.6	3.0	3.2

SOURCE: National Household Survey on Drug Abuse, NIDA 1988*a*.

Significant differences exist in the levels of nonmedical cocaine use by age group. The rates in lifetime, past year, and past month cocaine use are shown by age group in table 2. Young adults (18–25 years) had higher prevalence rates than any other age group for lifetime, past year, and past month cocaine use regardless of the year of the survey. In addition to the age group difference in absolute level of cocaine use, the groups also differed in the peak year of use. Current cocaine use peaked for young adults in 1979, for youth (12–17 years) in 1982, and for older adults (26 and over) in 1985.

Because young adults are the high-risk age group, it is useful to examine the recency of their cocaine use as an indicator of the level of experimental versus continual use. A measure of recency of use or continuation rates can be achieved by examining the proportion of those who had

TABLE 2. *Trends in percentage of U.S. household population reporting lifetime, past year, and past month use of cocaine by age group, selected years 1972–85*

Age	1972	1974	1976	1977	1979	1982	1985
12–17 years							
N*	(880)	(952)	(986)	(1,272)	(2,165)	(1,581)	(2,287)
Lifetime	0.5%	3.6%	3.4%	4.0%	5.4%	6.5%	4.9%
Past year	1.5	2.7	2.3	2.6	4.2	4.1	4.0
Past month	0.6	1.0	1.0	0.8	1.4	1.6	1.5
18–25 years							
N*	(772)	(849)	(882)	(1,500)	(2,044)	(1,283)	(1,804)
Ever used	9.1	12.7	13.4	19.1	27.5	28.3	25.2
Past year	NA	8.1	7.0	10.2	19.6	18.8	16.3
Past month	NA	3.1	2.0	3.7	9.3	6.8	7.6
26+ years							
N*	(1,613)	(2,221)	(1,708)	(1,820)	(3,015)	(2,760)	(3,947)
Lifetime	1.6	0.9	1.6	2.6	4.3	8.5	9.5
Past year	NA	†	0.6	0.9	2.0	3.8	4.2
Past month	NA	†	†	†	0.9	1.2	2.0

SOURCE: National Household Survey on Drug Abuse, NIDA 1988*a*.
* Unweighted sample sizes.
† Less than 0.5 percent.
NA Not available.

ever tried cocaine who were still using cocaine in the past month. In 1974, 24 percent of the young adults who had tried cocaine were using it currently; in 1979, 34 percent were using it currently, and in 1985, 30 percent were using it currently. While the overall prevalence rates for cocaine use were lower for youth than for young adults, it should be noted that in each survey year at least a fourth of the youth who tried cocaine used it currently.

In 1985, for the first time, a measure of the regularity of cocaine use in the past year was obtained. Young adults were more likely to have used cocaine at least monthly in the past year (4.1 percent) than youth (1.5 percent), adults aged 26–34 (3.0 percent), or adults aged 35+ (less than 0.5 percent). However, youth were almost as likely as young adults to use cocaine on a weekly basis (0.6 versus 0.7 percent).

AGE OF FIRST COCAINE USE (1979–85)

Older adults were the least likely to have ever used cocaine until 1982. Part of the increase in cocaine use among older adults may be due to the aging of the birth cohort raised during the peak years of drug use. When this hypothesis was tested, however, it was supported for marijuana but not for cocaine. Most of the older adult marijuana users began their use early and have simply continued to use the drug. In contrast, a significant number of the older cocaine users are new users, that is, they first used cocaine during their late twenties and thirties (Adams et al. in press).

As noted in several studies, the average age of first use of cocaine is quite different from that for marijuana. Marijuana users generally begin their first use in their early teens, while the peak period of risk for cocaine initiation is in the early twenties (National Commission on Marihuana and Drug Abuse 1973; Robins 1978; Clayton and Voss 1981; Kandel and Logan 1984; Kandel et al. 1985). Indeed, in a cohort of New York State students followed into their late twenties, Raveis and Kandel (1987) found relatively few new drugs initiated in young adulthood except cocaine.

The age of first use for cocaine and marijuana since 1979 was examined among users in the Household Survey. Among users, in all 3 years surveyed, the median age for first use of marijuana was 16 years and for cocaine, 19 years. It is interesting to note that in 1979 the average time from first opportunity to actual use of the drug for those who went on to use was 1.0 year for marijuana and 0.6 year for cocaine. By 1985, the delay between opportunity and first use was 1.3 years for marijuana and 0.8 year for cocaine. Among users, in all three surveys, cocaine use was initiated, on average, less than a year after the first chance to use it.

CHANCE TO USE COCAINE (1979–85)

Since the prevalence rates depend in part on the availability of the drug, trends were examined in reported opportunity to use cocaine. Because of the availability of data, these trends were examined from 1979, the peak year of most illicit drug use, to 1985, the most recent survey with available data.

The proportion of the general population who had a chance to use cocaine in their lifetime since 1979 is shown in table 3. The demographic characteristics of those at risk for cocaine use, that is, who had a chance to use the drug, are shown in table 4. Noteworthy is the fact that,

TABLE 3. *Trends in percentage of respondents reporting chance to use cocaine, U.S. household population aged 12 years and older, 1979, 1982, and 1985*

Opportunity	1979	1982	1985
N	(6,331)	(5,624)	(8,038)
No chance to use cocaine	81.1%	75.5%	79.4%
Chance but did not use	10.1	12.6	8.8
Chance and did use cocaine	8.8	11.8	11.8

SOURCE: National Household Survey on Drug Abuse, NIDA 1988*a*.

generally, a smaller proportion of each age group had a chance to use cocaine in 1985 compared with the earlier years; yet, as shown in table 5, a greater proportion of those with an opportunity to use cocaine did so in 1985. While only about 20 percent of the general population had a chance to use cocaine, over half with the chance did go on to use cocaine. Finally, by 1985, there were essentially no regional differences in availability as measured by the respondents' perceived chance to use cocaine.

TABLE 4. *Trends in percentage of respondents reporting chance to ever use cocaine, by demographic characteristics, 1979, 1982, and 1985*

Characteristics	1979	1982	1985
N	(6,331)	(5,624)	(8,038)
Total (12+ years)	23%	29%	21%
Sex			
Male	28	33	25
Female	19	25	17
Age group			
12–17 years	15	19	13
18–25 years	46	52	33
26–34 years	28	37	30
35+ years	7	10	7
Region			
Northeast	28	32	22
North central	20	25	21
South	18	25	21
West	30	38	27

SOURCE: National Household Survey on Drug Abuse, NIDA 1988*a*.

TABLE 5. *Trends in percentage who ever used cocaine among respondents reporting chance, by demographic characteristics, 1979, 1982, and 1985*

Characteristics	1979	1982	1985
Total (12+ years)	49%	53%	57%
Sex			
Males	52	50	60
Females	44	45	54
Age group			
12–17 years	37	30	38
18–25 years	58	54	60
26–34 years	45	51	65
35+ years	23	33	48
Region			
Northeast	48	51	58
North central	47	43	54
South	42	42	56
West	56	58	60

SOURCE: National Household Survey on Drug Abuse, NIDA 1988*a*.

CHARACTERISTICS OF COCAINE USERS (1979–85)

The demographic characteristics of those who have ever tried cocaine are shown in table 6. In all 3 years, more males and young adults and fewer Hispanics had tried cocaine, and the highest rates of use were in the West and Northeast. Rates of lifetime use remained about 13 percent in the Northeast, increased in the South (from 7.4 percent in 1979 to 9.4 percent in 1985), and decreased in the West (from 17.2 percent in 1979 to 15.3 percent in 1985). In 1985, even though there were essentially no regional differences in perceived opportunity to use cocaine, there were regional differences in actual use.

The number of times cocaine was used in the respondents' lifetime is shown in table 7. There was a slight increase between 1979 and 1982 in the proportion of the users who had used 100 or more times. Between 1982 and 1985, there was an increase in the proportion of experimenters.

TABLE 6. *Trends in lifetime prevalence of cocaine use, by demographic characteristics, 1979, 1982, and 1985*

Characteristics	1979	1982	1985
N	(6,331)	(5,624)	(8,038)
Sex			
Male	11.6%	15.3%	15.3%
Female	6.0	8.7	8.1
Age group			
12–17 years	5.4	6.5	4.9
18–25 years	27.5	28.7	25.2
26–34 years	13.3	21.7	24.1
35+ years	1.3	4.0	4.2
Race			
White	8.3	12.3	12.4
Black	9.6	11.6	9.9
Hispanic	NA	6.2	7.3
Region			
Northeast	13.5	13.8	13.1
North central	9.7	8.9	10.2
South	7.4	8.7	9.4
West	17.2	18.9	15.3

SOURCE: National Household Survey on Drug Abuse, NIDA 1988*a*.

TABLE 7. *Percentage of respondents who used cocaine at least once by number of times cocaine was used in their lifetime, 1979, 1982, and 1985*

Number of times cocaine used	1979	1982	1985
N	(807)	(701)	(981)
1–2	31%	32%	39%
3–10	36	34	37
11–99	27	26	18
100+	6	8	6

SOURCE: National Household Survey on Drug Abuse, NIDA 1988*a*.

CHANGES IN COCAINE USAGE

Some important changes have occurred in patterns of cocaine use. First, the purity of cocaine purchased by users has changed. Street levels of purity fluctuate from city to city and time to time, but estimates of the average purity levels were about 30 percent during 1978–82, about 35 percent during 1982–84, and between 50 and 65 percent during 1985–86 (NNICC 1987).

Second, the rates of cocaine users injecting and freebasing has increased (NIDA 1988*b*). Both the intravenous route of administration and smoking freebase or crack cocaine lead to more rapid absorption; thus, peak plasma concentrations of the drug are higher and are reached sooner. Dependence on cocaine can occur regardless of the route of administration, but the more rapidly cocaine is absorbed with its associated quicker positive reinforcement, the more rapidly the addictive process may be reached. "Speedballing" and other multiple drug use also seems to have increased. Speedballing is the intravenous combining of heroin with cocaine or amphetamines. These more hazardous methods of cocaine use have been reflected in increased rates of cocaine-related emergency room episodes, deaths (NIDA 1988*b*), and HIV infectivity (Watters et. al 1988).

Data on cocaine route of administration in the Household Survey were available only in 1985. Among the total cocaine users, most (95 percent) had sniffed, 21 percent freebased, 12 percent ingested, and 8 percent injected cocaine. Routes of cocaine administration ever used are shown in table 8 by age group. Smoking freebase or crack cocaine was most

TABLE 8. *Percentage of respondents who used cocaine at least once, by route of administration, 1985*

Route	Age 12–17	18–25	26–34	35+
N	(107)	(373)	(425)	(76)
Sniff	7.9%	95.3%	95.8%	92.4%
Smoke/freebase	45.9	21.0	18.9	19.9
Swallow/oral	18.8	12.5	14.6	1.0
Inject	3.1	5.6	8.0	12.7
Other	1.2	1.0	1.0	—

SOURCE: National Household Survey on Drug Abuse, NIDA 1988*a*.

predominant among young users. Among the cocaine users, twice as many youth (aged 12–17) as adults (aged 18 and over) had smoked cocaine (44 versus 20 percent). Older adults aged 35+ were more likely than users in any other age group to inject cocaine.

Among those who had used cocaine more than 10 times in their lives, 39 percent freebased and 17 percent injected it. More noteworthy is the fact that of the youth in this experienced cocaine-using group, 88 percent had freebased and 12 percent injected cocaine.

CRACK COCAINE—A PHENOMENON OF THE 1980s

In the latter part of the 1980s, due to the hazards of mixing ether with cocaine hydrochloride to produce freebase, "crack" was developed in the search for a new and safer form of freebase. The ease in marketing this cocaine in ready-to-smoke rock form in conjunction with the increased availability of high levels of cocaine purity led to the distribution of crack throughout the United States (Washton et al. 1986). The high rates of freebasing found among youth in 1985 may reflect the availability of crack at that time. Questions specifically concerning crack were not asked in the Household Survey at the time because the phenomenon was not identified until after the field work had begun.

While some see crack as another type of drug, users of crack are still at risk for cocaine-associated problems. Myocardial infarction, stroke, and other acute cardiovascular conditions have been identified as a consequence of nonmedical cocaine use (Isner et al. 1986; Levine et al. 1987), but pulmonary edema appears more common among crack users.

SUMMARY AND CONCLUSION

The nonmedical use of cocaine is related to a complex mix of availability or chance to use the drug, its pharmacological properties, and society's attitudes toward its addictive or harmful consequences. In the 1970s, when cocaine was more closely identified with heroin than with marijuana, rates of cocaine use were low. In the early 1980s, when only evidence of its psychological dependence-producing properties was avail- able, cocaine rates rose. In the late 1980s, however, discussions regarding psychological versus physiological dependence were overshadowed by the evidence of cardiovascular and other associated causes of cocaine-related mortality. Results from the National High School Senior Survey (Johnston 1988) indicated that, for the first time in this decade, cocaine use is decreasing. Recent surveys of attitudes toward nonmedical drug use indicate that antidrug sentiments continue to rise (Black 1988).

Trends in cocaine use since 1972 have differed from most other drugs, notably marijuana. Compared to marijuana, cocaine is available in a greater variety of forms (e.g., cocaine hydrochloride, crack, and coca paste) and routes of administration (sniffing, injecting, smoking, and absorbing through buccal or genital skin surfaces). Further, the period of initiation is longer, with the age of first use for cocaine later than for marijuana. The delay between the chance and actual use of cocaine, however, is shorter than with marijuana.

With its reduced cost and the increased availability of cocaine in any of its forms, cocaine could well replace marijuana as the illicit "gateway" drug. The high rates of freebase use in young cocaine users and the comparably easier logistics involved in distributing the less bulky crack compared with marijuana make crack cocaine a possible contender for the first illicit drug of initiation into nonmedical use. Further, some crack users do not identify it as cocaine but consider crack as a separate drug. Therefore, recent statistics on cocaine use need to clarify whether crack was identified for the respondents as a form of cocaine. Educational campaigns also need to indicate that crack or rock is a form of cocaine.

Further trends in cocaine use will depend upon an interaction between two powerful forces. On the one hand is cocaine's increased availability and ease in distribution as well as the aggressiveness of established cocaine distribution networks, that is, the "supply side." On the other hand, society in general and cocaine users in particular are becoming cognizant of cocaine's health dangers and less accepting of its use. This change in perceived risks and acceptability of cocaine use, i.e., the "demand side," is more difficult to alter. Yet, since the efforts of the last decade have indicated that it is impossible to completely eliminate the availability of cocaine, decreases in cocaine or any other illicit drug use will not occur until demand is diminished. Whether more or fewer people use cocaine in the future, important questions still remain: What happens to those who continue to use cocaine? What can we do to reduce those adverse consequences?

REFERENCES

Adams, E.H.; Rouse, B.A.; and Gfroerer, J.C. Populations at risk for cocaine use and subsequent consequences. In: Volkow, N.D., and Swann, A.C., eds. *Cocaine in the Brain*. New Brunswick, NJ: Rutgers, The State University of New Jersey, 1990.

American Hospital Formulary Service. *Drug Information 88.* Bethesda, MD: American Society of Hospital Pharmacists, 1988.

Black, G. *Media Partnership Campaign for a Drug Free America*. Preliminary Report. Rochester, NY: Gordon Black Corp., 1988.

Brower, K.J.; Hierholzer, R.; and Maddadian, E. Recent trends in cocaine abuse in a VA psychiatric population. *Hospital and Community Psychiatry* 37(12):1229–1239, 1986.

Clayton, R.R., and Voss, H.L. *Young Men and Drugs in Manhattan: A Casual Analysis.* National Institute on Drug Abuse Research Monograph No. 39, DHHS Pub. No. (ADM)81–1167. Washington, DC: Supt. of Docs., U.S. Govt. Print. Off., 1981.

Dezelsky, T.L.; Toohey, J.V.; and Shaw, R.S. Non-medical drug use behavior at five United States universities: A 15 year study. *Bulletin of Narcotics* 37(2–3):49–53, 1985.

Isner, J.; Estes, M.; and Thompson, P. Acute cardiac events temporally related to cocaine abuse. *New England Journal of Medicine* 315(23):1438–1443, 1986.

Johnston, L.D.; O'Malley, P.M.; and Bachman, J.G. *Drug Use Among American High School Students, College Students and Other Young Adults. National Trends Through 1987*. National Institute on Drug Abuse, Washington, DC: Supt. of Docs., U.S. Govt. Print. Off., 1988.

Kandel, D.B., and Logan, J.A. Patterns of drug use from adolescence to young adulthood: I. Periods of risk for initiation, continued use, and discontinuation. *American Journal of Public Health* 74(7):660–666, 1984.

Kandel, D.B.; Murphy, D.; and Karus, D. Cocaine use in young adulthood: Patterns of use and psychosocial correlates. In: *Epidemiologic and Clinical Perspectives.* National Institute on Drug Abuse Research Monograph 61, DHHS Pub. No. (ADM) 85–1414. Washington, DC: Supt. of Docs., U.S. Govt. Print. Off., 1985. pp. 76–110.

Levine, S.; Washington, J.; and Jefferson, M. Crack cocaine associated stroke. *Neurology* 37:1849–1853, 1987.

National Commission on Marihuana and Drug Abuse. *Drug Use in America: Problem in Perspective*. Second report of the Commission. Washington, DC: Supt. of Docs., U.S. Govt. Print. Off., 1973.

National Institute on Drug Abuse. *National Household Survey on Drug Abuse: Main Findings, 1985.* DHHS Pub. No. (ADM)88–1586. Washington, DC: Supt. of Docs., U.S. Govt. Print. Off., 1988*a*.

National Institute on Drug Abuse. "Overview of Selected Drug Trends." Division of Epidemiology and Statistical Analysis Working Paper, July 1988*b*.

National Narcotics Intelligence Consumers Committee (NNICC). *The Supply of Illicit Drugs to the United States From Foreign and Domestic Sources in 1985 and 1986.* The NNICC Report 1985–1986. June 1987.

Raveis, V.H., and Kandel, D.B. Changes in drug behavior from the middle to the late twenties: Initiation, persistence, and cessation of use. *American Journal of Public Health* 77(5), May 1987.

Robins, L.N. The interaction of setting and predisposition in explaining novel behavior: Drug initiations before, in and after Vietnam. In: Kandel, D., ed. *Longitudinal Research on Drug Use: Empirical Findings and Methodological Issues.* New York: Hemisphere Halsted Press, 1978. pp. 179–196.

Rouse, B.A.; Kozel, N.J.; and Richards, L.G. *Self-Report Methods of Estimating Drug Use. Meeting Current Challenges to Validity.* National Institute on Drug Abuse Research Monograph No. 57, DHHS Pub. No. (ADM)85–1402. Washington, DC: Supt. of Docs., U.S. Govt. Print. Off., 1985.

Van Dyke, C., and Byck, R. Cocaine. *Scientific American* 246(3):128–141, 1982.

Washton, A., and Gold, M. Recent trends in cocaine abuse: A view from the national hotline "800-COCAINE." *Advances in Alcohol and Substance Abuse* 6(2):31–47, Winter 1987.

Washton, A.M.; Gold, M.S.; and Pottash, A.C. Crack: Early report on a new drug epidemic. *Postgraduate Medicine* 80:52–58, 1986.
Watters, J.K.; Cheng, Y.-T.; Lewis, D.; Jang, M.; and Carlson, J. "Drug-Use Profile, Risk Participation, and HIV Exposure Among Intravenous Drug Users in San Francisco." Paper presented at the IV International Conference on AIDS, Stockholm, Sweden, June 12–16, 1988.
Weinstein, S.P.; Gottheil, E.; Smith, R.H.; and Migrala, K.A. Cocaine users seen in medical practice. *American Journal of Drug and Alcohol Abuse* 12(4):341–354, 1986.

AUTHOR

Beatrice A. Rouse, Ph.D.
National Institute on Drug Abuse
5600 Fishers Lane, Room 9–A–42
Rockville, MD 20857

Quantitative and Qualitative Changes in Cocaine Use Among American High School Seniors, College Students, And Young Adults

Patrick M. O'Malley, Lloyd D. Johnston, and Jerald G. Bachman

This chapter reports data on the prevalence of cocaine use, and related attitudes and beliefs, among American adolescents and young adults; it is thus an update and extension of a chapter in an earlier monograph on cocaine use (O'Malley et al. 1985). Some of the results have been reported elsewhere (Johnston et al. 1988). Here, the data specific to cocaine use are collated, and some new data related to cocaine use are reported.

SAMPLING AND SURVEY PROCEDURES

The *Monitoring the Future* project is an ongoing study conducted by the Institute for Social Research at the University of Michigan. The study design is described in more detail in Bachman et al. (1987) and Johnston et al. (1988). Briefly, it involves nationally representative surveys of high school seniors each year, plus followup surveys mailed each year to a subset of each senior class sample. This is called a cohort-sequential design, in which multiple cohorts are followed over time.

A three-stage national probability sample leads to questionnaire administration in about 135 high schools (approximately 120 public and 15 private) and yields between 15,000 and 19,000 senior respondents each year. The response rate is generally about 80 percent of all selected seniors. In order to include many different questions, five distinct forms are used; a random 20 percent of each class (approximately 3,400 seniors) is administered each form. A core set of demographic and drug use variables appears in all five forms.

From each senior class sample, 2,400 individuals are selected for followup, randomly divided into two equal-sized groups. The 1,200 members of one group are invited to participate the first year after graduation and every 2 years after that; those in the other group are invited to participate the second year after graduation and every 2 years after that. Respondents are paid $5 for each participation. Generally speaking, followup rates have been around 80 percent of the original group of sampled respondents, producing approximately 1,000 questionnaires per followup per class.

Three distinct populations are discussed in this chapter.

1. Nationally representative samples of *high school seniors*. Sample sizes have ranged between 15,000 and 19,000 each year since 1975. Dropouts and absentees were excluded from these and the other two populations.

2. *College students*, 1 to 4 years post high school. Sample sizes have been approximately 1,100 each year since 1980. Because dropouts would not be a significant portion of this group, the bias resulting from their exclusion is very slight. The exclusion of absentees creates only a very small bias.

3. *Young adults* in general, 1 to 10 years post high school (including college students). Sample sizes for this group were approximately 10,000 for the years 1986 and 1987.

Because of the small number of cases, one or more adjacent classes are generally combined in reporting post high school data.

PREVALENCE IN THREE POPULATIONS

In 1987, about one in every six seniors (15.2 percent) reported having used cocaine at some time in their lives (figure 1). Annual prevalence—any use in the past 12 months—was 10.3 percent, and monthly prevalence—any use in the past 30 days—was 4.3 percent. The percentage reporting use on a daily or near-daily level in the prior month (use on 20 or more occasions) was 0.3 percent. Among those seniors who reported having ever tried cocaine, about two-fifths (6.2 percent) used it only once or twice; this means that three-fifths of users, and 9.0 percent (1 in 11) of all high school seniors, used this substance more than just experimentally. Three percent reported having used cocaine 20 or more times in their lives. With each senior class representing approximately 3 million individuals, about 90,000 seniors in the class of 1987 had

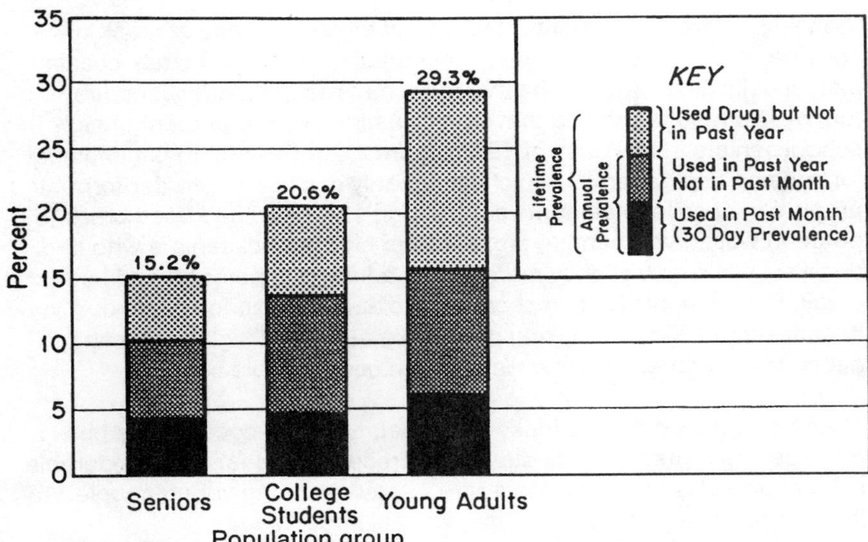

FIGURE 1. *Cocaine: Lifetime, annual, and monthly prevalence among high school seniors, college students, and young adults, 1987*

established a pattern of repeated use, thus placing themselves at considerably heightened risk of becoming dependent on this substance.

The levels of use of cocaine increased with age, and the prevalence rates were distinctly higher among the college and young adult populations, particularly in terms of lifetime prevalences. As of 1987, 21 percent of college students 1 to 4 years post high school and 29 percent of young adults 1 to 10 years post high school had at least tried cocaine. Among the older age groups, the lifetime prevalence rate stands at near 40 percent for those aged 27 and 28. As discussed in more detail elsewhere (Johnston et al. 1988), these lifetime prevalences are based on the respondents' most recent answers. A few respondents reported cocaine use in an earlier survey, but denied having ever used cocaine in a later survey. We believe that at least some of these respondents did, in fact, use cocaine and, therefore, using only the most recent responses probably underestimates prevalence by 1 to 3 percent.

Recent use was also higher among young adults compared to seniors. Annual prevalence among college students 1 to 4 years post high school was 13.7 percent, and the figure for young adults 1 to 10 years post high school was 15.7 percent.

The above figures are based on questions that do not distinguish among the various forms of cocaine. Because of the emergence of crack cocaine, in 1987 we added questions about frequency of crack cocaine use, specifically, to two of the five randomly assigned questionnaire forms. The results showed that crack was tried by 5.6 percent of high school seniors in the class of 1987 (figure 2). In contrast to the findings for cocaine use generally (which is primarily cocaine in powder form), the proportion of college students surveyed in 1987 who had used crack (3.3 percent) was lower than the proportion of high school seniors who had done so, while only slightly more young adults (6.3 percent) had used crack. Because this form of cocaine is relatively inexpensive, and because ingestion by smoking provides a quick and highly addicting effect, these figures must be viewed with considerable concern.

These prevalence figures make clear that, although cocaine use has been getting a great deal of attention in recent years for its considerable risk of harm, it is by no means a rare behavior among young people. And the new form, crack, has made substantial inroads.

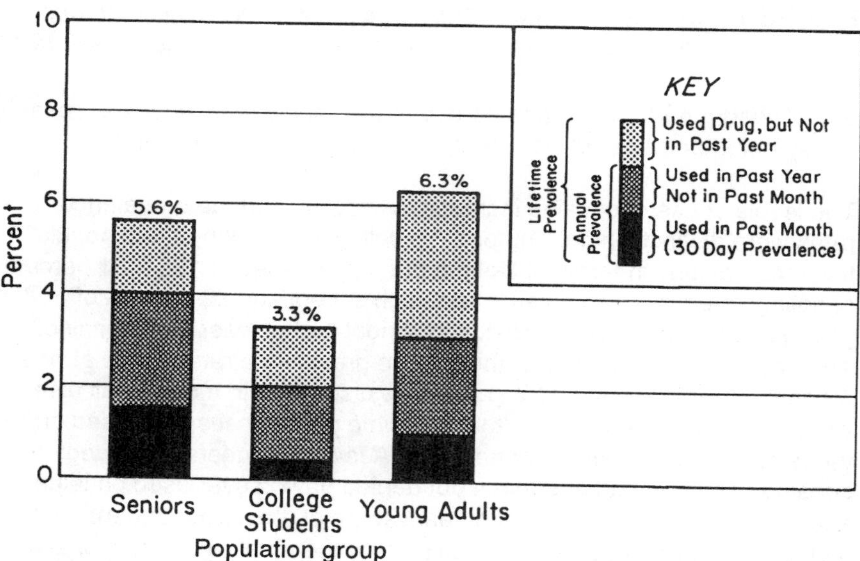

FIGURE 2. *Crack cocaine: Lifetime, annual, and monthly prevalence among high school seniors, college students, and young adults, 1987*

TRENDS IN PREVALENCE

From 1976 to 1979, cocaine use exhibited a dramatic and accelerating increase among high school seniors (figure 3): annual prevalence rose

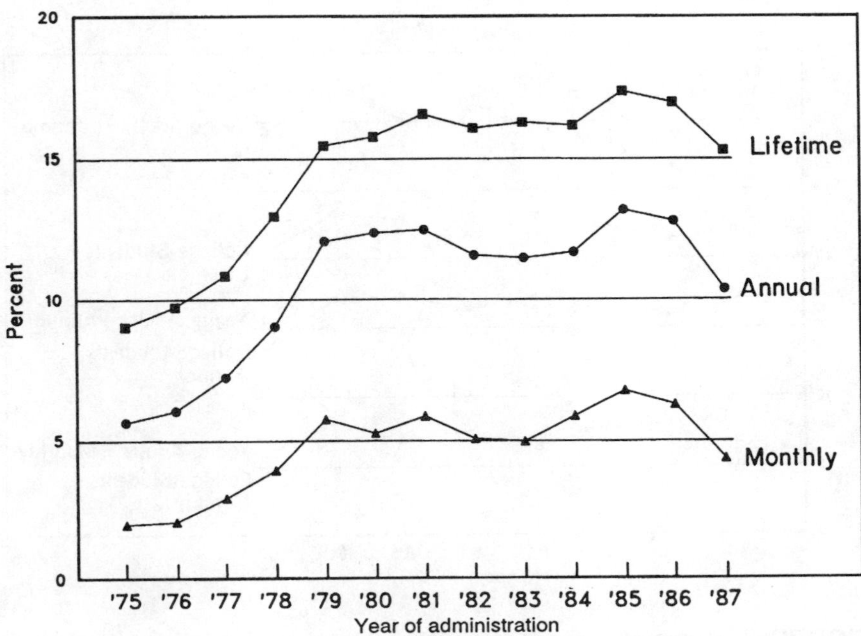

FIGURE 3. *Cocaine: Trends in lifetime, annual, and monthly prevalence among high school seniors*

from 6 to 12 percent, a twofold increase in just 3 years. There was some further gradual increase through 1985, with lifetime, annual, and 30-day prevalences reaching their peaks at 17.3, 13.1, and 6.7 percent, respectively. Cocaine use showed a very slight decrease in 1986 and a substantial decrease in 1987. Each of the prevalence measures in 1987 was at its lowest since 1979.

Although we do not have data for the post high school populations prior to 1980, levels of use undoubtedly increased substantially among them in the late 1970s. Among college students, overall levels of use remained relatively unchanged between 1980 and 1986, with significant declines in 1987 (figure 4). For example, annual prevalence dropped from 17.1 to 13.7 percent, a one-fifth decrease in just 1 year. Similarly, among young adults 1 to 10 years post high school, annual prevalence dropped from 19.7 percent in 1986 to 15.7 percent in 1987, also a one-fifth decrease.

Figure 5 provides some additional detail on trends among young adults by showing annual cocaine use by age group. Once again, it is clear that the downturn in 1986 and 1987 was very general, occurring among all age groups; indeed, the sharpest drops were among those aged 21 and over.

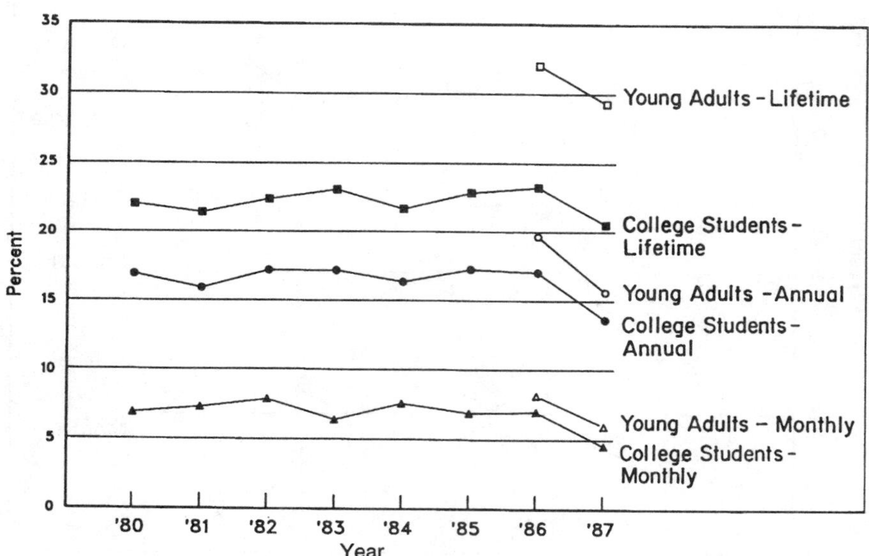

FIGURE 4. *Cocaine: Trends in lifetime, annual, and monthly prevalence among college students and young adults*

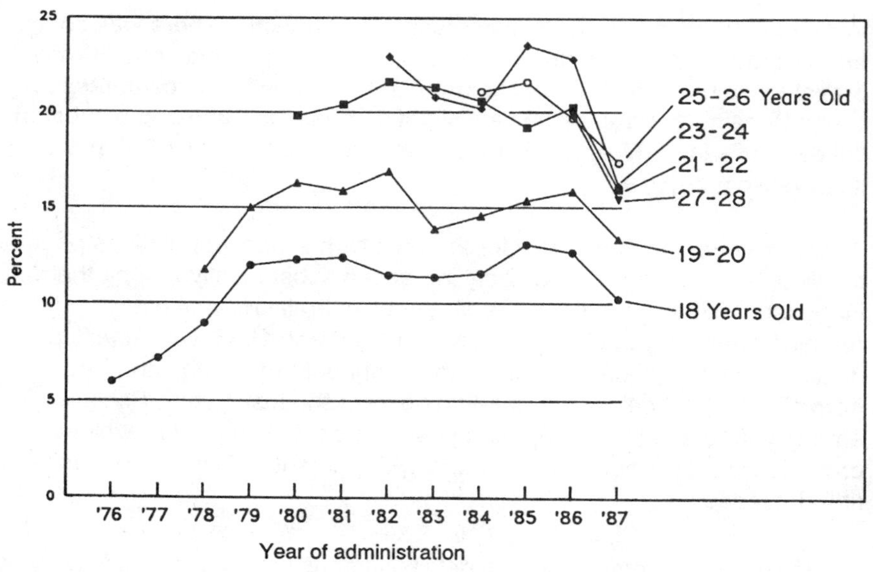

FIGURE 5. *Cocaine: Trends in annual prevalence among young adults by age group*

Two major points can be gleaned from the followup data. First, cocaine use rates rise sharply during the first few years after high school, but there is no convincing evidence of further age-linked changes in cocaine use after age 21 or 22. Second, an overall secular trend in cocaine use was evidenced by particularly dramatic increases in all age groups in the period between 1976 and 1981 or 1982. This secular trend and the age-linked changes combined to produce very high prevalences of cocaine use among young Americans. The increase in prevalence in the first few years after graduation is particularly striking because prevalence rates for most other illicit drugs showed little change or actually decreased on average during the same period (O'Malley et al. 1988).

In sum, the absolute numbers of young people using cocaine remains impressively high, although it appears that, as of 1987, many are beginning to get the message about the risks associated with the drug. As we will demonstrate later, the drop cannot be attributed to a decline in availability.

COMPARISONS FOR IMPORTANT SUBGROUPS

Gender

Cocaine use was greater among males than females (table 1); 16.5 percent of senior males had tried cocaine, compared to 13.6 percent of females. Similarly, annual prevalences were 11.3 percent and 9.2 percent, respectively. The higher rate of use among males was true among both college students and young adults as well.

The ratio of male-female prevalence rates in cocaine use was rather large in the mid–1970s, but there was a substantially sharper drop in use in 1986 and 1987 among males, and the sex differences are now substantially smaller. For example, among college students, 15.8 percent of males and 12.1 percent of females used cocaine in the previous year, whereas the corresponding figures for 1980 were 20.3 and 13.5 percent, respectively.

Among all three populations, males were generally more likely than females to have used the crack form of cocaine.

Region

Large and mostly consistent regional variations in cocaine use occurred in all three populations, with the lowest rates in the South and north-central United States, and higher rates in the Northeast and West. The

TABLE 1. *Cocaine and crack cocaine: Lifetime, annual, and monthly prevalence among high school seniors, college students, and young adults by gender, region, and population density, 1987 (in percentages)*

	Cocaine				Crack			
	(N)	Life	Annual	Monthly	(N)	Life	Annual	Monthly
Gender								
High school seniors								
Males	(7,746)	16.5	11.3	4.9	(2,861)	6.7	4.8	1.7
Females	(8,203)	13.6	9.2	3.7	(3,110)	4.2	3.1	1.1
College students (1-4 years post high school)								
Males	(528)	23.6	15.8	4.8	(235)	4.1	2.8	0.8
Females	(716)	18.4	12.1	4.4	(290)	2.6	1.4	0.1
Young adults (1-10 years post high school)								
Males	(3,099)	33.4	19.1	7.4	(1,237)	7.7	3.8	0.9
Females	(3,836)	25.9	12.9	4.8	(1,555)	5.1	2.5	1.0
Region								
High school seniors								
Northeast	(3,469)	18.5	13.3	5.4	(1,277)	5.9	4.1	1.5
North Central	(4,358)	11.1	7.5	3.0	(1,672)	4.8	3.6	1.4
South	(5,300)	11.3	7.0	2.9	(1,995)	4.1	2.9	0.8
West	(3,198)	23.7	16.4	7.4	(1,159)	8.9	6.3	2.7
College students								
Northeast	(273)	27.9	19.7	6.5	(113)	0.6	0.3	0.0
North Central	(370)	14.1	9.9	2.6	(155)	1.5	1.5	0.6
South	(371)	15.4	9.7	3.7	(160)	2.8	1.1	0.0
West	(211)	30.1	17.5	7.1	(91)	9.6	6.8	1.5
Young adults								
Northeast	(1,494)	35.4	20.7	8.0	(585)	6.5	3.3	1.4
North Central	(1,921)	25.3	13.1	4.7	(722)	5.6	2.9	0.6
South	(2,185)	23.1	11.9	5.0	(905)	4.8	2.2	0.8
West	(1,204)	39.7	20.8	8.0	(479)	10.1	5.1	1.4
Population density								
High school seniors								
Large SMSA	(4,211)	18.0	12.9	5.7	(1,543)	6.7	4.8	2.0
Other SMSA	(7,995)	15.7	10.1	4.1	(2,971)	5.3	3.5	1.1
Rural	(4,118)	11.3	8.1	3.4	(1,589)	4.9	4.1	1.7
College students								
Large SMSA	(415)	24.5	15.9	5.4	(168)	3.5	2.3	0.0
Other SMSA	(740)	19.1	12.7	4.5	(317)	3.1	2.0	0.7
Rural	(79)	14.4	10.4	1.3	(36)	1.0	1.0	0.0
Young adults								
Large SMSA	(2,357)	35.6	19.0	7.5	(964)	7.2	3.4	0.8
Other SMSA	(3,582)	27.5	15.9	5.7	(1,427)	6.2	3.1	1.2
Rural	(925)	20.2	9.6	3.3	(374)	4.7	2.7	0.7

NOTE: Cocaine data are based on five questionnaire forms; crack data are based on two questionnaire forms.

regional variations were more pronounced for crack cocaine, with the West being clearly higher. The difference was particularly striking among college students and, in this case, the Northeast was actually lowest. However, it must be pointed out that the regional data on crack among college students were subject to the largest sampling error because of much smaller numbers of cases (crack is asked about on only two of the five forms).

Population Density

Population density is defined differently between base-year and followup. In base-year, we use the designation assigned to the area where the school is located, which results in a 3-category code. In the followup, we ask the respondents to indicate where they live using a 9-point scale that ranges from "on a farm" to "a suburb of a very large city."[1] This measure is collapsed into a 3-point scale that is not very comparable to the base-year variable in terms of percentage distributions.

As with region, large differences were associated with population density. Among high school seniors, annual cocaine prevalence was half again as high in the large metropolitan areas (12.9 percent) as in the nonmetropolitan areas (8.1 percent). The smaller metropolitan areas were intermediate (10.1 percent).

Among young adults, cocaine use was distinctly more prevalent in the large and very large cities (population 100,000 plus) and their suburbs (19-percent annual prevalence) compared to the rural areas (9.6 percent), with the smaller towns and cities (and their suburbs) being intermediate (15.9 percent). The college students showed a similar pattern, although it was less pronounced.

Among high school seniors, use of crack cocaine was also highest in the large metropolitan areas (4.8 percent), but with this drug, the smaller metropolitan areas were slightly lower in usage rates than the nonmetropolitan areas. Among young adults generally, as with high school seniors, the differences in crack use by population density were not as strong as for cocaine in general: annual prevalence was 3.4 percent in the larger cities, 3.1 percent in the smaller cities, and 2.7 percent in the rural areas. Again, college students showed a pattern very similar to that of young adults generally, albeit less pronounced.

OTHER MEASURES RELATED TO COCAINE USE

Use at Earlier Grade Levels

The initiation of cocaine use occurs at older age levels than is true for most other illicit drugs. Of the 15 percent of the class of 1987 who had used cocaine, 80 percent (that is, 12 percent of the total population) first tried it in high school (10th, 11th, or 12th grade). Unlike most other drugs, there is less tendency for the rate of initiation to decline by 12th grade.

Most of the recent decline in cocaine use occurred only in 1986 and 1987, so these retrospective data on age of first use do not yet reflect the more recent changes, except for the lower proportion of class of 1987 initiating in 12th grade, compared to all the other senior classes in the 1980s.

Friends' Use of Cocaine

The decline in use of cocaine by seniors was also indicated by seniors' reports of use by their friends. Slightly less than half (44 percent) said that any of their friends take cocaine (figure 6). This trend mirrors the

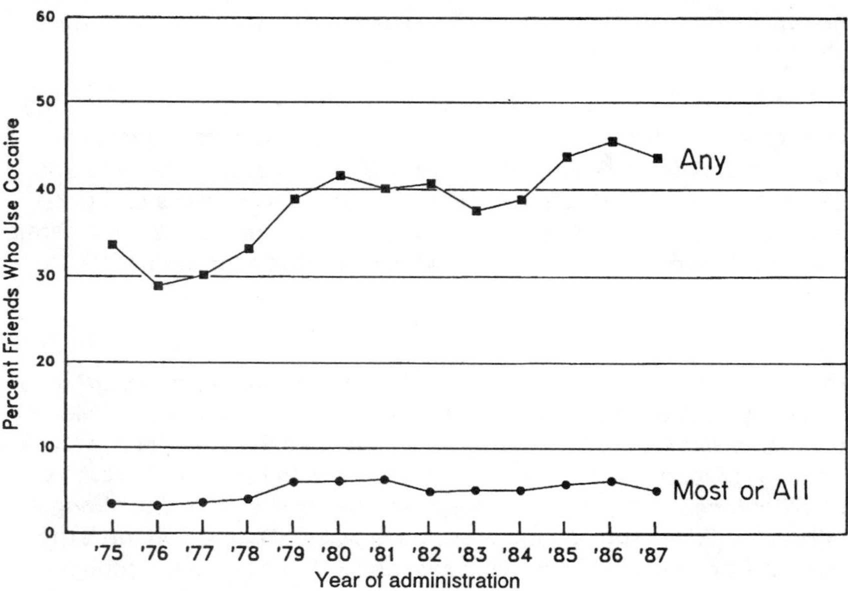

FIGURE 6. *Trends in proportion of friends using cocaine*

data on prevalence, showing an increase between 1976 and 1980 and a recent decrease. The percentage who said most or all of their friends take cocaine was 5.1 percent in 1987, down slightly from the previous year (6.2 percent).

Exposure to Cocaine Use

Seniors were asked how often during the previous 12 months they were around people who were taking cocaine to get high or for "kicks" (figure 7). About one-third (35 percent) of the class of 1987 had been exposed to such use at least once during the prior year; slightly more than half of these (19 percent) had been exposed only once or twice. Ten percent said they had been exposed "occasionally," and 6 percent said "often." (Note that 5 percent also said that most or all of their friends take cocaine.)

Trends in exposure to cocaine use closely follow the pattern of prevalence and use by friends, with one important exception: these measures did not show a substantial shift in 1987.

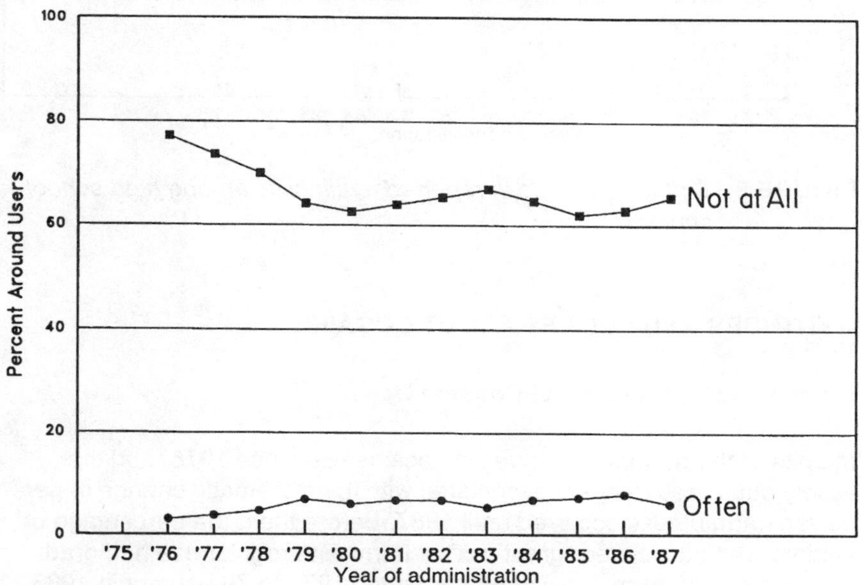

FIGURE 7. *Trends in exposure* to cocaine use among high school seniors*

*During the last 12 months, how often have you been around people who were taking (cocaine) to get high or for "kicks"?

Availability of Cocaine

More than half (54 percent) of 1987 seniors reported that it would be fairly easy or very easy to get cocaine (figure 8). This statistic was at the highest point ever in 1987. Therefore, it seems clear that the decline in use observed between the 1986 and 1987 surveys was not due to a decrease in perceived availability.

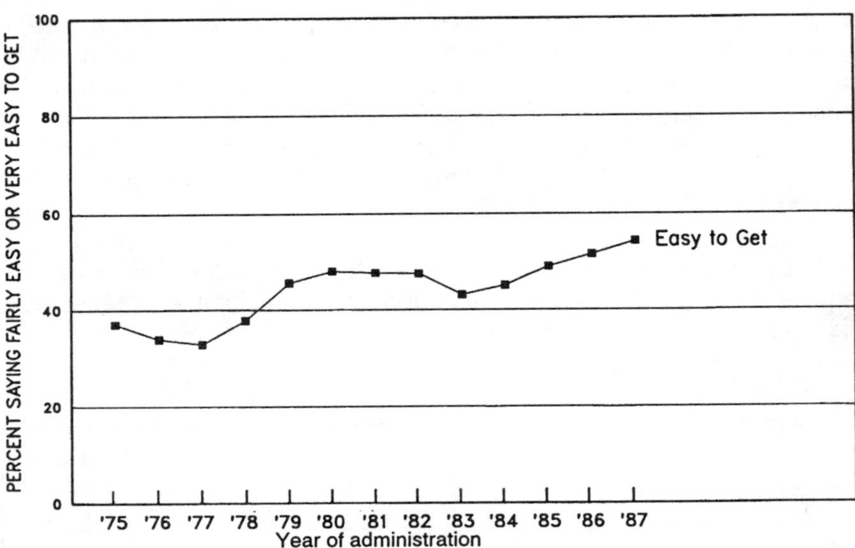

FIGURE 8. *Cocaine: Trends in reported availability among high school seniors*

ATTITUDES AND BELIEFS ABOUT COCAINE

Perceived Harmfulness of Cocaine Use

In spite of the dramatic changes in cocaine use since 1976, and the widely publicized dangers associated with it, no dramatic change in perceived harmfulness occurred until 1987. Before then, the percentage of seniors who associated "great risk" of harm with regular use had gradually increased, from a low of 68 percent in 1977 to 79 percent in 1985 (figure 9). On the other hand, using cocaine once or twice was seen as entailing great risk by *fewer* seniors in 1985 and 1986 (34 percent) than in 1977 (36 percent). The deaths in 1986 of two young athletes (Len Bias and Don Rogers)—along with the great deal of publicity about the drug's

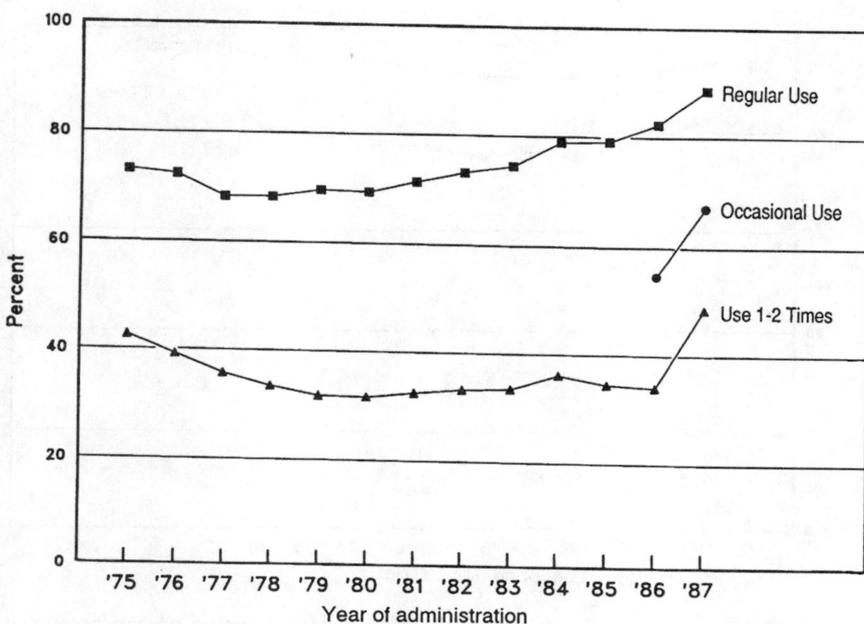

FIGURE 9. *Cocaine: Trends in perceived harmfulness among high school seniors*

dangers—undoubtedly had something to do with the changes seen in the 1987 survey. The proportion perceiving great risk in regular use went from 82 percent in 1986 to 89 percent in 1987, and the proportion perceiving great risk in trying cocaine went up a remarkable 14 percent, from 34 to 48 percent in just that 1 year. The risk associated with occasional use (which was not included until the 1986 survey) also showed a dramatic jump, from 54 to 67 percent in 1987.

With 89 percent of seniors perceiving great risk of harm, regular cocaine use is now viewed as somewhat more risky than regular use of LSD (84 percent), marijuana (74 percent), amphetamines (69 percent), or barbiturates (69 percent), and about as risky as heroin (89 percent).

Perceived Disapproval

Regular use of cocaine does not meet with approval among high school seniors; 97 percent of the class of 1987 said they personally disapprove of such behavior (figure 10). Throughout the study, this statistic has reflected a high level of disapproval; even at its lowest point in 1979–81, it was 91 percent. Trying cocaine once or twice was also disapproved by

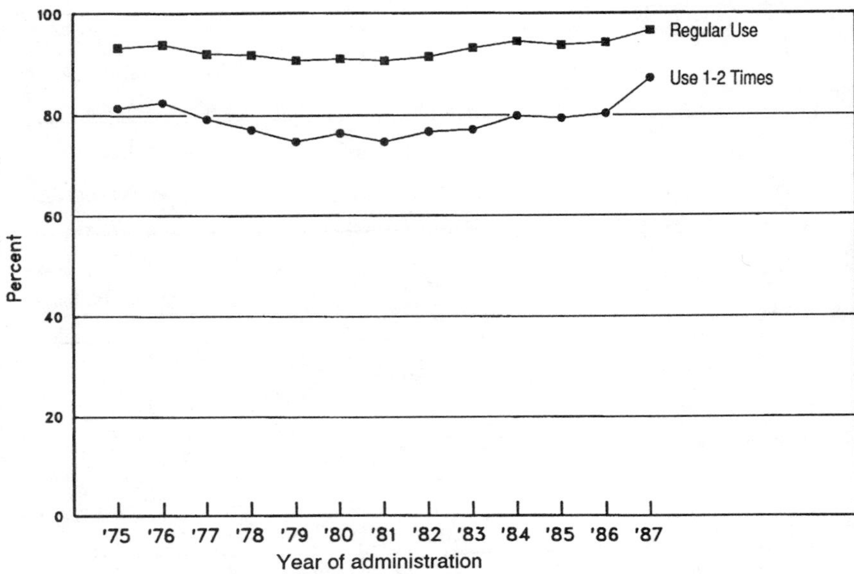

FIGURE 10. *Cocaine: Trends in proportions disapproving of use among high school seniors*

the great majority (87 percent) of 1987 seniors. This figure has increased substantially from its low of 75 percent in 1979 and 1981, with more than half of the increase occurring in 1987 (up 7 percent).

Probability of Future Use

The proportion of seniors indicating that they may use cocaine in the future increased somewhat between 1975 and 1979, to a high of 10 percent, and has been decreasing since then; about 3.4 percent of 1987 seniors said they will "probably" or "definitely" be using cocaine 5 years in the future. About 85 percent of the 1987 seniors said they "definitely will not" use cocaine 5 years in the future, up from a low of 73 percent in 1981. As with the perceived disapproval of experimenting with cocaine, more than half of the change occurred in 1987 (up 6.5 percent).

Virtually all the above statements about other variables related to cocaine use were true for the post high school populations as well as for high school seniors. The few differences were what would be expected from the higher levels of use in the post high school groups. For example, a higher proportion of young adults said most or all of their friends use cocaine. It is important to note that the very substantial increases in perceived harmfulness of cocaine observed among seniors were paralleled in the older groups as well. And perceived availability also increased among the post high school populations.

CHARACTERISTICS OF COCAINE USERS

The associations between use of cocaine in the past 12 months and various measures of background and lifestyle factors were examined (table 2). These measures were selected as potentially important correlates of drug use in general, as well as of cocaine in particular. Briefly, parents' education was a mean of father's and mother's educational level, each measured on a 6-point scale. Curriculum was a dichotomy (0=no, 1=yes) indicating whether the respondent was in a college preparatory curriculum. College plans was a 4-point scale indicating the likelihood of the respondent completing 4 years of college (1=definitely won't; 4=definitely will). High school grades were self-reported on a 9-point scale (1=D; 9=A). Truancy was a mean of two items, number of school days skipped in last 4 weeks (7-point scale) and number of classes skipped in last 4 weeks (6-point scale). Hours worked per week was an 8-point scale indicating the average number of hours that the respondent worked per week during the school year (1=none; 8=more than 30 hours). Total income per week was a 9-point scale indicating the respondent's average total income (1=none; 9=$112 or more). Religious commitment was a mean of two items, "How often do you attend religious services?" (4-point scale), and "How important is religion in your life?" (4-point scale). Political views was a measure of the respondent's political beliefs on a 6-point scale (1=very conservative; 6=radical). Evenings out for recreation indicated on a 6-point scale how many evenings per typical week the respondent went out for recreation (1=less than one; 6=six or seven). Frequency of dating indicated on a 6-point scale how often the respondents went out with a date (1=never; 6=over three times per week). Bachman et al. (1981, 1986) provided more details on these measures and their associations with smoking, drinking, and drug use.

Table 2 also provides results of multiple linear regression analysis in which all of the background and lifestyle factors were used to account for the variance in cocaine use. Regional and urbanicity variations aside, the most important factors accounting for variance in cocaine use are: truancy, evenings out for recreation, and race. Cocaine was generally thought to be a drug of particular appeal to people of high rather than low socioeconomic status. To the extent that amount of parental education was an indicator of socioeconomic status, there was no appreciable association with cocaine use; instead, the association was very weak (r=.011, β=.021). Another factor that might be expected to correlate well with cocaine use is amount of money available, but total income per

TABLE 2. *Background and lifestyle variables related to annual use of cocaine, high school class of 1987*

Independent variables	r[1]	ß[2]
Background variables		
Sex (M=1, F=2)	-.041**	-.007
Race (White=0, Black=1)	-.064**	-.052**
Parents' education	.011	.021
Number of parents in home	-.057**	-.039**
Urbanicity	-.059**	-.048**
Region		
Northeast	.041**	.051**
South	-.074**	.018
West	.105**	.092**
North central	-.053**	na[3]
Educational experiences and behaviors		
Curriculum (college prep)	-.089**	-.045
College plans	-.073**	-.019
High school grades	-.108**	-.037
Truancy	.265**	.196**
Occupation experiences and behaviors		
Hours worked per week	.077**	.000
Total income per week	.108**	.042
Lifestyle variables		
Religious commitment	-.131**	-.049**
Political views	.088**	.047**
Evenings out for recreation	.146**	.076**
Frequency of dating	.092**	.026
Percent variance explained		10.9%

1 The values in this column are product-moment correlations.

2 The values in this column are standardized regression coefficients. A standardized regression coefficient can be interpreted as the amount of change, in standard deviations, in the dependent variable that would result from one standard deviation change in the respective independent variable, holding all other independent variables constant.

3 Dummy variables were used for region, and therefore one region had to be excluded.

NOTE: The number of cases is approximately 16,000. Assuming a design effect of 3.7, the effective N is 4,324, the value used in calculating significance levels.

** = $p < .01$

week showed only a small association with cocaine use ($r=.108$, $\beta=.042$; the beta was not significantly different from zero at $p<.01$). In fact, this variable correlated slightly more strongly with marijuana use ($r=.133$). The rather small value of the standardized regression coefficient needs to be interpreted in the context of other variables included in the regression equation. In particular, there was a fair amount of overlap between income and hours worked per week ($r=.67$); if hours worked per week were left out of the equation, the regression coefficient for income would be significant at $p<.01$.

Only 10.9 percent of the variance in cocaine use was accounted for by background and lifestyle factors. It may be worth noting that in 1986, when there were more use of cocaine and greater variance to be predicted, 13.8 percent of the variance in cocaine use was explained by the set of predictors shown in table 2.

Cocaine Use and Use of Other Drugs

High school seniors who used cocaine tended to be consumers of other drugs as well. For example, of the 1987 seniors who were current cocaine users (that is, used at least once in the prior 30 days), 84 percent were current users of marijuana. By way of comparison, only 18 percent of those not currently using cocaine were current marijuana users. And more than a quarter (28 percent) of current cocaine users were daily marijuana smokers, compared to only 2 percent of those not currently using cocaine.

Alcohol and cigarette use was also far more prevalent among current cocaine users. About four-fifths (82 percent) of them reported having had five or more drinks in a row at least once in the prior 2 weeks (the corresponding figure was 35 percent for those not currently using cocaine), and more than half (53 percent) smoked cigarettes daily (compared to 17 percent among the others).

Similarly, users of other drugs were more likely to be cocaine users; one in six (17 percent) current marijuana users also were current cocaine users, compared to practically none (0.9 percent) of the those not currently using marijuana. Daily marijuana users were 12 times more likely than others to be current cocaine users (37 percent versus 3 percent). Among those reporting at least one occasion of heavy alcohol use, about 1 in 10 (9.5 percent) were current cocaine users, compared to less than 1 in 50 (1.3 percent) of the others. Finally, among daily cigarette smokers, 1 in 8 was a current cocaine user, compared to 1 in 40 of the others.

MEASURES FROM RECENT USERS ONLY

In one of the five questionnaire forms, respondents who indicated that they had used cocaine at least once in the prior 12 months were asked a series of additional questions regarding how high they became and how long they stayed high, their reasons for use, situations of use, use with other drugs, difficulty in stopping use, and methods of use. Although these questions are asked in both senior-year and followup questionnaires, only the senior-year data are discussed here.

Degree and Duration of Highs

Seniors who reported using cocaine in the past year were asked, "When you take cocaine, how high do you usually get?" and "How long do you usually stay high?" The responses indicated that cocaine was associated with fairly intense but relatively short highs. About one-quarter said they usually got "a little" or "not at all" high, another quarter said "very" high, and nearly half (44 percent) got "moderately" high. The remaining 4 percent said they "don't take cocaine to get high." Compared to other drugs, duration of the high is short: 45 percent stayed high about 1–2 hours, 29 percent said 3–6 hours, and 16 percent even longer. The remaining 10 percent claimed they "usually don't get high."

Some strong changes have occurred in the reported degree and duration of highs associated with cocaine use; both have declined in recent years. For example, in 1976, 40 percent said they usually got very high; the corresponding 1987 figure was 28 percent, which indicated that considerably fewer users were getting very high in 1987 compared to 1976. In 1976, only 28 percent said they were high for only 1–2 hours, and 23 percent had claimed to stay high 7 or more hours; in 1987, the corresponding figures were 45 and 16 percent, reflecting briefer highs. Both of these measures actually showed some reversal of the downtrend in 1987, although it should be kept in mind that the proportion of *users* reporting on these experiences declined.

Reasons for Use of Cocaine

Recent users were asked to indicate the most important reasons for cocaine use. The major reasons cited were to see what it's like (74 percent), to get high (70 percent), and to have a good time with friends (49 percent). Other reasons were to get more energy (41 percent), to stay awake (29 percent), to relax or to relieve tension (18 percent), because of boredom (15 percent), and to get away from problems or tensions (11 percent). All other reasons were cited by fewer than 10 percent of users.

Reasons for use have not changed much in recent years, except for some increase in use to get more energy (up from 14 percent in 1976 to 41 percent in 1987) and to stay awake (up from 12 percent in 1976 to 29 percent in 1987).

Situations of Use

About a quarter (26 percent) of high school seniors who used cocaine in the prior year used it when they were alone (table 3). A fair amount of use occurred in very small groups: 38 percent said they used most or every time with only one or two other people present. Use "at a party" most or every time was reported by 27 percent. (This compared to 29.5 percent for marijuana.) Sixteen percent used with a date (or spouse) most or every time. One-third (32 percent) had used with someone over age 30 present at least once. About 4 of 10 (42 percent) had used at home at least once, whereas less than half that many (18 percent) had used at school. (This latter figure was 29 percent for marijuana.) Just

TABLE 3. *Situations of use of cocaine by recent users, high school class of 1987 (in percentages)*

Situations of use*	Not at all	Few or sometimes	Most or every time
When you were alone	73.9	24.5	1.6
With just 1 or 2 others	12.5	49.4	38.0
At a party	33.2	39.4	27.4
When date or spouse was present	61.1	23.1	15.9
When people over age 30 were present	68.1	24.4	7.4
During the daytime (before 4 p.m.)	52.7	39.9	7.4
At your home (or apt. or dorm)	58.4	32.5	9.2
At school	81.5	16.2	2.2
In a car	46.0	42.8	11.2

NOTE: Recent users are those who report having used cocaine in the past 12 months. These questions appear on only one of the five questionnaire forms. (Number of respondents=329.)

* The question wording is: *When you used cocaine during the last year, how often did you use it in each of the following situations?*

over half (54 percent) used cocaine in a car, and about one of nine (11 percent) used most or every time in a car.

The above situations showed few consistent changes over time, with one exception. In 1976, one-third (33 percent) of users reported any use at school, compared to one-fifth (18 percent) in 1987.

Overlap With Other Drugs

Cocaine is often used with alcohol and marijuana. Twenty-eight percent of cocaine users said they used it with alcohol most or every time, but the same proportion never overlapped the two. Twenty percent reported using it with marijuana most or every time, but 37 percent never overlapped the two. Little overlapping use with other drugs was reported.

Trends in overlapping use with alcohol parallel trends in cocaine prevalence: increasing through 1980–81, with relatively little change until 1987, when it dropped, as did cocaine use. Overlap with marijuana use declined steadily throughout the 1976–87 period.

Mode of Administration

The great majority of senior users reported sniffing or snorting cocaine (93 percent in 1987). Many also reported smoking it (43 percent of users), and quite a few said “by mouth” (47 percent). Four percent of the users reported having injected cocaine.

Over time, the percentage reporting use by mouth changed, rising from about 25 percent of users in the 1970s to 47 percent in 1987. Many more now report smoking cocaine—43 percent of users in 1987 (4.5 percent of all seniors) compared to 19 percent of users (2.3 percent of all seniors) in 1979. The 1987 rate is actually down slightly from the peak reached in 1986 (5.7 percent of all seniors). But the trend toward more smoking suggests an important qualitative shift in cocaine use, away from the more traditional use of cocaine in powder form to the more dangerous smokable forms (freebase and crack).

Inability to Stop Using Cocaine

Another indicator suggesting a qualitative shift was a question about whether they had ever tried to stop using cocaine and found that they could not. Eight percent of users (0.8 percent of all seniors) in the high school class of 1987 responded affirmatively. This was the highest rate seen throughout the study, having increased from its lowest point of 0.7

percent in the class of 1979 (0.1 percent of all seniors). By way of comparison, 6.3 percent of marijuana users said they had tried to stop and found that they could not, as did 15 percent of cigarette smokers.

LONGITUDINAL PATTERNS OF USE

An important question that can be addressed by use of the followup data is: What implication does cocaine use at an earlier point have for use at a later point?

There are many ways to approach this question, and we have chosen a simple and straightforward one for presentation here. Analysis was restricted to those respondents who provided data at three different times: at base-year (as high school seniors), at 3 or 4 years post high school (corresponding to the second followup), and at 7 or 8 years post high school (corresponding to the fourth followup). These particular times were chosen to provide a long interval, while also allowing for a reasonably simple tabular presentation. We trichotomized the sample at each time point on the basis of cocaine use in the previous 12 months: no use, use on 1 to 9 occasions, and use on 10 or more occasions. One possible hypothesis, based on the fact that cocaine is a drug that easily produces high dependence in laboratory animals, is that use will progress. For example, individuals who reported no use at the base year and 1–9 occasions of use at the second followup might be expected to show a high rate of transition into the 10 or more category at the fourth followup.

Table 4 shows the pattern of use across time. The data in column one show senior-year percentages collapsed across several classes; 91.7 percent used no cocaine as high school seniors, 7.0 percent used on 1–9 occasions, and 1.3 percent used on 10 or more occasions. Following the top group across two followups, one can see that 77.43 percent did not use cocaine in the year prior to the second followup, and 70.85 percent did not use cocaine in the year prior to the fourth followup. In other words, by 7 or 8 years after graduation, 70.85 percent of the total sample of respondents had reported no use in the year prior to each of the three surveys. Annual prevalences were rather high (16 percent of young adults had used cocaine at least once), and quite a few 21- to 22-year-old Americans (5.0 percent) were using at relatively high rates (10 or more times a year) during this interval; the number of 25- and 26-year-old users was even a bit higher (5.7 percent).

One interesting group is the 11 percent of respondents who went from zero use in their senior year to 1–9 occasions of use in the second followup. Four years later, nearly half had reverted to no use, while about

TABLE 4. *Longitudinal patterns of annual use of cocaine classes of 1976–80 combined*

Use in base year	Use in 2nd followup	Use in 4th followup
91.67 None	77.43 None	70.85 None
		5.43 <Ten
		1.15 Ten+
	11.33 <Ten	4.97 None
		4.74 <Ten
		1.62 Ten+
	2.90 Ten+	0.60 None
		1.30 <Ten
		1.00 Ten+
7.03 <Ten	2.45 None	1.64 None
		0.59 <Ten
		0.22 Ten+
	2.96 <Ten	0.95 None
		1.39 <Ten
		0.63 Ten+
	1.63 Ten+	0.31 None
		0.66 <Ten
		0.66 Ten+
1.30 Ten+	0.34 None	0.24 None
		0.06 <Ten
		0.04 Ten+
	0.50 <Ten	0.20 None
		0.19 <Ten
		0.10 Ten+
	0.47 Ten+	0.06 None
		0.17 <Ten
		0.24 Ten+

NOTE: The number of weighted cases is 5,414.

the same percentage were still using at the 1–9 level, and about 14 percent, or 1.62 percent of the total sample, had increased their use.

Another interesting group comprised those who used cocaine on 1–9 occasions during the senior year of high school (7.03 percent of the sample). Three or four years later, at the second followup, slightly under half of them were still using at that level, and more of the remainder had decreased use than had increased (2.45 percent and 1.63 percent, respectively). And 4 years later, of those who were at the 1–9 level in the second followup, about half were using at that level (1.39 percent of 2.96 percent), about one-fifth had increased use, and one-third had decreased. These groups indicate that cocaine use certainly has the potential for becoming a relatively stable behavior.

The final base-year group comprised those who had used cocaine 10 or more times in the year prior to high school graduation. More than half of them were still using cocaine 7 to 8 years later (62 percent), and half of these persistent users had used cocaine 10 or more times. This again suggests that users tend to persevere in their use.

One way of summarizing these findings is to note that anyone having used cocaine at one point was more likely than not (probabilities ranging from .56 to .87) to be a user 3 or 4 years later, whereas a nonuser at any point was much more likely to remain a nonuser (probabilities ranging from .67 to .92). The other major point is simply the substantial proportions of users and repeat users; quite a few young adults place themselves at risk of becoming dependent on cocaine by using it more than just a few times, and they do so over very long intervals.

One other point may be worth making. Although the data in table 4 are weighted to correct to some extent for attrition, attrition would probably be higher among those who rapidly progress to addiction or dependence on cocaine. Thus, the respondents who remain in the study may underrepresent the proportion of all cocaine users who escalate their use.

SUMMARY AND CONCLUSIONS

Based on the data presented in this chapter, there is clearly no cause for complacency about the problem of cocaine use among the Nation's youth. Lifetime prevalence is at a disturbingly high 15 percent among high school seniors and over 20 percent among college students. Prevalence is considerably higher, around 30 percent, among young adults in the age range of 19 to 28, and reaches nearly 40 percent for people in their late twenties.

The use of cocaine is higher among males than among females; higher in the West and Northeast and lower in the North Central and South; and distinctly lower in rural, compared to more urban, areas.

The prevalence figures make clear that cocaine use has by no means become a rare behavior among young people. And the new form, crack, has made substantial inroads among these populations. Among high school seniors, more than 1 in 20 have tried crack cocaine.

Although these figures are very high, there is encouraging news in the slight downturn in prevalence that occurred in 1986 and particularly in the sharp decline in 1987. Clearly, these declines were not due to any reduction in perceived availability of cocaine, which actually increased. The declines appear to be due primarily to the increasing recognition that cocaine use is dangerous and carries substantial risk of harm.

On the other hand, there is reason to be concerned about the situation with respect to crack cocaine. Some indicators suggest that use of crack cocaine is not declining to the same extent that other cocaine use is. Moreover, this study does not represent well the populations of inner cities, with their extraordinarily high dropout rates; it may well be that the epidemic is continuing to grow there.

FOOTNOTES

1. The nine available responses were: (1) on a farm, (2) in the country, not on a farm, (3) in a small city or town (under 50,000 people), (4) in a medium-sized city (50,000-100,000), (5) in a suburb of a medium-sized city, (6) in a large city (100,000-500,000), (7) in a suburb of a large city, (8) in a very large city (over 500,000), (9) in a suburb of a very large city. Categories (1) and (2) were combined into "rural"; categories (3), (4), and (5) were combined as "small to medium-sized city or town"; categories (6), (7), (8), and (9) were combined as "large city."

REFERENCES

Bachman, J.G.; Johnston, L.D.; and O'Malley, P.M. Smoking, drinking, and drug use among American high school students: Correlates and trends, 1975–1979. *American Journal of Public Health* 71:59–69, 1981.

Bachman, J.G.; O'Malley, P.M.; and Johnston, L.D. *Change and Consistency in the Correlates of Drug Use Among High School Seniors: 1975–1986*. Monitoring the Future Occasional Paper No. 21. Ann Arbor, MI: Institute for Social Research, 1986.

Bachman, J.G.; Johnston, L.D.; and O'Malley, P.M. *Monitoring the Future: Questionnaire Responses from the Nation's High School Seniors, 1986*. Ann Arbor, MI: Institute for Social Research, 1987.

Johnston, L.D.; O'Malley, P.M.; and Bachman, J.G. Illicit drug use, smoking, and

drinking by America's high school students, college students, and young adults: 1975–1987. DHHS Pub. No. (ADM)89–1602. Washington, DC: National Institute on Drug Abuse, 1988.
O'Malley, P.M.; Johnston, L.D.; and Bachman, J.G. Cocaine use among American adolescents and young adults. In: Kozel, N.J., and Adams, E.H., eds. *Cocaine Use in America: Epidemiologic and Clinical Perspectives*. NIDA Research Monograph 61. Washington, DC: Supt. of Docs., U.S. Govt. Print. Off., 1985.
O'Malley, P.M.; Bachman, J.G.; and Johnston, L.D. Period, age, and cohort effects on substance use among young Americans: A decade of change, 1976–1986. *American Journal of Public Health* 78:1315–1321, 1988.

ACKNOWLEDGMENTS

This research was sponsored by research grant DA–01411 from the National Institute on Drug Abuse.

AUTHORS

Patrick M. O'Malley, Ph.D.

Lloyd D. Johnston, Ph.D.

Jerald G. Bachman, Ph.D.

Survey Research Center
Institute for Social Research
University of Michigan
426 Thompson Street
Room 2040
Ann Arbor, MI 48106–1248

Trends and New Developments In Cocaine Use in Canada

Reginald G. Smart

The history of cocaine use in Canada is similar to that in the United States, although present conditions are very different. In the early 1900s, cocaine was used in a wide variety of patent medicines, such as cough syrups, tonics, and catarrh and sinus remedies, as well as in cigarettes, chewing gum, and soft drinks. In addition, pharmacists sold cocaine in bulk to both addicts and recreational users without a medical pretext. Medical authorities agreed that cocaine was the "principal cause of the ruination of our young girls and . . . the demoralization of young boys" (Erickson et al. 1987).

Although the number of users in the early 1900s is unknown, it must have been very substantial. Cocaine was one of the first drugs to require a prescription in Canada, and its abuse helped to create the first legal controls in 1905 (Smart 1983). As in the United States, little was heard of cocaine until the outbreak of fashionable use in the 1970s. In the interim, cocaine was used a little by entertainers and a few sports figures, but it had no street market.

Although cocaine is more popular now than in the past 80 years, it is still not widely accepted in Canada. Rates of use are much lower than in many Latin American countries and far lower than in the United States. For example, 12.7 percent of U.S. high school seniors, but only 5.8 percent of the comparable age group in Ontario, used cocaine in the past year (Johnston et al. 1987). Among adults, the differences are even larger.

In general, stimulant drugs are not popular among Canadians. For example, the "speed" epidemic of the 1970s ended quickly in Canada and involved relatively few young people. Also, most stimulant drugs, such as amphetamines, were removed from the usual prescription lists in 1976. They can still be prescribed for rare disorders, such as catalepsy. However, their loss did not seem to be much noticed by young people or adults. Canadians tend to prefer depressant to stimulant drugs. For example, per capita alcohol consumption has traditionally been a little higher in Canada than in the United States. Canadian consumption rates for codeine and hydrocodone are much higher than the U.S. rates and are nearly the highest in the world.

Because cocaine is not very popular, few Canadians experiment with the newer and riskier ways of taking it. The preferred method is still sniffing the powder or crystalline form. Freebasing or smoking cocaine freebase seems to be rare, as is injecting. An initial flurry of interest in crack seems to have waned. About 60 percent of cocaine users are sniffers, 10 percent smoke freebase, 20–25 percent use crack, and 5–10 percent are injectors.

Although not overwhelming, there is certainly a cocaine abuse problem in Canada. In the early 1970s, virtually no cocaine users were admitted for treatment at the Addiction Research Foundation, and the street market was small. However, the numbers have continued to grow, and cocaine abusers now account for 15 percent of all admissions (but well behind alcohol and marijuana abusers). The total number of cocaine abusers requiring treatment in Canada still appears to be relatively small. Consequently, no large private cocaine treatment industry has developed nor is there much expansion of self-help groups such as Cocanon.

CONVICTIONS FOR COCAINE

One of the first indications that cocaine was being used again in Canada was the increase in convictions for cocaine possession and trafficking (table 1). There were only one or two convictions per year for the whole country in the late 1960s. In the early 1970s, the number increased rapidly, reaching 289 in 1975, 850 in 1980, and 1,953 in 1984.

The largest increases in cocaine offenses occurred after 1980. At the same time, convictions for cannabis offenses were falling rapidly, so that the number in 1984 was only 56 percent of that in 1981. Heroin and lysergic acid diethylamide (LSD) offenses have also been declining. Only cocaine shows any upward trend in convictions.

Cocaine convictions are most numerous in Quebec and Ontario, which account for 74 percent of the total. Cocaine use seems to be rare in the Maritime provinces, judging by convictions.

TABLE 1. *Convictions for various drugs, Canada, 1965–84*

Year	Drug			
	Cocaine	Cannabis	Heroin	LSD*
1965	3	60	266	—
1966	1	144	221	—
1967	0	586	348	—
1968	2	1,453	279	—
1969	1	3,191	310	—
1970	12	6,446	383	1,558
1971	19	10,045	502	1,644
1972	44	13,314	923	1,161
1973	123	24,052	1,290	970
1974	237	32,064	798	1,482
1975	289	30,471	511	1,570
1976	374	39,259	708	989
1977	448	41,281	636	710
1978	538	35,712	580	712
1979	592	36,103	509	1,272
1980	850	40,781	309	2,076
1981	1,246	43,755	250	2,208
1982	1,328	34,707	285	1,754
1983	1,555	28,632	289	1,391
1984	1,953	24,557	271	959

SOURCE: Bureau of Dangerous Drugs (compiled from annual reports).
* Not prohibited until 1970, under Part IV of the Food and Drugs Act.

COCAINE USE IN THE GENERAL POPULATION

Two recent surveys have documented the use of cocaine among Canadian adults: one in Ontario (Smart and Adlaf 1987; Smart et al. 1986) extending over several years and a national study conducted in 1985 (Health and Welfare Canada 1985). The latter indicated a very low level of use nationally—only 0.9 percent had used cocaine in the past year. Rates of stimulant use were typically higher in Ontario than in other parts of Canada. The Ontario study found that 3.3 percent of adults had used cocaine in 1984 and 6.1 percent in 1987. These rates were far lower than for comparable American studies, where 8.5 percent reported use of cocaine (Miller et al. 1982) in 1982. Rates of cocaine use are rising for both males and females aged 18 to 29 but not for other age groups. Although rates for lifetime use increased between 1984 and 1987 in Ontario, use in the past year did not. This suggests that the rate of increase in use of cocaine has slowed, and the peak may have been reached in 1985 or 1986. Unfortunately, no survey data are available for those years.

Cocaine is used infrequently by most people who try it. For example, only 31.4 percent of those who reported lifetime use in 1987 reported using it in the past year. About a quarter (27.6 percent) used it once a month or less, and only 3.6 percent reported using it weekly. No one reported daily use, but in a household study of 1,000 Canadian adults, one would not expect to find a daily cocaine user. Cocaine-using adults are very likely to have used other drugs. For example, 90 percent of cocaine users had used marijuana (Smart and Adlaf 1984). However, only 13 percent of marijuana users had used cocaine.

Table 2 shows the characteristics of adult cocaine users in Ontario in 1984 and 1987. Males were more often users than females, but females appear to be catching up. The largest number of users were under 30 years of age and almost no users were over 50. Rates of use were highest in Metropolitan Toronto in 1987 and lowest in northern Ontario. This probably reflects distribution problems, the isolation of the north, and the lower disposable incomes of northerners. However, it may also indicate their greater preference for alcohol, as per capita alcohol consumption is highest there. These differences between the north and other areas did not occur in 1984. Occupational differences in cocaine use were nonsignificant, but rates were a little higher among laborers. Marital status was related to use with "living as married" people reporting much higher use (18 percent) than others (2–4 percent).

The relationship of cocaine use to income in Canada is paradoxical. Some studies found higher use among those with high incomes (Smart et al. 1981); however, table 2 suggests a complex relationship. The problem may be that many users are students or unemployed people with low incomes. Those at the top and bottom of the income distribution reported the highest levels of cocaine use in 1987.

COCAINE USE AMONG STUDENTS

A large number of student surveys are available in Canada, but most do not have trend data over any substantial time. The variety of Canadian surveys does allow for a tentative assessment of regional variations, but the questions asked are somewhat different. Generally, they indicate that

TABLE 2. *Percentage of adults in Ontario who report having used cocaine in their lifetime, 1984 and 1987*

Characteristic	1984 (n=1,048) %	1987 (n=1,040) %	Effect	
Total sample	3.3	6.1	87 vs 84	**
Sampling error	1.4	1.9		
Gender			Gender	*
Male	4.8	7.2	Year	**
Female	1.9	4.7	G x Y	NS
Age			Age	***
18–29 years	7.1	13.6	Year	*
30–49 years	3.0	4.5	A x Y	NS
50 years and over	0.4	0.5		
Region			Region	***
Metropolitan Toronto	6.2	11.0	Year	**
Metropolitan outskirts	3.3	5.0	R x Y	NS
Eastern Ontario	0.6	5.4		
Western Ontario	1.0	2.9		
Northern Ontario	4.1	0.9		
Education			Education	***
Elementary	0.0	0.0	Year	**
Secondary	2.7	5.7	E x Y	NS
Postsecondary	5.2	7.6		
Occupation			Occupation	**
Professional/managerial	4.2	5.9	Year	**
Sales/clerical	2.9	6.5	O x Y	NS
Labor	5.2	7.8		
Other	1.9	4.5		
Gross family income (in thousands unadjusted)			Income (1987)	*
<10	3.8	12.7		
10–14.9	3.4	0.0		
15–19.9	3.3	12.6		
20–39.9	5.9	4.8		
40–49.9	—	5.4		
50 or more	—	10.1		

* p<.05.
** p<.01.
*** p<.001.
NS Not significant.

rates of use are highest in Vancouver (10.9 percent lifetime use, Hollander and Davis 1983), intermediate in Ontario (4.7 percent use in past year, Smart et al. 1986), and lowest in Prince Edward Island (1.8 percent used in past 6 months, Killorn 1982). These rates generally reflect differences in urbanization, income, and minor crime, which tends to be highest in the west and lowest in the Maritimes. Nationally, the rate of cocaine use among students is probably around 3.5 percent, but there is no national student survey to confirm this. The regional variations in student surveys are similar to those found in the conviction data.

COCAINE USE AMONG ONTARIO STUDENTS

Table 3 shows the overall rate of cocaine use and the characteristics of cocaine users in the Ontario school study. This is a large provincial trend study that began in 1977, although comparable studies were made as far back as 1968 in Toronto. It gathers data on a large, well-selected sample of students every 2 years. Cocaine use was first inquired about in 1977,

TABLE 3. *Percentage of Ontario students reporting cocaine use during prior year*

Characteristic	Year					
	1977 n=4,687	1979 n=4,794	1981 n=3,270	1983 n=4,737	1985 n=4,154	1987 n=4,267
Total	3.8±0.5	5.1±0.6	4.8±1.0	4.1±0.9	4.5±1.0	3.8±0.9
Gender						
Male	5.0±0.9	6.6±1.0	5.7±1.4	5.6±1.2	5.2±1.8	5.1±1.5
Female	2.6±0.6	3.4±0.7	3.7±1.3	2.7±0.8	3.6±0.9	2.4±0.9
Grade						
7	2.7±0.9	4.2±1.1	2.7±1.3	2.8±1.2	2.9±2.0	2.4±0.6
9	4.0±1.0	5.7±1.2	5.9±1.8	4.6±1.8	4.3±1.9	3.2±2.1
11	3.9±1.2	6.1±1.5	5.5±1.9	5.0±2.1	5.1±1.4	4.6±1.9
13	4.2±1.5	4.0±1.4	2.9±2.6	5.0±0.9	6.7±2.8	5.9±2.3
Age						
≤13	2.3±0.9	3.7±1.1	2.5±0.9	2.7±0.9	2.5±1.5	2.1±0.6
14–15	4.3±1.0	5.6±1.2	5.4±1.8	3.9±1.6	3.2±1.3	2.9±1.7
16–17	4.2±0.2	5.9±1.5	5.6±1.6	5.4±1.7	6.0±1.3	4.7±1.8
18+	4.3±1.5	5.3±1.6	3.6±2.3	5.9±1.6	7.3±2.5	6.9±2.0
Region[a]						
Metro			4.1±2.4	3.2±1.3	5.8±2.1	3.8±2.3
West			6.2±1.9	4.9±1.9	4.3±1.5	3.0±0.8
East			4.1±1.8	3.6±1.1	3.7±2.1	5.1±2.5
North			3.3±1.6	4.7±0.9	4.5±2.2	2.9±1.4

SOURCE: The Ontario school study.

a Regional stratification was different in 1977 and 1979 and is therefore not presented.

as this was the first time that any significant amount of use was expected. The study typically surveys 4,000–5,000 students in all areas of Ontario in grades 7, 9, 11, and 13. Boards of education, schools, and classes are chosen at random in keeping with a complex, single-stage, cluster design. In 1987, 24 boards, 215 classes, and 4,267 students participated. The nonresponse rate was very low and was due mostly to absenteeism (12.3 percent absent). The study inquired about the use of 17 drugs in the past year, including cocaine and crack.

Nearly 4 percent of students in grades 7 to 13 used cocaine in 1987. The rate of use was remarkably stable, with no significant change since 1977. As with adults, males were more often users than females, and no trend to greater male or female use was obvious. Older students, typically in grade 13, were much more likely than younger students to be cocaine users (6.9 percent and 2.1 percent for 18- and 13-year-olds, respectively).

Geographic differences in use rates were very small in 1987, but they were larger in 1981. This probably reflects difficulties in distribution in the early days of the cocaine fad. During the 1983–85 period, rates of cocaine use increased significantly in Toronto, but they had declined again in the 1985–87 comparison. As with adults, rates of use were higher in the United States, but the difference was smaller among students.

Student cocaine users take their drug infrequently. About 57 percent used cocaine only once or twice in the past year (table 4) in 1987, and 21 percent used it 10 or more times. However, about 10 percent of users

TABLE 4. *Frequency of cocaine use among total Ontario student sample and among users (in percents)*

Frequency	Total		Users	
	1985	1987	1985	1987
None	95.5	96.3	—	—
1–2 times	2.9	2.1	59.5	56.7
3–5 times	0.6	0.6	9.1	16.2
6–9 times	0.5	0.2	15.2	6.1
10–19 times	0.2	0.2	2.2	6.6
20–39 times	0.2	0.2	3.5	4.1
40 or more times	0.2	0.4	10.6	10.3

took it more than 40 times, and they would represent the heavy, problem users. Unfortunately, we know relatively little about their social and psychological problems except that they are heavy users of other drugs.

Sometimes, people express surprise that cocaine use appears not to be increasing among students in Canada. Given the large media and parental concern about drugs and the trends in the United States, this is striking. However, it should be noted that illicit drug use in general has not been increasing among Ontario students. No illicit drug has shown an upward trend since 1977, and several are declining significantly. For example, cannabis use involved only half the percentage of students in 1987 that it did in 1977 and 1979. Cannabis use often precedes cocaine use, and if we have fewer cannabis users, then cocaine use should also decline eventually. It appears that cocaine was introduced to the student population at a time of declining interest in illicit drugs and, incidentally, in drinking alcohol. The lack of student interest in cocaine may be temporary, but it is consistent with the more conservative approaches to cannabis and alcohol now being seen.

CRACK COCAINE

Although crack was described in 1986 as "a new drug epidemic" in the United States, its appearance in Canada came somewhat later. Newspaper reports of crack use appeared in early 1986, but virtually no crack users were found in the study of cocaine users in Ontario in 1986 (Erickson et al. 1987). Newspaper reports led us to expect an explosion of crack use among youth, but only four seizures of crack were made in Canada in 1986, all of small amounts. Figures for 1987 are not yet available. Seizures of cocaine amounted to more than 100 kg in 1986, and crack was a very small proportion of the total seized.

Two studies inquired about crack use in Canada. Only 0.7 percent of adults in Ontario reported crack use (Smart 1988); 6.1 percent had used cocaine. Nevertheless, 12.0 percent of cocaine users reported crack use. Crack users often used cannabis and sleeping pills, but none reported tranquilizer use. Most were daily drinkers, and almost all reported drinking five or more drinks at a sitting. Except for residence outside Toronto and heavy drug use, adult crack users were not very different from other cocaine users.

In the 1987 student study, 33 percent (n=52) of cocaine users reported the use of crack (1.4 percent of all students). Crack users were compared to those who used cocaine but not crack (n=116) and to a comparably sized random sample (n=95) of students who used neither. Crack users had an average age of 14.5 and were younger than other cocaine users and students in general. They were predominantly (71.2 percent) in grades 7–9. About 75 percent were male, a higher percentage than among cocaine users or students in general. A larger proportion lived in western Ontario than did the other groups.

Crack users, although young, were frequently users of licit and illicit drugs. For example, 58.8 percent had used cannabis, 27.1 percent glue, 37.3 percent nonprescription barbiturates, 31.4 percent heroin, 50 percent stimulants without a prescription, 30.6 percent tranquilizers without a prescription, 46.2 percent LSD, 37.3 percent phencyclidine (PCP), and 41.2 percent other hallucinogens in the past year (Smart 1988).

Drug use was higher among crack users than for the student population in general. When compared to cocaine users, a greater number of crack users used most drugs, the exceptions being tobacco, cannabis, alcohol, LSD, and other hallucinogens.

Crack use in Canada now involves a small proportion of adults and students. Since use rates are at a low level, crack use does not constitute an epidemic but is a growing concern. Continuous monitoring of crack use in the population is needed. As many current crack users are very young polydrug users, they will have considerable problems that may require future treatment for drug overdoses or addiction.

COCAINE USE IN SPECIAL HIGH-RISK GROUPS

Not much attention has been paid to cocaine users in high-risk groups. A study of Indians (Liban and Smart 1982) showed that 5.6 percent had used cocaine in the past year; however, this was similar to a matched group of non-Indians. The highest rate of cocaine use was found in a study of people arrested for cannabis possession (Erickson 1980). Nearly half had used cocaine, and 3 percent were using it once a month or more. These were not cannabis users in general; most were heavy users who intended to continue using cannabis. Since 1980, cocaine use has become more common and the cannabis-cocaine connection may be even closer, especially among heavy users of cannabis.

The largest special study of cocaine users was made by Erickson and colleagues (1987) of 111 "typical" users in the community. The sample was gathered by snowball methods and advertising. The typical user was a young (mean age 29) male, who was well educated and single. About 40 percent had attended university. Almost all were intranasal users. About half were infrequent users, that is, less than 10 times in the past year. About half used the drug in the month prior to the study and, of those, most used it one to five times. On the average, the participants reported using cocaine for about 7 years.

The average age for starting cocaine was about 22. That is much later than for cannabis, which was the most popular illicit drug. All the cocaine users reported having used cannabis, and many were daily users. However, 95 percent had used other hallucinogens, and 29 percent had used heroin. It appears that cocaine comes relatively late in drug-using careers, even those of heavy polydrug users. About one-third reported daily use of both alcohol and cannabis. Concurrent use of these drugs with cocaine was also common. Depressant drugs such as alcohol are often needed by cocaine users to help them calm down or get to sleep.

It was interesting to see the subjects' attitudes and behaviors related to legal issues. Most users reported easy access to cocaine and had obtained it from friends. Most were unfamiliar with the laws on cocaine, and few knew what the maximum sentence was. Despite this unfamiliarity, two-thirds thought that the cocaine laws should be changed, mostly toward greater leniency. Only 7 of the 111 had been arrested for a cocaine offense, but 44 percent knew someone who had. Almost none of the users (1.8 percent) thought that they might be caught by police. This was also true of users who had friends who had been caught. Perhaps the longer one uses a drug without legal repercussions, the more invulnerable to arrest one feels.

This study clearly showed that cocaine is not an addicting drug for all users. Many people tried it and gave it up as they did not like the stimulating effects. Others could use it intermittently without much ill effect. However, the longer cocaine was used, the more likely it was that problems would occur. About half the users reported one of the following serious effects: hallucinations, violent or aggressive behavior, paranoia, requiring medical attention at least once, frequent sore or bleeding nose, frequent mental or physical exhaustion, and frequent cravings to use cocaine. About 73 percent of users reported only one or two of these effects. However, 20 percent reported an uncontrollable urge or craving to use cocaine much of the time or always, and it would seem that these were the addicted users. How many cocaine users have problems depends very much on the definition. In our study, it appeared that about 20 percent were addicted (uncontrollable craving), and an additional 53 percent had some serious effect that may be viewed as a problem. About a quarter seemed to have no cocaine-related problems or serious adverse effects (Erickson et al. 1987).

THE FUTURE FOR COCAINE USE

In general, cocaine is a new and potentially important drug, although current use is at a relatively low level in Canada. Rates of use are highest among students, young males, and those in large cities, especially in Ontario and British Columbia. The rate of use is not increasing among students but may be among adults. Since cannabis use has decreased greatly among students and among males aged 18 to 29, cocaine use should be expected to not increase and may even decrease in the next few years. Many factors could change this tentative prediction. For example, a decrease in cocaine prices or increased availability, an increase in disposable income, or changes in attitudes about the safety of cocaine could make cocaine more attractive.

Continued monitoring of cocaine use is required, as is research on patterns of use. Followup studies of cocaine users are also needed to see how they cope with long-term use and its medical consequences. In addition, studies are needed on the extent of experimentation with newer forms of cocaine use, such as freebasing and crack. They promise to have serious consequences, and it is impossible to believe that Canadians will completely avoid them.

FOOTNOTE

The views expressed in this paper are those of the author and do not necessarily reflect those of the Addiction Research Foundation.

REFERENCES

Erickson, P.G. *Cannabis Criminals: The Social Effects of Punishment on Drug Users*. Toronto: Addiction Research Foundation, 1980.

Erickson, P.G.; Adlaf, E.M.; Murray, G.F.; and Smart, R.G. *The Steel Drug: Cocaine in Perspective*. Lexington, MA: Lexington Books, 1987.

Health and Welfare Canada (HWC). *Health Promotion Survey: Republication Results*. Ottawa: Health Promotion Studies Unit, Health and Welfare Canada, 1985.

Hollander, M.J., and Davis, B.L. *Trends in Adolescent Alcohol and Drug Use in Vancouver*. Vancouver: Ministry of Health, 1983.

Johnston, L.D.; O'Malley, P.M.; and Bachman, J.G. *National Trends in Drug Use and Related Factors Among American High School Students and Young Adults, 1975-1986*. Rockville, MD: National Institute on Drug Abuse, 1987.

Killorn, J. *Chemical Use Among P.E.I. Students*. Charlottetown, P.E.I.: Alcohol and Drug Problems Institute, 1982.

Liban, C.B., and Smart, R.G. Drinking and drug use among Ontario Indian students. *Drug and Alcohol Dependence* 9:161–171, 1982.

Miller, J.D.; Cisin, I.H.; and Gardner-Keaton, H. *National Survey on Drug Abuse: Main Findings*. Rockville, MD: National Institute on Drug Abuse, 1982.

Smart, R.G. *Forbidden Highs: The Nature, Treatment and Prevention of Illicit Drug Abuse*. Toronto: Addiction Research Foundation, 1983.
Smart, R.G. "Crack" cocaine use in Canada: A new epidemic. *American Journal of Epidemiology* 127(6):1315–1317, 1988.
Smart, R.G., and Adlaf, E.M. *Alcohol and Drug Use Among Ontario Adults in 1984 and Changes Since 1982*. Toronto: Addiction Research Foundation, 1984.
Smart, R.G., and Adlaf, E.M. *Alcohol and Other Drug Use Among Ontario Adults*. Toronto: Addiction Research Foundation, 1987.
Smart, R.G.; Liban, C.B.; and Brown, G. Cocaine use among adults and students. *Canadian Journal of Public Health* 72:433–438, 1981.
Smart, R.G.; Adlaf, E.M.; and Goodstadt, M.S. Alcohol and other drug use among Ontario students: An update. *Canadian Journal of Public Health* 77:57–58, 1986.

AUTHOR

Reginald G. Smart, Ph.D.
Addiction Research Foundation
33 Russell Street
Toronto, M5S 2S1
Ontario, Canada

Cocaine Use in Arrestees: Refining Measures of National Trends by Sampling the Criminal Population

Eric D. Wish and Joyce O'Neil

Estimates of the prevalence of drug use in the United States most frequently come from surveys of household or senior high school students. While these surveys yield valid estimates of drug use trends in persons who live in relatively stable households or who have stayed in school, they omit some of the most deviant drug abusers in the population. Persons who are hospitalized, detained by the criminal justice system, have dropped out of school, or are unlikely to be available at home are missed. While these surveys typically contain a caution that the samples have the above limitations, their estimates are often used to describe drug use in the entire population. It is questionable, however, whether a trend in drug use among high school students or household members is applicable to the deviant population detained by the criminal justice system.

A more comprehensive picture of the Nation's drug use trends could be obtained if surveys of these more deviant segments of the population were used to augment the estimates from the national surveys. Fortunately, a new monitoring system, the Drug Use Forecasting (DUF) system, is providing the first quarterly information about trends in the offender population.

In this chapter, we use information from the DUF system to describe the prevalence of recent cocaine use in persons who have been arrested and detained by the criminal justice system. In comparing DUF statistics with those in other chapters in this volume, it will become obvious that the prevalence of recent cocaine use in arrestees dwarfs the estimates of drug use derived from surveys of the general population.

THE DUF PROGRAM

In 1987, the National Institute of Justice (NIJ) established the DUF program, a data system for tracking drug use trends in arrestees in 25 of the largest cities in the United States. Every 3 months, a new sample of approximately 250 male arrestees in the booking facility in each participating city is asked to agree to a voluntary, anonymous interview about their drug abuse and treatment history. Each arrestee is also asked to provide a voluntary, anonymous urine specimen for analysis. Arrestees are usually interviewed while being processed in the city's central booking facility, within 24 hours of arrest.

Urine specimens are tested by EMIT® tests for 10 drugs: opiates, cocaine, PCP, marijuana, amphetamines (all amphetamine positives by EMIT are confirmed by gas chromatography), methadone, propoxyphene, barbiturates, methaqualone, and benzodiazepines. (The latter five drugs are rarely found in the DUF samples.) The urine tests are likely to detect use of heroin, amphetamines, or cocaine that occurred within the prior 24–72 hours. PCP and marijuana may be detected as long as 3 or 4 weeks after use.

DUF interviewers intentionally oversample persons charged with nondrug felony offenses. Prior research has demonstrated that persons charged with the sale or possession of drugs are most likely to test positive for drugs at arrest (Wish and Johnson 1986; Wish 1988). The DUF statistics would therefore be of little value if the samples mainly contained persons charged with drug offenses. To ensure obtaining an adequate number of persons charged with nondrug offenses, each site is instructed to limit the percentage of male arrestees charged with drug offenses to 25 percent. Although the seriousness of the arrest charge tends to be unrelated to whether a person tests positive for a drug, DUF interviewers also attempt to oversample persons charged with felony offenses.

The oversampling is achieved by asking the interviewers at each site to select arrestees in the following order: persons charged with a (1) nondrug felony, (2) nondrug misdemeanor, (3) drug felony, and (4) drug misdemeanor. The processing of arrestees in central booking facilities is often chaotic, and the sites vary in their ability to follow these priorities. The DUF estimates of drug use are robust, however, and do not change significantly even when the sample composition varies considerably along these dimensions. DUF statistics therefore describe arrestees charged with serious nondrug offenses and may underestimate the true level of recent drug use in the total arrestee population.

DUF interviewers typically station themselves in each city's booking facility for 10–15 consecutive evenings. The largest number of arrestees are processed during this period. Over 90 percent of the male arrestees who are approached agree to be interviewed, and approximately 80 percent of the interviewees provide a voluntary urine specimen.

In late 1987, five DUF sites began to collect information from female arrestees. Because the number of females arrested in a city is typically far below that of males, DUF staff interviewed all available female arrestees, regardless of charge. The goal was to interview and obtain urine specimens from 100 female arrestees in each site. (The response rates for female offenders were similar to those obtained for males.)

LIMITATIONS

Our findings about drug use patterns and injection are based upon voluntary self-reports. Although every effort is made to convince the arrestees of the anonymity of the findings and that the information cannot be used against them, the jail environment is inherently threatening and there is considerable underreporting of recent illicit behaviors. (Many more persons test positive for drugs than admit to recent drug use in the interview.) Because we know that some arrestees do conceal their illegal behaviors, our findings about injection and drug use should be viewed as minimal estimates of these behaviors in the arrestee population. On the other hand, we have found considerable internal consistency in the interview information. When persons do report illicit behaviors, the information appears valid (Wish 1988). For example, arrestees in Manhattan who tested positive for drugs and who self-reported dependence on drugs had worse criminal records, more prior arrests for drug offenses, and more severe drug abuse histories than persons who tested positive but denied dependence.

Although DUF interviewers ask each arrestee about the use of alcohol, we do not test the specimens for alcohol. This decision was made primarily because alcohol is a legal drug and urine tests can only detect heavy recent use. In our research with arrestees in Manhattan in 1984, we found that alcohol was the only drug that more persons reported using than tested positive by urinalysis (Wish et al. 1986*a*).

FINDINGS

DUF pilot studies highlighted cocaine use in arrestees in 1984. Early estimates of cocaine use in arrestees came from research that later became the basis of the DUF system. During a 6-month period in 1984, we interviewed and obtained voluntary urine specimens from 4,847 males arrested and processed in Manhattan Central Booking. The sample consisted primarily of persons charged with nondrug felony offenses. The study found that 42 percent of the arrestees tested positive for cocaine. (The EMIT® tests could detect cocaine used 24–72 hours prior to providing the specimen.) At all age levels, cocaine was more likely to be detected than opiates, methadone, or PCP (Wish et al. 1986*b*). These results provided some of the first indications of a high level of cocaine use in offenders, even before the use of "crack" cocaine became common. Previous statistics about widescale cocaine use had come primarily from the sample of persons calling the 800 Cocaine Hotline. The findings from the study of arrestees in Manhattan were subsequently included in Congressional testimony indicating that cocaine had become a street drug (President's Commission on Organized Crime 1984).

Test results documented offenders' increasing use of cocaine in the 1980s. We returned to Manhattan Central Booking in the fall of 1986 to pilot some of the procedures to be used in the DUF program. Voluntary and anonymous interviews and urine specimens were obtained from samples of 200 male arrestees in September, October, and November. Again, persons charged with drug offenses were undersampled while felony arrestees were oversampled. The urine test results from the 1984 sample of arrestees and the samples in 1986 appear in table 1.

Between 1984 and the fall of 1986, the prevalence of recent cocaine use almost doubled. This change in cocaine use was even more dramatic in the face of the stability of the findings for opiates and methadone. The decline in PCP over the same period (and subsequent results) suggested that newspaper reports of the popularity of combined use of PCP and crack may have been exaggerated.

The rising trend toward cocaine use in offenders was shown even more

TABLE 1. *Comparison of urine test results for arrestees in Manhattan in 1984 and 1986 (in percents)*

	1984 (n=4,847)	Sept.+Oct. 1986 (n=414)	Nov. 1986 (n=201)
Tested positive for:			
Cocaine	42%	83%	68%
Opiates	21	22	20
Methadone	8	8	10
PCP	12	4	3

SOURCE: Wish 1987.

clearly in the urine test results from the Washington, DC, pretrial testing program. (Washington, DC, is the only jurisdiction with a fully operational program that routinely tests all arrestees for recent drug use by urinalysis.) As figure 1 shows, 15 percent of males and females arrested in Washington in March 1984 tested positive for cocaine, compared with more than 60 percent of the arrestees in June 1988. These trends from New York City and Washington, DC, prompted the NIJ to establish the national DUF program in the largest cities across the country.

In the next section, we use information from the DUF program and the DC pretrial testing program to describe current levels of cocaine use in arrestees across the country.

More than one-quarter of all arrestees used cocaine within 2–3 days prior to arrest. Table 2 shows the percentage of male and female arrestees who tested positive for cocaine in eight cities in the DUF program during the first quarter of 1988. The percentage positive for cocaine in male arrestees ranged from 29 percent in Phoenix to 73 percent in Manhattan. Excluded from table 2 are cities where only males were tested. The cocaine results for male arrestees in these cities were: San

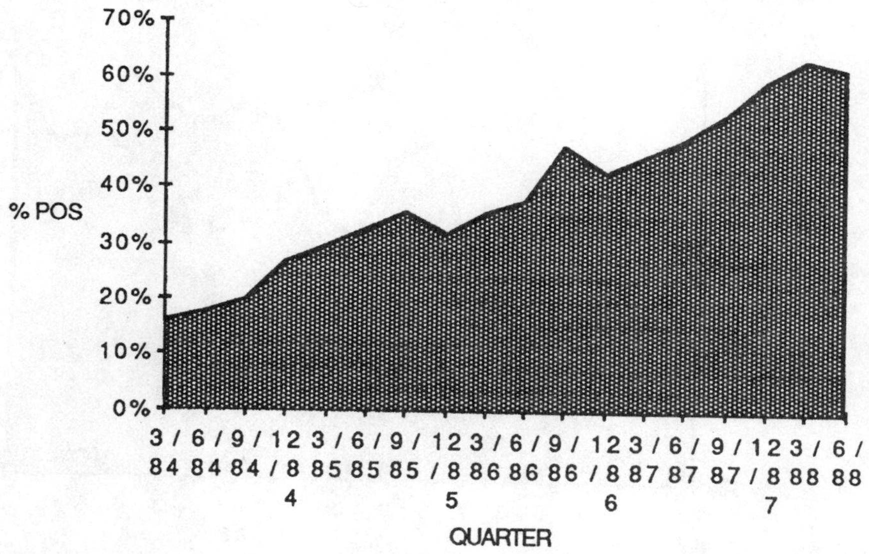

FIGURE 1. *Percentage of male and female arrestees in Washington, DC, who tested positive for cocaine, quarterly between 1984 and 1988*

SOURCE: Adult Drug Testing Program, DC Pretrial Services Agency.

TABLE 2. *Percentage of male and female arrestees positive for cocaine (results from January-March 1988)*

	Males	Females
Los Angeles	58%	66%
Portland	38	47
Phoenix	29	39
New Orleans	32	37
Chicago	55	70
Detroit	53	77
District of Columbia	59	73
New York	73	78

Diego—41 percent, Houston—44 percent, and Fort Lauderdale—52 percent. In all eight cities, females were more likely than males to test positive for cocaine. In five of these cities, more persons tested positive for cocaine than for marijuana.

Cocaine use is also growing in juvenile detainees. Data from the Washington, DC, Pretrial Service Agency, shown in figure 2, indicate an

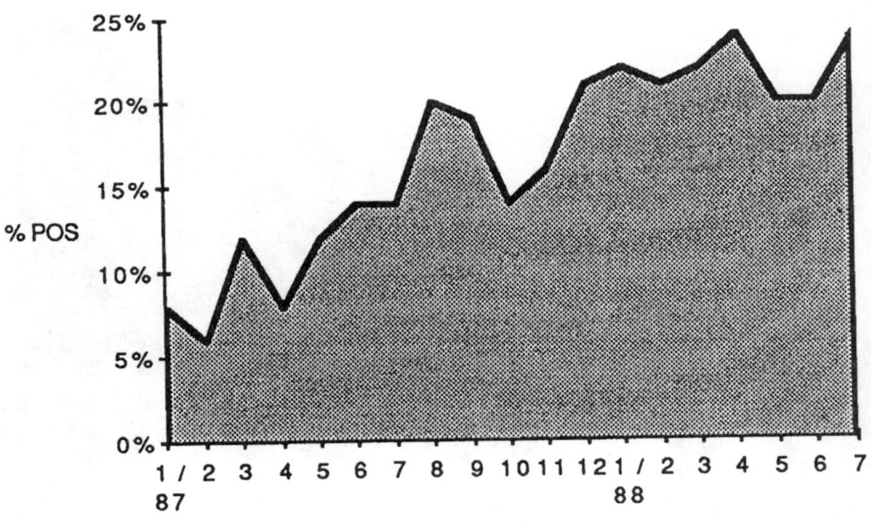

FIGURE 2. *Percentage of juvenile detainees in Washington, DC, who tested positive for cocaine during 1987 and 1988*

SOURCE: Juvenile Drug Testing Program, DC Pretrial Services Agency.

increase in cocaine among adolescent arrestees (aged 9–18). In January 1987, 8 percent of the adolescent detainees tested positive for cocaine. By July 1988, more than 21 percent tested positive for cocaine. (In January 1989, 19 percent tested positive.) Cocaine has replaced PCP as the most frequently detected drug in the juvenile arrestee population in Washington, DC.

Crack use and preferred route of administration. The urine test cannot differentiate the use of rock cocaine, crack, from use of other forms of the drug. Furthermore, the early DUF interviews did not obtain unambiguous information about crack use. However, when an arrestee reported having ever used cocaine, the interviewer did ask questions regarding the person's preferred route of administration. Table 3 shows the considerable geographical and gender differences. Male users in Detroit reported a preference for snorting (25 percent) and smoking or freebasing cocaine (64 percent). Few arrestees in Detroit reported injection as a preferred method (11 percent). In six cities, however, one-quarter or more of the cocaine users reported that injection was their preferred method. In all cities, female cocaine users were as or more likely to prefer injecting cocaine than were males. These findings are consistent with others showing that female arrestees are more likely to inject drugs (Wish et al. 1990). The large numbers who reported that they preferred to snort cocaine powder or inject the drug suggest that the high levels of cocaine use detected may not be attributable solely to the use of crack. It appears that these persons preferred a variety of forms of cocaine.

Table 4 lists the percentages of male and female arrestees who reported ever injecting drugs and their median age of first injection. With the exception of arrestees in New Orleans, Detroit, and Houston, approximately one-quarter or more of the males reported ever injecting any type of illicit drug. Female arrestees were more likely to report injecting drugs. (Remember that these self-reports probably constitute underestimates of injection in this population.) The median age at first injection varied between 17 and 22 years.

All persons who admitted injecting drugs were asked if they had ever injected heroin, cocaine, or amphetamines. While the majority of injectors had injected heroin, more than half had also injected cocaine. In Houston and Portland, more males reported injecting cocaine than heroin or amphetamines. Eighty-four percent of the female injectors in New Orleans had injected cocaine, while only 24 percent had ever injected heroin. Injection of amphetamines was limited to cities on the west coast. The high percentage who had injected heroin and cocaine indicates that injectors often had had experience with multiple drugs. One-quarter or

TABLE 3. *Self-reported preferred route of cocaine use in cocaine-using male and female arrestees (Persons arrested between January and March 1988 who reported ever using cocaine)*

	Los Angeles	San Diego	Portland	Phoenix	Houston	New Orleans	Detroit	New York
Males (N)	(239)	(157)	(176)	(149)	(73)	(61)	(106)	(177)
Snort	41	50	37	49	52	42	25	38
Smoke/base	40	21	28	18	11	28	64	37
Inject cocaine	11 } 19	12 } 29	26 } 35	25 } 33	34 } 37	20 } 30	8 } 11	4 } 25
Inject cocaine+heroin	8	17	9	8	3	10	3	21
	100%	100%	100%	100%	100%	100%	100%	100%
Females (N)	(172)		(75)	(65)		(34)	(40)	(69)
Snort	25		19	42		32	25	29
Smoke/base	49	NA	39	18	NA	9	60	46
Inject cocaine	13 } 26		19 } 42	28 } 40		53 } 59	8 } 15	9 } 25
Inject cocaine+heroin	13		23	12		6	7	16
	100%		100%	100%		100%	100%	100%

TABLE 4. *Self-reported drug injection in arrestees (persons arrested between January and March 1988)*

	Los Angeles	San Diego	Portland	Phoenix	Houston	New Orleans	Detroit	New York
Males (N)	(409)	(304)	(285)	(259)	(279)	(196)	(213)	(312)
Ever injected	24%	34%	35%	29%	14%	12%	18%	23%
Age first injected (median)	18	18	18	17	18	22	19	17
Percent of injectors who ever injected:								
Heroin	80%	79%	67%	76%	51%	75%	82%	75%
Cocaine	73%	72%	79%	84%	95%	75%	58%	71%
Amphetamines	38%	45%	64%	50%	21%	17%	5%	6%
Females (N)	(240)		(107)	(107)		(96)	(60)	(110)
Ever injected	37%		48%	41%		28%	32%	25%
Age first injected (median)	19		19	17		21	18	18
Percent of injectors who ever injected:								
Heroin	88%		80%	71%		24%	90%	93%
Cocaine	79%		75%	96%		84%	63%	95%
Amphetamines	32%		55%	30%		10%	16%	9%

more of the male and female injectors in each city reported ever having injected both heroin and cocaine (not necessarily simultaneously).

Table 5 shows the percentage of males who tested positive for cocaine, according to their top charge at arrest. (Results for female offenders are not presented because of the low numbers of females in each charge category.) As expected, persons charged with sale and possession of drugs were likely to test positive for cocaine. But persons charged with robbery, burglary, and larceny were also likely to be positive for cocaine. With some exceptions, persons charged with assault and sex offenses were least likely to test positive for cocaine. These findings are consistent with prior research showing that persons charged with violent offenses against persons are less likely to test positive for heroin or cocaine (Wish and Johnson 1986).

We aggregated the data for males and females across sites to look at the relationship of cocaine test results to age at arrest (figure 3). Male and female arrestees aged 15–20 were about equally likely to test positive for cocaine. The prevalence of cocaine use was consistently higher in females than males past the age of 20. Peak use of cocaine occurred in the late twenties for males and the early thirties for females. Why fewer of the arrestees older than 35 tested positive is unknown, but

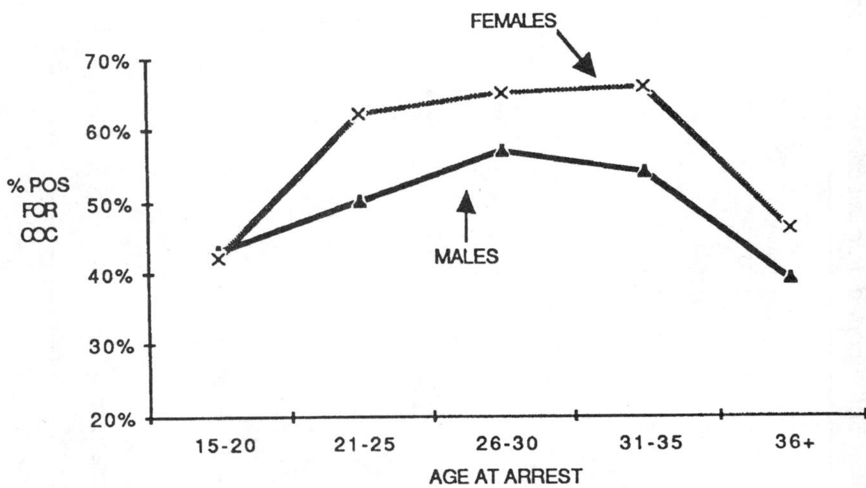

FIGURE 3. *Percentage of male and female arrestees who tested positive for cocaine, by age (N=2,292 males and 736 females)*

TABLE 5. *Percentage of male arrestees who tested positive for cocaine, by top arrest charge and city (combined information from two or more most recent quarters of data available)*

	Top charge at arrest							
	Drug sale or possession	Weapons	Robbery	Larceny	Burglary	Stolen property	Assault	Sex offense
Los Angeles	71%	33%*	67%	57%	68%	60%	42%	30%
San Diego	45	27	41	44	46	31	26	7*
Portland	55	36*	67	39	36	15	26	44*
Phoenix	44	25*	40	23	26	23	16	14
Houston	55	23	50	53	46	38	38	16
New Orleans	70	43	42	46	39	40	33	18
Chicago	63	57	41	54	49	53	33	46*
Detroit	59	52	56	67	58	56	25	46
New York	81	63	78	76	58	65*	61	33*

* Based on fewer than 20 persons.

possible explanations include maturing out of drug use, switching to alcohol use, and higher mortality rates for dysfunctional drug abusers.

We explored the relationship of ethnicity to cocaine test results. Table 6 shows that black male and female arrestees were most likely to test positive for cocaine, followed by Hispanics and whites. However, black arrestees were least likely to prefer injecting cocaine. A more detailed discussion of ethnic differences in drug injection appears in Wish, O'Neil, and Baldau (1990).

TABLE 6. *Cocaine use and injection, by sex and ethnicity*

	Black	White	Hispanic
Females			
Positive for cocaine	70% (354)	48% (252)	54% (102)
Percent of users who prefer to inject cocaine	23% (251)	40% (169)	45% (66)
Males			
Positive for cocaine	60% (1,075)	27% (680)	52% (497)
Percent of users who prefer to inject cocaine	18% (504)	36% (443)	33% (235)

DISCUSSION

The prevalence of the use of cocaine in the prior 2–3 days was more than 10 times greater among arrestees than that found in surveys of the general population, which typically measure use in the entire past month. Cocaine use was found in arrestees in all major cities included in the DUF system and at all age levels. Charge at arrest did not differentiate cocaine use; the drug was used by all types of offenders. Female arrestees reported higher levels of injection than male arrestees and in some cities were even more likely to test positive for cocaine. Cocaine (as well as other illicit drugs) was clearly a commonly abused drug among youths and adults who were detained by the criminal justice system in large urban areas.

This population administered cocaine by all routes, including smoking crack or freebase. Many persons preferred to snort cocaine powder, and a significant minority preferred to inject the drug. The levels of cocaine detected in these persons were therefore probably the result of a greater availability and reduced cost of all forms of cocaine.

In some cities, more intravenous drug-using arrestees had injected cocaine than heroin. Cocaine-using offenders constitute a group at high risk for AIDS (DesJarlais et al. 1987) and should be the target of treatment and prevention outreach efforts.

Finally, the dramatic levels of drug use found in arrestees show the pitfalls of relying solely on surveys of the general population to assess the Nation's drug problem and to design policy. A more comprehensive picture of drug trends in the entire country requires a consideration of the prevalence of drug use among the criminal and other hidden populations in addition to estimates obtained from samples from high school seniors and the household population.

REFERENCES

DesJarlais, D.J.; Wish, E.D.; Friedman, S.R.; Stoneburner, R.; Yancovitz, S.R.; Mildvan, D.; El-Sadr, W.; Brady, E.; and Cuadrado, M. Intravenous drug use and the heterosexual transmission of the human immunodeficiency virus—current trends in New York City. *New York State Journal of Medicine* 87:283–285, 1987.

President's Commission on Organized Crime. *Organized Crime and Cocaine Trafficking*. Record of Hearing IV, Washington, DC, Nov. 27–29, 1984. pp. 77–108.

Wish, E.D. "Drug Use Forecasting: New York 1984–86." Research in action report, National Institute of Justice, Feb. 1987.

Wish, E.D. Identifying drug abusing criminals. In: Leukefeld, C.J., and Tims, F.M., eds. *Compulsory Treatment of Drug Abuse: Research and Clinical Practice*. NIDA Research Monograph No. 86, DHHS Pub. No. (ADM)88–1578. Washington, DC: Supt. of Docs., U.S. Govt. Print. Off., 1988.

Wish, E.D., and Johnson, B.D. The impact of substance abuse on criminal careers. In: Blumstein, A.; Cohen, J.; Roth, J.; and Christy, A.V., eds. *Criminal Careers and Career Criminals, Volume II*. Washington, DC: National Academy Press, 1986.

Wish, E.D.; Chedekel, M.; Brady, E.; and Cuadrado, M. "Alcohol Use and Crime in Arrestees in Manhattan." Paper presented at the American Academy of Forensic Sciences meeting, New Orleans, Feb. 1986*a*.

Wish, E.D.; Brady, E.; and Cuadrado, M. "Urine Testing of Arrestees: Findings From Manhattan." Paper presented at the NIJ-sponsored conference, Drugs and Crime: Detecting Use and Reducing Risk, Washington, DC, June 5, 1986*b*.

Wish, E.D.; O'Neil, J.; and Baldau, V. Lost opportunity to combat AIDS: Drug abusers in the criminal justice system. In: *AIDS and IV Drug Users*. NIDA Research Monograph No. 93. Rockville, MD: NIDA, 1990. pp. 187–209.

ACKNOWLEDGMENTS

This work was supported by Visiting Fellow grant 87-IJ-CX-0008 from the National Institute of Justice, U.S. Department of Justice.

AUTHORS

Eric D. Wish, Ph.D.
Director
Center for Substance Abuse Research (CFSAR)
University of Maryland at College Park
Hartwick Office Building
4321 Hartwick Road, Suite 501
College Park, MD 20742

Joyce O'Neil
Director
Drug Use Forecasting Program
National Institute of Justice
633 Indiana Avenue, NW
Washington, DC 20531

Epidemiologic Evidence on Suspected Associations Between Cocaine Use and Psychiatric Disturbances

James C. Anthony and Kenneth R. Petronis

This chapter describes the historical background and context for epidemiologic study of potentially causal associations between cocaine use and psychiatric disturbances. It then gives an overview of work recently completed by our research group on the epidemiology of psychoactive drug hazards. This report on work in progress includes preliminary estimates that quantify the degree to which cocaine users experience specific psychiatric disturbances more frequently than nonusers. The report also includes an illustration of multivariable modeling to clarify the suspected causal association between cocaine use and psychiatric disturbances.

HISTORICAL BACKGROUND AND CONTEXT

The history of suspected causal associations between cocaine use and psychiatric disturbances began within 30 years of Nieman's extraction of cocaine from coca leaves. In 1886, Albert Erlenmeyer drew attention to a syndrome of cocomania, stressing physical signs and mental symptoms he observed in patients during cocaine intoxication and abstinence. Six years later, in an essay for Tuke's famous *Dictionary of Psychological Medicine*, Erlenmeyer set forth the prominent features of this syndrome as acute mania marked by delusions, as well as auditory and visual hallucinations. He also described the symptoms of depression after intoxication, saying "We have never observed in patients who suffer from morphia-poisoning, [the] crying and moaning, sighing and lamenting, loss of energy, and demoralization, or craving for stimulants, as in persons suffering from cocaine-poisoning."

In the 100 years following Erlenmeyer's work, evidence on psychiatric disturbances during and after cocaine use has mounted. Corroborating the initial reports about mania, depression, and psychosis-like experiences, later clinical observers also described cases in which cocaine seemed to have precipitated panic attacks and possibly panic disorder (Bose 1902; Gordon 1908; Chopra and Chopra 1958; Gay et al. 1975; Post 1975; Jeri et al. 1978; Lesko et al. 1982; Gold et al. 1985-86; Gawin and Kleber 1985; Aronson and Craig 1987). To bolster the clinical evidence, we now have basic laboratory research on cocaine's involvement in dopaminergic, serotonergic, and other brain systems that seem to affect mood, panic, and psychosis (summarized in Wise 1984; Adler et al. 1987; Gawin and Ellinwood 1988). These clinical and laboratory data directly address the biologic plausibility of suspected causal associations between cocaine use and psychiatric disturbances, strengthening the case for a causal linkage.

Nevertheless, even with the newest data, we are left with many unanswered questions about cocaine use and psychiatric disturbances. For example, it is possible that clinicians observe psychiatric conditions in relation to cocaine use solely because cocaine users with psychiatric complaints more often bring themselves for clinical attention and treatment, as compared to cocaine users without psychiatric complaints. If so, clinical data might implicate cocaine use as a cause of psychiatric conditions in the absence of any causal linkage. This would be a specific instance of a general error now known as "Berkson's bias" and "Berkson's fallacy" (Berkson 1946).

Moreover, it seems likely that cocaine use is not the only possible determinant of psychiatric disturbances in the reported cases. Some cases apparently had preexisting disturbances, and some may have had loadings on other risk factors for mania, depression, and other psychopathology. In the study of individual cases, it often is quite difficult to know which causal factors are operating to produce the disturbance. The apparent link to cocaine may be a confounded one, or spurious for other reasons. Thus, judged against standards of evidence proposed for tissue reactions to drugs (Irey 1976), the clinical case reports and judgments about cocaine are incomplete.

Finally, available clinical observations and laboratory data do not answer questions about the degree to which the risk of psychiatric disturbances might be elevated among cocaine users. A prerequisite for this quantitative estimate of the possibly increased risk is information about the occurrence of psychiatric disturbances under conditions of actual cocaine use relative to the occurrence of these disturbances in the absence of use.

In many instances, questions such as these might be answered with a series of well-controlled experiments in the modern biobehavioral laboratory, as illustrated in work by Fischman and colleagues (1976, 1980,

1983*a*, 1983*b*) and Resnick et al. (1977). However, adverse psychiatric reactions have been difficult to observe systematically in laboratory research on cocaine (Lesko et al. 1982), except under extraordinary conditions of exposure (see, for example, Sherer et al. 1988).

This situation may be due to precautions taken in the enrollment of subjects and in the guidelines governing conditions of cocaine use in the laboratory. For example, subjects for this type of research typically are experienced cocaine users for whom cocaine self-administration is rewarding—that is, sufficiently rewarding for them to spend considerable time in the laboratory to obtain access to cocaine. In addition, prescreening excludes subjects with prior major psychopathology and other contraindications. Just as unknown selection processes may lead clinicians to see an excess of cocaine users in psychiatric ill-health, these known selection processes of laboratory subject recruitment may lead pharmacologists to see an excess of cocaine users in whom adverse psychiatric reactions are rare relative to cocaine users in the general population.

For whatever reasons, the incidence of major psychiatric complications of cocaine use has been low in biobehavioral experiments. It may be that the incidence of these complications is so low that they cannot be studied systematically under controlled laboratory conditions without extraordinary dosage levels or methods of administration.

In this context, epidemiologic strategies are indispensable adjuncts to the clinical and laboratory work. Epidemiologic studies of potential drug hazards can go beyond the clinical or laboratory experience immediately in hand. Working toward a more complete picture of the population's experience with drugs, epidemiologic studies seek to avoid Berkson's bias and other sources of error faced when recruiting subjects by newspaper advertisement, word of mouth, and "convenience sampling." By study design or in statistical analyses, epidemiologic studies can take into account sources of spuriousness, for example, confounding factors that are difficult or impossible to control in clinical observations. Finally, epidemiologic studies can provide quantitative estimates of the degree to which drug users are at increased risk of adversity relative to nonusers. For these reasons, some issues of disease prevention and etiology have been addressed more definitively by epidemiologic research than by clinical and laboratory studies (e.g., links between dental caries and fluoridation of water; lung cancer and tobacco smoking; drug problems and antecedent maladaptation).

Epidemiologic findings are subject to their own set of limitations. In many circumstances, judgments about suspected causal associations cannot be made solely on the basis of evidence from epidemiologic studies. These judgments must be made in light of what can be learned from clinical and laboratory work as well. Taken together, results from clinical, laboratory, and epidemiologic research are complementary and can provide an especially strong foundation for causal judgments.

SURVEILLANCE OF DRUG EXPERIENCE IN HUMAN POPULATIONS

In the modern era of regulating new medicines, society has come to grips with the limited resolving power of clinical and laboratory studies by imposing requirements for postmarketing surveillance of the population's experience with new products. These requirements acknowledge that many adverse drug effects cannot be studied on the scale of laboratory experiments or even controlled clinical trials. Especially because the incidence of some important drug hazards can be quite low, the evidence of possible causal associations cannot be seen until after medicines have been marketed and a large number of patients have been exposed. The present state of knowledge about cocaine and psychiatric disturbances is analogous. This suggests consideration of postmarketing surveillance plans as a model for investigating the population's experience with cocaine.

One form of postmarketing surveillance involves direct questioning of drug users about adverse reactions. It is generally acknowledged that these reports about complications of drug use can provide helpful leads in postmarketing surveillance. Nevertheless, these reports cannot stand on their own because we cannot rely upon drug users' capacities to attribute effects to drugs with accuracy and completeness.

This problem with user-reported side effects may be seen by considering a frequently used interview question about social and occupational problems related to illicit drug use: "Did your use of this drug ever cause you considerable problems with your family, friends, on the job, at school, or with the police" (Anthony and Helzer in press). There is reason to be skeptical about many drug users' responses to such a question in view of observed associations between illicit drug use and aggressive or antisocial behavior (e.g., Robins 1966; Kellam et al. 1983; Anthony 1985), as well as an association between illicit drug use and concurrent use of alcoholic beverages (U.S. DHHS 1988). Those with a prior history of antisocial behavior and those who drink while using drugs illicitly face a special dilemma. The reported problems might have occurred in the absence of illicit drug use (e.g., because of a tendency for maladaptive behavior or because of drinking). Thus, as in the study of individual cases based on clinical observation, the epidemiologic study of *effects attributed to drugs by users* is vulnerable to the influence of confounding factors, even when reporting of drug experiences is complete.

Limitations such as these have prompted development of several strategies for postmarketing surveillance in which neither clinicians nor drug users are called upon to make causal attribution of drug effects in individual cases. One common element in these strategies is estimation of the risk of a suspected adverse outcome among persons exposed to the drug, as compared to the risk of the suspected adversity among persons not exposed to the drug. In the final analysis, occurrence of the adversity is expressed or modeled as a function of drug exposure and other important covariates, with the aim of estimating the degree to which drug-takers are at increased risk of the adversity, as compared to persons not taking the drug (Breslow and Day 1980).

SURVEILLANCE OF THE POPULATION'S EXPERIENCE WITH COCAINE

In our own work on cocaine experience, we began by studying what users report about the complications of cocaine use, based on data from the NIMH Epidemiologic Catchment Area (ECA) Program. This description of cocaine effects as attributed by cocaine users is unique in its use of large-scale probability samples of selected area populations in the United States during the middle of the epidemic of cocaine use in the 1980s, by inclusion of both household residents and residents of institutions, and by administration of the NIMH Diagnostic Interview Schedule (DIS). Because of these features of the work, we have been able to extend prior studies of user-reported cocaine effects completed by Gold, Chitwood, and others, which were based on samples of convenience (Gold et al. 1985–86; Chitwood 1985; Spotts and Shontz 1980; Hasin et al. 1988), as well as a preliminary report based on data from four ECA sites (Anthony et al. 1986). To our knowledge, the only other current published epidemiologic data of this type are reported in this volume (see Adams).

Owing to limitations of the data based on user-reported cocaine effects, our research also involved an epidemiologic strategy in which we modeled occurrence of specific psychiatric disturbances as a function of cocaine use, controlling for other covariates. For example, we have been able to estimate, for the first time, the degree to which cocaine users may be at increased risk of panic attacks, as compared to persons not using cocaine, while taking into account important potential confounding factors. This progress report presents a summary of findings from the work on panic attacks, as well as preliminary estimates from work on other specific psychiatric disturbances; details are reported elsewhere (Anthony et al. 1989; Anthony and Petronis submitted; Tien and Anthony in press).

MATERIALS AND METHODS

Key Features of the Epidemiologic Strategy Used in This Work

Table 1 lists key features of the general epidemiologic strategy our research group used to study risk of psychiatric disturbances in relation to cocaine use. This strategy is a form of case-control study nested within a cohort design (Kleinbaum et al. 1982, p. 71; Anthony 1988). It also might be regarded as a case-control analysis of cohort study data. As such, the research strategy limits the extent to which psychiatric disturbances precede cocaine use but does not rule out this possibility entirely (Anthony et al. 1989).

The strategy relied upon data from probability samples of defined area populations at the ECA sites. Within each sample, a baseline interview and tests were administered to each respondent. The baseline interview provided data on sociodemographic characteristics, previous history of psychiatric disturbances, and other factors that might be determinants of future occurrence of the specified psychiatric disturbances. The case definitions used in the ECA Program were based upon diagnostic criteria published in the American Psychiatric Association's *Diagnostic and Statistical Manual* (DSM–III), Third Edition (APA 1980).

With the baseline interview data, it was possible to identify candidates for future occurrence of each specific disturbance (that is, subjects with no prior history of the disturbance). Data from a followup interview conducted 1 year later were used to separate these candidates into two groups: (1) the incident (new) cases and (2) those who remained candidates for future occurrence of each disturbance.

The incident cases and the remaining candidates in the followup sample were sorted into substrata defined by neighborhood residence at baseline and, secondarily, by age at baseline. This step is a form of "post-stratification" or "matching" used to compensate for idiosyncrasies of sample selection and data gathering and also to provide for more thorough and cost-efficient analyses (Mantel 1973; Anthony et al. 1989).

Finally, we used conditional logistic regression to model the occurrence of each psychiatric disturbance during followup as a function of cocaine use and other drug use during followup, and also in relation to other

TABLE 1. *Key features of the epidemiologic strategy used to test for suspected causal associations*

1.0 Probability sample of defined population.

2.0 Baseline candidates for future occurrence of disturbance.
At baseline, administer standardized interview and tests to identify candidates for future occurrence of each disturbance (subjects with no prior history of the disturbance).

3.0 Incident cases of disturbance.
In a followup of the baseline sample, readminister interview and tests to identify new cases of the disturbance (incident cases).

4.0 Poststratification into homogeneous "risk sets."
Focusing on the followup sample, sort the remaining candidates for future occurrence and also the incident cases into substrata defined by neighborhood census tract at baseline.
Further sort the incident cases and remaining candidates into substrata defined by age.

5.0 Regression Modeling.
Using conditional logistic regression that accounts for the substrata, model the occurrence of the disturbance relative to drug use and other suspected risk factors. The logistic regression model can estimate the degree to which drug users are at increased risk of a disturbance relative to nonusers, with adjustment for other determinants.

- 5.1 Start with univariable models.
- 5.2 Proceed to build multivariable models within blocks of suspected risk factors.
- 5.3 Combine blocks and test for interactions.
- 5.4 Retest previously excluded terms, and check for overly influential observations.

---

suspected determinants measured at baseline. In its conditional form, the logistic regression model can take post-stratification or matching into account and can adjust for other covariates while producing an estimate of relative odds or relative risk (Breslow and Day 1980). In this instance, the antilogarithm of the regression coefficient served to estimate the degree to which users were at increased risk of a disturbance relative to nonusers. Alternately, it may be appropriate to interpret this antilogarithm as an estimate of the relative odds, not the relative risk (Rothman 1986). Even with this restriction, the estimates serve to index the strength of association between occurrence of psychiatric disturbance and drug use.

Our approach was to start with univariable models (one predictor at a time) and then to build multivariable models within prespecified blocks of covariates (sociodemographic block, drug use block, psychopathology block). Thereafter, we combined blocks into a single multivariable model and tested for multiplicative interactions. Finally, before settling on a final multivariable model, we tested whether previously eliminated covariates qualified for reinclusion either on the basis of statistical significance or influence on other regression coefficients (i.e., confounding). The method of Storer and Crowley (1985) was used to check for overly influential observations.

The Population Samples and Data Gathering

There were five sites in the ECA Program: New Haven, Baltimore, St. Louis, Durham-Piedmont, and Los Angeles. At each site, collaborators drew probability samples of area residents 18 years of age and older, including residents of prisons, psychiatric facilities, and other institutional group quarters, as well as of households. The samples were drawn and the baseline interviews were completed during 1980–84. The followup interviews were administered 1 year after the baseline interviews.

The number of sampled subjects who participated at baseline was 20,862. Most of these subjects were residents of households (n=18,572). The mean survey participation rate at baseline was close to 80 percent. There was 20–25-percent loss to followup at reinterview.

All study data on psychiatric disturbances, use of cocaine and other drugs, and other covariates were gathered with the DIS and other standardized interview methods. At baseline and followup, the interview items to assess psychiatric disturbances preceded those about drug use. Neither the subjects nor the interviewers were aware that cocaine-psychopathology associations would be tested.

To be consistent with clinical reports that cocaine-associated psychiatric disturbances occur within minutes, hours, or weeks of cocaine use, this study relied on the subjects' reports about drug use as elicited by the DIS at the time of followup. Within this framework, cocaine use referred to any reported use of cocaine during the period between baseline and followup (within an accumulated total of at least six lifetime occasions of use). Other survey details and data on DIS precision and accuracy have been reported elsewhere (Robins et al. 1981; Eaton et al. 1984; Eaton and Kessler 1985).

For the analyses of what cocaine users themselves reported about their experiences with cocaine, we present results from baseline DIS interviewing of the household and institutional samples at all sites. In some instances, data from the New Haven site are missing because some relevant drug questions were not included in the DIS until after the beginning of that site's fieldwork.

To model the occurrence of psychiatric disturbances as a function of cocaine use and other covariates, we used data from all five sites, but we restricted the analyses to the household samples and to young-adult and middle-aged subjects, the groups most likely to use cocaine (Anthony et al. 1986). As a result, the analyses reported here typically began with a baseline sample that included close to 8,500 young-adult and middle-aged subjects. By identifying the at-risk candidates and post-stratifying, the effective sample size was reduced to a more manageable level for conditional maximum likelihood estimation of the regression parameters. For example, the panic attack analyses were based on 509 subjects in 115 matched sets: 122 incident cases, 387 noncases.

Data Analyses

All of the logistic regression analyses were performed using the conditional regression computer program PECAN. PECAN provides maximum likelihood fitting of risk models to stratified data, yielding estimates of relative odds or relative risk for each covariate under study and also for multiplicative interaction terms (Storer and Crowley 1983).

RESULTS

Cocaine Consequences Reported by Users

The first set of results in this summary report is based upon cocaine users' responses to direct DIS questions about seven possible consequences of cocaine use: feeling dependent on cocaine, experiencing withdrawal sickness upon stopping or cutting down on cocaine use, being unable to cut down on cocaine use, experiencing tolerance to cocaine effects, health problems attributed to cocaine use, family or social problems attributed to cocaine use, and emotional or psychological problems attributed to cocaine use (Anthony and Helzer in press). If DIS questions accurately tap occurrence of these consequences, there should be an exposure-response relationship in the data. That is, subjects reporting 2 weeks of daily cocaine use ("daily users") should experience and report cocaine-related problems more frequently. In addition, cocaine users identified by sampling prisons, psychiatric facilities, and similar institutions may be prone to report these consequences more frequently.

Table 2 shows results based on household sample data. As expected, the daily users reported cocaine consequences more frequently—three to five times more frequently—than all identified cocaine users. For example, 24 percent of the daily users reported having felt dependent on cocaine, and 18 percent reported having experienced withdrawal sickness upon stopping or cutting down on cocaine use. By comparison, 6 percent of the identified cocaine users reported having felt dependent; 4 percent reported withdrawal sickness.

Subjects in the household samples were compared with those in the institutional samples at four sites (table 3). Whereas the total institutional sample size at these four sites (n=1,952) was only 14.4 percent of the total household sample size (n=13,538), 27 percent of the identified cocaine users were residents of institutions. Moreover, consistent with expectations, cocaine users in institutions reported cocaine consequences two to four times more frequently than users in the household sample. For example, 25 percent of cocaine users in the institutional samples reported having felt dependent on cocaine compared to 6 percent in the household samples.

TABLE 2. *Percent of identified cocaine users who reported consequences of cocaine use, by level of exposure*

Reported cocaine consequences	All identified daily users (n=125) N	%	All identified users (n=710)* N	%
Felt dependent on drug	30	24	41	6
Withdrawal sickness	23	18	25	4
Unable to cut down on use	18	14	29	4
Tolerance to effects	54	43	97	14
Health damage	14	11	17	2
Family or social damage	35	28	53	7
Psychological damage	35	28	62	9

SOURCE: Data from ECA household probability samples in New Haven, Baltimore, St. Louis, Durham-Piedmont, and Los Angeles, 1980–84.

* Not available at New Haven site.

TABLE 3. *Percent of identified cocaine users who reported consequences of cocaine use, by type of residence*

Reported cocaine consequences	Identified cocaine users: Institutional samples only (n=265)		Identified cocaine users: Household samples only (n=710)	
	N	%	N	%
Felt dependent on drug	67	25	41	6
Withdrawal sickness	33	12	25	4
Unable to cut down on use	41	15	29	4
Tolerance to effects	84	32	97	14
Health damage	14	5	17	2
Family or social damage	73	28	53	7
Psychological damage	44	17	62	9

SOURCE: Data from ECA household and institutional probability samples in Baltimore, St. Louis, Durham-Piedmont, and Los Angeles, 1980-84.

It is noteworthy that tolerance to cocaine effects was the most commonly reported cocaine consequence identified by the DIS. Fourteen percent of the cocaine users in the household samples reported having experienced tolerance, and 9 percent reported psychological problems related to cocaine. Among the daily cocaine users in the household sample, 28 percent reported having experienced psychological problems due to cocaine use.

Whereas these proportions seem to be large, they are smaller than corresponding values obtained from cocaine users identified in a clinical sample (Anthony and Petronis 1989). Moreover, very little is known about the clinical significance and meaning of cocaine users' reports about tolerance, psychological problems, and other effects attributed to cocaine. For example, whether reported cocaine tolerance is both necessary and sufficient as evidence of dependence on cocaine is an open question. It is possible that perceived tolerance to cocaine's effects develops soon after initiation to cocaine use, with no prognostic significance for later increasing involvement in cocaine use. If so, it would be a mistake to rely upon reported tolerance as a sole indicator of cocaine dependence, as suggested by others (Adams, this volume).

Are Cocaine Users at Increased Risk of Psychiatric Disturbances?

The occurrence of specific psychiatric disturbances was assessed and, separately by means of a statistical model, the odds of occurrence among subjects who use cocaine were related to the odds of occurrence among subjects not using cocaine. In many of these analyses, the resulting relative odds estimate serves well as an estimate of the degree to which cocaine users are at increased risk of the specific disturbance. The multivariable statistical model used in this strategy permits control of sociodemographic factors and other covariates that might otherwise function as confounders in the study of cocaine use and psychopathology.

Based on review of the literature, it seemed likely that cocaine users would be at increased risk of panic attacks, but possibly not autonomous DSM–III panic disorder. In parallel, we hypothesized that cocaine users would be at increased risk of syndromes involving depressed mood, with or without other symptoms of depression, but not DSM–III major depressive disorder; syndromes involving manic-like behavior, with or without other symptoms of mania, but not DSM–III manic episodes; and psychotic-like experiences of hallucinations and/or delusions, but not DSM–III schizophrenic disorders.

The basis for discounting cocaine users' increased risk for DSM–III disorders can be understood only by considering the diagnostic criteria. For each disorder, the criteria cannot be fulfilled if the disorder is considered to arise from an "organic mental disorder," including cocaine intoxication or withdrawal states. Thus, the DSM–III sets forth case definitions for these disorders that do not permit cocaine use to be a proximal cause. This topic is reviewed more thoroughly by Rounsaville (this volume).

The DIS method of identifying specific psychiatric disorders follows DSM-III guidelines. At several stages of the DIS method, there is an attempt to rule out psychiatric disturbances that seem to be caused by drug use or other organic factors. It is not possible to suppress this aspect of the method completely when using DIS data to study occurrence of psychiatric *disorders*. However, it can be completely suppressed when studying occurrence of specific symptoms, and it can be suppressed somewhat when studying occurrence of syndromes of depression and mania. Details about this aspect of the study are reported elsewhere (Anthony et al. 1989; Anthony and Petronis submitted; Tien and Anthony in press).

Table 4 gives estimates based upon univariable logistic regression analyses in which we modeled occurrence of each specific psychiatric disturbance as a function of cocaine use. Here, occurrence was defined as "occurrence for the first time"; subjects with prebaseline histories of the disturbance were excluded from the analysis. This exclusion improved the utility and interpretability of the relative odds estimate as an index of the degree to which cocaine users in the ECA household samples were at increased risk of developing the associated disturbance during the followup interval, as compared to subjects not using cocaine.

TABLE 4. *Estimated relative odds of psychiatric disturbances for cocaine users compared to nonusers based on univariable conditional logistic regression analyses*

Type of psychiatric disturbance	Number of new cases in substrata	Remaining candidates in substrata	Estimated relative odds*	p value
Panic attack	122	387	3.7	0.003
DSM Panic disorder	18	59	3.2	0.133
DSM Major Depression	192	621	1.7	0.148
Depression syndrome	259	776	2.0	0.017
Simple depression	232	591	1.8	0.121
DSM Manic Episode	24	104	11.8	0.031
Mania syndrome	42	164	5.5	0.006
Delusion/hallucination	477	1818	1.6	0.047

SOURCE: Data from ECA household probability samples in New Haven, Baltimore, St. Louis, Durham-Piedmont, and Los Angeles, 1980-84.

* Antilogarithm of logistic regression coefficient, interpretable as relative risk estimate (see text). Here, the issue is the extent to which univariable models showed cocaine users to experience the psychiatric disturbances more often than nonusers.

Panic: Unadjusted Estimates

Studying 122 incident cases of panic attack and 387 noncases in matched sets, we found cocaine use to be associated with an increased risk for panic attacks (p=0.003). Before adjustment for covariates, subjects reporting cocaine use during ECA followup were 3.7 times more likely to experience panic attacks compared to nonusing subjects. The 95-percent confidence interval for this relative risk estimate ranged from 1.6 to 8.2.

Studying 18 new cases of autonomous panic disorder and 59 noncases in their matched sets, we found a tendency for cocaine use to be associated with risk of panic disorder. The point estimate for relative risk was 3.2. However, the association was not statistically significant (p=0.133)—not surprising in view of the small number of new panic disorder cases in the sample.

Depression: Unadjusted Estimates

We studied three forms of depression. The case definition for Major Depression was determined by the DIS diagnosis for DSM–III Major Depressive Episode (Von Korff and Anthony 1982). For a subject to qualify as an incident case of Major Depression, the DIS data had to show a first-time episode of depression lasting 2 weeks or more, including at least four different types of allied symptoms also lasting 2 weeks or more. The DSM–III rules for excluding depression "due to organic mental disorders" could be dropped partially but not completely, forming the basis for our expectation that cocaine users might not be at increased risk for DSM–III Major Depression (Anthony et al. 1985).

The case definition for a second form of depression, termed "depression syndrome," required new occurrence of a spell of depressed mood or anhedonia accompanied by several allied symptoms such as sleep disturbance or feelings of guilt. The episode with this constellation of symptoms had to occur for the first time during the followup interval. As with Major Depression, the spell of depression itself had to last for at least 2 weeks but, in contrast with Major Depression, no single symptom during that spell was required to persist for 2 weeks. Owing to an unchangeable feature of the DIS method, it also happened that all incident cases of depression syndrome reported a lifetime history of at least three symptoms of Major Depression. Otherwise, when implementing this case definition, it was possible to suppress the DSM–III exclusion rules concerned with organic mental disorders.

The third form of depression, termed "simple depression," was defined in relation to Criterion A for DSM–III Major Depression. In brief, to be an incident case, a candidate had to report 2 weeks of depressed mood, dysphoria, or anhedonia in response to a single DIS question on this experience. In contrast with cases of Major Depression and the depression syndrome, these incident cases were not required to report accompanying symptoms of depression. Moreover, it was possible to completely drop the DSM–III exclusion rules concerned with organic mental disorders. Subjects with baseline data showing a history of Major Depression, the depression syndrome, or simple depression were not considered eligible candidates for first-time occurrence of simple depression.

Studying 192 incident cases and 621 noncases in their matched sets, there was a tendency for occurrence of Major Depression to be associated with cocaine use during followup, reflected in an estimate of 1.7. Nevertheless, this association was not statistically significant (p=0.148).

Studying 259 incident cases of the depression syndrome and 776 noncases in their matched sets, we found an association involving cocaine use. Subjects who reported cocaine use during followup were two times more likely to develop the depression syndrome as compared to subjects not identified as cocaine users (p=0.017). The 95-percent confidence interval for this estimate ranged from 1.1 to 3.6.

The analyses on simple depression were based upon 232 incident cases of simple depression and 591 noncases in their matched sets. In these analyses, we found a tendency for cocaine use to be associated with occurrence of simple depression during followup (estimate, 1.8). However, as with Major Depression, the association was not statistically significant (p=0.121). This may be due to unreliability in the single item assessment of simple depression.

Mania: Unadjusted Estimates

We studied two forms of mania-like experiences. An incident case of Manic Episode was required to qualify for the DIS–DSM diagnosis of Manic Episode. Thus, a subject's DIS data had to show a first-time episode of mania lasting 1 week or more, including at least three different types of allied symptoms also lasting 1 week or more. The DSM–III rules for excluding mania "due to organic mental disorders" could not be suppressed completely. Thus, we expected that cocaine use would not be associated with occurrence of DSM–III Manic Episode.

The case definition for a second form of mania-like experience, termed "mania syndrome," required new occurrence of a spell of mania, hypomania, or elation accompanied by several allied symptoms such as racing thoughts, sleep disturbance, or psychomotor agitation. The spell with this constellation of symptoms had to occur for the first time during the followup interval. As with DSM–III Manic Episode, the spell of mania or elation had to last for at least 1 week but, in contrast with Manic Episode, no single symptom during that spell was required to persist for 1 week. Because of an unchangeable feature of the DIS method, it also happened that all incident cases of mania syndrome reported a lifetime history of at least two symptoms of Manic Episode. Otherwise, when implementing this case definition, it was possible to suppress the DSM–III exclusion rules concerned with organic mental disorders.

Studying 24 incident cases of Manic Episode and 104 noncases in their matched sets, we found substantial association between DSM Manic Episode and cocaine use, contrary to our expectations. The strength of association was reflected in a relative odds estimate of 11.8, which was statistically significant at a p value of 0.031.

Studying 42 incident cases of the mania syndrome and 164 noncases in their matched sets, we found a statistically significant association involving cocaine. Subjects reporting cocaine use during followup were 5.5 times more likely to experience the mania syndrome (p=0.006). The 95-percent confidence interval for this estimate ranged from 1.6 to 2.9.

Psychosis-Like Experiences: Unadjusted Estimates

In an analysis organized by Dr. Allen Tien, 477 DIS-identified incident cases of delusions or hallucinations were studied in relation to 1,818 noncases in 390 matched sets (Tien and Anthony in press). Before adjustment for covariates, there was evidence of statistically significant association between cocaine use and occurrence of these psychosis-like experiences. Subjects reporting cocaine use during followup were 1.6 times more likely to experience DIS-identified delusions and hallucinations for the first time as compared to nonusing subjects (p=0.0466).

Panic Attack: Estimates Adjusted for Covariates

Whereas the univariable estimates reported in table 4 are informative and suggestive, they are preliminary. A major limitation of these univariable analyses is that they do not take into account potential confounding factors and other covariates that might influence the degree of association between cocaine use and occurrence of psychiatric disturbances.

In this section we present results to illustrate multivariable analysis of the association between cocaine use and occurrence of panic attacks (Anthony et al. 1989). Corresponding multivariable analyses on the other psychiatric disturbances have been submitted for publication (Anthony and Petronis submitted; Tien and Anthony in press).

The multivariable analysis on panic attacks was developed by sorting covariates into three blocks. As shown in table 5, sociodemographic factors and social role characteristics were grouped as one block of co-

TABLE 5. *Factors under study in the multivariable models*

Sociodemographic and Social Role Factors
Age
Gender
Marital status
Race-ethnicity
Past and current employment status
Years of schooling
Number of adults in household
Baseline occupational prestige score
Controlled Drug Factors*
Cocaine
Marijuana and cannabis products
Sympathomimetic drugs other than cocaine
Heroin
Opioids other than heroin
Psychedelics/hallucinogenics
Prebaseline Psychiatric and Behavioral Disturbances
Baseline DIS lifetime diagnoses for:
Major Depression; depression syndrome
Manic Episode; mania syndrome
Schizophrenia disorders
Phobic disorders
Panic disorder; panic attack
Alcohol abuse and/or dependence; heavy drinking

*Terms for any use during followup, as well as for 2 weeks of daily use during followup.

variates. Terms for use of cocaine and other controlled drugs were considered as a separate block. Finally, baseline DIS variables on preexisting psychopathology and alcohol problems constituted a third block.

Considered individually, only five factors in the sociodemographic block had statistically noteworthy associations with occurrence of panic attacks ($p<0.10$). These factors were gender ($p=0.05$), being separated or divorced at baseline ($p=0.04$), working for pay at baseline ($p=0.009$), and having earned at least a bachelor's degree ($p=0.025$). In addition, there was an inverse association between occupational prestige and occurrence of panic attacks ($p<0.002$).

When the five factors were analyzed together in the multivariable analysis, three factors retained statistical significance: separation/divorce, working for pay, and occupational prestige. After statistical adjustment for these covariates, neither gender nor having earned a bachelor's degree improved the fit of the multivariable model ($p>0.40$). Further, addition of previously excluded sociodemographic factors did not improve the fit of this model.

Considered individually, cocaine use and marijuana use were the only two Schedule I or II drugs whose use was found to be associated with occurrence of panic attacks at a level of statistical significance ($p<0.05$). When terms for cocaine and marijuana use were joined with the sociodemographic model, and after retesting of previously excluded terms, the best-fitting model included terms for the following factors: use of cocaine during followup, but not marijuana; use of marijuana during followup, but not cocaine; use of both cocaine and marijuana during followup; gender; separation/divorce; working for pay; and occupational prestige. Whereas the cocaine-marijuana multiplicative interaction term improved the fit of the model, no other interaction term did so.

At this stage of the analysis, we tested for confounding by psychiatric disturbances detected at baseline, which might otherwise account for associations between cocaine use and occurrence of panic attacks. This was accomplished by introducing terms for factors in the psychopathology block that had proved to be statistically significant in univariable analyses ($p<0.05$). These factors were preexisting DIS-identified Major Depression, Manic Episode, schizophrenic disorders, alcohol abuse or dependence, and heavy drinking. The best-fitting and final multivariable model included terms for DSM Major Depression and heavy drinking. No other psychopathology variable nor previously eliminated covariate added to this final model in terms of statistical significance or appreciable effect on the regression coefficients (i.e., confounding).

The estimates from this final multivariable model are shown in table 6. Each estimate is adjusted for all other terms in the model. The cocaine-marijuana multiplicative interaction term retained its statistical significance. Thus, to understand the occurrence of panic attacks, it was not possible to consider cocaine use during followup without also considering marijuana use during followup. Subjects reporting cocaine use but not marijuana use during followup were at especially increased risk of developing panic attack for the first time (estimated relative risk=13.02). This association had statistical significance ($p=0.004$), though the confidence interval for the estimate was broad because the sample included only eight subjects. This interaction and the overall pattern of findings

TABLE 6. *Estimated relative odds for occurrence of panic attack, based on multivariable logistic regression model with gender, job prestige, drug terms, and psychiatric conditions*

Suspected risk factors	Referent category	Estimated relative odds	95% confidence interval	p value
Job prestige score	NA*	0.99	0.977–0.997	0.015
Female	No	1.90	1.11–3.26	0.020
Marijuana use, no cocaine use	Neither	1.64	0.87–4.78	0.125+
Cocaine use, no marijuana use	Neither	13.02	2.24–75.84	0.004
Marijuana and cocaine use	Neither	2.59	0.94–7.19	0.067+
DSM Major Depression	Absent	4.05	1.90–8.60	<0.0001
DSM heavy drinking	Absent	2.26	1.01–5.07	0.048

SOURCE: Data from ECA probability samples in New Haven, Baltimore, St. Louis, Durham-Piedmont, Los Angeles, 1980-84 (115 matched sets: 122 cases; 387 noncases).

* Not applicable. This score, ranging from low prestige (0 percent) to high prestige (100 percent), was not catergorized.

+ In this model, the interaction coefficient by itself was statistically significant (p=0.041); the joint effect, which is a linear combination of the two main effect coefficients and the interaction coefficient, was at the margin of statistical significance (p=0.067). The main effect for marijuana use lost statistical significance (p=0.125), but is retained because the interaction coefficient remained significant.

are discussed in more detail elsewhere (Anthony et al. 1989). A post hoc conjecture about the interaction is that different results might be obtained in controlled laboratory studies of cocaine effects if the laboratory subjects were recruited specifically from the pool of cocaine users with no recent marijuana experience (e.g., no marijuana use within 1 year of the experiment).

DISCUSSION

A point of departure for our research on cocaine and psychiatric disturbances was Erlenmeyer's clinical observations on cocomania, made more than 100 years ago. Since Erlenmeyer's day, there have been major advances in clinical and laboratory research, with corresponding increases in the plausibility of causal linkage between cocaine use and these disturbances. Nevertheless, progress has been hindered by the apparently limited resolving power of clinical and laboratory research about the linkage.

In this chapter, we suggest that epidemiologic research is in a unique position to complement clinical and laboratory research on cocaine and the occurrence of psychiatric disturbances. If we are correct, epidemiology can help us better understand associations between cocaine and these disturbances, adding to the knowledge base for causal judgments.

Some of the potential value of epidemiology in the study of cocaine hazards is illustrated in this progress report. Taking advantage of the ECA data, which were not gathered with research on cocaine hazards specifically in mind, we have gained a better view of what drug users themselves report about the adverse consequences of cocaine use.

There is good reason to retain a healthy skepticism about self-reported dependence, tolerance, and other consequences of cocaine use. Much remains to be learned about the meaning and clinical significance of these reports (Anthony and Petronis 1989). Nevertheless, the observed pattern of findings showed daily cocaine users to be more likely to report adverse consequences, as were the cocaine users identified in prisons, psychiatric facilities, and other institutions. These relationships may be a first step toward adducing construct validity of the DIS assessment of cocaine consequences, a validation problem that deserves more attention than it has received.

Notwithstanding the value of data on consequences of cocaine use reported by users themselves, epidemiologists can move beyond the basically descriptive issues addressed by these data. In this spirit, our research group focused on suspected causal associations between cocaine use and occurrence of specific psychiatric disturbances. To proceed, we had to take the clinical observations seriously. This meant some suspension of trained disbelief and skepticism about individual case reports and case series described by clinicians (Hogarth 1980). As part of the process, it was necessary to evaluate which suspected cocaine hazards had biologic plausibility in relation to accumulating laboratory evidence on cocaine and the neurobiology of psychiatric disorders. Thereafter, we had to invest some degree of trust in the validity of the ECA data and in its coverage of potentially confounding covariates. Finally, we had to approach the ECA dataset with a strategy that allowed for use of recent advances in epidemiology, biostatistics, and statistical computing.

As shown in the reported estimates for relative risk, this line of epidemiologic research holds promise for a more complete understanding of suspected hazards of cocaine use. This is not to say that the results are unequivocal. As described in our original papers, some limitations of the work must be considered with care. For example, there was only partial control over the possibility that psychiatric disturbances actually preceded or led to use of cocaine during the ECA followup interval. Further, the study's assessment of cocaine use in terms of frequency, route of administration, and other relevant characteristics was not comprehensive. Even so, the potential weaknesses of this work cannot be considered in the abstract. They must be balanced against the strengths of the epidemiologic strategy and placed in relation to weaknesses of clinical and laboratory research on associations between cocaine use and psychiatric conditions. This leads back to the theme of complementarity in clinical, laboratory, and epidemiologic study of cocaine hazards.

In conclusion, the cocaine research reported here may be most valuable as a demonstration that advanced epidemiologic and biostatistical strategies can speak to issues of cocaine hazards in human populations. Our goal is to use these strategies to complement those of the laboratory and clinic. In so doing, we hope for valuable new contributions to an understanding of drug effects.

REFERENCES

Adler, M.; Anthony, J.C.; Balster, R.; Brady, J.; Byck, R.; Croker, K.; Dewey, W.; Dunwiddie, T.; Ellinwood, E.; Finnegan, L.; Fischman, M.; Harris, L.; Hollister, L.; Isner, J.; Jaffe, J.; Jatlow, P.; Johanson, C.E.; Jones, R.; Kaganowich, G.; Kellam, S.; Killam, K.; Kleber, H.; Kreek, J.M.; Lorion, R.; Macdonald, D.; Martin, B.; Schuster, C.R.; Smith, J.; Waranch, M.; Washton, A.; Weiner, N.; Woods, J. Scientific perspectives on cocaine abuse. *Pharmacologist* 29:20–24, 1987.

American Psychiatric Association. *Diagnostic and Statistical Manual (DSM–III)*, 3rd ed. Washington, DC: American Psychiatric Association, 1980.

Anthony, J.C.; Folstein, M.; Romanoski, A.J.; Von Korff, M.R.; Nestadt, G.E.; Chahal, R.; Merchant, A.; Brown, C.H.; Shapiro, S.; Kramer, M.; and Gruenberg, E. Comparison of the Diagnostic Interview Schedule with a standardized psychiatric examination: Experience in eastern Baltimore. *Archives of General Psychiatry* 41:667–675, 1985.

Anthony, J.C. Young adult marijuana use in relation to antecedent misbehaviors. In: Harris, L.S., ed. *Problems of Drug Dependence, 1984*. Washington, DC: Supt. of Docs.; U.S. Govt. Print. Off., 1985. pp.238–244.

Anthony, J.C.; Ritter, C.J.; Von Korff, M.R.; Chee, E.M.; and Kramer, M. Descriptive epidemiology of adult cocaine use in four U.S. communities. In: Harris, L.S., ed. *Problems of Drug Dependence, 1985*. National Institute of Drug Abuse Research Monograph No. 67. DHHS Pub. No. (ADM) 86–1448. Washington, DC: Supt. of Docs., U.S. Govt. Print. Off., 1986. pp. 283–289.

Anthony, J.C. The epidemiologic case-control strategy, with applications in psychiatric research. In: Henderson, A.S., and Burrows, G.D., eds. *Handbook of Social Psychiatry*. Amsterdam: Elsevier Science, 1988. pp. 157–172.

Anthony, J.C.; Tien, A.Y.; and Petronis, K.R. Epidemiologic evidence on cocaine use and panic attacks. *American Journal of Epidemiology* 129: 543–549, 1989.

Anthony, J.C., and Petronis, K.R. Cocaine and heroin dependence compared: Reconsideration with evidence from an epidemiologic field survey. *American Journal of Public Health* 79(10):1409–1410, 1989.

Anthony, J.C., and Helzer, J. Syndromes of drug abuse and dependence. In: Robins, L.N., and Regier, D.A., eds. *Psychiatric Disorders in America*. New York: Free Press, in press.

Anthony, J.C., and Petronis, K.R. Cocaine use and other suspected risk factors for depression. Submitted.

Aronson, T.A., and Craig, T.J. Cocaine precipitation of panic disorder. *American Journal of Psychiatry* 143:643–645, 1987.

Berkson, J. Limitations of the application of fourfold table analysis to hospital data. *Biometrics Bulletin* 2:47–53, 1946.

Bose, K.C. Cocaine intoxication and its demoralizing effects. *British Medical Journal* 1:1020–1022, 1902.

Breslow, N.E., and Day, N.E. Statistical methods in cancer research. Vol. I. *The Analysis of Case-Control Studies*. Lyon: International Agency for Research on Cancer, 1980. pp. 248–279.

Chitwood, D. Patterns and consequences of cocaine use. In: Kozel, N.J., and Adams, E.H., eds. *Cocaine Use in America: Epidemiologic and Clinical Perspectives*. National Institute on Drug Abuse Research Monograph No. 61. DHHS Pub. No. (ADM)85–1414. Washington, DC: Supt. of Docs., U.S. Govt. Print. Off., 1985. pp. 111–129.

Chopra, I.C., and Chopra, R.N. The cocaine problem in India. *Bulletin on Narcotics* 10:12–24, 1958.

Eaton, W.W., and Kessler, L.G., eds. *Epidemiologic Field Methods in Psychiatry: The NIMH Epidemiologic Catchment Area Program*. New York: Academic Press, 1985.

Eaton, W.W.; Holzer, C.E.; Von Korff, M.R.; Anthony, J.C.; Helzer, J.E.; George, L.; Burnam, M.A.; Kessler, J.G.; and Locke, B.Z. The design of the Epidemiologic Catchment Area surveys: The control and measurement of error. *Archives of General Psychiatry* 41:942–948, 1984.

Erlenmeyer, A. Cocomania. In: Tuke, D.H., ed., *Dictionary of Psychological Medicine*. Vol. I. London: J.& A. Churchill, 1892. Reprint. New York: Arno Press, 1976. pp. 236–237.

Fischman, M.W.; Schuster, C.R.; Resnekov, L.; Schick, J.F.E.; Krasnegor, N.A.; Fennel, W.; and Freedman, D.X. Cardiovascular and subjective effects of intravenous cocaine administration in humans. *Archives of General Psychiatry* 33:983–989, 1976.

Fischman, M.W., and Schuster, C.R. Cocaine effects on sleep-deprived humans. *Psychopharmacology* 72:1–8, 1980.

Fischman, M.W.; Schuster, C.R.; and Hatano, Y. A comparison of the subjective and cardiovascular effects of cocaine and lidocaine in humans. *Pharmacology, Biochemistry, and Behavior* 18:123–127, 1983*a*.

Fischman, M.W.; Schuster, C.R.; and Rajfer, S. A comparison of the subjective and cardiovascular effects of procaine and cocaine in humans. *Pharmacology, Biochemistry, and Behavior* 18:711–716, 1983*b*.

Gawin, F.H., and Ellinwood, E.H. Cocaine and other stimulants: Actions, abuse, and treatment. *New England Journal of Medicine* 318:18:1173–1182, 1988.

Gawin, F.H., and Kleber, H.D. Cocaine use in a treatment population: Patterns and diagnostic distinctions. In: Kozel, N.J., and Adams, E.H., eds. *Cocaine Use in America: Epidemiologic and Clinical Perspectives*. National Institute on Drug Abuse Research Monograph No. 61. DHHS Pub. No. (ADM) 85–1414. Washington, DC: Supt. of Docs., U.S. Govt. Print. Off., 1985. pp. 182–192.

Gay, G.R.; Inaba, D.S.; Sheppard, C.W.; and Newmeyer, J.A. Cocaine: History, epidemiology, human pharmacology, and treatment. A perspective on a new debut for an old girl. *Clinical Toxicology* 8:149–178, 1975.

Gold, M.S.; Dackis, C.A.; Pottash, A.L.C.; Extein, I.; and Washton, A. Cocaine update: From bench to bedside. *Advances in Alcohol and Substance Abuse* 5:35–60, 1985–1986.

Gordon, A. Insanities caused by acute and chronic intoxication with opium and cocaine. *JAMA* 51:97–101, 1908.

Hasin, D.S.; Grant, B.F.; Endicott, J.; and Harford, T.C. Cocaine and heroin dependence compared in poly-drug abusers. *American Journal of Public Health* 78:567–569, 1988.

Hogarth, R.M. Judgement, drug monitoring, and decision aids. In: Inman, W.H.W., ed. *Monitoring for Drug Safety*. Philadelphia: Lippincott, 1980. pp. 439–478.

Jeri, F.R.; Sanchez, C.C.; Pozo, T.; Fernandez, M.; and Carbajal, C. Further experience with the syndromes produced by coca paste smoking. *Bulletin on Narcotics* XXX:3:1–11, 1978.

Kellam, S.K.; Brown, C.H.; Rubin, B.R.; and Ensminger, M.E. Paths leading to teenage psychiatric symptoms and substance abuse: Developmental epidemiological studies in Woodlawn. In: Guze, S.B.; Earls, F.J.; and Barrett, J.E., eds. *Childhood Psychopathology and Development.* New York: Raven Press, 1983. pp.17–51.

Kleinbaum, D.G.; Kupper, L.L.; and Morgenstern, H. *Epidemiologic Research: Principles and Quantitative Methods*. Belmont, CA: Lifetime Learning Publications, 1982.

Lesko, L.M.; Fischman, M.W.; Javaid, J.I.; and Davis, J.M. Iatrogenous cocaine psychosis. *New England Journal of Medicine* 307:1152, 1982.

Mantel, N. Synthetic retrospective studies and related topics. *Biometrics Bulletin* 29:479–486, 1973.

Post, R.M. Cocaine psychosis: A continuum model. *American Journal of Psychiatry* 132:225–231, 1975.

Resnick, R.B.; Kestenbaum, R.S.; and Schwartz, L.K. Acute systemic effects of cocaine in man: A controlled study by intranasal and intravenous routes. *Science* 195:696–699, 1977.

Robins, L.N. *Deviant Children Grown Up*. Baltimore: Williams and Wilkins, 1966.

Robins, L.N.; Helzer, J.E.; Croughan, J.; and Ratcliff, K.A. National Institute of Mental Health Diagnostic Interview Schedule: Its history, characteristics, and validity. *Archives of General Psychiatry* 38:381–389, 1981.

Rothman, K.J. *Modern Epidemiology*. Boston: Little, Brown, 1986.

Sherer, M.A.; Kumor, K.M; Cone, E.J.; Jaffe, J.H. Suspiciousness induced by four-hour intravenous infusions of cocaine. *Archives of General Psychiatry* 45:673–677, 1988.

Spotts, J.V., and Shontz, F.C. *Cocaine Users*. New York: Free Press, 1980.

Storer, B.E.; Wacholder, S.; and Breslow, N.E. Maximum likelihood fitting of general risk models to stratified data. *Applied Statistics* 32:172–181, 1983.

Storer, B.E., and Crowley, J.C. A diagnostic for Cox regression and general conditional likelihood. *Journal of the American Statistical Association* 80:139–147, 1985.

Tien, A.Y., and Anthony, J.C. Epidemiologic analysis of alcohol and drug use as risk factors for psychotic experiences. *Journal of Nervous and Mental Disease*, in press.

U.S. Department of Health and Human Services, National Institute on Drug Abuse. *National Household Survey on Drug Abuse: Main Findings, 1985*. Washington, DC: Supt. of Docs., U.S. Govt. Print. Off., 1988.

Von Korff, M.R., and Anthony, J.C. The NIMH Diagnostic Interview Schedule modified to record current mental status. *Journal of Affective Disorders* 4:365–371, 1982.

Wise, R.A. Neural mechanisms of the reinforcing action of cocaine. In: Grabowski, J., ed. *Cocaine pharmacology, effects, and treatment of abuse*. National Institute of Drug Abuse Research Monograph No. 50, DHHS Pub. No. (ADM)84–1326. Washington, DC: Supt. of Docs., U.S. Govt. Print. Off., 1984. pp.15–33.

ACKNOWLEDGMENTS

Other members of the psychoactive drug hazard research group during the period of this work were Christian Ritter, Allen Tien, Howard Chilcoat, and Ahmed Aboraya. This research was supported by a grant from the National Institute of Drug Abuse (DA0392).

AUTHORS

James C. Anthony, Ph.D.

Kenneth R. Petronis

Department of Mental Hygiene
The Johns Hopkins University
School of Hygiene and Public Health
615 N. Wolfe Street
Baltimore, MD 21205

Preliminary Findings of an Epidemiologic Study of Cocaine-Related Deaths, Dade County, Florida, 1978–85

A. James Ruttenber, Patricia A. Sweeney, James M. Mendlein, and Charles V. Wetli

Fatal cocaine overdoses in the United States, as reported by the Drug Abuse Warning Network of the National Institute on Drug Abuse, increased ninefold from 1978 to 1985 (NIDA 1987). Though theories have been proposed for the etiology of the epidemic of fatal cocaine overdoses that occurred throughout the country, no study has clarified the relation between the increase in these deaths and potentially contributing factors, such as the prevalence of cardiovascular disease in a population of cocaine users, the concentration of cocaine in street-level samples, or measures of the street availability of cocaine. Commonly, local epidemics are attributed to increases in purity of street-level cocaine (Wetli 1987).

Many reports have been made recently of the association between cocaine overdose and various cardiovascular diseases, particularly cardiac arrhythmias and myocardial infarction (Cregler and Mark 1986; Isner et al. 1986). To date, these events have been described only for groups of selected cases. These case reports have not determined whether cardiovascular diseases are risk factors for cocaine overdose or merely coincidental findings in the population of cocaine users. Furthermore, case reports cannot be used to establish the prevelance of cardiovascular anomalies in selected populations of cocaine users and fatal overdose victims.

This chapter describes preliminary data for an ongoing study of fatalities associated with cocaine use in Dade County, Florida. We examined risk factors for fatal overdose through traditional case-control analysis. We also analyzed the temporal distribution of fatal cocaine overdoses and risk factors for the preliminary study period 1978–85, when fatal cocaine overdose assumed epidemic proportions in metropolitan Miami.

METHOD

The jurisdiction of the Metropolitan Dade County Medical Examiner Department (MDCMED) encompasses all of Dade County and includes the city of Miami and other municipalities. The population of Dade County was 1,625,781 in 1980, and 1,771,000 in 1985. Since 1983, the county population has increased by about 1.3 percent per year. During the period of this study, the MDCMED routinely performed medicolegal investigations of all deaths from causes other than natural ones. Forensic pathologists identified the victim, evaluated the scene environment and circumstances of death, and autopsied the victim to determine the cause and manner of death.

Before 1985, testing of biologic fluids was done only when drugs were suspected to have played a role in death or when there was evidence that the death was associated with violence. Since 1985, the urine from each decedent has been screened for common drugs of abuse, and positive results have been confirmed by quantitative analysis of blood. During the study period, blood cocaine was quantified in flouride-preserved blood with a gas-liquid chromatographic procedure using a nitrogen detector. Enzyme-multiplied immunoassay was also used to detect benzoylecgonine in the urine, and for selected subjects, gastric contents and nasal swabs were screened for cocaine with thin-layer chromatography (Mittleman and Wetli 1984).

All subjects were selected from deaths investigated by the MDCMED. A cocaine-related death (CRD) was defined as a death that was investigated by the MDCMED and, based on medical judgment, was attributed to the toxic effects of cocaine alone or cocaine in combination with another drug or with the effects of a cardiovascular or cerebrovascular disease. These deaths were the cases in the case-control analysis. A control was defined as a person who died from causes not associated with cocaine use and who had cocaine detected in blood at autopsy.

Subjects who survived for 7 or more hours after overdose, or who died after hospitalization for an overdose, were eliminated from the case control analyses that included toxicologic data. This was done to minimize spurious results caused by the rapid deterioration of cocaine in postmortem blood. In the analysis of temporal trends for CRDs, the concentration of cocaine in blood was excluded from analysis for only those decedents who were hospitalized prior to death.

Descriptions of all pathologic findings for cases and controls were reviewed by a medical epidemiologist with training in pathology.

Coronary artery arteriosclerosis was categorized as mild, moderate, or severe, based on written descriptions of gross and microscopic pathology in the autopsy reports. Subjects for whom quantitative estimates of coronary artery occlusion were made were classified according to the following criteria for the most occlusive lesion: mild, 1–24 percent; moderate, 25–74 percent; and severe, 75 percent or more.

Median values and the Wilcoxon signed rank-sum test were used to compare variables for cases and controls, because the values were not normally distributed in each variable we examined. Crude odds ratios were estimated by the Mantel-Haenszel method. The median blood cocaine concentration for cases was used to create a dichotomous variable for computing odds ratios.

We used multiple logistic regression models to adjust for the confounding effects of significant risk factors identified in the crude analyses. A full regression model that included all the variables with significant crude odds ratios was first used to simultaneously adjust odds ratios for confounding between variables. We employed a backward stepwise elimination procedure (Kleinbaum et al. 1982) to retain only the variables that had a significant association with the distribution of cases and controls ($p \leq 0.05$). Ninety-five-percent confidence intervals for all odds ratios were calculated with unconditional maximum likelihood estimates.

Annual measures of the incidence of CRDs, median blood cocaine concentrations for cases and controls, and the frequency of other risk factors for CRD in cases and controls were computed for the period 1976–85. Trends in these variables were graphically described and compared to develop hypotheses for the etiology of the epidemic of CRDs in Dade County. For some years during the study, there were no subjects in the selected categories, or no subjects with measurements of the variables of interest. In these instances, no annual data were plotted.

RESULTS

Case-Control Analysis

From the records of the 401 decedents who had cocaine detected in blood, we identified 125 CRDs (cases) and 238 controls. The majority of controls (66 percent) were victims of firearm-related homicide, 12 percent were victims of suicide, and 8 percent died in motor vehicle accidents (table 1). Thirty-eight decedents were excluded from the case control analyses because they exhibited effects of cocaine atypical for accidental overdose or because factors in addition to cocaine toxicity

TABLE 1. *Manner of death for controls*

Manner of death	N	(%)
Suicide*	29	(12)
Homicide, with firearm	157	(66)
Homicide, stabbed or beaten	16	(7)
Homicide, other	10	(4)
Accident, motor vehicle	18	(8)
Accident, other	7	(3)
Other	1	(0)
Total	238	(100)

* Manner of death other than drug overdose.

contributed to death. The excluded subjects were primarily "body packers" (Mittleman and Wetli 1981), victims of drowning, and cocaine-induced suicides.

Cases differed significantly from controls with respect to all categorical variables shown in table 2. The majority of subjects were male. Forty-eight percent of cases were white and non-Hispanic, while 40 percent of the controls were white and Hispanic. The route of administration of cocaine prior to death was not consistently reported, particularly for control decedents. Intranasal and intravenous administration were the most commonly noted routes for cases. Needle tracks and morphine in urine were detected more frequently for cases than for controls.

Cases and controls were comparable in age, height, body weight, and heart weight (table 3). Cases differed significantly from controls with regard to lung and liver weight. Blood ethanol levels were higher in controls, and blood cocaine and morphine levels were higher in cases. The only cardiovascular diagnoses consistently reported in MDCMED autopsy reports were ventricular hypertrophy and coronary arteriosclerosis. Six percent of the cases and only 1 percent of the controls had severe coronary arteriosclerosis.

Crude odds ratios for selected variables are presented in table 4. Though the presence of any arteriosclerosis was not associated with CRD, the crude odds ratios for both severe coronary arteriosclerosis and ventricular hypertrophy were both significantly elevated. The odds ratios

TABLE 2. *Descriptive data for selected categorical variables*

Variable	Category	Cases* (N=125) N (%)	Controls (N=238) N(%)	p+
Sex	Male	86 (69)	203 (85)	
	Female	39 (31)	35 (15)	<0.001
Race	White, non-Hispanic‡	60 (48)	42 (18)	
	White, Hispanic	29 (23)	95 (40)	
	Black, non-Hispanic	33 (26)	82 (34)	
	Black, Hispanic	2 (2)	20 (8)	
	Other, Pacific Island	1 (1)	0 (0)	<0.001
Route of administration	Intranasal	28 (44)	3 (38)	
	Freebased, smoked	2 (3)	5 (63)	
	Injection	28 (44)	0 (0)	
	Vaginal, rectal	2 (3)	0 (0)	
	Other	3 (5)	0 (0)	<0.001§
	Not reported	62	230	
Pulmonary edema	Yes	86 (70)	50 (21)	
	No	36 (30)	184 (79)	<0.001
Urine morphine	Positive	15 (13)	10 (5)	
	Negative	99 (87)	210 (95)	<0.005
Presence of needle tracks	Yes	32 (26)	14 (6)	
	No	89 (74)	217 (94)	<0.001
Presence of fresh injection sites	Yes	37 (31)	5 (2)	
	No	84 (69)	224 (98)	<0.001

* For each route, percentage was based only on those subjects for whom evidence was available.

+ Chi-square test (2-tailed) for significance.

‡ Hispanic surname.

§ Eighty percent of the observations are unknown; chi square may be an invalid test

TABLE 3. *Measure of central tendency* for continuous variables*

Variable	Cases+	Controls+	p
Age (years)	29 (125)+	30 (237)	0.2015
Height (inches)	68 (123)	68 (233)	0.6711
Weight (pounds)	152 (123)	150 (235)	0.2880
Heart weight (grams)	350 (118)	340 (235)	0.0501
Combined lung weight (grams)	1140 (122)	810 (236)	<0.0001
Liver weight (grams)	1815 (120)	1540 (237)	<0.0001
Blood ethanol (mg/100 ml)	16[z](110)	54[z](232)	<0.0001
Blood cocaine (mg/L)	1.800 (113)	0.230 (232)	<0.0001
Blood morphine (mg/L)	0.029[z](112)	0.004[z](228)	0.0090

* Unless otherwise specified, median values express central tendency, and significance is evaluated with Wilcoxon rank-sum test.

+ Parentheses indicate number of subjects.

z Median=0, mean reported.

TABLE 4. *Crude odds ratios for case control analysis*

	Odds ratio	95% confidence interval
Blood cocaine (≥ 1.80 mg/L* vs. < 1.80 mg/L)	20.4	11.2–37.0
Fresh injection sites (present vs. absent)	19.7	9.3–41.9
Needle tracks (present vs. absent)	5.6	3.0–10.42
Arteriosclerosis (severe vs. mild, moderate, or none)	4.7	1.3–16.5
Ventricular hypertrophy (present vs. absent)	3.5	1.5–8.3
Blood morphine (positive vs. negative)	3.4	1.3–9.0
Urine morphine (positive vs. negative)	3.2	1.4–7.09
Race (white vs. all other)	1.8	1.1–2.9
Arteriosclerosis (any vs. none)	1.6	0.9–3.0
Sex (male vs. female)	0.4	0.2–0.6
Blood ethanol (≥100 mg/100 ml vs. <100 mg/100 ml)	0.1	0.0–0.3

* Median concentration for cases.

for a blood cocaine concentration greater than or equal to 1.80 mg/L and for the detection of morphine in either blood or urine were significantly elevated. The odds ratio for a blood ethanol concentration greater than 100 mg/100 ml was significantly less than one. We also found significantly elevated odds ratios for the presence of both fresh injection sites and needle tracks.

In the crude and stratified analyses, the presence of both fresh injection sites and track marks were similarly associated with cases, but not with controls. We chose evidence of fresh injection sites to reflect intravenous cocaine use in the final logistic regression model (table 5). In this model, adjusted odds ratios were significantly elevated for blood cocaine concentration, severe arteriosclerosis, ventricular hypertrophy, and the presence of injection. The odds ratios for a blood ethanol concentration greater than 100 mg/100 ml was significantly less than one.

TABLE 5. *Logistic regression model*

Variable	Odds ratio	95% confidence limits
Fresh injection sites (present vs. absent)	18.6	(6.4—54.2)
Arteriosclerosis (severe vs. mild, moderate and none)	17.0	(2.9—100.6)
Ventricular hypertrophy (present vs. absent)	5.1	(1.4—17.6)
Blood cocaine concentration (mg/L, continuous)	2.1	(1.6—2.9)
Blood alcohol (≥ 100 mg/100 ml vs. <100 mg/100 ml)	0.2	(0.1—0.9)

Analysis of Temporal Trends

The annual incidence of CRDs in Dade County rose from 8 in 1978 to 30 in 1985 (figure 1). The incidence of CRDs nearly doubled between 1981 and 1982 and between 1983 and 1985. The annual median blood cocaine concentrations for CRDs in these years had no relation to the frequency of CRDs (figure 2). In fact, median blood cocaine concentrations rose markedly between 1978 and 1981, when the incidence of CRDs was stable, and actually declined during both periods of substantial increase for CRDs. The median blood concentrations for controls were stable throughout this period.

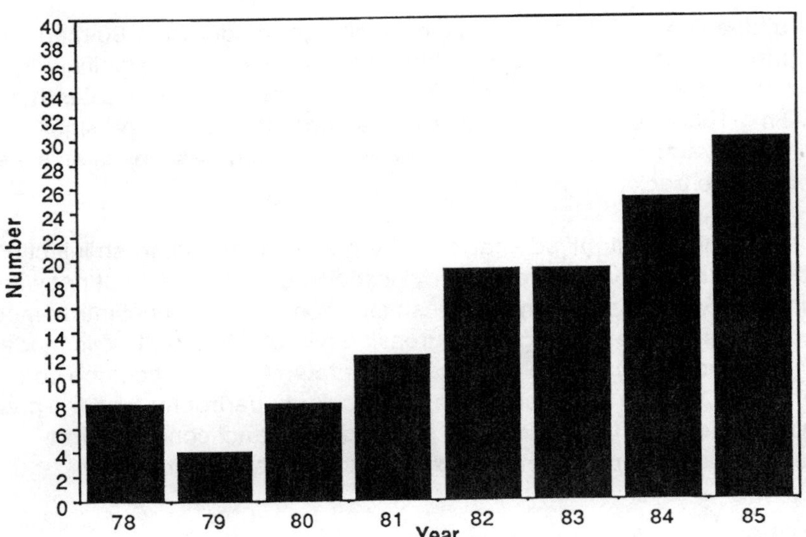

FIGURE 1. *Annual incidence of cociane-related deaths in Dade County, Florida*

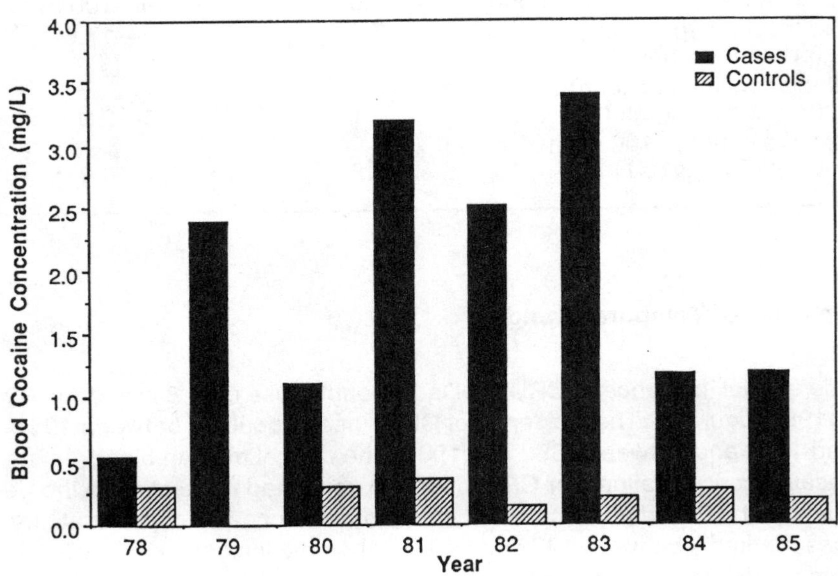

FIGURE 2. *Annual median blood cocaine concentrations in cases and controls*

Assessment of the temporal distribution of cardiovascular risk factors for CRD reveals that arteriosclerosis was not diagnosed in decedents before 1980. The diagnosis of severe arteriosclerosis in CRDs was first made in 1982. The frequency of this finding doubled between 1983 and 1984, but returned to the original level in 1985 (figure 3). Severe arteriosclerosis was rarely diagnosed for controls. Evidence of any coronary arteriosclerosis was first reported for controls in 1980 and for cases in 1981 (figure 4). Ventricular hypertrophy was commonly diagnosed in 13 to 17 percent of cases between 1978 and 1981, but declined to 6 percent between 1982 and 1983 (figure 5). Ventricular hypertrophy was less common in controls.

The frequency of seizures reported prior to death for cases was highest in 1981 and declined in subsequent years (figure 6). The median age for cases increased from 25 in 1978 to 30 in 1985 and increased in a similar manner for controls (figure 7). The frequency of detection of ethanol in the blood was fairly stable for cases, but increased substantially for controls between 1981 and 1985 (figure 8).

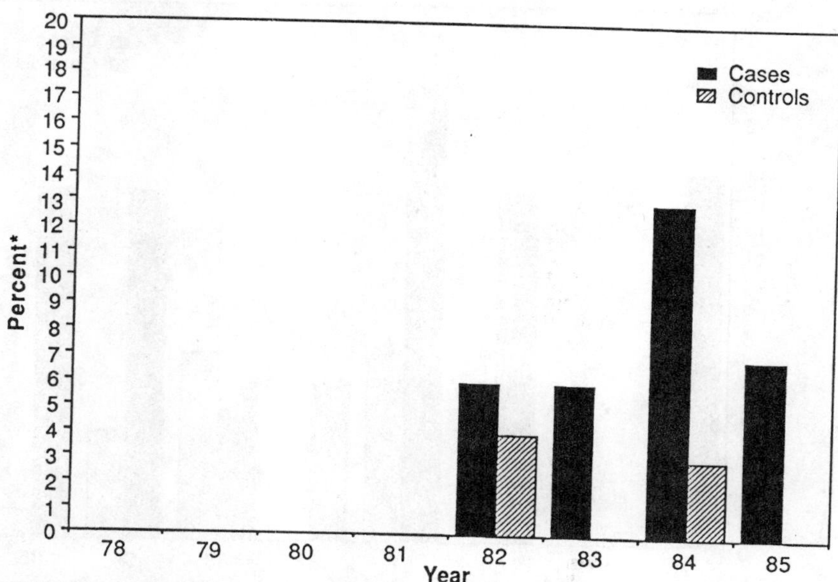

FIGURE 3. *Annual frequency of cases and controls with severe coronary arteriosclerosis*

* Percent of those cases or controls with adequate descriptions of gross pathology.

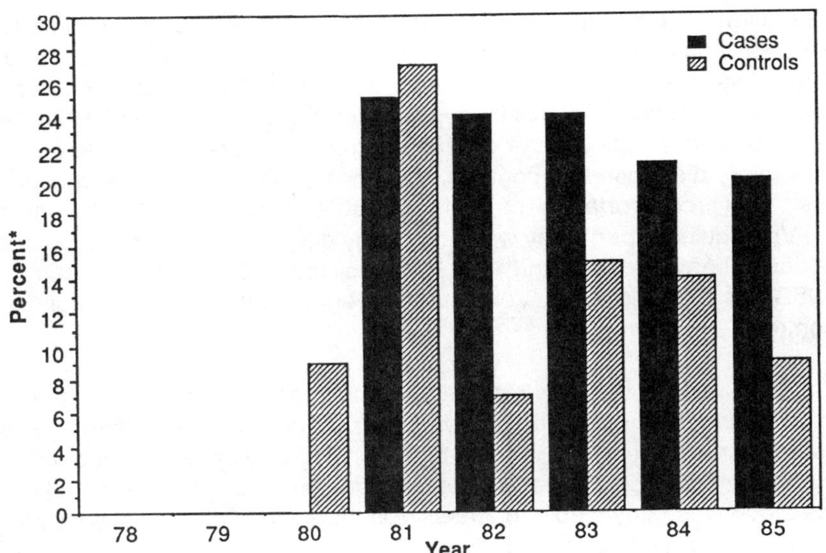

FIGURE 4. *Annual frequency of cases and controls with any evidence of coronary arteriosclerosis*

* Percent of those cases or controls with adequate descriptions of gross pathology.

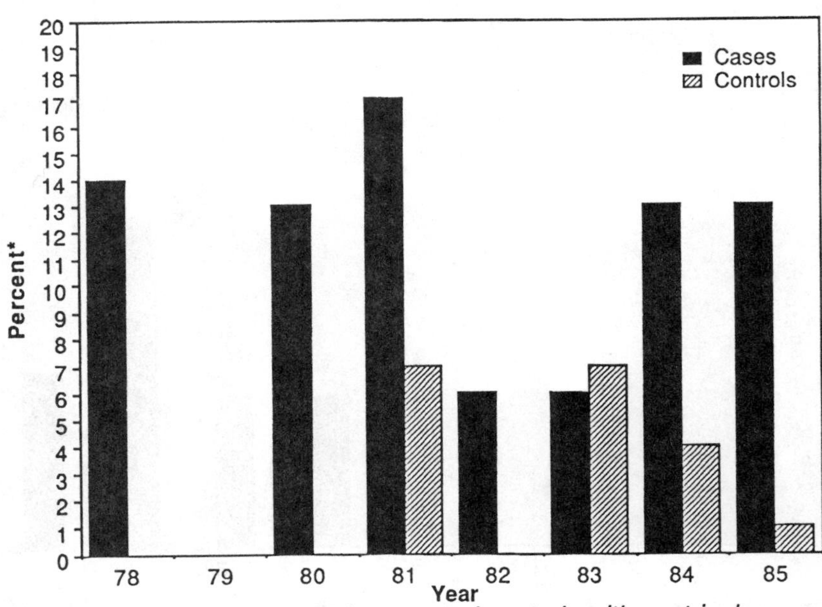

FIGURE 5. *Annual frequency of cases and controls with ventricular hypertrophy*

* Percent of those cases or controls with adequate descriptions of gross pathology.

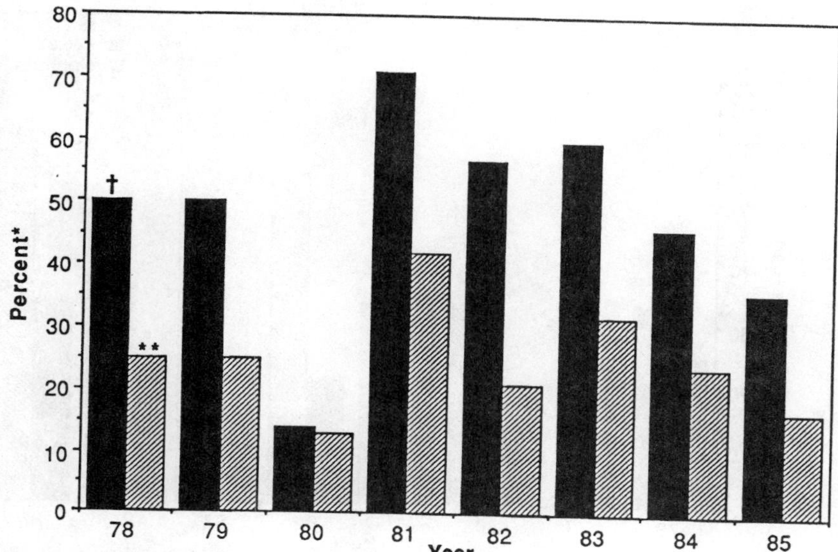

FIGURE 6. *Annual frequency of cases with seizures prior to death*
* Percent of those cases or controls with adequate descriptions of gross pathology.
† Percent of those cases with adequate descriptions of signs and symptoms of overdose.
** Percent of all cases.

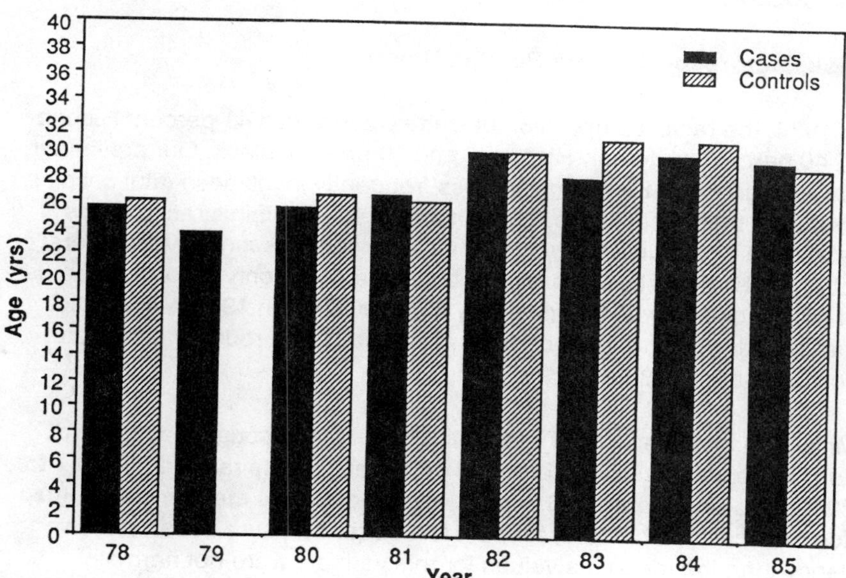

FIGURE 7. *Annual median age of cases and controls*

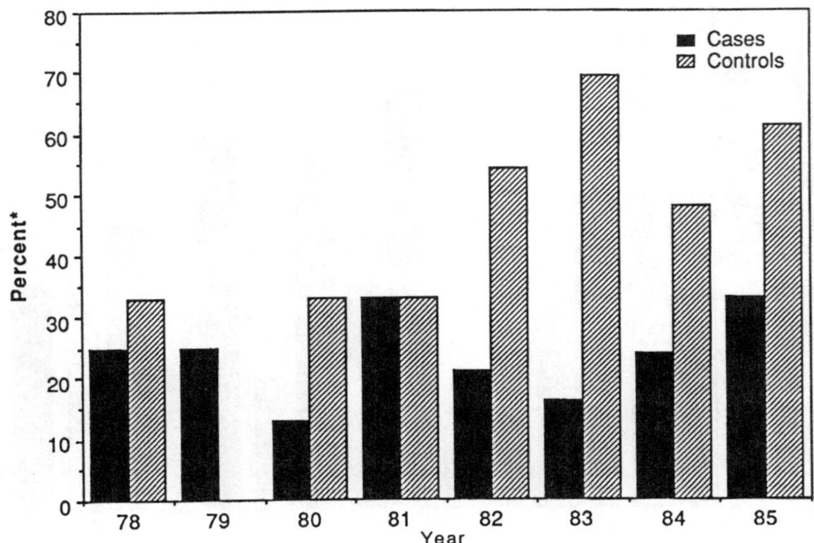

FIGURE 8. *Annual frequency of cases and controls with ethanol in blood*

DISCUSSION

Risk Factors for Cocaine-Related Death

In 1984, the racial composition of Dade County was 41 percent Hispanic, 40 percent white non-Hispanic, and 19 percent black. Our preliminary data suggest that Hispanics are less frequently involved in fatal cocaine overdose than other races. Though the route of administration of the fatal dose of cocaine was usually not specified by scene investigators, intranasal administration and injection were commonly reported. The use of crack cocaine was first noted by the MDCMED in 1985. We predict that smoking will be more commonly reported as a route of administration in data for 1986 and 1987.

Mittleman and Wetli (1984) determined that blood cocaine concentrations in decedents who overdosed on street cocaine ranged from 0.1 to 20.9 mg/L and averaged 6.2 mg/L. We reported the median concentration of cocaine in blood because it is a better measure of central tendency than the mean, as values for this variable were not normally distributed. In our preliminary study, the median blood cocaine concentration for CRDs was substantially lower than the average previously reported for CRDs, but the average concentration, 5.2 mg/L, was only slightly lower. Because there are yearly changes in median blood cocaine concentrations and the frequency of risk factors for CRD, it may be important to consider the year of death and other contributing causes of death in comparisons between blood cocaine concentrations for CRDs.

Through the computation of crude odds ratios, we identified a number of variables that were either positively or negatively associated with fatal cocaine overdose. Blood cocaine concentration in excess of the median concentration for cases was the variable with the highest crude odds ratio, indicating that the amount of cocaine used is related to a high likelihood of fatal overdose. Indicators of intravenous administration are also substantial risk factors. These variables suggest that the intensity of cocaine use and the rate at which cocaine enters the bloodstream could both increase the risk of fatal overdose.

The finding that whites are at greater risk for fatal overdose than other races is probably an artifact, because the majority of controls were homicide victims, who were more commonly black and Hispanic than white. This same bias is probably responsible for the identification of male sex and high blood ethanol concentration as protective factors. Both white race and male sex were not retained in the final logistic regression model, indicating that these variables were probably confounded by other variables with stronger influences on the model.

We identified severe coronary arteriosclerosis and ventricular hypertrophy as significant risk factors for CRD. Cregler and Mark (1986) summarized 17 cases of fatal myocardial infarction following cocaine use and noted a consistent temporal relationship between use of cocaine and subsequent myocardial infarction. Twelve of these decedents had either preexisting angina or a previous myocardial infarction that was not related to cocaine use. The remaining five, each under 40 years of age, had no previous history of heart disease. Isner et al. (1986) described 26 fatal cardiac events that followed administration of cocaine by inhalation or smoking. Underlying heart disease was not common in these deaths, and at least seven of the subjects had normal coronary arteriograms.

Our data show that many CRDs had coronary artery disease, but only a few had disease that was significant enough by epidemiologic criteria to have contributed to fatal overdose. It is not clear whether these victims died from myocardial infarction or from arrhythmia. We also found ventricular hypertrophy to be a significant risk factor for fatal cocaine overdose. To our knowledge, this disease has not been previously associated with CRDs. This finding is consistent with the recognized relation between ventricular hypertrophy and cardiac arrhythmia (Huston et al. 1985; McLenachan et al. 1987) and suggests that ventricular hypertrophy and perhaps other manifestations of myocardial thickening or chamber enlargement could enhance the arrhythmogenic effects of cocaine. The influence of ventricular hypertrophy on CRD may be similar to the risk for fatal arrhythmia noted in athletes with athletic heart syndrome (Huston et al. 1985).

Though we found both severe coronary artery disease and ventricular hypertrophy to have strong and significant influences on the risk for CRD, only 6 percent of the cases in our study had severe coronary arteriosclerosis, and only 11 percent had ventricular hypertrophy. These risk factors, therefore, appear to explain only a portion of the CRDs that occurred during our study period.

Analysis of Temporal Trends: Cocaine-Related Deaths And Associated Risk Factors

Though the factors responsible for the epidemic of CRDs in Dade County have not been clearly identified, there is little evidence to suggest that the epidemic is merely a result of increasingly strong preparations of cocaine. Blood cocaine concentrations in victims of fatal overdose may not exactly reflect the purity of street cocaine preparations, but this measurement is probably one of the best that is available. To our knowledge, no reliable data exist for establishing temporal changes in the cocaine concentration and chemical composition of street preparations of cocaine in Dade County or in other U.S. communities. The fact that blood cocaine concentrations for controls remained stable throughout the study period suggests that laboratory error or change in laboratory procedure are unlikely explanations for declining blood cocaine concentrations in cases.

Possible explanations for the epidemic of CRDs include: (1) an increase in the absolute number of cocaine users who had underlying cardiovascular disease severe enough to contribute to fatal overdose; (2) the presence of toxic compounds other than cocaine in street preparations of cocaine; (3) sensitization of the heart and the sympathetic nervous system to the toxic effects of cocaine or the development of coronary artery obstruction through chronic use of this drug (Fischman et al. 1976; Simpson and Edwards 1986); and (4) increases in the frequency of other risk factors as yet unidentified.

The temporal distribution of the frequency of coronary arteriosclerosis and ventricular hypertrophy suggests that these risk factors became more frequent in the case group during the epidemic. This increase may be due to the increase in the number of cocaine users during the period of study and, hence, the absolute number of persons with cardiovascular disease. Gross pathologic evidence for this risk was not noted frequently enough, however, to explain the majority of deaths during the epidemic. Perhaps some CRDs had early disease that was clinically significant but not severe enough to have led to gross pathologic changes observable at autopsy.

Montagne and Rinfret (this volume) provide evidence for the expanded availability of cocaine during our preliminary study period. Montagne documents a striking increase in the worldwide production of coca leaf in the early 1980s and in the illicit importation of cocaine into the United States, Canada, and Europe between 1983 and 1985. Both of these changes occurred during periods noted for high rates of CRDs in the Dade County epidemic. Even more interesting is the stabilization of the frequency of CRDs between 1982 and 1983, when Bolivia suffered a major drought that caused a temporary reduction in cocaine production (Montagne, this volume).

In the laboratory, seizures can be induced in animals by increasing the dose of cocaine administered (Ritchie and Greene 1985), and seizures followed by respiratory arrest are frequently noted in humans who have consumed large quantities of cocaine (Simpson and Edwards 1986; Wetli 1987). Our data indicate that the percentage of CRDs with seizures declined during the epidemic, a finding that is consistent with the toxicology data. Perhaps the cause of CRD in decedents with comparatively low concentrations of blood cocaine is different from that for those with high concentrations. Because the majority of CRDs we studied did not have seizures, they may have died from the effects of cardiac arrhythmia (Ritchie and Greene 1985), uncomplicated by the effects of cocaine upon the central nervous system.

The finding that cocaine concentrations in CRDs declined during the epidemic is also consistent with the hypothesis that compounds other than cocaine contributed to these deaths. Many compounds that occur naturally in the coca plant or that can be made during cocaine processing (Lee 1986) are psychoactive and also might increase risk for cardiac arrhythmia (El-Imam et al. 1985; Novak et al. 1984). A major change in the location of coca processing laboratories from Chile and Brazil to Colombia occurred in the early 1980s (Montagne, this volume). At the same time, coca paste was diverted to South Florida and Caribbean nations for processing, in response to importation restrictions on ether in Colombia (Inciardi, this volume). Both of these alterations in the traditional processing of cocaine could have stimulated interest in increasing the yield of marketable white powder from processed coca leaves, which might contain toxic compounds other than cocaine (Lee 1986).

We have not analyzed data relevant to the hypothesized effect of chronic cocaine use on both potentiating the toxic effects of cocaine and damaging coronary vasculature. We have collected, but have not yet analyzed, data on the history of drug abuse for cases and controls. We did note a slight increase in the median age of CRDs during the preliminary study period, and this finding is consistent with the hypothesized effects of chronic cocaine use. This finding is also consistent with the recruitment into the population of cocaine users of older persons who may have been at greater risk for cardiovascular disease.

CONCLUSION

Our preliminary analyses show that cardiovascular disease appears to increase the risk for fatal cocaine overdose. The association of ventricular hypertrophy with CRD is a new finding, but one that is consistent with the known toxic effects of cocaine. The fact that in the 1980s, CRDs seem to be related to these cardiovascular risk factors (but not to the occurrence of seizures before death) and that the median blood cocaine concentration in CRDs declined during the epidemic suggests that the mechanism for many fatal cocaine overdoses is cardiac arrhythmia and not respiratory arrest precipitated by a seizure.

The new findings in this preliminary study will be evaluated in more detail in the final analysis of all CRDs that occurred in Dade County between 1971, the year of the first reported CRD, and the end of 1987. The preliminary analysis strongly suggests, however, that factors in addition to the dose of cocaine administered before death are involved in the etiology of fatal cocaine overdose. A clarification of risk factors, mechanisms, and the toxicology of coca alkaloids may help provide public health measures that can reduce the epidemic of CRDs in Dade County and in the United States.

REFERENCES

Cregler, L.L., and Mark, H. Medical complications of cocaine abuse. *New England Journal of Medicine* 315:1495–1500, 1986.

El-Imam, Y.M.A.; Evans, W.C.; and Plowman, T. Alkaloids of some South American *Erythroxylum* species. *Phytochemistry* 24:2285–2289, 1985.

Fischman, M.W.; Schuster, C.R.; Resnekov, L.; Shick, J.F.; Krasnegor, N.A.; Fenneii, W.; and Freedman, D.X. Cardiovascular and subjective effects of intravenous cocaine administration in humans. *Archives of General Psychiatry* 33:983–989, 1976.

Huston, T.P.; Puffer, J.C.; and Rodney, W.M. The athletic heart syndrome. *New England Journal of Medicine* 313:24–32, 1985.

Isner, J.M.; Estes, N.A.M.; Thompson, P.D.; Costanzo-Nordin, M.R.; Subramanian, R.; Miller, G.; Katsas, G.; Sweeney, K.; and Sturner, W.Q. Acute cardiac events temporally related to cocaine abuse. *New England Journal of Medicine* 315:1438–1443, 1986.

Kleinbaum, D.G.; Kupper, L.L.; and Morgenstern, H. *Epidemiologic Research, Principles and Quantitative Methods*. Belmont, CA: Lifetime Learning Publications, 1982. pp. 477–491.

Lee, D. *Cocaine Handbook*. Berkeley, CA: And/Or Press, 1986. pp 32–39.

McLenachan, J.M.; Henderson, E.; Morris, K.I.; and Dargie, H.J. Ventricular arrhythmias with hypertensive left ventricular hypertrophy. *New England Journal of Medicine* 317:787–792, 1987.

Mittleman, R.E., and Wetli, C.V. The body packer syndrome, toxicity following ingestion of illicit drugs packaged for transportation. *Journal of Forensic Science* 26:492–500, 1981.

Mittleman, R.E., and Wetli, C.V. Death caused by recreational cocaine use—An update. *JAMA* 252:1889–1893, 1984.

National Institute on Drug Abuse. *Trends in Drug Abuse Related Hospital Emergency Room Episodes and Medical Examiner Cases for Selected Drugs, DAWN 1976–1985*. DHHS Pub. No. (ADM)87–1524. Washington, DC: Supt. of Docs., U.S. Govt. Print. Off., 1987.

Novak, M.; Salemink, C.A.; and Khan, I. Biological activity of the alkaloids of *Erythroxylum coca* and *Erythroxylum novogranatense*. *Journal of Ethnopharmacology* 10:261–274, 1984.

Ritchie, J.M., and Greene, N.M. Local anesthetics. In: Gilman, A.G.; Goodman, L.S.; Rall, T.W.; and Murad, F., eds. *The Pharmacological Basis of Therapeutics*. 7th ed. New York: Macmillan, 1985.

Simpson, R.W., and Edwards, W.D. Pathogenesis of cocaine-induced ischemic heart disease. *Archives of Pathology Laboratory Medicine* 110:479–484, 1986.

Wetli, C.V. Fatal cocaine intoxication, a review. *American Journal of Forensic Medical Pathology* 8:1–2, 1987.

Wetli, C.V. Fatal reactions to cocaine. In: Washton, A.M., and Gold, M.S., eds. *Cocaine, a Clinician's Handbook*. New York: Guilford Press, 1987. pp. 33–54.

AUTHORS

A. James Ruttenber, Ph.D., M.D.

Patricia A. Sweeney

James M. Mendlein, Ph.D.

DEHHE, CEHIC
Koger F28
Centers for Disease Control,
1600 Clifton Road
Atlanta, GA 30333.

Charles V. Wetli, M.D.
Dade County Medical Examiner Office
1851 Northwest 9th Avenue
Miami, FL 33136

Frequency of Cocaine Use and Violence: A Comparison Between Men and Women

Paul J. Goldstein, Patricia A. Bellucci, Barry J. Spunt, and Thomas Miller

The relationship between drugs and violence has been characterized by three models: psychopharmacological, economic-compulsive, and systemic. This tripartite conceptual framework was fully discussed in previous publications (Goldstein 1985, 1986, 1989).

The psychopharmacological model suggests that some individuals, as a result of long- or short-term ingestion of specific substances, may become excitable and irrational and may act out in a violent fashion. Also, some persons' behavior may be modified by drug ingestion in such a way as to bring about their own violent victimization. A classic example of this phenomenon is the inebriate who is boisterous and obnoxious until somebody punches him in the nose. The irritability associated with withdrawal syndrome, that is, the absence of a drug rather than its presence, may also lead to psychopharmacological violence.

The economic-compulsive model suggests that some drug users engage in economically oriented violent crime to support their costly drug use. Robbery is an example. Economic-compulsive violence is instrumental rather than expressive and may be precipitated by the need to overcome a victim's resistance or to effectuate an escape.

The systemic model refers to the traditionally aggressive patterns of interaction within the system of drug use and distribution. Systemic violence includes disputes over territory between rival drug dealers, enforcement of normative codes within drug-dealing hierarchies, punishment for selling adulterated or phony drugs, and punishment for failing to pay one's drug-related debts.

To test the viability of usefulness of this tripartite conceptualization, two separate field studies were undertaken on the lower east side of New York City between 1984 and 1987. The first study examined the drugs/

violence nexus among males. The second study focused on females. Both studies aimed at documenting the nature, scope, and drug relatedness of all violent perpetrations and violent victimizations occurring during the study period.

The intent of this chapter is to examine the role played by cocaine in the violent events reported by research subjects. General information on the characteristics of the sample and the reported violent events is presented first. Then the relationship between cocaine and these violent events is elaborated upon. Male and female data are presented separately for comparative purposes.

METHODS

Research subjects were drug users or distributors who lived in, or frequented, the lower east side. They were recruited from field contacts, through snowball sampling techniques, and from a local methadone maintenance treatment program (MMTP). Only persons over the age of 18 were eligible to participate in the study. All interviewing took place in an ethnographic field station established solely for these projects.

Upon recruitment for the study, all subjects were first given a Life History Interview (Goldstein et al. 1987, 1988) that focused on a wide range of issues. After completing the interview, subjects were put on a weekly reporting schedule for at least 8 weeks. The analytic time unit for the weekly interview was the day. Data covering 7 discrete days were collected each week. Special taped interviews were conducted around topics or events of special interest to project staff. In addition to the structured interviews and special tapings, project staff spent considerable time on the street with subjects and took copious ethnographic field notes.

The concept of violence is rather vague and confusing. There has been little agreement among researchers on an appropriate operational definition. For the purposes of this research, violence was defined as the use, or the threat of use, of physical force or harm.

With regard to domestic violence, an unfortunate lack of comparability occurred between the data collected from males and females. In the female study, project staff had been instructed to probe specifically for incidents of domestic violence. Although male subjects were questioned about violent encounters with spouses or lovers, specific questions and probes were addressed only to the female subjects.

Violence against children turned out to be an especially difficult issue in this research, both conceptually and methodologically. In the male study, which began first, we probed for all instances of violence, but did not probe specifically for violence against children. No such cases were reported. In the female study, we did probe specifically for violence against children. A large number of such cases were reported.

However, none of these cases dealt with serious child abuse. Most of the incidents involved disciplining children in ways that are generally socially approved. Examples included threatening a child, spanking, slapping a hand, and so on. While such cases did fall within the stated definition of violence, they tended to skew the data in unfortunate directions. For example, including these data tended to overrepresent females as perpetrators of violence. These cases of "violent" disciplining of children were therefore omitted from the analysis reported here. To have included them in the analysis would have created a serious lack of comparability between male and female data. However, the authors are planning a future paper focusing specifically on violence against children that will examine the drug relatedness of these cases.

No data were systematically collected during this research concerning type of cocaine or mode of cocaine ingestion. When the research began in 1984, crack-cocaine was not an issue. As the crack problem escalated, project staff considered whether to add questions that would specify forms of cocaine use. This was rejected, primarily because of issues of comparability between data collected early in the study and that collected at a later date. Since interviewing of males predated females, it is likely that crack use was less common among the men.

SAMPLE

Table 1 presents basic demographic characteristics of the male and female samples. In general, the two samples were quite similar. There was a somewhat greater proportion of blacks in the female sample and a correspondingly greater proportion of whites in the male sample. Hispanics comprised about 20 percent of both samples.

A few characteristics of these samples should be highlighted. Subjects tended to be better educated than many other samples of drug users recruited from the streets. The majority of both the men and women were high school graduates, and substantial proportions had attended college. In part, this may be a function of the eclectic character of the lower east side. This is an ethnically diverse neighborhood that has traditionally been the center of New York's bohemian underground. Art galleries and

TABLE 1. *Sample characteristics by gender (in percentages)*

Characteristic	Males (n=152)	Females (n=133)
Ethnicity		
Black	43	53
White	34	26
Hispanic	20	20
Other	3	2
Median age (years)	32	32
Education		
Less than high school graduate	40	47
High school graduate	28	26
Some college/college graduate	31	27
Marital status		
Single	59	57
Formerly married	32	30
Married	8	13
Current living situation		
Shelter	49	40
Spouse/lover	16	10
Family	8	24
Friend	7	16
Alone	13	5
Vagrant	7	4
Currently employed	13	7

punk rock clubs currently coexist with ethnic enclaves of recent and not-so-recent immigrants. Research subjects exemplified the diversity of the surrounding neighborhood.

The modal living situation for both men and women was in shelters for the homeless. The lower east side not only contains the greatest concentration of shelters in New York City, but the main processing centers for shelters located throughout the city were only a few blocks from our field site. The authors are planning future papers focusing on the topics of drug use among the homeless, and on drug use and distribution in the shelters. Two such reports have already been presented (Bellucci et al. 1986, 1987).

Few men or women were employed. However, this research probably overrepresents unemployed drug users because, for the most part, interviewing was conducted during normal business hours. Drug users who were employed during the day found it difficult to participate in the study.

Male subjects had a higher rate of completion in this research than females. About 66 percent of the men completed the interview process (a Life History and eight weekly interviews) compared to only 52 percent of the women. Reasons why subjects failed to complete included being incarcerated, hospitalized, seriously injured, or killed; moving out of the study area; and enrolling in residential drug treatment. Some subjects were also terminated by project staff for lying or for engaging in certain proscribed behaviors at the field site. Such behaviors included acting out violently against project staff, stealing, using or distributing drugs in the field office, and being so consistently stoned or drunk that little of coherent value could be learned from them.

The higher dropout rate for women appeared to be the consequence of a number of factors. Some stopped coming to the field site because of problems with their children at home. Others dropped out because suspicious boyfriends or husbands ordered them to do so. Others developed relationships with men who took care of them and thus they no longer needed the $10 interview fee. Some homeless women were able to move in with men who lived outside of the study area. Finally, drug-using women appeared more likely than drug-using men to be welcomed back into their families. Many left the study area for this reason.

DIVISION INTO COCAINE-USING GROUPS

All subjects completing the process provided information on 8 weeks (56 days). The sample was divided with regard to reported frequency of cocaine use. *Regular users* were defined as those who used cocaine an average of 3 or more days per week (a total of 24 or more of the 56 days). *Moderate users* were defined as those who used cocaine for 1–23 days. *Nonusers* reported no cocaine use during the 56-day reporting period, though they may have had a prior history of cocaine use or may have used other drugs during the reporting period. Table 2 shows the division of the sample by frequency of cocaine use for both males and females.

The majority of both the men and the women were moderate cocaine users. Little relationship was found between frequency of cocaine use and mean amount of cocaine used. Male moderate users used cocaine for a mean 9.5 days and a mean $31 worth of cocaine per cocaine use

TABLE 2. *Frequency of cocaine use by gender*

Frequency	Males (n=152) n	(%)	Females (n=133) n	(%)
Nonusers	28	(18)	30	(23)
Moderate users	83	(55)	75	(56)
Regular users	41	(27)	28	(21)

day. Male regular users used cocaine for a mean 38.5 days and a mean $40 worth of cocaine per cocaine use day.

The difference between frequency and amount used was even less among the women. Female moderate users used cocaine for a mean 8.7 days and spent a mean $31 per cocaine use day. Female regular users used cocaine for a mean 36.7 days and a mean $30 worth of cocaine per cocaine use day.

Table 3 reveals some interesting differences both within and between sexes when the sample was divided according to frequency of cocaine use. Male regular cocaine users were more likely to be black, while non-users were more likely to be white (X^2=9.2, p=.01). About equal proportions of female regular users were white and black. However, since about twice as many black females as white females were in the sample, white females were clearly overrepresented as regular cocaine users (X^2=7.5, p=.02). Because of the small number of subjects within the non-user and regular user groups, these results should be interpreted with caution.

The male user groups were not significantly different in age. However, a significant difference was found between mean ages of female nonusers and female regular users (F=4.51, p=.01). In general, male regular users were the oldest group and female regular users were the youngest.

When looking at duration of cocaine use, current male regular users tended to have used cocaine for significantly longer durations (F=6.48, p=.002) than current nonusers or moderate users. Among the females, moderate users had a significantly lengthier history of cocaine use than nonusers or regular users (F=3.3, p=.04).

TABLE 3. *Characteristics of subjects by gender and cocaine use*

	Male (n=152)			Female (n=133)		
	Nonuser (n=28)	Moderate (n=83)	Regular (n=41)	Nonuser (n=30)	Moderate (n=75)	Regular (n=28)
Ethnicity						
White	61%	30%	24%	30%	17%	43%
Black	29	39	61	47	61	39
Hispanic	11	25	15	23	20	14
Other	—	6	—	—	1	4
Mean age	31.5	32.2	33.5	34.9	31.7	30.2
(SD)[1]	(6.7)	(8.7)	(7.5)	(6.4)	(5.9)	(6.7)
Mean years						
using cocaine	5.5	6.5	10.3	6.7	9.4	7.2
(SD)	(5.5)	(5.7)	(6.8)	(5.0)	(5.8)	(4.3)
Treatment						
Ever in MMTP[2]	64%	52%	46%	60%	56%	46%
No. of times in						
MMTP	2.5	1.6	.89	1.2	1.5	.82
(SD)	(3.0)	(2.5)	(1.5)	(1.6)	(2.0)	(1.2)
Mean months in						
MMTP	44.1	36.7	24.9	38.6	28.7	20.6
(SD)	(56.6)	(57.4)	(49.2)	(65.2)	(48.2)	(44.3)
Currently in						
MMTP	56%	43%	15%	37%	39%	21%
Education						
<High school grad	43%	42%	34%	50%	48%	43%
High school grad	36%	26%	27%	20%	32%	14%
College	21%	30%	39%	30%	20%	43%
Marital status						
Single	63%	61%	54%	60%	59%	50%
Formerly married	33%	30%	34%	33%	28%	32%
Married	4%	—	12%	7%	13%	18%

[1]Standard deviation.
[2]Methadone maintenance treatment program.

Current and prior methadone maintenance treatment may be related to the frequency of current cocaine use. Both male and female currently regular cocaine users were least likely to have ever been in methadone treatment, had the fewest and the shortest methadone treatment experiences, and were the least likely to be in methadone programs during the study period. However, the only one of these relationships that attained statistical significance was number of times in MMTP for males. An earlier paper examined the effects of methadone maintenance treatment on the drugs/violence nexus within the male sample only (Spunt et al. 1990).

The relationship between methadone treatment and frequency of cocaine use indicated that many regular cocaine users were also heroin users. In fact, frequency of heroin use and frequency of cocaine use were strongly associated. During the study period, male regular cocaine users used heroin for a mean 28 days, as compared to a mean 3 days of heroin use for nonusers of cocaine. In addition, use of heroin and cocaine was reported on the same day for a mean 23 days for regular users compared to 3.5 mean days for moderate users. A similar relationship existed for the females. Female regular cocaine users used heroin for a mean 23 days during the study period. Female nonusers of cocaine only used heroin for a mean 7 days. Same day use of heroin and cocaine for regular users was a mean 20 days compared to 1.4 mean days for moderate users. Male regular users of cocaine also had significantly lower frequencies of tranquilizer use. No other significant relationships were found between frequency of cocaine use and frequency of other drug use.

Both male and female regular cocaine users tended to be better educated and were more likely to be married when compared to nonusers. Nonusers were only slightly more likely to be regularly employed. No significant differences were found between user groups with regard to current living situations.

With one notable exception, no significant differences were found between current cocaine use groups on a variety of measures of prior criminality. These measures included self-reported arrest histories, incarceration histories, and past criminal behavior.

The one exception to this finding was female prostitution. While 57 percent of the female current nonusers of cocaine reported never having been prostitutes, only one woman of the current regular users reported never having prostituted herself. This was a white, unmarried, Italian-American woman with an eighth-grade education who was 22 years old when she became a subject in our study. She had been living with her boyfriend and some other friends in an apartment on the lower east side for the previous 3 years. She reported being in an all-girl hard rock band, but only worked at this for 2 days of the 56-day reporting period. During the study period, she was hospitalized for 1 week for endocarditis. She described her cocaine career in the following manner:

> When I was 17, I worked for a production company. After it went out of business, I found out that the owner was a cocaine dealer. At first, I was buying grams from him. When I could not buy it any more, I gave him blow jobs to get cocaine

> from him. After a while, he told me that I could earn more money from selling it and then buying my own. He became my connection. I would buy a quarter of an ounce and then break it down with a lot of mix and then sell it in bars in Queens. I did this for 2 years.

She began using cocaine in 1981 and dealt from 1981 to 1983. During this phase of her cocaine career, she reported using about $300 worth of cocaine per day. She reported first injecting cocaine in 1984. Soon afterward, she stopped selling cocaine and reduced the volume of her consumption. She explained this reduction in cocaine use and distribution by stating that she was forced to move out of Queens because she owed so many people money and because she had begun dealing "dummy" bags. She was afraid that people were after her. She moved to the lower east side. When she began her interviews, she reported using about $30 worth of cocaine per day. She used cocaine on 34 of the 56 reporting days and used a mean $17 worth per day. She stated that most of the cocaine that she used during the study period was given to her by her boyfriend or by her sister, whom she termed a "rich junkie."

Some persons might argue that this woman's exchange of sexual favors for cocaine with her ex-boss constituted a form of prostitution. However, the subject herself did not define it as such during the interview. Trading sex for drugs has been historically commonplace in the drug world. In the vivid vernacular of the streets, such women have been referred to as "bag brides" and, more recently, as "strawberries." But there is little agreement among female drug users as to whether this practice should be considered a form of prostitution. (For a more complete discussion of this phenomenon, see Goldstein 1979, pp. 45–50.)

During the current crack epidemic, much publicity has been given to women trading sex for crack. Some of our female research subjects reported violent encounters after they had accepted crack from a man who mistakenly presumed that he would be given sex in return. Whether these expectations arose from past experiences or from reading the newspapers is not clear. A few examples of such events follow.

> This guy bought me one crack and then wanted to have sex. I told him no. He got angry and twisted my arm and threw me to the ground. He got scared. He thought that I was hurt. He called Emergency Medical Service. They looked at me and said I was OK and left. He was high on crack.

I was with this boy who wanted me to have sex and I said no. He then got mad at me because I wouldn't, and he punched me in my nose three times. I was high from smoking a lot of crack. He got violent and really did a number on me. No revenge. I left because I was scared.

I was hanging out with a friend of mine, male, and his friend, male. We were at his mother's house smoking crack and talking when the next thing I know, they had me on the floor and they both raped me. I went to the precinct and told the police. They took me to the hospital for a checkup. I was smoking crack. So was one of the boys. We only smoked 10 dollars between the two of us.

CRIME

Table 4 presents information on selected crimes reported by the male and female sample during the study period. Among males, regular users of cocaine were most likely to report committing every offense, with the exception of prostitution. Male prostitution in this sample was either overtly gay or was practiced by transvestites who were frequently able to

TABLE 4. *Reported criminal activity by gender and cocaine use*

Criminal activity	Males			Females		
	Nonuser (n=28)	Moderate user (n=83)	Regular user (n=41)	Nonuser (n=30)	Moderate user (n=75)	Regular user (n=28)
Shoplifting						
Any activity	32%	23%	37%	13%	44%	39%
Mean days	16	4	7	14	4	8
Burglary						
Any activity	4%	7%	17%	—	3%	4%
Mean days	2	2	2	—	1	1
Robbery						
Any activity	4%	11%	12%	3%	5%	7%
Mean days	1	3	2	1	1	1
Prostitution						
Any activity	4%	12%	10%	20%	32%	79%
Mean days	2	12	13	11	8	23
Con games						
Any activity	7%	16%	46%	10%	12%	21%
Mean days	3	2	4	4	2	2
Theft						
Any activity	32%	24%	56%	10%	23%	46%
Mean days	3	3	6	2	2	4

pass as females with male customers. The most striking differences with regard to increased criminality of male regular users of cocaine occurred in the categories of theft and con games. These con games frequently occurred in the context of the drug trade, for example, selling phony drugs.

Among females, regular users of cocaine were also more likely to report committing most offenses. The one exception was shoplifting. As with the males, female regular cocaine users were more likely to report theft or con games. The most dramatic differences appeared in the category of prostitution. About 79 percent of the female regular cocaine users reported prostituting themselves, and they reported doing so for a mean 23 days of the 56-day reporting period. The range was from 1 to 49 days. Only 32 percent of the female moderate users reported prostitution, and they reported a much lower frequency of this activity: a mean 8 days.

VIOLENT EVENTS

Table 5 shows the overall participation in violent events by the different cocaine-using groups. The 152 males were involved in 212 violent events during the 8-week reporting period. The 133 females reported participating in 172 violent events. About 55 percent of the male sample and about 59 percent of the female sample reported some participation in violence.

The three categories of cocaine users contributed to the totality of violent events in proportions commensurate with their proportion of the sample. For example, regular users of cocaine comprised 27 percent of the male sample and accounted for 21 percent of the violent events. Further, with the exception of female regular cocaine users, roughly equal proportions of each group reported some violence.

Male moderate users and female nonusers reported the highest mean number of violent events per participant. While female regular users clearly had the highest proportion reporting at least one violent act, this group reported one of the lowest mean numbers of violent events per participant.

The phrase "violent participation" denotes the full range of potential connections that an individual can have to a violent event. A violent participation can involve perpetration, victimization, or codisputancy in which no differentiation between perpetrator and victim is possible. An example of codisputancy follows.

TABLE 5. *Overall participation in violence by gender*

Frequency/violence	Males	Females
Nonusers		
Percent of sample	18	23
Percent of violent events	13	25
Percent reporting any violent participation	57	47
Mean violent events per participant	1.8	3.1
Moderate users		
Percent of sample	55	56
Percent of violent events	66	49
Percent reporting any violent participation	55	53
Mean violent events per participant	3.1	2.1
Regular users		
Percent of sample	27	21
Percent of violent events	21	25
Percent reporting any violent participation	51	86
Mean violent events per participant	2.0	1.9

> We got some tools and we spread them out on the street in front of this store. The owner comes out and told us to move. An argument started and he called in the store for more help. I got hit with a milk crate My friend got hit with a chair. We lost the tools. We went to the police to lodge a complaint. Then I went to the emergency room to get my lip stitched [10 stitches].

In addition, a small number of violent events are included in our data base that were witnessed by subjects, but in which they were not active participants. Table 6 presents data regarding the nature of violent participations for both male and female subjects.

While frequency of cocaine use appeared to have little effect on the overall number of violent participations, it had a definite effect on the nature of those participations. Interestingly, however, that effect appeared to be rather different for men than for women. Male nonusers of cocaine were the victims in 50 percent of the violent events that they participated in, while male regular users were the victims in only 29 percent of their

TABLE 6. *Cocaine user status in violent events*

	Perpetrator	Victim	Codisputant	Witness	Number of violent events
Males (n=212)					
Nonusers	21%	50%	25%	4%	28
Moderate users	35%	23%	40%	2%	135*
Regular users	41%	29%	24%	7%	42⁺
Females (n=172)					
Nonusers	27%	33%	33%	7%	40‡
Moderate users	23%	45%	30%	2%	83
Regular users	20%	59%	11%	11%	46

*Information missing for 6 cases.
⁺Information missing for 1 case.
‡Three cases of violent self-abuse by a nonuser are excluded from this table.

violent events. Conversely, male regular users of cocaine were the perpetrators in 41 percent of their violent participations compared to only 21 percent of the violent participations by nonusers. Male moderate users were most often codisputants (X^2=13.5, p=.04).

Females were most likely to be victims in every cocaine user category, that is, nonuser, moderate user, and regular user. However, female nonusers were the victims in 33 percent of their violent participations; female regular users were victimized in 59 percent of their violent participations (X^2=22.0, p=.005). While male regular users were about twice as likely as nonusers to be perpetrators, female regular users were slightly less likely than nonusers to be perpetrators.

Among men, increased frequency of cocaine use was associated with a greater likelihood of being a perpetrator rather than a victim of violence. An opposite relationship was found among the women; increased frequency of cocaine use was associated with a greater likelihood of being a victim of violence.

Table 7 shows the relationship between our research subjects and the other parties in the violent events. Once again, interesting differences were apparent both between sexes and within sexes between user groups.

TABLE 7. *Relationship of other participants to subjects during violent events (in percentages)*

	Males*			Females+		
	Nonusers (n=24)	Moderate users (n=130)	Regular users (n=42)	Nonusers (n=43)	Moderate users (n=83)	Regular users (n=46)
Spouse/lover	—	7	2	35	31	20
Friend/acquaintance	38	21	19	35	24	24
Stranger	21	28	14	7	11	13
Shelter coresident	21	23	12	14	8	2
Drug relation	13	12	36	—	8	17
Prostitution relation	—	7	—	5	7	20
Police officer	8	3	10	—	—	2
Other	—	—	7	5	10	2

NOTE: Column percentages may not add up to 100 owing to rounding error.
*Includes data on 196 violent events. Relationship between participants was unknown in 16 cases.
+Includes data on 172 violent events.

Male nonusers were most often involved in violent events with friends or acquaintances, followed by strangers and shelter coresidents. Some examples follow.

> I went up to a friend's room with my radio to drink some wine. We drank. I went down to get more wine. When I came back I see my radio is gone. I said, "Where's my radio?" He said, "What radio?" We argued. He picked up a pipe and hit me in my ribs. I got a big stick and hit him in his back. I went to the hospital on Saturday. They told me my ribs were broke.

> Whacked guy [shelter coresident at Ward's Island] over head with cane. I think he's the guy who took my methadone bottles. What I did was dirty, but that's what I did. He didn't fight back. He got stitches.

Male regular users of cocaine were most often violently involved with drug relations. This category includes drug sellers, drug buyers, and drug business associates. Fingers, a 24-year-old black male, who used a mean $76 per day worth of cocaine over his 24 days of cocaine use reported the following incident.

> Friday in an afterhours place. Some guy came in and Fingers said he'd sell him coke. The guy said, "Yeah." So Fingers took him outside and robbed him with an ice pick. Fingers had some alcohol in him. The other guy was a little drunk. Fingers got $525. Fingers did him once, punch to face hard, when the guy pleaded with him to leave him some rent money.

Males reported few violent encounters with spouses or lovers. For women, however, violent encounters with spouses or lovers contributed a substantial proportion of the total violence reported in all cocaine use categories. The proportion of violence involving spouses/lovers was highest in the nonuser group. It should be noted that many of our male and female subjects were engaged in domestic relationships with one another. Females were more likely than their male partners to report incidents of domestic violence during their interviews.

Women who did not use any cocaine during the study period were most often involved in violence with spouses/lovers, friends/acquaintances, and, to a lesser extent, shelter coresidents. An account of violence involving a 26-year-old black female subject who did not use any cocaine during the study period and a shelter coresident follows.

> A girlfriend told me not to drink the coffee. A girl at the shelter was going around dropping pills in the coffee. I had already drank the coffee. I told them at the shelter that I wanted to go to the hospital. I didn't want anything to happen to my baby. I went up to the girl and punched her in the mouth. She was high. They found the pills in her purse, little green pills.

Spouse/lover and friend/acquaintance were also relevant categories for the regular cocaine users. However, a high frequency of cocaine use was associated with increased violent events involving drug and prostitute relations. Prostitute relations included customers, pimps, and other prostitutes. The following example of prostitution-related violence involved a 34-year-old white female who used a mean $30 per day worth of cocaine on 42 of her 56 reporting days.

> Last night a guy slapped me. I have a jagged tooth and as I was giving him a blow job in his car, I moved to get in a comfortable position. I scratched him on his you-know-what and he hollered, "You bitch! You hurt me." I think he was high on coke.

CIRCUMSTANCES OF VIOLENT EVENTS

Table 8 presents data on the circumstances of the violent events for males and females. The most common circumstances of violence for both men and women were robberies or other economic crimes, nondrug-related disputes, and drug-related disputes. However, the distribution of violence within these three categories varied between men and women.

For men, violence was fairly evenly divided among the three principal categories. Robbery or other economic crime violence constituted the greatest proportion of violent events for the moderate and regular users. A robbery involving a 35-year-old black male who was a moderate cocaine user (using a mean $63 worth of cocaine on 10 days) is described below.

> Partner with knife took dude off. I just watched his back. Partner wanted coke money. He was high on coke, dope, and Placidyls when he did it. Partner took $60. I got $40. I had just been smoking marijuana. We were walking down the street.

TABLE 8. *Circumstances of violent events*

	Nonuser	Moderate user	Regular user
Males*	(n=25)	(n=136)	(n=40)
Robbery/other economic crime	24%	40%	30%
Nondrug-related dispute	28	32	20
Drug-related dispute	20	13	28
Altercation with police officer	8	2	8
Other	20	13	15
Females⁺	(n=41)	(n=79)	(n=46)
Robbery/other economic crime	12%	16%	24%
Nondrug-related dispute	49	54	24
Drug-related dispute	15	13	28
Forcible sex crime	5	8	11
Prostitution	5	4	4
Other	15	5	8

NOTE: Columns may not add up to 100 percent because of rounding errors.
*Includes information on 201 violent events. Circumstances were unknown in 11 cases.
⁺Includes information on 166 violent events. Circumstances were unknown in 6 cases.

> Partner says, "Watch my back." He goes across the street, puts knife to this guy's throat. The guy was just playing cards with another guy. I watched and helped hold him down while partner got into his pockets. When we got away he gave me my share. Forty dollars.

Nondrug-related disputes constituted the greatest proportion of violence among those men who did not use any cocaine during the study period. An account involving a 35-year-old white male follows.

> I hear kicking on downstairs door at 7 a.m. I say get out. He puts metal spiked wrist thing in hand. I pull my knife out. I kick him in his ass and he flew through the door. Shortly afterward I hear more banging. I throw my hot plate out the window at him. He takes the hot plate and throws it through the front door window. I run downstairs. He's ready to fight. I grab him. People are saying, "Hit him!" I start punching him in the face, one after another. I held him on the floor, sitting on him. He's dazed. Then [the cops] came. They didn't want to touch him. Afraid of AIDS. He is gay. He was hurt bad.

Regular users of cocaine participated in the largest proportion of violence stemming from drug-related disputes. None of the differences between male user groups within the three main circumstance categories was very substantial.

However, the relationship between violent event participants within specific circumstance categories manifested some variability depending on frequency of cocaine use. Economic crime violence among nonusers tended to involve friends/acquaintances (67 percent of the time). A scenario involving a 36-year-old Hispanic male follows. The subject was high on alcohol, tranquilizers, and antidepressants at the time.

> On Friday night I took a nap in the park before I went to the shelter. Three guys attacked me. They got $10 and a ring. To get the ring off, one guy bit my finger. They didn't show any weapons. They took my boots, a delaying tactic. I know one of the guys. I'm going to get him.

Economic crime violence among moderate users tended to involve strangers (58 percent of the time). The following event happened to a 53-year-old white male who used a mean $44 worth of cocaine over 7 reporting days. At the time of the event, he was high on alcohol and tranquilizers.

> I took this girl to cop coke. When I was coming down the stairs, there was two Puerto Ricans with sticks. I started to go back up the stairs and there was one more waiting for me on top. They said, "Give it up. I said I ain't got no money. They started to beat and kick me. I was unconscious. I don't know how long. They took $30 and my methadone ID. I'll know the Puerto Ricans if I see them again, but if I do anything, I'll probably get hurt worse.

Economic crime violence among regular users of cocaine tended to involve drug relations (64 percent of the time). Nondrug-related disputes tended to involve friends or acquaintances in all cocaine user categories. Drug-related disputes tended to involve drug relationships in all user categories.

The situation was somewhat different among women. For both nonusers and moderate users, the majority of violent participations occurred in the context of nondrug-related disputes. Substantial proportions of these events involved domestic violence. The encounter described below involved a 37-year-old black female who was classified as a moderate cocaine user. She used cocaine on 13 of her reporting days, with a mean use of $17 worth per cocaine-use day.

> [On a shelter line] this girl kept bumping into me. I went to the bathroom and when I came back she was arguing with my girlfriend. I asked what's up. She attacked me. Started to choke me. The guards broke it up. They told her to leave. As she was going down the stairs, the guards told us to take a walk. In other words, they were telling us to kick her ass outside. I went up to her and stabbed her. She didn't get hurt too bad. She had on a heavy coat. No drugs on either me or my friend's part. Other girl, either she was high on crack or just plain crazy.

The preponderance of nondrug-related dispute violence was not apparent among the female regular users. They had a rough comparability in magnitude among the three main categories of violence that was similar to that of the men.

The proportion of violence involving forcible sex crimes increased with higher frequencies of cocaine use. However, prostitution appears to be a critical intervening variable in this regard. Women who were regular users of cocaine were often raped while engaging in prostitution. Prostitutes, because they have intimate liaisons with strange males in relatively uncontrolled environments, such as automobiles, rooftops, and parks, are at great risk for rape. One such incident happened to Beverly, a regular cocaine user.

> On Saturday morning, Beverly was picked up by a trick and driven to a parking lot and raped. The guy slapped her several times and forced her to give him a BJ and sex. She didn't press any charges, but she did get his plate number. No weapon. He didn't look like he was on drugs. She was neither dope sick nor high. Her body still aches from it.

Not all prostitution-related violence involved forcible sex crimes. Rachel, another regular cocaine user, reported the following event during her fourth weekly interview.

> Some guy pulled a knife. He was all coked up. He couldn't get off. I told him, "Five more minutes. That's all." He still couldn't get off. I got up to go and he put a knife to my neck. I got scared and started to cry. He ran away.

It should be noted that prostitutes often claim that they were raped when a customer refuses to pay after receiving sexual services. No such incidents are included here. All recorded forcible sex crimes involved a violent assault on the person. A much smaller number of forcible sex crimes were reported by the men. These incidents were homosexual rapes that took place in shelters for homeless males.

For the women, violence surrounding nondrug-related disputes tended to involve spouses or lovers in all user categories. Robbery or other economic crime violence tended to involve friends/acquaintances (80 percent) among nonusers, strangers (50 percent) among moderate users, and drug relations (33 percent) or prostitute relations (33 percent) among regular users. Drug-related disputes tended to occur between friends/acquaintances (67 percent) among nonusers, between spouses/lovers (60 percent) among moderate users, and between friends/acquaintances (31 percent) or drug relations (31 percent) among the regular users.

TRIPARTITE CONCEPTUAL FRAMEWORK

The drug relatedness of violent events was classified in a two-step process. First, it was determined whether any of the three posited dimensions of drug relatedness were present in the event and which drugs were associated with each identified dimension. Second, a main reason for the event was inferred from the available data.

For example, a heroin user experiencing withdrawal symptoms decides to commit a robbery to obtain money with which to purchase heroin. He spots an obviously inebriated person on the street and decides that this is an easy mark. He hits the drunk over the head and takes his money. This event would be classified as containing two drug-related dimensions. An economic compulsive/heroin dimension motivated the perpetrator. A psychopharmacological/alcohol dimension targeted the victim. The main reason, or primary motivating force, for the event taking place would be classified as economic-compulsive/heroin.

Before actual coding began, all coders were thoroughly grounded in the tripartite theoretical framework. All interviews were coded independently. About 10 percent of interviews were cross-coded. A reliability coefficient of 90 percent or better was obtained between coders.

It was not unusual for drug-related information to be vague or incomplete. Interviewing drug-using subjects in the field can be difficult for the best of interviewers. To deal with this problem, specific rules were developed to address situations in which information was missing. For example, if subjects reported that the other individual in a violent event appeared to be high, but they weren't sure, then we coded the psychopharmacological dimension as missing information. If the subject used drugs on the day of a violent event, and the drug use could have been reasonably, but not certainly, connected to the violent event, then we again coded this as missing information. For the economic-compulsive dimension, the subject may have engaged in a robbery and in drug use on the same day; however, if the coder could not make a clear connection between the two events, such cases were also coded as missing information. In other words, the guiding principle in coding drug relatedness was to classify events as *not* drug related if we were certain of that fact; to classify events as positively drug related if we were certain; and to classify events as missing information if there was some reason to believe they might have been drug related, but we could not be completely sure of this relationship.

Table 9 shows the proportion of violent events manifesting each dimension of drug relatedness for each of the cocaine user groups. Psychopharmacological dimensions were clearly the most prevalent throughout both the male and female samples. Increased frequency of cocaine use was associated with a higher proportion of violent events containing an economic-compulsive dimension among males only. However, it should

TABLE 9. *Drug-related dimensions of violent events (in percentages)*

	Nonuser	Moderate user	Regular user
Males	(n=28)	(n=141)	(n=43)
Psychopharmacological	44[a]	44[b]	33[c]
Economic-compulsive	—	7[d]	16[a]
Systemic	25	18	54
Females	(n=43)	(n=83)	(n=46)
Psychopharmacological	39[e]	48[f]	47[g]
Economic-compulsive	7	5	7[g]
Systemic	2	8	33

[a] Missing information for 3 cases.
[b] Missing information for 41 cases.
[c] Missing information for 10 cases.
[d] Missing information for 8 cases.
[e] Missing information for 2 cases.
[f] Missing information for 6 cases.
[g] Missing information for 1 case.

be emphasized that only 16 percent of the violent participations by male regular cocaine users contained an economic-compulsive dimension. The proportion of violent events containing economic-compulsive dimensions remained consistently low throughout the three categories of female users. This reflects the fact that females in need of money for drugs are more apt to resort to prostitution.

Frequency of cocaine use had the greatest impact in the systemic category. The proportion of violent participations containing a systemic dimension increased dramatically between moderate users and regular users for both males (a threefold increase) and females (a fourfold increase). It should be noted, however, that female regular users still had a greater proportion of violent events with a psychopharmacological dimension than with a systemic dimension. Also, unlike females, male nonusers and moderate users had substantial proportions of systemic violence.

Table 10 displays these dimensions by the specific drug involved. The percentages reported in each cell specify the proportion of violent events within each user group that contained a drug-specific dimension of violence. For example, 28 percent of the violent events (n=25) involving

TABLE 10. *Drug-specific dimensions of violence (in percentages)*

	Males			Females		
	Non-users	Moderate users	Regular users	Non-users	Moderate users	Regular users
Psychopharma-cological						
Heroin	—	7	11	—	2	15
Cocaine	—	6	6	—	11	32
Alcohol	28	22	14	23	32	11
Economic-compulsive						
Heroin	—	3	5	2	1	4
Cocaine	—	6	14	5	2	4
Alcohol	—	1	2	—	—	—
Systemic						
Heroin	8	6	15	—	1	14
Cocaine	—	4	23	—	1	21
Alcohol	—	—	—	—	1	—

male nonusers of cocaine contained an alcohol-related psychopharmacological dimension, and 8 percent contained a heroin-related systemic dimension.

This table contains overlap, both within and across the dimensions of drug relatedness. For example, an event that contains a psychopharmacological dimension may involve the use of more than one drug in any single event. In addition, an event might have both a psychopharmacological and economic-compulsive dimension and involve the same or different drugs across the separate dimensions. In such cases, both dimensions and each specific drug related to each dimension were included. Only heroin, cocaine, and alcohol are listed because these three substances were responsible for more than 60 percent of the reported drug-related dimensions of violence.

Combining the male and female samples, a total of 383 violent events were reported. About 25 percent of these events contained an alcohol-related dimension, about 23 percent contained a cocaine-related dimension, and about 16 percent contained a heroin-related dimension. These categories were not mutually exclusive. For example, a single event might involve both alcohol and cocaine.

For both males and females, alcohol was a major contributor in the psychopharmacological category. Females, especially regular cocaine users, were more likely than males to report cocaine-related psychopharmacological violence. It has already been shown that most of the female cocaine-related psychopharmacological violence involved victimization.

Table 11 presents the main reasons for violent events for the male and female samples. The category "multidimensional" refers to cases that contained two or more of the three dimensions of drug relatedness in roughly equal magnitude with regard to causation. The category "other drug related" refers to cases that could not be classified according to the tripartite conceptualization. The fact that 21 cases were unclassifiable in the male sample, and only 1 case was unclassifiable in the female sample, reflects an increased proficiency due to experience on the part of interviewers in obtaining the information necessary to make causal inferences.

One of the more striking findings was the relatively high proportion of violent events reported by this sample of street drug users and distributors that was not drug related. About 43 percent of the male violent participations and about 61 percent of the female violent participations were not primarily drug related. This finding supports the notion that such persons live in a subculture in which both drugs and violence are relatively commonplace, and that the two may occur in conjunction with one another or either may occur separately.

TABLE 11. *Main reasons for violent events (in percentages)*

	Males*			Females+		
	Nonusers (n=26)	Moderate users (n=125)	Regular users (n=40)	Nonusers (n=42)	Moderate users (n=83)	Regular users (n=46)
Psychopharmacological	35	18	13	14	17	11
Economic-compulsive	—	4	13	—	2	4
Systemic	23	14	33	—	6	24
Multidimensional	—	5	7	7	4	9
Other drug related	8	4	2	14	4	4
Not drug related	35	55	32	64	68	48

*n=191. Classification of drug relatedness was undetermined in 21 cases.
+n=171. Classification of drug relatedness was undetermined in one case.

It was also clear that the female regular users of cocaine were more likely than the other two user groups to report that their violent participations were drug related. For the males, however, both the regular users and nonusers of cocaine were more likely than moderate users to report drug-related violent participation.

Male nonusers of cocaine reported a higher proportion of psychopharmacological violent events than the female nonusers. The higher proportion of psychopharmacological violent events can be accounted for by the preponderance of alcohol-related violence. For example, of the nonuser violent events that were classified as psychopharmacological, 66 percent involved only the use of alcohol, and an additional 11 percent involved alcohol, tranquilizers, and other types of drugs. In our samples of male and female drug users and distributors, cocaine-related psychopharmacological violence was rare. Rather, alcohol was the drug most commonly associated with psychopharmacological violence.

In addition, male nonusers of cocaine reported a higher proportion of systemic violent events compared to female nonusers. These systemic violent events involved drugs other than cocaine, including heroin and marijuana. However, for both male and female regular users, the greatest proportion of their drug-related violence was systemic, that is, occurring in the context of drug distribution activities. Male regular users of cocaine also reported higher levels of economic-compulsive violence.

DISCUSSION

The relationship between drug use/distribution and violence in general, and between cocaine and violence specifically, is clearly very complex. Regular users of cocaine reported volumes of violence that were fairly similar to the volumes of violence reported by nonusers and more moderate cocaine users. However, regular cocaine users were more likely to report that their violence was drug related. These finding cannot be generalized beyond the street users and distributors from New York City's lower east side who comprised the research sample.

Important differences were found between males and females. Regular cocaine use among males was more strongly associated with the perpetration of violence. Regular cocaine use among females was more strongly associated with violent victimization.

Prostitution appeared to be an important intervening variable in the cocaine/violence nexus for females. Regular cocaine use was associated with increased involvement in prostitution. Prostitution proved to be a social context in which violence was a frequent occurrence. Most often, the prostitute was the victim of violence. The research was not designed to address issues of whether cocaine use was more likely to lead to prostitution, or whether prostitution was more likely to lead to cocaine use. Previous research (Goldstein 1979) has indicated that both sequences of events appear, probably in roughly equal proportions.

Heroin use appeared as a confounding variable. Regular users of cocaine, both men and women, also had the highest frequencies of heroin use. Because individuals tended to use the two substances at the same time, it was difficult to separate the effects of one from the other. Further analysis will be devoted to this issue.

Analysis of all violent events combined indicated that cocaine-related violence occurred more frequently than heroin-related violence. Alcohol was the substance most often related to violence, occurring in about 25 percent of the reported events. Cocaine appeared in about 23 percent of the events and heroin in about 16 percent. Alcohol was almost always related to psychopharmacological violence. Cocaine and heroin were most often related to both systemic and psychopharmacological violence. Economic-compulsive violence appeared relatively rarely, with the exception of cocaine-related economic-compulsive violence among male regular cocaine users.

This chapter discusses only a single measure of cocaine use, that is, frequency of use. This measure was useful in providing certain insights into the cocaine/violence nexus. However, it is not the only possible measure that could have been used. For example, examining volume of cocaine used (independent of frequency) provides additional insights and understanding (Goldstein et al. 1990).

FOOTNOTES

NOTE: Preparation of this report was supported by grants DA-03182, "Drug Related Involvement in Violent Episodes (DRIVE)," and DA-04017, "Female Drug Related Involvement in Violent Episodes (FEMDRIVE)," from the National Institute on Drug Abuse.

REFERENCES

Bellucci, P.A.; Goldstein, P.J.; Spunt, B.J.; Miller, T.; Cortez, N.; Khan, M.; and Lipton, D.S. "Violence Among Homeless Drug Users in New York City: Preliminary Findings." Paper presented at the meeting of the American Society of Criminology, Atlanta, 1986.

Bellucci, P.A.; Goldstein, P.J.; Spunt, B.J.; Miller, T.; Cortez, N.; and Khan, M. "Homeless Drug Users in New York City: Patterns of Drug Use." Paper presented at the meeting of the Society for the Study of Social Problems, Chicago, 1987.
Goldstein, P.J., *Prostitution and Drugs*. Lexington, MA: Lexington Books, 1979.
Goldstein, P.J. The drugs/violence nexus: A tripartite conceptual framework. *Journal of Drug Issues* 15:493–506, 1985.
Goldstein, P.J. Homicide related to drug traffic. *Bulletin of the New York Academy of Medicine* 62:509–515, 1986.
Goldstein, P.J. Drugs and violent crime. In: Weiner, N.A., and Wolfgang, M.E., eds. *Pathways to Criminal Violence*. Newbury Park, CA: Sage, 1989.
Goldstein, P.J.; Lipton, D.S.; Spunt, B.J.; Bellucci, P.A.; Miller, T.; Cortez, N.; Khan, M.; and Kale, A. "Drug Related Involvement in Violent Episodes (DRIVE)." Interim Final Report to the National Institute on Drug Abuse, July 1987.
Goldstein, P.J.; Bellucci, P.A.; Spunt, B.J.; Miller, T.; Cortez, N.; Khan, M.; Durrance, R.; and Vega, A. "Female Drug Related Involvement in Violent Episodes (FEMDRIVE)." Final Report to the National Institute on Drug Abuse, March 1988.
Goldstein, P.J., Bellucci, P.A., Spunt, B.J., and Miller, T. Volume of cocaine use and violence: A comparison between men and women. *Journal of Drug Issues*, in press.
Spunt, B.J.; Goldstein, P.J.; Bellucci, P.A.; and Miller, T. Drug related violence among methadone maintenance treatment clients. *Advances in Alcohol and Substance Abuse*, in press.

AUTHORS

Paul J. Goldstein, Ph.D.
Patricia A. Bellucci
Barry J. Spunt, Ph.D.
Thomas Miller

Narcotic and Drug Research, Inc.
11 Beach Street
3rd Floor
New York, NY 10013

Stealing and Dealing: Cocaine and Property Crimes

Dana Hunt

This chapter examines the relationship between cocaine use and acquisitive crimes, that is, crimes whose primary intent is to generate income. These crimes include burglary, robbery, shoplifting, con games, forgery, prostitution, and drug dealing. Some aspects of this relationship are covered in Dr. Goldstein's chapter in this volume, as many property crimes may also involve violence.

Unfortunately, the public is prone to a rather simplistic view of the relationship between cocaine (or any expensive drug, for that matter) and criminal activity. The image, often reinforced in the media, is that drug use automatically propels the user into income-generating crimes because of the need for money to buy drugs. Both logic and much of the drugs/crime literature suggest that people with an expensive drug habit may resort to illegal activities to support that habit. The research literature has long indicated a strong relationship between the use of another expensive drug, heroin, and criminal activity (McGlothin 1979; Gandossy et al. 1980; Wish et al. 1981; Chaiken and Chaiken 1982; Ball et al. 1983; Hunt et al. 1984; Johnson et al. 1985; Anglin and Speckart 1986).

While teasing out the relationship between heroin and crime is difficult, cocaine presents an even more complicated task. Less than 1 percent of the population in the United States uses heroin, and the majority of users are low-income individuals concentrated in urban areas. Cocaine use is quite different. Epidemiological data and data from the National Institute on Drug Abuse (NIDA) household and high school surveys reported elsewhere in this volume indicate that a large number and wide variety of persons have used and currently use cocaine. Indeed, among high school students, it is one of the few drugs whose use seems to have increased or at least remained the same over the past few years, in spite of an overall decline in drug use in this group. This drug is not confined to the inner city nor to populations already linked to criminal activity for other reasons. Needless to say, the question of producing criminal activity in this large number of users is of great interest, apart from any health risks or social disruption cocaine use presents. Millions of Americans have used or currently use cocaine. Are they involved in crime?

Goldstein's conceptualization of the three types of violence related to drug use is useful to keep in mind in this discussion: crimes resulting from the psychopharmacological aspects of use such as violence related to alcohol consumption; crimes resulting from the drug distribution system such as violence in the drug trade; and crimes driven by economic need such as theft to support a heroin habit. Only the final type of crime is addressed in this chapter.

The economic-compulsive explanation for a relationship between cocaine and crime argues that the relationship between expensive drug use and criminal activity is a direct function of physical need (addiction or compulsion) producing economic needs unmet through traditional channels. An alternative explanation is that the relationship is a function of a deviant lifestyle that includes both drugs and crime, and that both activities are a function of discretion or choice rather than one necessitating the other.[1] For example, Anglin and Speckart (1986) reported that some crimes, such as dealing, are enduring parts of the drug abuser's life and may persist even during periods of reduced use or abstinence among users with limited incomes. Jorquez (1983) found in his sample of "retiring" heroin addicts that retirement from drugs did not necessarily mean cessation of criminal activity or decreased involvement in the lifestyle of the drug world.

This chapter briefly examines the relationship between use of cocaine and criminal activity. A number of studies are drawn on for these analyses. These sources were chosen for their explanations and descriptions and do not by any means constitute an exhaustive review of the literature.

IS COCAINE USE RELATED TO INCOME-GENERATING CRIME?

The first question is whether any use of cocaine is related to criminal activity. A great deal of evidence suggests that the general, infrequent user of cocaine is not significantly more likely to be involved in criminal activity than the nonuser. The majority of users in the NIDA household and high school surveys confine use to experimental "tries" or infrequent use and are not involved in property crimes. This may be particularly true with cocaine, which attracts a substantial number of upper or middle-income users who do not generally need to support limited use through illegal means. The exceptions to this are the middle-income users whose costs related to high-frequency use exceed their income and who may, as some reports from cocaine hotlines indicate, deplete their resources and/or resort to small amounts of stealing or dealing (Washton and Gold 1984).

There are few studies of middle-income cocaine users, particularly those who are not seriously involved with the drug, in treatment or concurrently involved with other drugs. Waldorf (1977) and others (Siegal 1982; Chitwood and Morningstar 1985; Murphy et al. 1986; Zinberg 1984) reported that they found middle-income moderate users rarely involved in traditional property crimes, although some were involved in small-scale distribution of cocaine through sharing and/or selling small amounts to friends. More than 10 years ago, Waldorf (1977) described a group of middle-income cocaine users who, despite use patterns ranging from infrequent to heavy use, were not involved in property crimes. Reinterviewing them 10 years later, he found that, regardless of periods of heavy use and abstinence, with one exception the criminal activity of this group of 27 users was still confined to dealing amounts related to their own use (Murphy et al. 1986).

More recent studies by Reinarman, Waldorf, and Murphy (1986) reported on a San Francisco-based group of heavy cocaine users (n=60) representing a wide range of occupations, including blue-collar workers, lawyers, and social workers. This group consisted of persons who consumed an average of 2 or more grams of cocaine per week for more than a year; 40 percent used it daily for at least 6 months. In each case, the users funded their use through work and low-level dealing. Increases in the quantity used changed the ratio of expenditures on nondrug to drug items or increased dealing activities, but did not trigger other crimes such as burglary or robbery.

Other small studies (Spotts and Schontz 1982) also found that the relationship between use and crime was not direct in users with some flexibility in income and little prior criminal experience. A summary of the data from many studies on drug use and crime by Chaiken and Chaiken (1990) substantiates these smaller study findings.

The reader should not infer, however, that no relationship exists between cocaine abuse and criminal activity; it is simply far more complex than economic impulse alone. If cocaine use and property crime are viewed as intersecting circles, there is a shaded area where cocaine use and crime overlap. The literature suggests that involvement in that shaded area is related to:

- the disposable income of the user;
- the frequency of use and/or involvement in the drug lifestyle; and
- the user's prior experience with crime as an income producer.

Consequently, most persons falling into the shaded area share the following characteristics:

- low or limited income in relation to the level of cocaine use;
- fairly high level of cocaine use; and
- some prior experience with crime as an income producer.

This report focuses on the user/offender. Other persons are users but not involved in acquisitive crimes, and many property offenders do not use cocaine. These would include burglars, robbers, con men, and so forth, who do not use cocaine, as well as nonusing cocaine dealers, distributors, and money launderers. These latter groups are certainly involved with cocaine-related crime, though they may not be users themselves. Because of the hidden nature of all these groups, it is difficult to estimate the extent of the overlap among them.

COCAINE AND CRIME

Unfortunately, the majority of our information about cocaine use and criminal activity is derived from populations already endowed with heavy drug use, marginal incomes, and some prior experience with both criminal activity and other drugs, that is, persons at arrest, in jail, or in drug treatment. Many studies have examined the drug use, particularly narcotics use, and criminal activity in these populations (Ball et al. 1983; Nurco et al. 1985; Inciardi 1985; Johnson et al. 1985), though most have not delineated cocaine for separate analysis.

Collins, Hubbard, and Rachel (1985) examined heroin and cocaine use and criminal activity in the 1980 cohort sample from the Treatment Outcome Prospective Study (TOPS). They found that daily users of cocaine reported drug expenditures averaging more than $18,000 in the year prior to entrance into treatment, $2,000 more than daily heroin users reported. Persons who used both drugs reported expenditures of $21,000. The relationship between these high drug expenditures and criminal income was also consistently significant in this sample. The higher the use level, the higher the reported criminal income level. While populations such as these are skewed toward higher levels of both use and crime, they can be used profitably to examine the nature of the drugs/crime relationship.

One such group consisted of 368 methadone treatment clients randomly selected from four programs in the northeast in the early 1980s, a period of high availability and popularity of cocaine in the area studied but prior to the widespread availability of crack-cocaine. This population was at risk for involvement with both crime and drugs, had prior histories of use and, in most cases, had prior criminal involvement. They were, in general, poorly skilled, and almost two-thirds were unemployed. The characteristics of this sample have been discussed widely in other publications (Hunt et al. 1984, 1985; Strug et al. 1985; Goldsmith et al. 1985).

The relationship between any use of cocaine and income-generating crime was examined in this population, which was well versed in both drugs and criminal activity. Half the sample had at least one prior arrest for property crimes, and almost one-third had a prior arrest for a personal crime (Hunt et al. 1984). The current criminal activity of this group was quite varied: 68 percent reported no involvement in property crime, and 71 percent reported no involvement in drug-dealing crime (table 1). The question of whether any use of cocaine was related to the criminal activity occurring in the sample was particularly salient in this low-income/high-unemployment group, whose disposable income was likely to be small.

Persons who reported any cocaine use in the prior week had significantly higher levels of criminal activity than those reporting no current cocaine

TABLE 1. *Criminal activity in the period 2 weeks prior to interview by cocaine use in the week prior to interview of methadone clients*

Crime/frequency	No cocaine use n=240		Cocaine use n=128		Total n=368	
Property crimes						
None	75%	(180)	54%	(70)	68%	(250)
1–4 times	12%	(29)	26%	(33)	17%	(62)
5 or more times	13%	(31)	20%	(25)	15%	(56)
Chi square=15.84, df=2 p=.001						
Drug-dealing crimes						
None	78%	(186)	58%	(74)	71%	(260)
1–4 times	19%	(45)	34%	(43)	24%	(88)
5 or more times	4%	(9)	9%	(11)	5%	(20)
Chi square=13.63, df=2 p=.001						

use. Only 25 percent of abstainers reported current property crimes, and 23 percent engaged in drug dealing, compared to 45 percent of the users reporting property crimes and 42 percent, drug dealing. The relationship between use and crime remained significant whether the individual was employed or not, though 85 percent with the heaviest drug use and the heaviest criminal involvement were unemployed.

Persons in this sample who used cocaine were also more likely to be involved in income-generating crimes such as dealing stolen merchandise, theft, prostitution, or robbery. Of the seven who reported committing a robbery in the prior 2 weeks, five reported using cocaine during that period.

These figures are somewhat misleading, however. Fifty-two percent of the sample who reported cocaine use used it only once or twice and might be classified as infrequent or occasional users. Of this group, only a third reported property crime, and 31 percent reported drug dealing in the prior 2-week period. As table 2 indicates, the low-frequency users were still more involved in crime than the abstainers, but not nearly as involved as high-frequency users. The low-frequency user committed, on the average, one property crime in a 2-week period, while the more frequent user was committing an average of five property crimes, a significant difference that was repeated across all types of crime. The daily users in this population were very criminally active; 46 percent reported committing more than five property crimes, and 25 percent reported committing more than five drug-dealing crimes in the prior 2 weeks.

TABLE 2. *Criminal activity in the period 2 weeks prior to interview by frequency of cocaine use by methadone clients*

Crime/frequency	Cocaine use in prior week			
	1–2 times n=67	3–5 times n=37	7 or more n=24	Total n=128
Property crimes				
None	67% (45)	54% (20)	21% (5)	55% (70)
1–4 times	24% (16)	24% (9)	33% (8)	26% (33)
5 or more times	9% (6)	22% (8)	46% (11)	20% (25)
Chi square=13.67, df=4 p=.03				
Drug-dealing crimes				
None	69% (46)	57% (21)	29% (7)	58% (74)
1–4 times	28% (19)	35% (13)	46% (11)	34% (43)
5 or more times	3% (2)	8% (3)	25% (6)	9% (11)
Chi square=19.96, df=4 p=.01				

The influence of other drugs besides cocaine was also apparent in this group. As other investigators have pointed out, heavy use of cocaine alone is uncommon; most often, the heavy user combines cocaine with depressants such as alcohol, tranquilizers, or heroin to counteract the "wired" effect of too much cocaine. Twelve percent of the methadone treatment sample used both heroin and cocaine in the week prior to interview. Of those who used cocaine three or more times a week, 38 percent combined it with heroin. Not surprisingly, these heroin/cocaine users were also the most involved in crime in the sample.

These data mirror the findings of other investigators. High frequency of criminal offenses is found among high-frequency cocaine users, particularly those who combine cocaine with heroin. Johnson and Wish (1986) reported that cocaine is the drug of preference among seriously drug-involved offenders, and heroin is often present as a secondary drug of choice. Wish, reporting data from the Drug Use Forecasting System (personal communication 1988), said that 42 percent of arrestees tested positive for cocaine and that while cocaine was frequently the only drug detected on urinalysis among arrestees aged 18-25, heroin and cocaine together were frequently found in those over 30. Similarly, Inciardi (1985) found that crime rates were as high among cocaine-using females as among female heroin addicts. Chaiken and Johnson (1988) also reported that the most seriously involved drug-using offenders were those who were daily users of heroin and cocaine. In each of these cases, the crimes tended to be varied, with few "specializing" in a type of crime.

DEALING COCAINE

Even among cocaine users who commit no other crime, dealing small amounts of cocaine is common. Frequent users deal as a way of obtaining consistent supplies, larger quantities, or quantities at a reduced price. Even occasional users may buy more than they need and sell or share a portion with other using friends as a way to defray costs or "treat" others. The frequent user may also find dealing cocaine the only way to maintain an adequate supply affordably. Faupel and Klockers (1986) argued that any competent drug user would at some time stumble upon an opportunity to distribute some amount for profit and would take it, either as a "break even" enterprise or sometimes for substantial profit.

Dealers in bulk or "weight" amounts of cocaine, however, are not usually heavy users, though they may consume it recreationally. Data indicate that 80 percent of the Federal drug violators are not regular drug users (Bureau of Justice Statistics 1984). Work by Adler (1985) and Chaiken and Johnson (1988) also substantiated these findings. These upper level or high-quality dealers may be binge users, but are rarely addictive users. Adler (1985) reported that among her middle to upper income cocaine dealers, those who became heavily involved with the drug "broke" or "ruined" their businesses. In these cases, dealing cocaine was an income-producing enterprise, unrelated to the dealers' own use of the drug.

Street-level dealers of cocaine, however, may be users. Of the persons arrested for possession in the Drug Use Forecasting System nationwide, over half tested positive for cocaine on urine screening (National Institute of Justice 1988). The street-level dealer of cocaine is also likely to be a low-income, minority status user, likely to be arrested and to be involved in a variety of criminal activities. The recent appearance of crack-cocaine has produced a number of young, inner-city crack dealers in some areas who sell and may even produce the crack pellets (Hunt 1987). Upper or middle-income users may be "dealing" in that they are sharing or distributing to friends, but they are unlikely to be operating public commercial enterprises like their less-well-heeled brothers.

Again, as with property crimes, the most active street-level drug dealers, those for whom dealing is a primary income, are most likely to be daily or near daily users of cocaine and other expensive drugs (Anglin and Speckart 1986; Collins et al. 1985; Chaiken and Chaiken 1982). For these active user/dealers, dealing is likely to be only one of a battery of illegal activities in which they are involved.

SUMMARY

A common thread in all studies of this nature is the level of use of cocaine and/or the concomitant use of other drugs, suggesting that economic necessity plays a role in the decision to commit crimes to help defray the costs of use. While a truly causal link between use and crime remains unclear, the relationship between escalating use and criminal activity in marginal income populations is apparent. Whether that association is driven primarily by economics or lifestyle considerations is not answered by simple examination of the numbers.

Statisically, the use of cocaine is related to criminal activity as a function of the income level and prior criminal experience of the user. This relationship is better defined by looking at the threshold effect in marginal income groups, where use that goes beyond what the pocket can bear produces a significantly greater chance that illegal sources will be found. However, many occasional users or even regular users with resources are able to fund their use through routine sources and never resort to criminal activity or to unconventional financial resources. A large number of cocaine users probably fall into this middle ground: they are neither the "high rollers" that often make the media nor the traditional heroin/ cocaine addicts. For them, criminal activity may surface when use exceeds funds or not at all. For still others, cocaine is part of a criminal lifestyle rather than a motivation for it.

Statistically, all these cocaine users look the same, though the relationship between their use and their crime may be quite varied. The descriptions of three cases discussed in an earlier paper (Hunt et al. 1985) clarify this point. The first case was a 32-year-old white male former heroin addict and former drug dealer who reported cocaine use intravenously three to four times a month, smoked marijuana weekly, and used no other drugs. He was married, working, and had a small child. He also reported dealing in stolen merchandise and clothing that he got from someone else to sell. This pattern had been his custom for several years, observed at close hand by the author, and he had not been arrested for many years, though he had a prior history of arrests dating back more than 15 years. This individual did not link his selling stolen merchandise with his cocaine use. He linked it with the need for supplementary funds and was as likely to deal goods for Christmas money as for cocaine.

In the second case, a direct link between use of cocaine and crime was reported by the individual. This case involved a beautiful young Hispanic female reporting a varying amount of cocaine use each week, averaging about $100–150 worth but ranging as high as $600 some weeks. Although she worked full time in a clerical position, she supplemented her income with weekend prostitution, an occupation she clearly disliked. She reported that the funds from the prostitution went toward the support of her cocaine use, and that she would have no interest or need for such activity if she stopped using cocaine. She smoked marijuana a few times a month and used no heroin.

The third case was a 42-year-old white male who was an active heroin user, though currently in methadone treatment. He reported the use of cocaine three times a week and heroin almost daily. He supported himself through dealing stolen merchandise, steering others to drug dealers, and acting as a runner for persons who wished to buy drugs. He described cocaine as a "bonus" rather than a primary drug of abuse, though he was eloquent in singing its praises. For him, cocaine was part of a lifestyle of hustling, crime, and drug use, rather than a motivation for his criminal activity. Without the added costs of cocaine, he would continue in his activities, as he had done in periods of abstinence from both heroin and cocaine.

These three cocaine users are not unusual. They may look similar in the level of use and, at times, in the level of criminal activity, but they were dramatically different in the relationship between their use and crime. They were all marginal in terms of income, though two were working steadily at legitimate jobs. All had prior histories of incarceration and drug use. In the first two cases, heroin use was in the past, as was active participation in "the life." In the first case, criminal activity was revived for extra money, whether that money was for a special need or for cocaine. In the second, criminal activity was seen as a distasteful necessity given a desire for cocaine; and in the last case, criminal activity was part of the lifestyle, social activity, and even the personality of the individual.

The distinction between lifestyle and economic motivation is critical in understanding the connection between cocaine use and crime. Cocaine use may propel individuals, particularly moderate-income users, into an economic squeeze in which they look to illegal sources of funds. It may also propel them into an ongoing lifestyle in which drugs and crime are routine activities not causally linked to each other. The weighting of cocaine use as a causal factor, however, is based on the resources of the users, their involvement in a drug-using lifestyle, and their economic resources.

FOOTNOTE

1. For a summary of the two models, see Collins et al. 1985.

REFERENCES

Adler, P. *Wheeling and Dealing*. New York: Columbia Press, 1985.

Anglin, D., and Speckart, G. Narcotics use, property crime and dealing: Structural dynamics across the addiction career. *Journal of Quantitative Criminology* 2(4):355–375, 1986.

Ball, J.; Shaffer, J.; and Nurco, D. The day to day criminality of heroin addicts in Baltimore—A study in the continuity of offense rates. *Drug and Alcohol Dependence* (12):119–142, 1983.

Ball, J.; Corty, E.; Petroski, S.; Bond, H.; and Tommasello, A. "Patient Characteristics, Services Provided and Treatment Outcome in Methadone Maintenance Programs in Three Cities." Unpublished report, University of Maryland School of Medicine, Baltimore, MD, 1987.

Bureau of Justice Statistics. *Report to the Nation on Drugs and Crime*. Washington, DC: U.S. Dept. of Justice Bureau of Justice Statistics, 1984.

Chaiken, J., and Chaiken, M. Drugs and predatory crime. In: Wilson, J., and Tonry, M. *Drugs and Crime*. Crime and Justice Series. Washington, DC: National Institute of Justice, 1990.

Chaiken, J., and Chaiken, M. *Varieties of Criminal Behavior*. Santa Monica, CA: Rand Corporation, 1982.

Chaiken, M., and Johnson, B. Characteristics of different types of drug involved offenders. *Issues and Practices*. Washington, DC: National Institute of Justice, 1988.

Chitiwood, D., and Morningstar, P. Factors which differentiate cocaine users in treatment from non-treatment users. *International Journal of the Addictions* 20(3):449–459, 1985.

Collins, J.; Hubbard, R.; and Rachel, V. Expensive drug use and illegal income: A test of explanatory hypotheses. *Criminology* 23(4):743–764, 1985.

Faupel, C., and Klockers, C. Drugs-crime connections: Elaborations from the life histories of hard core heroin addicts. *Social Problems* 34(1):54–68, 1986.

Gandossy, R.; Williams, J.; Cohen, J.; and Harwood, H. *Drugs and Crime: A Survey of the Literature*. Washington, DC: Supt. of Docs., U.S. Govt. Print. Off., 1980.

Goldsmith, D.; Hunt, D.; Lipton, D.; and Strug, D. Methadone folklore: Beliefs about methadone side effects. *Human Organization* 2(1):59–71, 1985.

Hunt, D. *Crack*. Drug Abuse Monitoring Series. Sacramento, CA: State of California, 1987.

Hunt, D.; Lipton, D.; Goldsmith, D.; and Strug, D. An instant shot of 'aah': Cocaine use among methadone clients. *Journal of Psychoactive Drugs* 16:217–227, 1984.

Hunt, D.; Lipton, D.; and Spunt, B. Patterns of criminal activity among methadone clients and current narcotics users not in treatment. *Journal of Drug Issues* Fall:687–702, 1984.

Hunt, D.; Spunt, B.; and Lipton, D. The costly bonus: Cocaine related crime among methadone treatment clients. *Advances in Alcohol and Substance Abuse* Fall:111–142, 1985.

Inciardi, J. *The War on Drugs*. Palo Alto, CA: Mayfield Press, 1985.

Johnson, B., and Wish, E. "The Robbery-Hard Drug Connection." Paper presented at the meeting of the American Sociological Association, Chicago, IL, 1987.

Johnson, B., and Wish, E. "Highlights of Research on Drug and Alcohol Abusing Criminals." Unpublished report, National Institute of Justice, Washington, DC, October 1986.

Johnson, B.; Goldstein, P.; Preble, E.; Smeidler, J.; Lipton, D.; Spunt B.; and Miller, T. *Taking Care of Business: The Economics of Crime by Heroin Users*. Lexington, MA: Lexington Books, 1985.

Jorquez, J. The retirement phase of heroin using careers. *Journal of Drug Issues* Summer:343–365, 1983.

McGlothlin, W.H. Drugs and crime. In: DuPont, F ; Goldstein, A.; and O'Donnell, J., eds. *Handbook on Drug Abuse*. Rockville, MD: National Institute on Drug Abuse, 1979.

Murphy, S.; Reinarman, C.; and Waldorf, D. "An 11-year Follow-up of a Network of 27 Cocaine Users." Paper presented at the meeting of the Society for the Study of Social Problems, New York City, 1986.

National Institute of Justice. *Research in Action: Drug Use Forecasting*. Washington, DC: U.S. Dept. of Justice, Office of Justice Programs, Jan. 1988.

Nurco, D.; Cisin, I.; and Ball, J. Crime as a source of income for narcotics addicts. *Journal of Substance Abuse Treatment* (2):113–115, 1985.

Reinarman, C.; Waldorf, D.; and Murphy, S. "Cocaine and the Workplace." Paper presented at the meeting of the Society for the Study of Social Problems, New York City, 1986.

Siegal, R. Cocaine use and sexual dysfunction: The curse of Mama Coca. *Journal of Psychoactive Drugs* 14(1-2):71–74, 1982.

Spotts, J., and Schontz, F. *Lifestyles of Nine Cocaine Users*. DHEW Pub. No. 76–392. NIDA Monograph Series. Rockville, MD: National Institute on Drug Abuse, 1976.

Strug, D.; Hunt, D.; Lipton, D.; and Goldsmith, D. Patterns of cocaine use among methadone clients. *International Journal of the Addictions* 20(8):1163–1175, 1985.

Waldorf, D. *Doing Coke: An Ethnography of Cocaine Users and Sellers*. Washington, DC: Drug Abuse Council, 1977.

Washton, A., and Gold, M. Chronic cocaine use: Evidence for adverse effects on health and functioning. *Psychiatric Annals* (14):733–743, 1984.

Wish, E.; Klumpp, K.; Moorer, A.; Brady, E.; and Williams, K. *An Analysis of Drugs and Crime Among Arrestees in the District of Columbia*. Washington, DC: National Institute of Justice, 1981.

Zinberg, E. *Drug, Set and Setting: The Basis for Controlled Intoxicant Use*. New Haven, CT: Yale University Press, 1984.

AUTHOR

Dana Hunt, Ph.D.
Abt Associates Inc.
55 Wheeler Street
Cambridge, MA 02138

Cocaine Use in a National Sample of U.S. Youth (NLSY): Ethnic Patterns, Progression, and Predictors

Denise B. Kandel and Mark Davies

Epidemiological surveys have established that following a sharp increase in the late 1970s and a seeming stabilization in the 1980s, cocaine use in the general population is starting to decline (Adams 1988; Rouse 1988; Johnston et al. 1989). However, data are consistently presented for the American population as a whole. Potential ethnic differences and/or similarities in patterns of cocaine use are rarely discussed. An exception is the recently released report on the 1985 National Household Survey on Drug Abuse (National Institute on Drug Abuse 1987*a*).

In this chapter, we take advantage of a large data set of young American adults, the Youth Cohort of the National Longitudinal Survey of the labor force experience of young Americans (NLSY), to investigate in some detail patterns of cocaine use and selected risk factors for such use not only in the total youth population but also among three major ethnic groups, namely, whites, blacks and Hispanics.

Specifically, we address the following three issues: (1) What is the prevalence of the use of cocaine and other drugs among young Americans reported by the three ethnic groups? (2) What is the order of initiation into the use of cocaine and other illicit drugs? Can one identify developmental patterns of involvement with cocaine? Are these patterns similar among the three ethnic groups? (3) What are the predictors of cocaine use among young adults? Are they different for whites, blacks and Hispanics?

DATA SOURCE

Sample

The data derive from the NLSY, a study of 12,069 young adults conducted since 1979 by the Center for Human Resource Research of Ohio

State University (Wolpin 1983). In 1984, with support from the National Institute on Drug Abuse (NIDA), 5 minutes of drug-related questions were included in the interview schedule administered to participants in the sixth wave of the survey. Respondents were then 19 to 27 years old. The Youth Cohort sample is a multistage stratified area probability sample representative of individuals born in the years 1957–64 in the coterminous United States. The study includes youths who are usually not well represented in national samples, not only members of minority groups but also high school dropouts and the unemployed. Blacks (N=2,172), Hispanics (N=1,480), and economically disadvantaged white youths (N=1,643) were oversampled for a supplemental sample, and 1,280 young persons in the military (as of September 1978) were also included. Respondents have been interviewed annually through personal household interviews averaging about 1½ hours in length. The completion rate for the base year was 89.7 percent for the cross-sectional sample, 88.7 percent for the basic supplemental sample, and 71.5 percent for the military sample (Frankel et al. 1983). Reinterviewing rates have been consistently very high, with 95 percent of the original cohort—6,062 males and 6,009 females aged 19-27 years—interviewed for the sixth time in 1984.

Data Collection Instrument

While the initial focus of the survey was primarily on the labor force experience of young people, a number of lifestyle and health-related questions were added in successive waves. In 1984, a series of drug-related questions was included along with the earlier battery of questions on education, labor force participation, marriage, fertility, and alcohol usage. The alcohol questions ascertained lifetime experience and current extent of alcohol consumption. Limited questions on psychological characteristics, attitudes, and delinquency were included in a single wave of the survey.

The drug questions were answered directly to the interviewer rather than on self-administered forms. Respondents were asked separate questions about their use of cigarettes and marijuana. For seven classes of illicit drugs other than marijuana and nonmedical use of pills and tranquilizers, respondents were shown a card, read a list of drugs, and asked for each whether or not they had ever used it. For each drug used, further questions inquired about lifetime frequency of use, recency of use in the last year, frequency of use in the last month, and age at first use. Response categories were designed to ensure comparability with the two major national drug-related surveys, Monitoring the Future (Johnston et al. 1989) and the National Household Survey on Drug Abuse (Adams

1988; NIDA 1987*a*; Rouse 1988). Additional questions were asked about lifetime, last-year, and last- month frequency of use for each of three classes of medically prescribed psychotropics (sedatives, stimulants, and minor tranquilizers). Refusal rates were less than 1 percent for most illicit drug questions.

As in preceding waves of data collection, respondents were assured complete confidentiality. No names appeared on the interview schedule, only an identification number. In addition, to assure the confidentiality of the drug- related reports, a grant of confidentiality was specifically obtained from the Surgeon General guaranteeing that none of the records could be subpoenaed for any legal proceedings, whether at the local, State, or Federal levels.

The field work was carried out by NORC of the University of Chicago. As reflected in the very high completion rates, participation in the study has been excellent. There was no reason to expect less than candid answers. It is important to note, as background to the epidemiological data presented below, that underreporting of the use of certain drugs, especially illicit drugs other than marijuana and the medically prescribed drugs, may have occurred (Mensch and Kandel 1988). Furthermore, underreporting is not randomly distributed in the sample but is more prominent among certain social groups, in particular, school dropouts and blacks.

EPIDEMIOLOGY OF COCAINE USE: ETHNIC PATTERNS

Eighteen percent of the total cohort reported having ever used cocaine compared to 25 percent reported by the comparable age group (18 to 25) in the 1985 National Household Survey on Drug Use (NIDA 1987*a*, 1988). The striking finding is that blacks consistently reported lower rates of cocaine use than whites, with Hispanics in between these two groups (table 1). These differences appear whether one considers lifetime prevalence of use, use in the past year, or use in the last month. Blacks also reported lower rates of use of illicit drugs other than cocaine. Close to two and a half times as many whites as blacks reported using an illicit drug other than marijuana or cocaine.

Ethnic differences in patterns of cocaine use were more pronounced among women as compared to men. Black and Hispanic women also reported lower rates of use of the legal drugs and marijuana than did whites. Among men, ethnic differences appeared only with respect to illicit drugs other than marijuana.

TABLE 1. *Lifetime, past year, and past month use of selected drugs by sex and ethnicity (NLSY 1984)*

	Percent who used:					
	Alcohol	Cigarettes	Marijuana	Cocaine	OID–C[b]	N
Lifetime						
Men						
White	98	83	69	23	31	4,240
Black	93	81	68	15	13	839
Hispanic	95	81	63	18	22	382
Women						
White	97	83	62	15	26	4,024
Black	89	74	48	6	9	831
Hispanic	88	70	44	12	17	375
Last 12 months[a]						
Men						
White	NA	48	40	15	16	4,243
Black	NA	52	40	10	6	840
Hispanic	NA	50	36	12	12	384
Women						
White	NA	50	30	9	13	4,022
Black	NA	44	24	4	5	830
Hispanic	NA	41	19	8	9	376
Last 30 days						
Men						
White	82	41	25	6	5	4,243
Black	69	47	28	4	3	840
Hispanic	75	43	22	7	5	384
Women						
White	69	43	14	4	5	4,022
Black	50	38	14	2	2	830
Hispanic	53	31	10	3	3	376

[a] 12-month data for alcohol not available.
[b] Illicit drugs other than marijuana and cocaine.

The lower prevalence of reported use of cocaine and other illicit drugs by blacks as compared to whites is also observed in most surveys that have reported on ethnic differences, whether the data are obtained by household interviews, as in the National Household Survey, or in self-administered questionnaires within a school setting (Kleinman and Lukoff 1978; Maddahian et al. 1986; NIDA 1987*a*; Skager and Maddahian 1983; Trimble et al. 1987; Welte and Barnes 1987; Zabin et al. 1985).

O'Donnell et al.'s (1976) survey of a national sample of young men interviewed in 1974 is the only representative national study to report overall higher rates for blacks than for whites. The only population surveys to report very high rates of illicit drug use for blacks are community surveys of urban low-income blacks (Brunswick et al. 1985). Such surveys, however, typically do not have matched comparison groups of poor urban whites.

A comparison of rates of cocaine use reported by different ethnic groups in the restricted sample of NLSY youths, who reside in urban areas throughout the United States, reveals differentials similar to those observed in the total sample (table 2). Blacks report the lowest rates of cocaine use. However, in the urban sample restricted to the northeastern region, the differences are attenuated for lifetime experience and disappear for use reported for the last year and the last month among men and for the last month among women. Thus, while fewer blacks than whites may initiate the use of cocaine, those who do so in large urban

TABLE 2. *Lifetime, past year, and past month use of cocaine in urban areas by sex and ethnicity (NLSY 1984)*

Urban region	Lifetime %	Last 12 months %	Last 30 days %	Total N ≤
Men				
All urban				
White	28	17	7	(3,247)
Black	16	12	5	(613)
Hispanic	17	12	8	(312)
Northeastern				
White	28	20	9	(726)
Black	24	19	10	(131)
Hispanic	21	17	13	(59)
Women				
All urban				
White	18	11	4	(3,403)
Black	7	5	2	(659)
Hispanic	12	8	3	(325)
Northeastern				
White	24	16	5	(750)
Black	16	10	6	(129)
Hispanic	16	10	6	(67)

centers in the Northeast are more likely than whites to persist in the use of the drug. The ratio of those who reported using within the last 30 days over those who ever used is .42 among black men compared to .31 among whites. As we will discuss shortly, blacks are also more likely than whites to become heavily involved in cocaine.

These ethnic differences appear to be related to age and to characterize the population younger than 35 years old. Data from the National Household Survey (NIDA 1988) showed that almost twice as many blacks as whites aged 35 and over reported any lifetime experience with cocaine (7 versus 4 percent), while the reverse was true for each of the three major age groupings younger than 35. Thus, 14 percent of blacks aged 26 to 34 reported any lifetime experience with cocaine compared to 28 percent of whites. Similarly, Robins (1985) reported that, for Epidemiological Catchment Area (ECA) respondents, blacks had higher rates of alcohol abuse than whites among those 45 or older, but lower rates among those younger than 45. Historical factors may explain these ethnic patterns. In discussing similar age-related trends regarding alcohol abuse, Robins (1985) suggested as one interpretation that "the middle-aged black group is the first black cohort to have a large proportion of its members reared in inner cities" (p.13). Lack of familiarity of black families with the stresses of urban life may have increased the children's vulnerability to alcohol.

General Population Versus Treated Cases: A Paradox

The juxtaposition of data on cocaine use from general population samples and those from cases that come to the attention of various treatment centers presents two striking and puzzling paradoxes. One is the contrast between the striking increase in the number of treated cases and the stable or declining trends observed since the 1980s in the number of individuals in general population samples who report any experience with cocaine. This is discussed by Adams in this volume.

Another paradox pertains to racial differences. A smaller proportion of blacks than whites report having experimented with illicit drugs, with Hispanics generally in an intermediate position. Yet, cocaine users who have come to the attention of various treatment, medical, or criminal institutions, such as drug-related emergency rooms, treatment programs, or medical examiner offices, consistently show an overrepresentation of blacks compared to their distribution in the population. Large national samples, however, may not be the best source of data with which to compare the ethnic distribution of treated cases, which tend to come disproportionately from large urban centers (Brunswick 1988). For example, of cocaine-related emergency room episodes recorded in 1985, 35 percent were white and 46 percent black (NIDA 1987*c*). Among clients with a primary cocaine problem who were admitted in 1985 to 15 State-monitored treatment programs that reported to NIDA, 56 percent were white and 35 percent black (NIDA 1987*b*). In these samples, blacks were overrepresented compared to their representation in the population (NIDA undated).[1] By contrast, in both the 1985 household sample and the NLSY, over 80 percent of the self-reported lifetime cocaine users were white and only 9 percent were black.

The similarity in the ethnic distribution of cocaine users in the two general population samples is remarkable. The proportion of blacks among cocaine users from the northeastern urban centers in the NLSY increased slightly to 11 percent, compared to the 9 percent observed in the total sample, but was still substantially lower than the proportions recorded in treated cases or casualties. What accounts for this discrepancy? One common explanation advanced to account for such ethnic differences is a bias involved in who appears for treatment, especially at publicly funded centers. Whites may seek care from private physicians and may be underrepresented in government-financed programs.

Another factor may also be operative. That is, although *fewer* blacks than whites experiment with various illicit drugs, a *higher* proportion of blacks than whites becomes heavily involved and develops problems with these drugs. As noted above, following initial experimentation with cocaine, blacks are more likely than whites to persist in their use. Self-acknowledged black cocaine users in general population surveys also report heavier involvement than either whites or Hispanics. For instance, 22 percent of black men in the NLSY who reported having used cocaine within the last 30 days, reported using it on 10 or more days as compared to 14 percent of white men and 13 percent of Hispanics. Similarly, among those in the National Household Survey on Drug Abuse who used cocaine in the last year, three times as many blacks (15 percent) as whites (5 percent) aged 18 to 25 used it at least once a week; 13 percent of the Hispanics did so. Among those older than 25 who used cocaine in the last year, 18 percent of the blacks aged 26–34 and 21 percent of those 35 and older used cocaine at least once a week compared to none of the whites; 15 percent of the Hispanics aged 26–34 and none of those 35 and older did so (based on data presented in NIDA 1987*a*).

Finally, the ECA surveys, which ascertained the distribution of cases of substance abusers meeting DSM–III criteria, found a higher proportion of diagnosed substance abuse cases among blacks than among whites (Robins et al. 1984). In particular, in Baltimore, 7.3 percent of blacks 18 and older received such a diagnosis compared to 4.9 percent of whites. The ethnic differences in the ECA would be accentuated if the rates were calculated among those who ever used an illicit drug rather than in the total samples of each ethnic group. In the ECA study, any potential respondent selection bias that could be reflected in statistics on treated cases is absent.

AGE OF ONSET AND PROGRESSION INTO DRUGS

A clear progression in stages of drug use, from alcohol and/or cigarettes to marijuana and from marijuana to one or more of the other illicit drugs has been consistently documented (Donovan and Jessor 1983; Hamburg et al. 1975; Huba and Bentler 1983; Kandel 1975; O'Donnell and Clayton 1982; Welte and Barnes 1985; Yamaguchi and Kandel 1984*a*, 1984*b*). In these investigations, illicit drugs other than marijuana were generally grouped together, and not much work has been done to identify particular sequences among them. When each illicit drug is considered separately, such an order is actually difficult to determine (Single et al. 1974). We have now approached the problem by singling out cocaine in addition to marijuana and grouping together users of illicit drugs other than marijuana and cocaine, such as stimulants, other pills, psychedelics, and heroin. Such a strategy reveals a strong and regular pattern of progression among illicit drugs.

The analyses of progression were based on the mean ages of onset of use of each class of drugs: marijuana, cocaine, and other illicit drugs. First, we examined each pair of drugs at a time. Because respondents had been asked about age of first experimentation rather than specific month and year, ties were observed, in which individuals mentioned having started two classes of drugs at the same age (table 3). The proportion of ties was very low for marijuana and cocaine but reached more than 30 percent of the sample among black users of cocaine and illicit drugs other than marijuana and cocaine.

For all ethnic groups, marijuana preceded cocaine in the overwhelming majority of cases, and illicit drugs other than marijuana preceded cocaine. These trends appeared to be stronger for whites than for blacks or for Hispanics.

We then determined the sequences of progression among those who reported using all three classes.[2] The patterns were based on the three-way cross-tabulation of the pairwise classification of sequential patterns of initiation. Each pairwise classification has three categories, with the middle category representing a tie and the other two the order of initia-

TABLE 3. *Order in which illicit drugs were used among male and female users of pairs of substances (NLSY 1984)*

Proportions using	Men White %	Men Black %	Men Hispanic %	Women White %	Women Black %	Women Hispanic %
Marijuana and cocaine						
Marijuana first	97	92	90	92	94	85
Both same age	2	4	6	7	4	15
Cocaine first	1	4	4	1	3	0
Marijuana and OID–C[a]						
Marijuana first	76	82	74	69	75	68
Both same age	14	10	12	21	15	14
OID–C first	10	8	14	10	9	18
OID–C[a] and cocaine						
OID–C first	73	57	66	73	54	72
Both same age	21	35	24	21	33	17
Cocaine first	5	8	10	6	12	10

[a] Illicit drugs other than marijuana and cocaine.

tion of each member of the pair of drugs. Certain patterns are logically impossible; others are empirically very rare. The five major patterns of progression observed among each ethnic group are displayed in figure 1. The first four are patterns in which marijuana initiation clearly preceded initiation into any other illicit drugs, or, in a minority of cases, occurred at the same age as initiation to another illicit drug. Only 4 out of the 1,037 young men who used all three classes of drugs initiated cocaine prior to marijuana; 6 of the 618 women did so.

In the most prevalent pattern, marijuana clearly preceded onset into other illicit drug use, and these drugs preceded cocaine experimentation. This pattern was most prevalent among whites, where it accounted for 50 percent of the multiple users among men and women, and least prevalent among blacks. In the next most prevalent pattern, marijuana clearly preceded all other illicit drugs, but cocaine and other illicit drugs were initiated at the same age. In a reversal from the ethnic differences observed for the first pattern, the second pattern was more prevalent among blacks than among whites or Hispanics. These two patterns, in which marijuana clearly precedes the use of any other illicit drugs and cocaine is the last drug used, account for approximately 70 percent of the men in each ethnic group and 60 percent of the women.

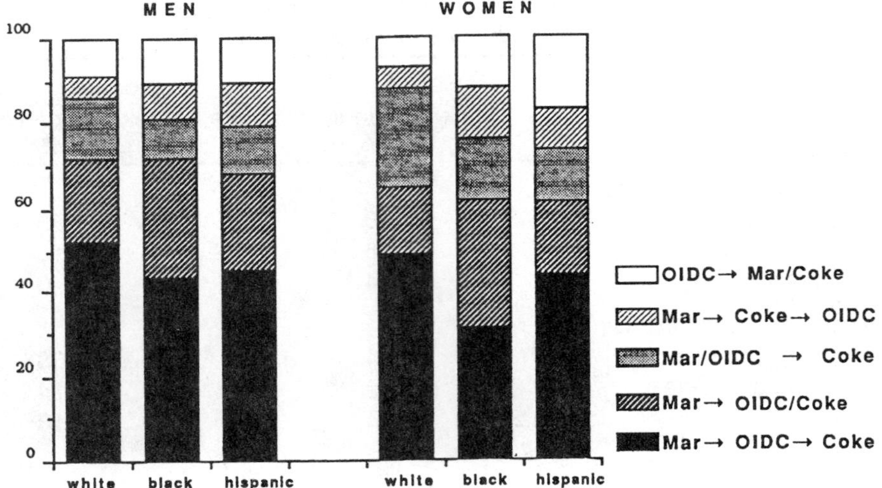

FIGURE 1. *Patterns of progression into illicit drugs by sex and ethnicity (NLSY 1984)*

The next three patterns were much less frequent. They included one in which marijuana and other illicit drugs were experienced at the same age but prior to cocaine, and a variety of other patterns in which cocaine followed marijuana but preceded other illicit drugs. This pattern was least prevalent among whites.

Finally, for about 10 percent of all men and white and black women, an illicit drug other than marijuana or cocaine preceded the use of marijuana. This proportion of young people who had used an illicit drug prior to marijuana was higher in the NLSY than in the cohort of young adults from New York State high schools who have been followed up to age 29 (Kandel and Yamaguchi in press).

It is clear that there are well-delineated stages of progression into cocaine and that, for the overwhelming majority of young people, not only does marijuana precede experimentation with cocaine, but experimentation with an illicit drug other than marijuana is a precursor to cocaine as well.

On the average, among males, initiation into marijuana use took place at age 16, and initiation into illicit drugs other than marijuana and cocaine took place 1 or 2 years later, depending upon ethnicity (table 4). Initiation into cocaine use occurred at about the same age for all groups—age 19. This represents on the average a 2-year lag for whites, but only a 1-year lag for blacks and a slightly longer lag for Hispanics. Nonwhite females generally initiated illicit drugs at a later age than nonwhite males.

TABLE 4. *Age of onset into drugs by ethnicity and sex (NLSY 1984)*

	White $\overline{X}$ age	Black $\overline{X}$ age	Hispanic $\overline{X}$ age
Men			
Marijuana	16.1	16.2	16.0
N	(3,388)	(560)	(237)
OID–C[a]	17.3	18.3	17.2
N	(1,515)	(107)	(84)
Cocaine	19.2	19.4	18.9
N	(1,130)	(120)	(68)
Women			
Marijuana	16.5	17.3	16.7
N	(2,953)	(397)	(164)
OID–C[a]	17.4	19.0	17.9
N	(1,202)	(70)	(61)
Cocaine	19.0	20.2	19.6
N	(698)	(51)	(45)

[a] Illicit drug other than marijuana and cocaine.

Indeed, while the patterns of progression were very similar for the three ethnic groups, the rates of progression differed. The ages of initiation and duration in each state were examined among those who had used all three classes of drugs (table 5). Extent of involvement in drugs varied by age of onset. Those who went through the entire sequence and used cocaine as well as marijuana and other illicit drugs, initiated marijuana use more than a year earlier on the average than each sex/ethnic cohort as a whole (compare tables 4 and 5).

Black and white male adolescents who progressed to cocaine initiated marijuana use at approximately the same age. However, blacks remained longer in the stage of marijuana use before progressing to illicit drugs other than marijuana and cocaine, and stayed in the marijuana stage for a much shorter period of time before progressing to cocaine.

TABLE 5. *Duration of use at one stage before progression to higher stage among men and women users of three types of illicit drugs, by ethnicity (NLSY 1984)*

	White	Black	Hispanic
Men			
Age at marijuana onset	14.9	15.1	14.6
Duration (in years):			
Marijuana	2.0	2.6	2.3
OID–C[a]	2.1	1.4	1.8
Age at cocaine onset	19.0	19.1	18.7
Women			
Age at marijuana onset	14.8	15.9	15.5
Duration (in years):			
Marijuana	1.7	2.4	1.7
OID–C[a]	2.3	1.6	2.1
Age at cocaine onset	18.8	19.9	19.3

[a] Illicit drugs other than marijuana and cocaine.

White males stayed on the average 8 months longer than blacks in the other-illicit-drugs stage before progressing to cocaine—2.1 years compared to 1.4 years. As for most other drug-related behaviors, Hispanics were in the middle, between whites and blacks. Black women similarly spend more time than whites in the marijuana stage and less time in the other-illicit-drug stage before progressing to cocaine. Both black and Hispanic women initiated marijuana and cocaine at a later age than did whites.

Adolescents who used cocaine as well as illicit drugs other than marijuana were the most seriously involved in drugs of any youths. Adolescents were classified into five mutually exclusive groups: (1) never used any illicit drugs, (2) used marijuana only, (3) used other illicit drugs, except cocaine, (4) used cocaine, no other illicit drug than marijuana, (5) used cocaine and other illicit drugs, in addition to marijuana. The latter group had started use of all classes of illicit drugs at the earliest age (table 6) and had much more extensive experiences with marijuana and cocaine than any other group (tables 7 and 8). Illustrative data for whites are displayed for age of onset in table 6 and for all three ethnic groups for extent of use of marijuana and cocaine in tables 7 and 8, respectively. The results were similar for blacks and Hispanics. Similar results were reported earlier for another cohort (Kandel et al. 1985).

TABLE 6. *Mean age of onset into illicit drugs use by lifetime pattern of drug use among white men and women (NLSY 1984)*

	Marijuana only $\bar{X}$ age	OID[a]/no cocaine $\bar{X}$ age	Cocaine/ no OID[a] $\bar{X}$ age	Cocaine and OID[a] $\bar{X}$ age	Difference in years $\bar{X}$ age
White men					
Marijuana	16.9	15.9	15.9	14.9	-2.0
N	(1690)	(550)	(184)	(926)	
OID–C[b]		18.0		16.9	-1.1
N		(584)		(926)	
Cocaine			20.1	19.0	-1.1
N			(182)	(919)	
White women					
Marijuana	17.2	16.2	16.1	14.8	-2.4
N	(1645)	(574)	(130)	(583)	
OID–C[b]		18.2		16.5	-1.7
N		(641)		(561)	
Cocaine			20.1	18.8	-1.3
N			(130)	(557)	

[a] Illicit drugs other than marijuana.
[b] Illicit drugs other than marijuana and cocaine.

TABLE 7. *Extent of marijuana use by pattern of drug use in last 12 months, by sex and ethnicity (NLSY 1984)*

Proportion who used marijuana 20+ times in last 30 days:	Marijuana/ no OID[a] %	OID[a]/no cocaine %	Cocaine/ no OID[a] %	Cocaine/ OID[a] %
Men				
White	7	16	15	24
N	(984)	(363)	(263)	(416)
Black	10	15	33	36
N	(240)	(19)	(51)	(30)
Hispanic	6	11	14	29
N	(82)	(19)	(20)	(25)
Women				
White	3	6	4	15
N	(690)	(351)	(196)	(235)
Black	9	11	36	22
N	(155)	(23)	(16)	(16)
Hispanic	5	2	8	18
N	(40)	(19)	(14)	(15)

[a] Illicit drugs other than marijuana.

TABLE 8. *Extent of cocaine use in last 30 days by pattern of drug use in last 12 months, by sex and ethnicity (NLSY 1984)*

Proportion who used cocaine 6+ times in last 30 days:	Cocaine/No OID[a]		Cocaine/OID[a]	
	%	N	%	N
Men				
White	2	(260)	13	(423)
Black	12	(51)	17	(31)
Hispanic	9	(20)	25	(25)
Women				
White	3	(200)	16	(241)
Black	12	(16)	14	(15)
Hispanic	15	(14)	20	(15)

[a] Illicit drugs other than marijuana

PREDICTORS OF COCAINE USE

Which young adults use cocaine?

A positive relationship between adolescent drug use and early sexual experimentation and permissive attitudes about sexual behavior have been documented by prior investigators. Ensminger and Kane (1985) reported that sexually active young black women are 7 times as likely to have used marijuana, and active young black men are 10 times as likely as their nonactive peers. Parallel findings have been reported by Zabin et al. (1986). Similarly, Elliott and Morse (1985) found in a large national sample that, among men and women aged 15 to 21 in 1981, the proportions sexually active within the last year ranged from 21 percent among those who had used no drugs to 45 percent among those who used marijuana and to 89 percent among those who experimented also with illicit drugs other than marijuana. Sexual experimentation had a stronger relationship with drug use than with delinquency. The relationships between sexual experience and drug use obtained not only for illicit drugs but also for cigarettes and alcohol (Harford 1986; Jessor and Jessor 1977; Miller and Simon 1974; Rachal et al. 1980; Vener and Stewart 1974; Zucker and Devoe 1975). To the best of our knowledge, no study has yet examined the relative impact of marijuana and sexual activity specifically on cocaine.

Analysis of the predictors of drug use in the NLSY was limited by the availability of relevant measures. Very few psychological or attitudinal variables were measured. However, variables were available from domains that have been identified in prior studies as being important correlates or predictors of illicit drug use in general, and cocaine in particular (e.g., Hawkins et al. 1985; Kandel 1980; Kandel et al. 1985; Newcomb and Bentler 1987). In addition, the data set had information about one behavior that is rarely covered in surveys of cocaine use, namely, information about the young person's sexual behavior. This is an important factor in predicting subsequent cocaine involvement.

Logistic regressions were carried out predicting involvement in cocaine, both lifetime and within the last year, using the SPSS–X package. Variables from five domains were included in the models: sociodemographic factors, current participation in social roles of adulthood, deviance, degree of involvement with various classes of drugs, and region of the country where residing. The variables are described in detail in the appendix. Sociodemographic variables included age, race, educational attainment, whether or not the youth had ever dropped out of high school, score on the Armed Forces Qualification Test (AFQT), and whether the youth was raised in an intact family when an adolescent. Deviance was measured by questions asked in 1980 on number of delinquent acts from among 13 in which participated in the last year, whether had ever been stopped by the police, arrested, and/or convicted by 1980, and frequency of religious attendance. In order not to lose additional cases in the analysis, a dummy variable was included for those who did not answer the delinquency question in 1980, i.e., 2.8 percent of men and 1.8 percent of women. Information about ever having had sexual intercourse and age of first intercourse was also available. Other predictors included measures of current participation in adult roles (whether currently working, marital and parenthood status), extent of involvement with alcohol, cigarettes, and marijuana, and region of the country. The drug use variables measured recency and frequency of involvement. The categories ranged from having never used the drug to used 20 or more times in the last 12 months and reflected increasing involvement in each class of drugs.[3]

Two models were run to predict lifetime cocaine use. Each estimated a different aspect of sexual experience: any lifetime sexual experience and age of onset. The first model was based on the total sample and included a covariate for ever having had sex. The second model was restricted to nonvirgins and included a covariate for age of first sexual experience. The second model was also run to predict cocaine use within the last year among all nonvirgins and among blacks, Hispanics, and whites separately to obtain estimates for each ethnic group. Ninety-three percent of all men and 88 percent of all women had ever had sex. The proportions by ethnicity among men were 91 percent for whites, 97 percent for blacks, and 92 percent for Hispanics; and among women 88, 93, and 81 percent, respectively. The logistic regression coefficients predicting lifetime use of cocaine among men and women for the total sample are presented in table 9 and for nonvirgins in table 10. Sex-specific regressions restricted to nonvirgins predicting cocaine use in the last year are presented for the total sample in table 11, for whites in table 12, for blacks in table 13, and for Hispanics in table 14.

In order to compare and evaluate the relative impact of the different covariates in each group, the logistic regression coefficients were transformed into standardized odds ratios. These express the change in the odds for experiencing the event (i.e., cocaine use ever or in the last year), for a change in a categorical variable, or for a change in one standard deviation for continuous variables. The values are obtained by exponentiating regression coefficients for categorical variables or the product of each logistic regression coefficient by the standard deviation of the relevant predictor for continuous variables. For example, consider two hypothetical groups that share identical covariate patterns except for the independent variable of interest. For this particular independent variable, the hypothetical groups differ by one standard deviation. The odds ratio between these two groups is the exponentiated product of the regression coefficient and the standard deviation.[4]

In addition, to provide a substantive interpretation of the results, the proportions of individuals expected to be using cocaine for selected categories of selected covariates were estimated[5] and are presented in tables 15 and 16.

Almost all the variables included in the models were statistically significant predictors of lifetime cocaine involvement. Almost the same variables that predicted lifetime involvement among nonvirgin men and women also predicted current cocaine involvement. With several exceptions, the same variables predicted cocaine involvement among men and women. Fewer variables reached statistical significance among blacks and Hispanics than among whites, probably because of smaller sample sizes.

In the total sample, an important factor for lifetime cocaine involvement among men and women was having experienced sexual intercourse (table 9). The odds ratios were 3.5 for men and 3.0 for women. A second important factor was recency/frequency of marijuana involvement (odds ratios of 2.7 for men, 2.5 for women), with a stopped-by-the police or having-ever-been-convicted tied for second place for women. Among nonvirgins, the largest effect on lifetime cocaine use was recency/

TABLE 9. *Logistic regression predicting lifetime use of cocaine by sex (NLSY 1984—unweighted)*

Predictors	Men			Women		
	Standard deviation	β	Odds ratios[c]	Standard deviation	β	Odds ratios[c]
Age	2.295	.084***	1.2	2.261	.086**	1.2
Highest grade completed	2.134	.122***	1.3	2.043	.028	1.0
Ever dropped out (vs. never)	a	.306*	1.4	a	.412**	1.5
Ethnicity						
Black (vs. white/other)	a	–.518***	0.6	a	–.596***	0.6
Hispanic	a	–.206	0.8	a	.178	1.2
Intact family at age 14 (vs. broken)	a	–.364***	0.7	a	–.038	1.0
Armed Forces Qualification Test	23.249	.016***	1.5	21.162	.024***	1.7
Church attendance (1980)	1.677	–.070*	0.9	1.695	–.166***	0.8
Number of delinquent acts (1980)[b]	2.698	.110***	1.3	1.672	.142***	1.3
Police contacts						
Stopped (vs. not)	a	.232*	1.3	a	.670***	2.0
Arrested	a	.102	1.1	a	.694**	2.0
Convicted	a	.378**	1.4	a	.914***	2.5
Ever had sexual intercourse (vs. never)	a	1.266***	3.5	a	1.106***	3.0
Currently working (vs. not)	a	–.048	1.0	a	–.034	1.0
Marital status						
Never married (vs. marr)	a	.188	1.2	a	.364**	1.4
Separate/divorce/widow	a	–.046	0.9	a	.064	1.1
Ever a parent (vs. never)	a	–.116	0.9	a	–.382**	0.7
Cigarettes Q/F	2.422	.130***	1.4	2.361	.104***	1.3
Alcohol Q/F	1.684	.066*	1.1	1.278	.194***	1.3
Marijuana Q/F	1.983	.506***	2.7	1.614	.544***	2.5
Region						
North Central (vs. East)	a	–.782***	0.5	a	1.006***	0.4
South	a	–.322**	0.7	a	–.630***	0.5
West	a	.330*	1.4	a	.140	1.1
Intercept		.577			.899	
Chi Square		4342			4110	
DF		4690			5128	

a Categorical variable.

b A categorical variable was entered for those who did not answer question (less than 3 percent of sample).

c Odds ratios are displayed for categorical variables and for changes in one standard deviation of the variable for continuous variables.

⁺p<.10; *p<.05; **p<.01; ***p<.001.

TABLE 10. *Logistic regression predicting lifetime cocaine use by sex among nonvirgins (NLSY 1984—unweighted)*

Predictors	Men: Standard deviation	Men: β	Men: Odds ratios[c]	Women: Standard deviation	Women: β	Women: Odds ratios[c]
Age	2.279	.092***	1.2	2.221	.126***	1.3
Highest grade completed	2.138	.150***	1.4	2.058	.084*	1.2
Ever dropped out (vs. never)	a	.296*	1.3	a	.294⁺	1.3
Ethnicity						
Black (vs. white/other)	a	–.704***	0.5	a	–.792***	0.4
Hispanic	a	–.210	0.8	a	.280⁺	1.3
Intact family at age 14 (vs. broken)	a	–.324*	0.7	a	–.056	0.9
Armed Forces Qualification Test	22.959	.018***	1.5	21.115	.022	1.6
Church attendance (1980)	1.654	–.058⁺	0.9	1.681	–.140***	0.8
Number of delinquent acts (1980)[b]	2.733	.102***	1.3	1.709	.138***	1.3
Police contacts						
Stopped (vs. not)	a	.214⁺	1.2	a	.712***	2.0
Arrested	a	.064	1.1	a	.520***	1.7
Convicted	a	.342*	1.4	a	.682**	2.0
Age at 1st sexual intercourse	2.644	–.118***	0.7	2.122	–.252***	0.6
Currently working (vs. not)	a	–.048	1.0	a	.000	1.0
Marital status						
Never married (vs. marr)	a	.202	1.2	a	.402*	1.5
Separate/divorce/widow	a	–.136	0.9	a	–.040	1.0
Ever a parent (vs.never)	a	–.168	0.8	a	–.540***	0.6
Cigarettes Q/F	2.417	.118***	1.3	2.373	.078**	1.2
Alcohol Q/F	1.685	.062*	1.1	1.291	.198***	1.3
Marijuana Q/F	1.986	.490***	2.6	1.650	.518***	2.2
Region						
North Central (vs. East)	a	–.758***	0.5	a	–1.008***	0.4
South	a	–.346***	0.7	a	–.710***	0.5
West	a	.328*	1.4	a	.106	1.1
Intercept		1.923			2.974	
Chi Square		3964			3729	
DF		4301			4462	

a Categorical variable.
b A categorical variable was entered for those who did not answer question (less than 3 percent of sample).
c Odds ratios are displayed for categorical variables and for changes in one standard deviation of the variable for continuous variables.
⁺p<.10; *p<.05; **p<.01; ***p<.001.

TABLE 11. *Logistic regression predicting cocaine use in the last 12 months by sex among nonvirgins (NLSY 1984—unweighted)*

Predictors	Men			Women		
	Standard deviation	β	Odds ratios[c]	Standard deviation	β	Odds ratios[c]
Age	2.279	.026	1.1	2.221	.058	1.1
Highest grade completed	2.138	.094*	1.2	2.058	.108*	1.2
Ever dropped out (vs. never)	a	.088	1.1	a	.092	1.1
Ethnicity						
Black (vs. white/other)	a	–.302⁺	0.7	a	–.482*	0.6
Hispanic	a	–.030	1.0	a	.598**	1.8
Intact family at age 14 (vs. broken)	a	–.326**	0.7	a	–.054	0.9
Armed Forces Qualification Test	22.959	.016***	1.5	21.115	.014**	1.3
Church attendance (1980)	1.654	–.038	0.9	1.681	–.084⁺	0.9
Number of delinquent acts (1980)[b]	2.733	.086***	1.3	1.709	.142***	1.3
Police contacts						
Stopped (vs. not)	a	.230⁺	1.3	a	.410*	1.5
Arrested	a	.058	1.1	a	.030	1.0
Convicted	a	.012	1.0	a	–.190	0.8
Age at 1st sexual intercourse	2.644	–.066**	0.8	2.122	–.216***	0.6
Currently working (vs. not)	a	–.000	1.0	a	.092	1.1
Marital status						
Never married (vs. marr)	a	.748***	2.1	a	.552**	1.7
Separate/divorce/widow	a	.530*	1.7	a	.456⁺	1.6
Ever a parent (vs. never)	a	–.108	0.9	a	–.806***	0.4
Cigarettes Q/F	2.417	.096***	1.3	2.373	.070*	1.2
Alcohol Q/F	1.685	.146***	1.3	1.291	.310***	1.5
Marijuana Q/F	1.986	.588***	3.2	1.650	.612***	2.8
Region						
North Central (vs. East)	a	–1.150***	0.3	a	–1.158***	0.3
South	a	–.564***	0.6	a	–.840***	0.4
West	a	.214	1.2	a	–.058	0.9
Intercept		1.868			2.875	
Chi Square		3313			3279	
DF		4296			4457	

a Categorical variable.

b A categorical variable was entered for those who did not answer question (less than 3 percent of sample).

c Odds ratios are displayed for categorical variables and for changes in one standard deviation of the variable for continuous variables.

⁺p<.10; *p<.05; **p<.01; ***p<.001.

TABLE 12. *Logistic regression predicting last year cocaine use for whites among nonvirgins (NLSY 1984–unweighted)*

Predictors	Men			Women		
	Standard deviation	β	Odds ratios[c]	Standard deviation	β	Odds ratios[c]
Age	2.279	.016	1.0	2.218	.059	1.1
Highest grade completed	2.194	.067	1.2	2.049	.114*	1.3
Ever dropped out (vs. never)	a	–.022	0.8	a	.079	1.1
Intact family at age 14 (vs. broken)	a	–.336*	0.7	a	–.091	0.9
Armed Forces Qualification Test	20.447	.018***	1.5	18.423	.012*	1.3
Church attendance (1980)	1.650	–.035	0.9	1.700	–.078	0.9
Number of delinquent acts (1980)[b]	2.777	.088***	1.3	1.698	.144***	1.3
Police contacts						
Stopped (vs. not)	a	.204	1.2	a	.328	1.4
Arrested	a	–.031	1.0	a	.379	1.5
Convicted	a	–.303	0.7	a	.028	1.0
Age at 1st sexual intercourse	2.379	–.106**	0.8	2.155	–.174***	0.7
Currently working (vs. not)	a	–.026	1.0	a	.133	1.1
Marital status						
Never married (vs. marr)	a	.836***	2.3	a	.494*	1.6
Separate/divorce/widow	a	.764*	2.1	a	.451	1.6
Ever a parent (vs. never)	a	–.279	0.8	a	–.974***	0.4
Cigarettes Q/F	2.525	.064*	1.2	2.468	.038	1.1
Alcohol Q/F	1.709	.158***	1.3	1.355	.266***	1.4
Marijuana Q/F	1.955	.570***	3.0	1.622	.658***	2.9
Region						
North Central (vs. East)	a	–.918***	0.4	a	–1.154**	0.3
South	a	–.390***	0.7	a	–.622**	0.5
West	a	.470*	1.6	a	.127	1.1
Intercept		2.433			2.507	
Chi Square		2025			1815	
DF		2542			2624	

a Categorical variable.

b A categorical variable was entered for those who did not answer question (less than 3 percent of sample).

c Odds ratios are displayed for categorical variables and for changes in one standard deviation of the variable for continuous variables.

+p<.10; *p<.05; **p<.01; ***p<.001.

TABLE 13. *Logistic regression predicting last year use of cocaine for blacks among nonvirgins (NLSY 1984—unweighted)*

Predictors	Men: Standard deviation	Men: β	Men: Odds ratios[c]	Women: Standard deviation	Women: β	Women: Odds ratios[c]
Age	2.234	.062	1.1	2.199	.004	1.0
Highest grade completed	1.879	.246*	1.6	1.734	–.008	1.0
Ever dropped out (vs. never)	a	.235	1.3	a	–.234	0.8
Intact family at age 14 (vs. broken)	a	–.360	0.7	a	.483	1.6
Armed Forces Qualification Test	19.455	.005	1.1	17.820	.002⁺	1.5
Church attendance (1980)	1.658	–.037	0.9	1.590	–.033	0.9
Number of delinquent acts (1980)[b]	2.626	.082⁺	1.2	1.780	.198*	1.4
Police contacts						
Stopped (vs. not)	a	.084	1.1	a	.110	1.2
Arrested	a	–.015	1.0	a	–1.029	0.4
Convicted	a	.742⁺	2.1	a	—	—
Age at 1st sexual intercourse	2.750	–.003	1.0	1.953	–.210*	0.7
Currently working (vs. not)	a	–.031	1.0	a	–.296	0.7
Marital status						
Never married (vs. marr)	a	.621	1.9	a	.238	1.3
Separate/divorce/widow	a	–.981	0.4	a	1.007	2.7
Ever a parent (vs. never)	a	.202	1.2	a	–.552	0.6
Cigarettes Q/F	2.289	.182**	1.5	2.183	.164⁺	1.4
Alcohol Q/F	1.559	.196**	1.4	1.131	.432***	1.6
Marijuana Q/F	2.069	.592***	3.4	1.725	.532***	2.5
Region						
North Central (vs. East)	a	–1.666***	0.2	a	–1.302**	0.3
South	a	–.998***	0.4	a	–1.396***	0.2
West	a	–.091	0.9	a	–.705	0.5
Intercept		.163			3.573	
Chi Square		871			1021	
DF		1092			1164	

a Categorical variable.

b A categorical variable was entered for those who did not answer question (less than 3 percent of sample).

c Odds ratios are displayed for categorical variables and for changes in one standard deviation of the variable for continuous variables.

⁺p<.10; *p<.05; **p<.01; ***p<.001.

TABLE 14. *Logistic regression predicting last year use of cocaine for Hispanics among nonvirgins (NLSY 1984—unweighted)*

	Men			Women		
Predictors	Standard deviation	β	Odds ratios[c]	Standard deviation	β	Odds ratios[c]
Age	2.215	.038	1.1	2.232	.149	1.4
Highest grade completed	2.173	.043	1.1	2.419	.125	1.4
Ever dropped out (vs. never)	a	.306	1.4	a	.177	1.0
Intact family at age 14 (vs. broken)	a	–.431	0.6	a	–.276	0.8
Armed Forces Qualification Test	21.682	.038***	2.3	20.676	–.000	1.0
Church attendance (1980)	1.603	–.078	0.9	1.614	–.135	0.8
Number of delinquent acts (1980)[b]	2.739	.094⁺	1.3	1.588	.045	1.1
Police contacts						
Stopped (vs. not)	a	.880*	2.4	a	1.312*	3.7
Arrested	a	.388	1.5	a	–.283	0.8
Convicted	a	.765⁺	2.1	a	–.274	0.8
Age at 1st sexual intercourse	2.448	–.074	0.8	2.152	–.546***	0.3
Currently working (vs. not)	a	.152	1.2	a	.388	1.5
Marital status						
Never married (vs. marr)	a	.161	1.2	a	1.232*	3.4
Separate/divorce/widow	a	.481	1.6	a	–.037	1.0
Ever a parent (vs. never)	a	–.312	0.7	a	–.952⁺	0.4
Cigarettes Q/F	2.094	.156*	1.4	2.026	.182⁺	1.5
Alcohol Q/F	1.652	–.007	0.9	1.147	.584***	2.0
Marijuana Q/F	1.960	.756***	4.4	1.582	.640***	2.8
Region						
North Central (vs. East)	a	–1.504⁺	0.2	a	–.041	1.0
South	a	–.600	0.5	a	–.654	0.5
West	a	–.251	0.8	a	–.042	1.0
Intercept		1.451			4.699	
Chi Square		434			356	
DF		618			630	

a Categorical variable.

b A categorical variable was entered for those who did not answer question (less than 3 percent of sample).

c Odds ratios are displayed for categorical variables and for changes in one standard deviation of the variable for continuous variables.

⁺p<.10; *p<.05; **p<.01; ***p<.001.

TABLE 15. *Proportion of young adults expected to have ever used cocaine by ever sex, age of first intercourse, or frequency of marijuana use, and sex, controlling for other covariates in the model (NLSY 1984)*

	Proportions expected to have ever used cocaine			
	Total sample		Nonvirgins	
	Men %	Women %	Men %	Women %
Ever sex				
No	7.5	5.3	—	—
Yes	22.3	14.5	—	—
Odds ratios[a]	3.5	3.0		
Age at first sex[b] (male/female)				
13/14	—	—	28.4	27.6
15/16	—	—	23.9	18.7
17/18	—	—	19.9	12.2
Odds ratios[a]			1.6	2.7
Frequency marijuana use				
Never used	8.8	7.0	9.2	7.5
Used 6–11 months ago	20.9	18.2	21.3	18.6
Last month, 1–5 times	42.1	39.8	41.8	39.2
Last month, 20+ times	66.7	66.3	65.7	64.5
Odds ratios[a]	20.8	26.2	18.9	22.4

[a] Odds ratio between highest and lowest categories.

[b] Ages for men before slash, ages for women after slash.

frequency of involvement with marijuana (table 10). The odds ratios were 2.6 for men and 2.2 for women. Among nonvirgins, age of first sexual intercourse had a much smaller impact than marijuana use on lifetime cocaine use. The other significant predictors of lifetime cocaine experience included a mix of factors that reflected simultaneously high achievement in certain conforming activities as well as participation in deviance. Those who were older, had completed more years of education, scored higher on the AFQT or had dropped out of high school, had committed delinquent acts, used cigarettes, or drank alcohol, and women who never married and had no children were more likely to have experimented with cocaine. Men from intact families, men and women who are black, and those who were religious were less likely to have done so. Young adults in the North Central and Southern regions of the United

TABLE 16. *Proportion of young adult nonvirgins expected to have used cocaine in the last year by age of first intercourse, frequency of marijuana use, race, and sex, controlling for other covariates in the model (NLSY 1984)*

	Proportions expected to have used cocaine last year			
	White %	Black %	Hispanic %	All %
Age at first sex				
Men				
Age 13	21.5	10.8	17.2	16.9
Age 15	18.2	10.8	15.2	15.1
Age 17	15.2	10.7	13.4	13.5
Odds ratios[a]	1.5	1.0	1.3	1.3
Women				
Age 14	16.9	7.9	43.8	16.0
Age 16	12.5	5.4	20.7	11.0
Age 18	9.2	3.6	8.1	7.4
Odds ratios[a]	2.0	2.3	8.9	2.4
Frequency of marijuana use				
Men				
Never used	5.4	3.3	3.7	4.7
Used 6–11 months ago	15.1	10.1	14.7	13.9
Last month, 1–5 times	35.7	26.9	44.9	34.7
Last month, 20+ times	63.5	54.6	78.0	63.6
Odds ratios[a]	30.6	34.9	93.3	34.0
Women				
Never used	4.0	2.4	4.7	3.9
Used 6–11 months ago	13.5	6.6	15.1	12.0
Last month, 1–5 times	36.9	17.1	39.1	31.7
Last month, 20+ times	68.5	37.4	69.8	61.3
Odds ratios[a]	51.8	24.3	46.5	39.3

[a] Odds ratio between highest and lowest categories.

States were less likely to have used cocaine than adults in the East, and men in the West were more likely to have done so.

The predictors of last year cocaine use among nonvirgins were similar to the predictors of lifetime use (compare tables 10 and 11). Frequency/recency of marijuana use was an important factor. For men and women, the role played by early sexual experimentation is less important for cocaine use within the last year than for lifetime experience. Several variables that were significant for lifetime experimentation were not significant for use in the last year. These include age and police arrests for men and women, being a school dropout, race, and residing in the West for men. Educational attainment had stronger effects for lifetime experimentation than for last year use among men, as did religiosity among women. Thus, certain factors, especially sociodemographic ones, were more important determinants of initiation than of continued cocaine use. When compared to predicting lifetime use, however, family-related factors gained increased importance in predicting use in the last year: not being married predicted increased use for men, while being a parent decreased the risk for women more than it did for men. Two consistent and striking gender differences appeared both for lifetime and last year cocaine use: the negative impact of being a parent was present only for women, while the negative impact of having been raised in an intact family in adolescence was present only for men. While family intactness in adolescence was an important protective factor for males, for females this variable was not significant.

The patterns of relationships regarding the predictors of current cocaine use in young adulthood show similarities as well as important differences among the three ethnic groups (tables 12–14). Fewer predictors were significant among blacks and Hispanics than among whites, in part because of differences in sample size. Use of other drugs, and especially marijuana, was the strongest predictor of cocaine use among males and females of all three ethnic groups. The major ethnic differences included the lack of significance of AFQT scores among black males compared to the other two groups and the greater importance of family factors in adulthood among white males compared to blacks and Hispanics. Males and females of all three groups who were married were much less likely to report having used cocaine within the last year than those who never married and/or were separated or divorced. While living with both their parents at age 14 was a statistically significant factor in reducing cocaine use in adulthood only among white males, the absolute size of the coefficient was similar to those observed for that variable among blacks and Hispanics. Among black women, however, family intactness in adolescence led to a greater risk of cocaine experimentation, although the effect was not statistically significant. Other differences included the lack of importance of early sexual initiation among nonwhite males compared to whites and the greater importance of police contacts among blacks and Hispanics than among whites. There were also ethnic variations in the effect of regional residence. Western residence was related to increased cocaine use only for white males. Age of first intercourse was a relatively more important predictor for females than for males among blacks and, especially, Hispanics but not whites. The relative impact of marijuana use and age at first sex was the same among men and women, except Hispanics. In this group, the relative effect was greater among women than among men.

The substantive impact of different factors can be observed more clearly when the logistic regression model is used to estimate proportions expected to be using cocaine for different categories of specific covariates. Tables 15 and 16 present the predicted lifetime and last year prevalence of cocaine use for ever having had sexual experience, for different ages at first intercourse, and for different levels of marijuana use, by gender and ethnicity, keeping all other factors in the model constant. The odds ratios between the first and last categories of each variable are also presented. Because of differences in the mean ages of first sex for males and females, different ages were selected for contrast for each sex.

Early sexual intercourse, age 13 for males and age 14 for females, was associated with elevated lifetime cocaine use for males and females and recent cocaine use for females of the three ethnic groups and for white and Hispanic males. Controlling for other covariates, for women, the odds ratios for using cocaine in the last year between first intercourse at age 14 versus age 18 are approximately 2 for whites and blacks and approximately 9 for Hispanics. A reduction of 4 years in the age of first sex for women from 18 to 14 led to a reduction in the proportions expected to be using cocaine within the last year from 8 to 44 percent among Hispanics, 4 to 8 percent among blacks, and 9 to 17 percent among whites. Early sex was an especially serious risk factor for cocaine use among Hispanic women. For men, the odds ratios of first intercourse at age 13 versus age 17, are 1.5 for whites, 1.0 for blacks, and 1.3 for Hispanics (table 16).

The strong association between marijuana use and cocaine use is evident in tables 15 and 16. The odds ratios for lifetime cocaine use between nonusers of marijuana and those who use at least 20 times in the last 30 days (i.e., the daily users) range from over 19 for men and over 22 for women. The odds ratios for recent cocaine use range from

31 for white males to 93 for Hispanic males. Nine percent of males were expected to have ever used cocaine if they never used marijuana compared to 67 percent of those who used marijuana 20 times or more in the month preceding the interviews. With the exception of the black females, over half of the daily marijuana users were predicted to have used cocaine in the past year. For whites and Hispanics of either sex, at least one-third were predicted to have used cocaine in the past year if they had used marijuana one to five times in the last month. It is also of great interest to note that sex differences in the lifetime prevalence of cocaine use were eliminated when degree of marijuana involvement was controlled.

The important role played by sexual experience for cocaine initiation and the lesser role of early sex for initiation and for sustained use in early adulthood was documented by these data. The analyses have not examined the precise timing of onset into sex and cocaine use, an issue that we plan to pursue further. However, on average, the mean age of first sexual intercourse took place several years before first use of cocaine. For males, the mean ages of first sex were 16.7 years for whites, 14.4 for blacks, and 16.1 for Hispanics; for women, the corresponding ages were 17.5 years, 16.8 years, and 17.7 years. Thus, the inference from these data is that sexual experience precedes and predicts cocaine experimentation. The much lower mean age of first sexual experimentation among black males may account for its lack of importance as a predictor of cocaine involvement.

These patterns of sexual behavior in adolescence, which are related to greater experimentation with cocaine, are reflected as well in the current sexual activity of cocaine users in young adulthood among white and black males, although not as systematically among Hispanic males or among females of all three ethnic groups. The extent of current sexual activity of young adult men and women tends to increase with increasing drug involvement. White and black men who used cocaine in the last year preceding the survey had had more sexual experiences within the last 30 days than those who used no illicit drugs (table 17). The differences among Hispanic men were smaller. Although age of first sexual experience did not differentiate black men who subsequently used cocaine as young adults from those who did not, sexual activity in adulthood did. As young adult users, black cocaine users who also used illicit drugs other than marijuana were the most active.

Early sexual initiation and/or greater sexual activity characterized young men and women who use cocaine in young adulthood.

TABLE 17. *Mean frequency of intercourse in last 30 days among nonvirgins by pattern of drug use in last 12 months and ethnicity among men and women (NLSY 1984)*

	No illicit %	Marijuana/ no OID[a] %	OID[a]/no cocaine %	Cocaine/ no OID[a] %	Cocaine/ OID[a] %
Men					
White	6.4	7.3	7.2	10.3	9.5
N	(2212)	(923)	(360)	(259)	(409)
Black	6.5	7.3	9.4	8.3	11.7
N	(439)	(236)	(19)	(49)	(30)
Hispanic	7.0	6.8	5.6	8.1	8.8
N	(188)	(78)	(17)	(20)	(25)
Women					
White	7.0	7.3	8.8	9.7	7.5
N	(2508)	(619)	(324)	(188)	(234)
Black	4.6	5.3	7.3	7.2	3.8
N	(518)	(150)	(23)	(14)	(14)
Hispanic	6.8	7.1	7.2	7.2	7.1
N	(207)	(35)	(16)	(13)	(14)

[a] Illicit drugs other than marijuana.

CONCLUSION

In conclusion, we focus on three findings: the sequential order of involvement with different drugs, the role of sexual experimentation as a precursor to cocaine involvement, and the differential role of family-related factors among men as compared to women.

As is already well known from prior work on developmental stages of involvement with drugs (Kandel 1975; Yamaguchi and Kandel 1984*a*, 1984*b*), very few young people experiment with illicit drugs other than marijuana without prior experimentation with marijuana. However, while the analyses carried out on the NLSY sample confirmed this pattern, a new finding has emerged pertaining to the order of involvement among illicit drugs other than marijuana and the position of cocaine in that sequence. For most cocaine users, the transition is not directly from marijuana to cocaine, but rather from marijuana to an illicit drug other than cocaine, and from these drugs to cocaine. This order holds among men and women and among whites, blacks, and Hispanics. Those who get involved with cocaine are the most involved of all drug users and those most likely to suffer health consequences from the use of drugs. These consequences derive not only from their use of cocaine but from their use of other illicit drugs. Preventing the use of cocaine would greatly reduce the casualties associated with the use of cocaine and other illicit drugs. The most efficient strategy would be to reduce involvement with marijuana. The best strategy to reduce involvement with marijuana is to reduce involvement with its precursor drugs, alcohol and cigarettes (see Kandel et al. 1985; Robins 1984; Kandel and Yamaguchi 1985).

A major contribution of the present analysis is the documentation that early sexual experimentation is an important risk factor for cocaine use, in addition to the risk created by marijuana use, and the specification of the relative risk attributable to each variable. Prior attempts to identify early risk factors that would predict subsequent cocaine involvement have consistently implicated marijuana use as the major factor. Furthermore, early onset of marijuana use and degree of marijuana involvement are crucial components of marijuana experimentation as a precursor to the use of cocaine. We found in the NLSY sample, as we had found earlier in the New York State cohort (Kandel et al. 1985), that those who subsequently experimented with cocaine in addition to illicit drugs other than marijuana had initiated marijuana 2 to 3 years earlier on the average than those who experimented with marijuana exclusively.

Thus, participation in certain activities, including use of marijuana and sex, emerge as crucial risk factors for progression to cocaine. Not only do young adults who use cocaine initiate sexual behavior early in adolescence, but as young adults they are also more sexually active than young adults who do not use cocaine. The role of sexual experimentation in increasing the risk of involvement in cocaine and other illicit drugs has important public health implications with respect to the current AIDS epidemic. If sexual experimentation cannot be postponed, at least efforts should be pursued to teach adolescents proper contraceptive practices and less risky manners of engaging in sex. While at present, most such efforts are developed within the school setting, they should involve other important socialization agents, in particular the family.

The differential impact of family-related factors on cocaine use found in our analyses suggest that involving the family in such efforts may be more difficult for certain youths, especially males. Thus, a broken family in adolescence is a risk factor for subsequent cocaine involvement among males but not females. The risk appears to be approximately the same for minority youths as for whites.

The differential negative effect of a nonintact home for cocaine use among men as compared to women is consonant with much of the literature on the effect of single-parent homes for the psychosocial development of boys and girls. Most such homes are headed by mothers and are generally associated with more problematic behaviors among males than among females (e.g., Hetherington 1981; Collins 1984), although Dornbusch et al. (1985) found almost equally strong negative effects among male and female adolescents. As documented by the present study, these negative effects persist into early adulthood.

The role of the broken family among blacks compared with whites has been extensively studied with respect to delinquent involvement, but rarely with respect to illicit drug use. Inconsistent results have been obtained. Some investigators find that family intactness is a more important protective factor against delinquency for blacks than for whites (Matsueda and Heimer 1987; Moynihan 1965), while others find the reverse (Chilton and Markle 1972), and others find no difference among ethnic groups (Berger and Simon 1974; Dornbusch et al. 1985). As pointed out by Matsueda (Matsueda 1982; Matsueda and Heimer 1987), to the extent that a broken home has an effect on delinquency, the process by which it operates is the same among all ethnic groups. A broken home reduces the extent of parental supervision, "which in turn increases delinquent companions, prodelinquent definitions and, ultimately, delinquent behavior." (Matsueda and Heimer 1987, p.836). In mother-only families, parental control is reduced and adolescent decisionmaking is increased, especially when another adult is not present in the household (Dornbusch et al. 1985).

As stressed by Kellam (Kellam et al. 1977), the crucial variable with respect to family structure may not be so much father absence as mother aloneness. It has been argued that the extended family may play a particularly crucial role in childrearing, particularly within the black community (Wilson 1988). Thus, the presence of a grandmother in black families appears to protect children against social maladaptation (Kellam et al. 1977) as does another adult among black and white adolescents, especially among the males (Dornbusch et al. 1985). The specific structure of respondents' parental family, beyond the simple intact-not intact dichotomy, could not be established in this study.

The impact of the family orientation and the family of procreation on the use of illicit drugs by young people is an area in need of greater investigation.

FOOTNOTES

1. Similar trends characterize legal drugs. Expected increases in rates of lung cancer by 1990 are higher among blacks than whites (American Cancer Society 1983). Rates of alcohol-related mortality are twice as high among blacks as among whites (Herd 1986). See also Botvin et al. 1987.

2. A progression can also be determined if, at a particular time, someone has only used one class of drugs or two classes rather than all three. Furthermore, since the cohort ranged in age from 19 to 27, not every individual was past the risk of initiation into certain illicit drugs, especially cocaine, for which the risk terminates at an older age (Kandel and Logan 1984).

3. These ordinal variables were treated as continuous variables in the regressions since they had a linear association with lifetime cocaine use. An analysis of variance was performed with the marijuana index as the grouping factor and lifetime cocaine use as the dependent variable. A polynomial regression was fit through the means of lifetime cocaine use as a function of the categories of marijuana use. Of the total variability in the means, 95.5 percent of the variability was due to the linear component of the polynomial regressors. Although deviations from the linear trend were statistically significant, we decided not to model any effects for the marijuana index other than the linear term.

4. In a logistic regression with two independent variables (X_1, X_2) the odds, p/(1-p) for using cocaine are:

$$P/(1-p) = \exp\,[b_0 + b_1X_1 = b_2X_2] \qquad (1)$$

For two groups (a,b) that have identical values for X_2 and differ on X_1 by one standard deviation, σ, of X_1, the odds ratio is

$$(P_b/(1-P_b))/(P_a/(1-P_a)) =$$

$$\{\exp[b_0 + b_1\,(X_1 + \sigma) = b_2X_2]\} \,/\, \{\exp[b_0 + b_1X_1 + b_2X_2]\,\} \qquad (2)$$

This expression can be simplified to

$$(P_b/(1-P_b))/(P_a/(1-P_a)) =$$

$$\exp\,[b_0 + b_1X_1 + b_1\,\sigma + b_2X_2 - b_0 - b_1X - b_2X_2] \qquad (3)$$

or

$$(P_b/(1-P_b))/(P_a/(1-P_b)) = \exp [b_1 \sigma] \quad (4)$$

Thus the odds ratio between the two groups is the exponentiated product of the regression coefficient, b_1, and the standard deviation, σ, of the corresponding variable. Furthermore, (4) can be rewritten

$$P_b/(1-P_b) = [\exp(b_1 \sigma)] [P_a/(1-P_a)] \quad (5)$$

Thus, to obtain the odds for group b, where the value of only one of the variables is increased by one standard deviation, the odds for group a are multiplied by $\exp[b_1 \sigma]$.

5. To calculate these expected changes, we evaluated the regression function at the mean of all the independent variables except the variable of interest. This variable was assigned the value presented in the table and the predicted log odds was obtained. The expected percentage at each value is:

$$P = \frac{odds}{odds+1} x\ 100$$

REFERENCES

American Cancer Society. *Cancer Facts and Figures for Black Americans: 1983*. New York: the Society, 1983.

Berger, A.S., and Simon, W. Black families and the Moynihan report: A research evaluation. *Social Problems* 22:145–61, 1974.

Botvin, G.J.; Palleja, J.; Moncher, M.S.; Schinke, S.P.; Orlandi, M.A.; and Schilling, R.F. *Preventing Substance Abuse Among Minority Group Adolescents: Applications of Risk-Based Interventions*. St. Louis, MO: Center for Adolescent Mental Health, Washington University, 1987.

Brunswick, A.F. Young black males and substance use. In: Gibbs, J.T.; Brunswick, A.F.; Connor, M.E.; et al., eds. *Young, Black, and Male in America*. Dover, MA: Auburn House, 1988. pp.166–187.

Brunswick, A.F.; Merzel, C.R.; and Messeri, P.A. Drug use initiation among urban black youth. *Youth & Society* 17:189–215, 1985.

Chilton, R., and Markle, G. Family Disruption, Delinquent Conduct, and the Effects of Sub-Classification. *American Sociological Review* 37:93–99, 1972.

Collins, W.A., ed. *Development During Middle Childhood*. Washington, DC: National Academy Press, 1984.

Donovan, J.E., and Jessor, R. Problem drinking and the dimension of involvement with drugs: A Guttman Scalogram Analysis of adolescent drug use. *American Journal of Public Health* 73:543–552, 1983.

Dornbusch, S.M.; Carlsmith, J.M.; Bushwall, S.J.; Ritter, P.L.; Leiderman, H.; Hastorf, A.H.; and Gross, R.T. Single parents, extended households, and the control of adolescents. *Child Development* 56:326–341, 1985.

Elliott, D.S., and Morse, B.J. "Drug Use, Delinquency and Sexual Activity." Paper presented at NIDA Technical Review on Drug Abuse and Adolescent Sexual Activity, Pregnancy and Parenthood, March 1985.

Ensminger, M.E., and Kane, L.P. "Adolescent Drug and Alcohol Use, Delinquency and Sexual Activity: Patterns of Occurrence and Risk Factors." Paper presented at NIDA Technical Review on Drug Abuse and Adolescent Sexual Activity, Pregnancy and Parenthood, March 1985.

Frankel, M.R.; McWilliams, H.A.; and Spencer, B.D. *National Longitudinal Survey of Labor Force Behavior, Youth Survey, Technical Sampling Report*. Chicago: National Opinion Research Center, 1983.

Hamburg, B.A.; Kraemer, H.C.; and Jahnke, W.A. Hierarchy of drug use in adolescence: Behavioral and attitudinal correlates of substantial drug use. *American Journal of Psychiatry* 132:1155–1163, 1975.

Harford, T.C. Drinking patterns among black and nonblack adolescents: Results of a national survey. In: *Alcohol and Culture: Comparative Perspectives from Europe and America. Annals of the New York Academy of Sciences*. 472:130–141, 1986.

Hawkins, J.D.; Lishner, D.; and Catalano, R.F., Jr. Childhood predictors and the prevention of adolescent substance abuse. In: Jones, C.L., and Battjes, R.J., eds. *Etiology of Drug Abuse: Implications for Prevention*. Rockville, MD: National Institute on Drug Abuse, 1985. pp.75–126.

Herd, D. A review of drinking patterns and alcohol problems among U.S. blacks. In: Malone, T.E., Chair. *Report of the Secretary's Task Force on Black and Minority Health: Volume VII: Chemical Dependency and Diabetes*. GPO Pub. No. 491–313/44709. Washington, DC: Supt. of Docs., U.S. Govt. Print. Off., 1986. pp. 77–140.

Hetherington, E.M. Children and divorce. In: Henderson, R.W., ed. *Parent-Child Interaction*. New York: Academic Press, 1981. pp. 33–58.

Huba, G.J., and Bentler, P.M. Test of a drug use causal model using asymptotically distribution free methods. *Journal of Drug Education* 13:3–14, 1983.

Jessor, R., and Jessor, S.L. *Problem Behavior and Psychosocial Development: A Longitudinal Study of Youth*. New York: Academic Press, 1977.

Johnston, L.D.; O'Malley, P.; and Bachman, J.G. *Drug Use, Drinking, and Smoking: National Survey Results From High School, College, and Youth Adult Populations*. Rockville, MD: National Institute on Drug Abuse, 1989.

Kandel, D. Stages in adolescent involvement in drug use. *Science* 190:912–914, 1975.

Kandel, D. Drug and drinking behavior among youth. In: Coleman, J; Inkeles, A.; and Smelser, N., eds. *Annual Review of Sociology*. 6:235–285, 1980.

Kandel, D. "Cocaine Use in Young Adulthood: Patterns of Use, Psychosocial Correlates and Predictors of Use at Age 29." Paper presented at Seminar in Epidemiology and Preventive Medicine, Dept. of Public Health, Cornell University Medical College, Jan. 1986.

Kandel, D.B., and Logan, J.A. Patterns of drug use from adolescence to young adulthood - I. Periods of risk for initiation, stabilization and decline in use. *American Journal of Public Health* 74:660–666, 1984.

Kandel, D.B., and Yamaguchi, K. Developmental patterns of the use of legal, illegal and medically prescribed psychotropic drugs from adolescence to young adulthood. In: Jones, C.L., and Battjes, R., eds. *Etiology of Drug*

Abuse: Implications for Prevention. NIDA Research Monograph 56. Washington, DC: Supt. of Docs., U.S. Govt. Print. Off., 1985. pp. 193–235.

Kandel, D.B., and Yamaguchi, K. Stages of progression in drug involvement from adolescence to adulthood: Further evidence for the gateway theory. *Journal of Studies on Alcohol* in press.

Kandel, D.B.; Murphy, D.; and Karus, D. Cocaine use in young adulthood: Patterns of use and psychosocial correlates. In: Kozel, N., and Adams, E., eds. *Cocaine Use in America: Epidemiological and Clinical Perspectives*. NIDA Research Monograph 61. Washington, DC: Supt. of Docs., U.S. Govt. Print. Off., 1985. pp. 76–110.

Kellam, S.G.; Ensminger, M.E.; and Turner, R.J. Family structure and the mental health of children. *Archives of General Psychiatry* 34:1012–1022, 1977.

Kleinman, P.H., and Lukoff, I.F. Ethnic differences in factors related to drug use. *Journal of Health and Social Behavior* 19:190–199, 1978.

Maddahian, E.; Newcomb, M.D.; and Bentler, P.M. Adolescents' substance use: Impact of ethnicity, income, and availability. In: Maddahian, E.; Newcomb, M.D.; and Bentler, P.M., eds. *Alcohol and Substance Abuse in Women and Children*. New York: The Haworth Press, 1986. pp.63–78.

Matsueda, R.L. Testing control theory and differential association: A causal modeling approach. *American Sociological Review* 47:489–504, 1982.

Matsueda, R.L., and Heimer, K. Race, family structure, and delinquency: A test of differential association and social control theories. *American Sociological Review* 52:826–840, 1987.

Mensch, B.S., and Kandel, D.B. Underreporting of substance use in a national longitudinal cohort. *Public Opinion Quarterly* 52:100–124, 1988.

Miller, P.Y., and Simon, W. Adolescent sexual behavior: Context and change. *Social Problems* 22:58–76, 1974.

Moynihan, D.P. *The Negro Family: The Case for National Action*. Washington, DC: Office of Policy Planning and Research, U.S. Department of Labor, 1965.

National Institute on Drug Abuse. *Drug Abuse Among Minorities*. Prepared by the Division of Epidemiology and Statistical Analysis for the HHS Task Force on Black and Minority Health, undated.

National Institute on Drug Abuse. *National Household Survey on Drug Abuse: Population Estimates 1985*. Rockville, MD: the Institute, 1987*a*.

National Institute on Drug Abuse. *Demographic Characteristics and Patterns of Drug Use of Clients Admitted to Drug Abuse Treatment Programs in Selected States: Annual Data 1985*. Rockville, MD: the Institute, 1987*b*.

National Institute on Drug Abuse. *Trends in Drug Abuse Related Hospital Emergency Room Episodes and Medical Examiner Cases for Selected Drugs, DAWN 1976-1985*. Rockville, MD: the Institute, 1987*c*.

National Institute on Drug Abuse. *National Household Survey on Drug Abuse: Main Findings 1985*. DHHS Pub. No. (ADM)88–1586. Washington, DC: Supt. of Docs., U.S. Govt. Print. Off., 1988.

Newcomb, M.D., and Bentler, P.M. Cocaine use among young adults. *Advances in Alcohol & Substance Abuse* 6:73–96, 1987.

O'Donnell, J.A., and Clayton, R.R. The stepping-stone hypothesis: A reappraisal. *Chemical Dependency* 4:229–241, 1982.

O'Donnell, J.; Voss, H.; Clayton, R.; Slatin, G.; and Room, R. *Young Men and Drugs—A Nationwide Survey*. NIDA Research Monograph No. 5. Washington, DC: Supt. of Docs., U.S. Govt. Print. Off., 1976.

Rachal, J.V.; Guess, L.L.; Hubbard, R.L.; Maisto, S.A.; Cavanaugh, E.R.; Waddell, R.; and Benrud, C.H. *Adolescent Drinking Behavior, Volume 1. The*

Extent and Nature of Adolescent Alcohol and Drug Use: The 1974 and 1978 National Sample Studies. Research Triangle Park, NC: Research Triangle Institute, 1980.

Robins, L.N. The natural history of adolescent drug use. *American Journal of Public Health* 74:656–657, 1984.

Robins, L.N. "Alcohol Abuse in Blacks and Whites as Indicated in the ECA." Paper presented at NIAAA Conference on Epidemiology of Alcohol Use and Abuse Among U.S. Ethnic Minorities, September 1985.

Robins, L.N.; Helzer, J.E.; Weissman, M.M.; Orvaschel, H.; Gruenberg, E.; Burke, J.D., Jr.; and Regier, D.A. Lifetime prevalence of specific psychiatric disorders in three sites. *Archives of General Psychiatry* 41:949–958, 1984.

Rouse, B. "Trends in Cocaine Use in the General Population of the United States." Paper presented at NIDA Technical Review Meeting on the Epidemiology of Cocaine Use and Abuse, May 3, 1988.

Single, E.; Kandel, D.B.; and Faust, R. Patterns of multiple drug use in high school. *Journal of Health and Sociological Behavior* 15:344–357, 1974.

Skager, R., and Maddahian, E. *A Survey of Substance Use and Related Factors Among Secondary School Students in Grades 7, 9, and 11 in the County of Orange*. Fall 1983, Report No. 224. Los Angeles: Center for Study of Evaluation, Graduate School of Education, University of California, 1984.

Trimble, J.E.; Padilla, A.M.; and Bell, C.S., eds. *Drug Abuse Among Minorities*. DHHS Pub. No. (ADM)87–1474. Washington, DC: Supt. of Docs., U.S. Govt. Print. Off., 1987.

Vener, A.M., and Stewart, C.S. Adolescent sexual behavior in middle America revisited: 1970-1973. *Journal of Marriage and the Family* 36:728–735, 1974.

Welte, J.W., and Barnes, G.M. Alcohol: The gateway to other drug use among secondary-school students. *Journal of Youth and Adolescence* 14:487–498, 1985.

Welte, J.W., and Barnes, G.M. Alcohol use among adolescent minority groups. *Journal of Studies on Alcohol* 48:329–336, 1987.

Wilson, M.N. The black extended family: An analytical consideration. *Developmental Psychology* 22:246–258, 1986.

Wilson, M.N. *The Truly Disadvantaged*. Chicago: The University of Chicago Press, 1987.

Wolpin, K. *The National Longitudinal Surveys Handbook 1983-1984*. Columbus, OH: Center for Human Resource Research, The Ohio State University, 1983.

Yamaguchi, K., and Kandel, D.B. Patterns of drug use from adolescence to early adulthood - II. Sequences of progression. *American Journal of Public Health* 74:668–672, 1984*a*.

Yamaguchi, K., and Kandel, D.B. Patterns of drug use from adolescence to early adulthood—III. Predictors of progression. *American Journal of Public Health* 74:673–681, 1984*b*.

Zabin, L.S.; Hardy, J.B.; Smith, E.A.; and Hirsch, M.B. Baltimore as a case study: Substance abuse and its relation to sexual activity among inner-city adolescents. *Journal of Adolescent Health Care* 7:320–331, 1986.

Zabin, L.S.; Hardy, J.B.; Smith, E.A.; and Hirsch, M.B. "Substance Use and Its Relation to Sexual Activity Among Inner-City Adolescents." Paper presented at NIDA Technical Review on Drug Abuse and Adolescent Sexual Activity, Pregnancy and Parenthood, March 1985.

Zucker, R.A., and Devoe, C.I. Life history characteristics associated with problem drinking and antisocial behavior in adolescent girls: A comparison with male findings. In: Wirt, R.D.; Winokur, V.; and Roff, M., eds. *Life History Research in Psychopathology*. Vol. 4. Minneapolis, MN: University of Minnesota Press, 1975. pp.109–134.

APPENDIX

Variables Entered in Logistic Regressions

Sociodemographic

- Age: age at time of 1984 survey
- Race: three categories: black, Hispanic, white and others
- Family structure: two parents present in household when respondent was 14
- Education: highest grade completed by 1984 survey
- Dropout status: ever interrupted schooling before finishing high school
- AFQT score: score based on performance on ASVAB exam. Range 0 to 105.

Deviance/Conformity

- Frequency of attendance at religious services in past year.
  - 1 = Not at all
  - 2 = Infrequently
  - 3 = Once per month
  - 4 = 2-3 times per month
  - 5 = Once per week
  - 6 = More than once per week
- Delinquent actions: number of positive responses to questions posed in 1980 about involvement within the last year in 13 activities, such as "Skipped a full day of school without a real excuse", "Purposely damaged or destroyed property that did not belong to you", "Gotten into a physical fight at school or work" or "Helped in a gambling operation". Excludes drug-related actions.
- Delinquent actions information missing: information not available because of non-interview or respondent refusal.
- Police contact: four categories: (1) no police contact, (2) ever stopped by police, but not arrested or convicted; (3) ever arrested, but not convicted, (4) ever convicted.
- Age at first intercourse

Participation in Social Roles of Adulthood

- Current activity: most common activity for survey week was working.
- Marital status: two variables used, one for never having been married and one for currently separated, widowed, or divorced.
- Parental status: has respondent ever had a child.

Drug Use

- Cigarettes: quantity/frequency within the last 12 months/30 days
  - 0 = Never used
  - 1 = Used, not last year
  - 2 = Used, 6–11 months ago
  - 3 = Used, 1–5 months ago
  - 4 = Used in the last 30 days, 1–5 cigs/day
  - 5 = Used in the last 30 days, ½ pack/day
  - 6 = Used in the last 30 days, 1 pack/day
  - 7 =Used in the last 30 days, ≥1½ packs/day
- Alcohol use quantity/frequency within the last 30 days (Information beyond prior 30 days is not available.)
  - 0 = never drank + did not drink in the 30 days prior to the interview
  - 1= drank on 3 or fewer occasions in the last 30 days
  - 2 = drank on 4 to 16 days of the last 30 but have not had more than 3 drinks on any one day
  - 3 = drank on 4 to 16 days of the last 30 and have had more than 3 drinks on at least one day
  - 4 = drank on 17 or more days of the last 30 but have not had more than 3 drinks on any one day
  - 5 = drank on 17 or more days of the last 30 and have had more than 3 drinks on 1 to 10 of those days
  - 6 = drank on 17 or more days of the last 30 and have had more than 3 drinks on 11 or more of those days
- Marijuana: quantity/frequency within the last 12 months/30 days
  - 0 = Never used
  - 1 = Used, not within the last year
  - 2 = Used 6–11 months ago
  - 3 = Used 1–5 months ago
  - 4 = Used 1–5 times in the past 30 days
  - 5 = Used 6–19 times in the past 30 days
  - 6 = Used 20+ times in the past 30 days
- Cocaine: quantity/frequency within the last 12 months/30 days
  Same categories as for marijuana.

Ecological variables

- Region of residence: east north central, south, and west.

ACKNOWLEDGMENTS

This research was partially supported by grant DA03525 and by Research Scientist Award DA00081 from the National Institute on Drug Abuse, and by grant HD22194 from the National Institute on Child Health and Human Development.

AUTHORS

Denise B. Kandel, Ph.D.
Department of Psychiatry and School of Public Health
Columbia University College of Physicians and Surgeons and
New York State Psychiatric Institute
722 West 168th Street
New York, N.Y. 10032

Mark Davies, M.S.
Department of Child Psychiatry
New York State Psychiatric Institute
722 West 168th Street
New York, N.Y. 10032

Factors Influencing Initiation of Cocaine Use Among Adults: Findings From the Epidemiologic Catchment Area Program

Christian Ritter and James C. Anthony

Cocaine use in the United States has received considerable research attention in recent years, due in part to a dramatic jump in prevalence of cocaine use between 1975 and 1982 (Clayton 1985; Abelson and Miller 1985; Anthony et al. 1986; Johnston et al. 1987; Ritter 1988). Epidemiologic interview data showing increased prevalence of cocaine use during that period are complemented by epidemiologic and clinical evidence of greater numbers of patients in treatment facilities for cocaine-related problems as well as more deaths related to cocaine use (Adams and Durell 1984; Kozel et al. 1982).

Prevalence of cocaine use and cocaine problems in the population are determined by an interplay of many processes and factors, some of them involving environmental characteristics such as the cost and relative availability of cocaine. Others involve characteristics of users or would-be users. For example, the reported correlates of cocaine use include an individual's use of marijuana and other illicit drugs, the use of drugs by friends, a perceived availability of cocaine, and the stated intention to use cocaine (Siegel 1984; Adams et al. 1985; Abelson and Miller 1985; Kandel et al. 1985; O'Malley et al. 1985; Ritter 1988; White 1988).

In some studies, initiation of cocaine use was related to the same types of factors that seem to influence illicit use of other federally controlled drugs such as marijuana (e.g., O'Malley et al. 1985). However, there may be some potentially important differences between predictors of the use of cocaine and predictors of the use of other illicit drugs. For example, data from one research group (Kandel et al. 1985) indicated that the risk of initiating cocaine use remains high between ages 20 and 30, in contrast with a typically declining risk of initiating use of other illicit drugs, alcohol, and tobacco. Another difference was suggested by the work of

Ritter (1988), who found perceived availability of cocaine to be related to cocaine use while perceived availability of marijuana did not seem to determine marijuana use. One possibility is that an increasing trend in actual cocaine availability has promoted a perception of greater cocaine availability, with a subsequent increase in size of the pool of would-be cocaine users. This might lead to persistence of a cocaine epidemic in the form of increased demand over and above demand determined by other factors and processes (Adams and Durell 1984; O'Malley et al. 1985).

Epidemiologic issues of this type generally cannot be resolved through analyses of data on the prevalence of cocaine use or through study of current and past cocaine users. These issues require information on the initiation of cocaine use and the factors associated with becoming a cocaine user. In studies of such risk factors, prevalence data come up short, because prevalence is influenced not only by initiation of cocaine use, but also by persistence or duration of use (Anthony and Helzer in press). Prevalence correlates may or may not be risk factors; they can be related to duration or persistence of use, but not related to initiation of use.

The analyses of Epidemiologic Catchment Area (ECA) data prepared for this chapter are partial steps toward a better understanding of factors associated with risk of becoming a cocaine user, as distinct from correlates of prevalence. The ECA surveys involved drawing samples of the adult population and conducting two waves of personal face-to-face interviews. Followup interviews 1 year after baseline interviews identified individuals who initiated cocaine use during the followup interval and who had progressed to six or more occasions of cocaine use (Anthony et al. 1986). Comparing characteristics of these individuals with characteristics of persons who reported not using cocaine on six or more occasions, we sought to identify factors that influence initiation and progression of cocaine use in adult life. Taking advantage of unique diagnostic and social data from the ECA surveys, we looked beyond basic sociodemographic characteristics of cocaine users to examine whether a syndrome of depression might influence risk of cocaine use (e.g., Khantzian 1985; Newcomb and Bentler 1987) and also whether any social roles or role transitions promote or retard initiation or progression of drug use (Brown et al. 1974; Single et al. 1975; Yamaguchi and Kandel 1985; O'Malley et al. 1985; Kandel and Yamaguchi 1987). Extending prior research on social roles and illicit drug use, these analyses focus specifically on cocaine and consider potential effects of losing social roles on the initiation and progression of cocaine use.

MATERIALS AND METHODS

The Epidemiologic Catchment Area Program was a multisite collaborative study of prevalence and incidence of mental disorders sponsored by the National Institute of Mental Health, with surveys completed between 1980 and 1985. The five ECA sites were New Haven, Baltimore, St. Louis, Durham, and Los Angeles.

The ECA collaborators selected subjects for the surveys by drawing probability samples of adult residents from sampled households in various parts of the metropolitan area at each site. For example, the Durham investigators sampled nearby rural areas in addition to a central urban county at their site; the Los Angeles investigators sampled West Los Angeles and a geographically separate area of East Los Angeles where the population included a sizable proportion of Hispanic Americans (Holzer et al. 1985).

Subjects agreeing to participate were interviewed at baseline and again at followup roughly 1 year later. The interviews showed that cocaine use was very rare among persons aged 45 years and older (Anthony et al. 1986). Thus, our analyses were based on 18- to 44-year-olds in the samples. Interview completion rates for designated respondents in this age range were close to 80 percent at both baseline and followup.

The Diagnostic Interview Schedule (DIS) was the primary interview instrument at all ECA sites, with supplementary questions to gather data on sociodemographic characteristics of each subject, recent social role transitions, and other pertinent factors. Three sites (Baltimore, Durham, Los Angeles) used a version of the DIS modified by Von Korff and Anthony to gather data on recency of psychiatric symptoms and illicit drug use (Von Korff and Anthony 1982; Robins et al. 1981). The recency data were needed to identify subjects who initiated cocaine use during followup and to assess illicit drug use in the year prior to baseline. Hence, analyses for this chapter are based on data from these three sites only.

At each site, the investigators hired and trained a team of lay interviewers, who administered the DIS at baseline and at followup without knowledge of specific study hypotheses. These face-to-face interviews were conducted privately for 60 to 90 minutes, with an assurance of confidentiality covered by a DHHS Certificate of Confidentiality. Other details about the ECA Program and the DIS interviewing have been reported elsewhere (Eaton and Kessler 1985; Anthony and Petronis this volume).

Measurement of Cocaine Use

Cocaine use at baseline was measured by DIS questions that assessed whether the subject had ever been an illicit drug user, had engaged in illicit drug use on more than five occasions, had used cocaine on more than five occasions, and if yes, the recency of cocaine use (Anthony and Helzer in press). These questions and corresponding questions on use of marijuana and other illicit drugs were repeated during the followup interview.

In baseline interviews with 19,417 ECA participants, a total of 3,925 reported six or more occasions of illicit drug use, and of these, 975 reported six or more occasions of cocaine use (Anthony and Helzer in press). To focus on progression into cocaine use, our analysis was restricted to the 4,394 18- to 44-year-old subjects whose baseline interview data showed no history of cocaine use and who completed personal interviews at followup.

The DIS data did not allow us to distinguish new initiators from individuals who progressed from one to five occasions of cocaine use to more than five occasions of use. Moreover, there may be some unidentified individuals whose new cocaine use did not progress to six or more occasions of use during followup. This limitation of the DIS precludes identification of factors specifically related to risk of becoming a cocaine user. However, this approach does allow for study of factors related to initiation and progression of cocaine use at a relatively early stage in the course or natural history of an individual's cocaine use. Throughout this chapter, for ease of presentation, we have used the term "initiation" to refer to changes in cocaine use from less than six occasions to six or more occasions.

Control Selection

Factors associated with initiating the use of cocaine can be revealed by measuring the characteristics of respondents and comparing the characteristics of those who initiated cocaine use with those who did not (Schlesselman 1982). In a study such as this one, selection of the control subjects depends not only upon the substantive focus of the research, but also upon the manner in which the cocaine users are sampled and identified. For example, in analyses for this chapter, the focus was on depression, social role transitions, prior illicit drug use, and sociodemographic characteristics that might influence progression in cocaine use. Broad age-related variations have been examined elsewhere (Anthony et al. 1986). The ECA data gathering did not extend to characteristics of the environment such as cost or availability of cocaine, or to local neighborhood or subcultural variations in attitudes and behaviors related to cocaine.

With these considerations in mind, we specified a control group for this study in relation to age and to location of household residence. Specifically, after identifying the new cocaine users, we identified other ECA respondents who lived near them who did not initiate cocaine use. Via a poststratification strategy (Schlesselman 1982), each subject was assigned to a subgroup defined by census tract of household residence—this feature of the design provided a means of holding constant neighborhood characteristics such as actual cost of cocaine in the neighborhood, as well as house effects and other intersite methodologic differences that might contribute to artifactual differences between subjects (Anthony and Petronis this volume). Within each of these neighborhood subgroups, we found age-matched (within 2 years) control subjects for each cocaine initiator. This age-matching feature of the design was intended to take into account and hold constant previously observed age-related variation in cocaine use (Anthony et al. 1986).

Suspected Determinants of Initiating Cocaine Use

The selection of age-matched and residence-matched control subjects allowed a sharper focus on depression, social role transitions, prior illicit drug use, and other personal characteristics that might influence initiation into cocaine use. In this study, the DIS measured lifetime history of a syndrome of persistent depressed mood with allied symptoms (specified by Anthony and Petronis this volume) and occurrence of the depression syndrome during the followup interval.

The social role transitions under study involved changes in employment and marital status during the followup interval. These transitions consisted of moving into the labor force (unemployed who gained a job), moving out of the labor force (employed who became unemployed), becoming married, and becoming separated or divorced during followup. We expected that transitions into the social roles of work and marriage might be related negatively to initiation into cocaine use, that is, they might retard the initiation. We expected that having social roles come to an end might be positively related to initiation into cocaine use, that is, might promote initiation. We reasoned that transitions into work or marriage might serve as protective factors because, for example, as one acquires social roles, one also acquires additional responsibilities that could limit opportunities for involvement in illicit drug use. Conversely, transitions out of social roles (i.e., out of marriage, becoming unemployed) might increase opportunities for involvement in illicit drug use. For example, without associated role obligations, an individual might be more likely to initiate behavior otherwise incompatible with these obligations.

As backdrop to this focus on depression and social role transitions, we also examined use of marijuana and other illicit drugs, which are plausible alternative determinants of initiation into cocaine use (Clayton 1985). We also took into account the possible importance of several sociodemographic characteristics available for study in the ECA data set. These included race-ethnicity, personal income, household income, educational achievement, occupational prestige, employment status at baseline, and marital status at baseline. The two terms for income were 18-point rank-order variables that were scaled to the subject's own annual earnings, and separately, earnings for the household in the year prior to baseline ($0–$1,999=1, $2,000–$2,999=2 , . . . , $35,000–$49,999=17, $50,000 and up =18).

Statistical Analysis

We used the conditional logistic regression model to test for suspected differences between ECA subjects who initiated cocaine use and those who did not initiate or progress. This model took age- and residence-matching into account while estimating the strength of association between each suspected determinant and initiation of cocaine use. Under this model, the strength of association is indexed by a relative odds estimate obtained by taking the antilogarithm of the regression coefficient. Under the circumstances of this study, the relative odds estimates typically approximate estimates of relative risk, that is, the degree to which one subgroup is at greater risk of initiating cocaine use compared to another subgroup. When more than one term is included in conditional logistic regression models, each regression coefficient is adjusted for the influence of all other included terms—that is, the potentially determining influences of the other variables are held constant (Breslow and Day 1980).

To study the initiation of cocaine use over the followup interval, we completed a series of conditional logistic regression analyses. First, a dichotomous outcome variable was created to index initiation (cocaine use=1, other=0), and this variable was regressed separately on each suspected determinant. Results from these univariate regressions were used to guide selection of variables for subsequent multivariate modeling.

In the multivariate modeling, we first developed separate models that contained sociodemographic variables only, prior illicit drug use only, depression variables only, and role-transition variables. Terms that were statistically significant ($p<0.05$) in the illicit drug use model were then added to the sociodemographic model. Finally, statistically significant depression and role transition variables were tested in a model that included all of the above. In this sequence, factors that were no longer statistically significant were dropped. However, in the last step of the model-building process, the previously eliminated covariates were tested to determine whether any would qualify for entry into the final model, either on the basis of statistical significance or because their inclusion led to appreciable change in the regression coefficients corresponding to the depression or role transition variables. This series of regressions provided a final model that contained all four types of covariates. Statistically significant ($p<0.05$) factors were retained in the final multivariate model, as were potentially confounding factors that had an appreciable influence on the magnitude of other coefficients.

RESULTS

Among the 4,394 18- to 44-year-old candidates for initiation into cocaine use, it was possible to identify 78 individuals (1.8 percent) whose followup interview data indicated initiation or progression of cocaine use during the followup interval. The 78 cases resided in 58 separate census tracts, and it was possible to match almost all of them to a total of 131 controls after poststratification into risk sets defined by location of household residence and by age. Five cases and eight potential controls had to be dropped from the regression analyses due to missing data on key covariates, or because no age-matched control was available in the residence-matched risk set. Thus, the regression analyses compared 73 matched sets, each including 1 case and from 1 to 4 controls. Except when missing data led to exclusion of a potential control subject, all available age-matched controls within the risk sets were included in the analyses.

Table 1 shows the distribution of characteristics of the 78 observed cases and the 131 matched controls. Despite careful age-matching to within 2 years, the cases were slightly younger than the controls ($p<0.05$); thus, a term for age was retained in all subsequent multivariate models. Moreover, cases were less likely to be married at baseline and had slightly higher personal income levels at baseline ($p<0.05$). Several other suspected sociodemographic covariates were studied, but they did not qualify for inclusion in the study models on the basis of either statistical significance ($p<0.05$) or impact on regression coefficients for other covariates. The eliminated sociodemographic variables were labor force participation, occupational prestige (Nam and Powers 1968), annual

TABLE 1. *Selected characteristics of individuals with initiation or progression into cocaine use and matched controls*

Suspected determinants	Cocaine users (N=78) n (%)	Control subjects (N=131) n (%)	Initial relative risk estimate	p-value
Age (25 years or older)†	35 (44.9)	70 (53.4)	0.55	0.1127
Married at baseline	13 (16.7)	50 (38.2)	0.07	0.0025
Personal income above median*	39 (53.4)	62 (50.5)	1.17	0.0494
Recent use of marijuana only	42 (53.9)	20 (15.3)	40.50	0.0001
Recent use of other illicit drugs (but not marijuana)	1 (1.4)	0 (0.0)	‡	‡
Recent use of both marijuana and other illicit drugs	6 (7.7)	2 (1.5)	112.50	0.0681
Depression syndrome during followup	12 (15.4)	5 (3.8)	18.70	0.0289
Transition from unemployment to employment during followup	13 (16.7)	12 (9.2)	7.30	0.0828
Gender (male)	42 (54.9)	62 (47.3)	0.30	0.3153
Race (black)	19 (24.4)	27 (20.6)	0.33	0.6084
Race (other)	16 (20.5)	39 (29.8)	–0.77	0.1133

†Relative risk estimate and p-value for age estimate are based on an unrecoded variable. This also is true for the personal income estimate.

* For personal income cases N=73, controls=123 due to missing data.

‡The relative risk and p-value were not estimated due to sparse data.

household income at baseline, and educational achievement. Although race and gender were not significantly related to cocaine use, and were eliminated in subsequent analyses, they are retained in table 1 because they are traditionally important variables in epidemiological research.

Results from the multivariate sociodemographic model are shown in table 2. In univariate models, risk of initiating cocaine use was significantly associated with age, marital status at baseline, and level of personal income at baseline. Nevertheless, after holding age and personal income constant, the association with marital status was at the margin of

TABLE 2. *Adjusted relative risk of initiating or progressing in cocaine use, based on a model that included sociodemographic variables only*

Suspected determinant	Reference category	Adjusted estimate for relative risk	Estimated 95% confidence limits for relative risk	Estimated regression coefficient	p-value
Age	*	0.6	0.40, 0.95	–0.485	0.029
Being married at baseline	Not married	0.5	0.21, 1.05	–0.762	0.067
Personal income at baseline	†	1.1	1.02, 1.21	0.105	0.012

*Age was not recoded to a dichotomous variable. Within each risk set, each control subject was matched to the index case's age within 2 years.

†Personal income was coded as a rank-order scale ranging from 1 to 18 (see text). The adjusted relative risk estimate indicates that relative risk of initiating or progressing in cocaine use increased by a factor of 1.1 with every unit increase in the personal income score.

statistical significance (p=0.067). The risk of initiating cocaine use declined with increasing age (adjusted relative risk, aRR=0.6; p=0.029). With each increment in ranked personal income, risk of initiation of cocaine use increased by a factor of 1.1 (p=0.012). Candidates who were currently married at baseline were only half as likely to progress in cocaine use compared to the never-married, separated, or divorced candidates (aRR=0.5; p=0.067).

Compared to the reference group of subjects who reported no use of illicit drugs in the year prior to baseline, subjects who reported marijuana use in the year prior to baseline were 7.5 times more likely to initiate or progress in cocaine use during the followup interval (aRR=7.5; p<0.001), even when holding constant age, marital status at baseline, and personal income at baseline. This is shown in table 3. Compared to the same reference group, subjects who used other illicit drugs as well as marijuana were 29.5 times more likely to initiate or progress in cocaine use during followup (aRR=29.5; p=0.031). There was no statistically significant association with use of other illicit drugs but not marijuana in the year prior to baseline (p=0.87). This pattern of illicit drug use without marijuana use occurred rarely; as a result, the estimated regression coefficient was extremely imprecise.

TABLE 3. *Adjusted relative risk of initiating or progressing in cocaine use, based on a model that included sociodemographic variables and drug variables only*

Suspected determinant	Reference category	Estimated relative risk	95% confidence limits for estimated relative risk	Estimated regression coefficient	p-value
Illicit drug use in the year prior to baseline:					
Marijuana use only	No use[#]	7.5	3.05, 18.4	2.012	<0.001
Use of marijuana and other illicit drugs	No use	29.5	1.37, 633.0	3.383	0.031
Use of other illicit drugs but not marijuana	No use	(Not estimated due to sparse data)			0.870
Age	*	0.4	0.25, 0.72	–0.857	0.001
Being married at baseline	Not married	0.5	‡	–0.714	0.161
Personal income at baseline	†	1.1	1.00, 1.22	0.092	0.063

*Age was not recoded to a dichotomous variable. Within each risk set, each control subject was matched to the index case's age within 2 years.

†Personal income was coded as a rank-order scale ranging from 1 to 18 (see text). The adjusted relative risk estimate indicated that relative risk of initiating or progressing in cocaine use increased by a factor of 1.1 with every unit increase in the personal income score.

#"No use" refers to subjects with no use of either marijuana or other illicit drugs during the year prior to baseline, as assessed in the baseline interview.

‡The p-value exceeded 0.10 and the confidence limits were not estimated.

In univariate analyses, either occurrence of a depressive syndrome or gaining a job during followup was associated with increased risk of initiating cocaine use (table 1). Even so, neither a prior history of the depression syndrome (at baseline), getting married during followup, becoming separated or divorced during followup, nor becoming unemployed during followup were associated with initiation of cocaine use (p>0.05). Thus, contrary to what we had expected, a new marriage and its attendant role obligations did not signal reduced risk for involvement with cocaine.

Further, job loss and marital breakup did not increase risk for cocaine involvement.

As table 4 shows, occurrence of the depression syndrome during followup was associated with initiation or progression of cocaine use during followup. This association was strong and statistically significant, even when holding constant other covariates (aRR=11.4; p=0.034). Those who gained a job during followup were 4.3 times more likely to initiate or

TABLE 4. *Adjusted relative risk of initiating or progressing in cocaine use, based on a model that included all variables listed below*

Suspected determinant	Reference category	Adjusted estimate for relative risk	95% confidence limits for estimated relative risk	Estimated regression coefficient	p-value
Syndrome of depression during followup	None	11.4	1.20, 108.3	2.435	0.034
Job gain during followup	No job gain	4.3	1.00, 18.96	1.469	0.051
Illicit drug use in the year prior to baseline:					
Marijuana use only	No use#	10.3	3.46, 30.6	2.331	<0.001
Both marijuana and other illicit drugs	No use	33.4	1.29, 867.9	3.510	0.035
Other illicit drugs, but not marijuana	No use	(Not estimated due to sparse data)			0.871
Age	*	0.4	0.23, 0.70	–0.916	0.001
Being married at baseline	Not married	0.5	0.17, 1.35	–0.739	0.164
Personal income at baseline	†	1.1	0.99, 1.24	1.015	0.087

#"No use" refers to subjects with use of neither marijuana nor other illicit drugs during the year prior to baseline, as assessed in the baseline interview.

*Age was not recoded to a dichotomous variable. Within each risk set, each control subject was matched to the index case's age within 2 years.

†Personal income was coded as a rank-order scale ranging from 1 to 18 percent (see text).

progress in cocaine use compared to subjects who had no change in job status, but the association was at the margin of statistical significance in the multivariate model (p=0.051). Adding terms for depression and job gain to the multivariate model produced a minor change in coefficients for the illicit drug use terms, well within the statistical margin of error for these estimates (table 4 estimates versus table 3 estimates).

The association between job gain and the initiation of cocaine use was estimated via analyses comparing those who moved from unemployment to employment during the followup interval to those who did not gain a job during this time. Since we were concerned with the impact of role transitions on drug use, this approach was appropriate. Nevertheless, the approach left open several questions, especially whether the association involving job gain would remain significant when the comparison groups were defined in a different way. Specifically, the association we observed in the preceding analysis might not hold if those who gained a job were compared to those who remained unemployed.

To explore the observed association between job gain and the initiation of cocaine use in more detail, we created dummy-coded (0/1) variables to represent job gain, job loss, and continuing employment. The reference category was those who were unemployed at baseline and also at followup. The three dummy-coded variables were then used in the model presented in table 4 instead of the single dummy variable of job gain. The results of the new model are presented in table 5. The association between job gain and initiation of cocaine use was no longer statistically significant; the parameter estimates for the other predictors remained essentially unchanged.

Despite the drop in statistical significance of the association with job gain (from a p-value of 0.051 to a p-value of 0.094), it would be premature to conclude that job gain is not a risk factor for the initiation of cocaine use. Comparison of tables 4 and 5 indicates that the relative risk estimate for job gain actually increased under the second model, from 4.3 to 4.7. Thus, the drop in statistical significance has to do with an increase in the standard error of the estimate, not to a decline in strength of association. This increase is a consequence of adding terms to a model with a relatively small number of cases (i.e., cocaine users). In this context, it is noteworthy that there was no appreciable improvement in the goodness-of-fit statistics for the regression model when the new dummy variables were added to the model depicted in table 4.

TABLE 5. *Adjusted relative risk of initiating or progressing in cocaine use, based on final multivariate model*

Suspected determinant	Reference category	Adjusted estimate for relative risk	Estimated 95% confidence limits for relative risk	Estimated regression coefficient	p-value
Syndrome of depression during followup interval	None	11.6	1.22, 110.56	2.452	0.033
Job gain during followup	Unemployed at both interviews	4.7	0.77, 28.77	1.547	0.094
Illicit drug use in the year prior to baseline:					
Marijuana use only	No use#	10.0	3.36, 30.82	2.307	<0.001
Both marijuana and other illicit drugs	No use	32.5	1.19, 889.84	3.482	0.039
Use of other illicit drugs but not marijuana	No use	(Not estimated due to sparse data)			0.871
Age	*	0.4	0.23, 0.70	–0.909	0.001
Being married at baseline	Not married	0.5	0.17 1.33	–0.752	0.157
Personal income at baseline	†	1.1	0.97, 1.24	0.096	0.125
Job loss during followup	Unemployed at both interviews	0.9	0.19, 4.71	–0.066	0.937
Being employed at baseline and also at followup	Unemployed at both interviews	1.2	0.29, 5.15	0.206	0.779

#"No use" refers to subjects with no use of either marijuana or other illicit drugs during the year prior to baseline, as assessed in the baseline interview.

*Age was not recoded to a dichotomous variable. Within each risk set, each control subject was matched to the index case's age within 2 years.

†Personal income was coded as a rank-order scale ranging from 1 to 18 (see text).

DISCUSSION

This analysis of prospective data from the ECA surveys pointed toward some suspected determinants of initiation or progression in cocaine use, including social role transitions, occurrence of depression, and several sociodemographic factors. Each of these associations is discussed below.

Social Role Transitions

Contrary to our expectations, subjects who made the transition from unemployed at baseline to employed during followup were more likely to initiate or progress in cocaine use; the association was at the margin of statistical significance in our final models. We had expected to find a reduced risk of cocaine involvement associated with new role obligations of work.

Several explanations might account for this unanticipated finding. One explanation that we were able to explore partially concerns personal income. It is quite plausible that cocaine use is facilitated by increases in income; gaining a job is associated with increased personal income and having more money to spend on illicit drug use. To explore this possibility, we added personal income at followup to the multivariate model. This made little difference in the results: regression coefficients for personal income at baseline and for the job gain term remained virtually unchanged; personal income at followup did not improve the statistical fit of this model. In future work, we hope to examine alternative model specifications that might clarify this issue.

Another plausible explanation for the observed association is that entry into the labor force increased the actual or perceived availability of cocaine, with subsequent impact on initiation in cocaine use. As one moves from a period of unemployment to employment, new acquaintances are made, possibly involving increased contact with cocaine users or others who could supply cocaine for illicit use. This potential increase in availability of cocaine through workplace connections may be a partial explanation for the observed association. This reasoning is consistent with related findings reported by Ritter (1988), but a more specific and empirical test is needed.

As a third explanation, we cannot rule out the possibility that ECA sample attrition from baseline to followup was greater for those who gained a job and did not initiate or progress in cocaine use compared to those who gained a job and used cocaine. With no corresponding imbalance among those who did not gain a job, this selective attrition might create the observed association as an artifact.

Finally, it has not escaped our attention that a certain proportion of transitions from unemployed to employed status represents temporary jobs for a segment of the population that is homeless, indigent, or otherwise not fully enjoying or participating in the benefits of a productive economy. To some extent, the transition from unemployment to employment may be a nonspecific and noncausal marker for the longstanding vulnerabilities in this segment of the population, which has often been found to have increased rates of alcohol and drug problems (e.g., Fischer et al. 1986). Possibilities along these lines could be clarified by more intensive study of the histories of the 78 ECA cases of cocaine initiation/progression, which also could show whether specific industries, occupational titles, or job characteristics were overrepresented among cocaine users.

Besides providing needed replications of the observed association between cocaine use and job gain, future inquiries into this matter can be designed for assessment of dynamic processes that might underlie the observed pattern of associations. For example, job change and mobility have been shown to be related to illicit drug use (Kandel and Yamaguchi 1987). One extension of this line of research would be to assess whether repetitively changing from one job to another is a signal for reinforcement contingencies or other characteristics of the environment that might promote use of cocaine once the drug becomes available.

Other measures of social role transition were not found to be associated with initiation or progression into cocaine use as we had expected. Subjects who became unemployed were no more likely to initiate or progress in cocaine use, possibly because availability of cocaine did not change as a function of job loss as it might with job gain. Another possibility consistent with observed data showing no association with marital separation or divorce is that cocaine initiation or progression is unaffected by role losses. Although this finding was not expected, it is plausible that social role loss, in contrast with job gain, typically involves limited differentiation of social networks; it actually may promote a constriction of these networks. In addition, it is possible that the 1-year followup interval in the ECA study was too short to observe delayed impact of role losses: the induction period for this impact may be long.

Cocaine Use and Depression

In this study, we found a strong and statistically significant association between occurrence of a syndrome of persisting depression and initiation/progression in cocaine use among persons who previously had minimal or no experience with cocaine. The observed association is congruent with other work on cocaine and depression, including other ECA analyses suggesting that individuals who use cocaine are at increased risk of this syndrome of persisting depression (Anthony and Petronis this volume; Chitwood 1985; Gawin and Kleber 1985; Khantzian and Treece 1985; Siegel 1985).

The cocaine-depression relationship may be a manifestation of self-medication, a possibility suggested by others (e.g., Khantzian and Treece 1985; Newcomb and Bentler 1987). However, if self-medication were to account for the cocaine-depression association, then one might expect a measurable predictive association between the depression syndrome as detected at baseline and the subsequent occurrence of cocaine initiation or progression. In our analyses, we found no such association, and thus there is countervailing evidence not consistent with the self-medication hypothesis. Of course, the null finding may be due to selective attrition, inadequate measurement of depression or cocaine use, or to other methodologic features of the ECA analyses such as the year-long followup interval. These are questions for resolution through future research, including replication and more detailed inquiry.

Social Class and Other Sociodemographic Determinants

Age, marital status at baseline, and personal income at baseline were found to be associated with initiation or progression in cocaine use in univariate analyses; there was some change in statistical significance once other covariates were taken into account. These three variables, as well as social class indicators and other sociodemographic variables, were included in the analyses primarily to improve specification of our analytic model and to avoid potential confounding in the study of associations involving cocaine use, social role transitions, and depression. At the same time, these characteristics qualify as possible determinants of initiating cocaine use deserving of attention by themselves.

The strong and statistically significant inverse association between age and initiation or progression in cocaine use, in the context of a closely age-matched design, points toward a central importance of age as a determinant of cocaine use. Consistent with prior work (e.g., Kandel et al. 1985; Anthony et al. 1986), these analyses suggest that the risk of initiating cocaine use does not become negligible in adult life, though it seems to have dropped rather than increased with increasing age.

Initial analyses showed statistically significant inverse associations between cocaine initiation or progression and being married at baseline. These associations were diminished in magnitude somewhat and were reduced in statistical significance when other covariates were added to the sociodemographic model, a matter requiring some comment. Although it might seem plausible that the association between marital status and initiation or progression of cocaine use was confounded by use of marijuana, the evidence from this study suggests otherwise; the relative risk estimates changed very little when a term for marijuana use was added to the regression model.

The observed association between personal income and initiation or progression in cocaine use was consistent with prior speculation that higher income promotes cocaine use, though it was not consistent with all prior epidemiologic data (O'Malley et al. 1985; Clayton 1985). Further, data from the ECA samples did not suggest that cocaine use is limited to those with high incomes.

Overview of Possible Limitations

This study identified a set of personal characteristics associated with initiation or progression in cocaine use midway through an epidemic period of cocaine use in the United States. Estimated risk of initiating or progressing in cocaine use was more likely at higher levels of personal income, among persons with recent prior use of marijuana, and especially among those with recent prior use of marijuana and other illicit drugs, among persons who experienced a syndrome of persisting depression, and among unemployed persons who gained a job. Estimated risk of initiating or progressing in cocaine use was lower among married persons, and it diminished with increasing age.

It is quite legitimate to ask whether these results are generalizable, and this is a question to be resolved through replications in other places and at other times. Use of a nationally representative sample will not necessarily resolve the question, since results obtained with a national sample might not be generalizable to specific metropolitan areas or regions of the country. Moreover, even with local control over ECA survey fieldwork, it was not possible to rule out differential survey participation at baseline or followup as potential sources of artifactual associations. The problems of sample nonresponse and attrition during followup might be felt more acutely in a nationally representative sample compared to local area samples.

To some extent, measurement of the study variables is a source of concern with respect to the outcome variable as well as the predictor variables. The outcome variable was a compromise crafted from DIS questions intended to identify subjects who qualified for a diagnosis of Cocaine Abuse, not to identify first-time users of cocaine. In consequence, the variable for initiation and progression in cocaine use was only partially sensitive and specific. It did not include individuals who started using cocaine but did not progress to more than five occasions of use. Although this might be a relatively rare occurrence during a 1-year followup of 4,394 adults aged 18–44 years, it would not be an impossibility. Thus, some of the study's "control" subjects might actually have belonged with the cases. Further, the specification did not allow a complete differentiation of cocaine initiators from those who progressed from initial occasions of use to more than five occasions of use. As a result, the statistically significant predictor variables are not unambiguous risk factors, though the present results suggest that they are related to either initiation of cocaine use or progression in cocaine use to more than five occasions of use.

The predictor variables were measured without attention to subjects' replies to the cocaine variables. Moreover, the interviewers were not aware that specific hypotheses about use of cocaine or other illicit drugs would be tested. In part, these characteristics of study design limit the extent to which spurious associations might arise as a function of systematic measurement error or to differential probing and measurement by interviewers. Nevertheless, to some extent, shared methods covariation may lead to an artifactually high estimated degree of association between cocaine use and certain other factors such as illicit marijuana use. That is, individuals willing to report about their marijuana use may be more likely to be willing to report about their cocaine use. Conversely, those unwilling to discuss marijuana use may be less likely to report cocaine use. The result would be a spuriously high degree of association between marijuana and cocaine use. Whether this potential source of bias also affects coefficients for characteristics such as depression, perceived availability of cocaine, and other suspected determinants is now unknown and is an urgent matter for future epidemiologic interview research on illicit drug use.

In the discussion of associations involving role losses, it was suggested that the followup interval of 1 year might be too short: the induction period from role loss to initiation or progression in cocaine use might be longer than 6–12 months. It also might be said that the followup interval was too lengthy in the case of cocaine and depression, where the induction period may be a matter of hours or days, as opposed to months or years. This issue can be resolved only through studies with a relatively fine-grained measurement and analysis of time-related events, including initiation of cocaine use, progression in cocaine use, occurrence of depression, and social role transitions.

Finally, in retrospect, the analysis could have been statistically more powerful if the risk sets had not been further restricted by age-matching—that is, if all residence-matched controls had been used. Via age-matching, we had hoped to address difficult-to-model nonlinear associations between subjects' ages and initiation or progression in cocaine use. Since it proved to be necessary to include a term for age in analytic models for the study, addition of suitable covariates for age might have been a more direct solution to the problem.

CONCLUSIONS

Despite the several imperfections and unresolved issues, the analyses reported in this chapter have provided new information and a partial step toward better understanding of factors associated with initiation of cocaine use and its progression. The major conclusions are that chronological age and a syndrome of persisting depression are significantly associated with initiation or progression in cocaine use, as is a social role transition from unemployed to employed status. In addition, it appeared that use of other illicit drugs such as marijuana did not account for observed associations between cocaine use and both personal income and current marital status. Besides providing important leads for future etiologic research on cocaine use in the population, these findings also suggest a variety of questions to be asked about dynamic processes and the role of individual risk factors in determining who initiates cocaine use and who progresses beyond a period of minimal experimentation. In many instances, questions about this study can be answered through future extensions of this work that should include more specific and detailed information about the suspected linkages between cocaine use, depression, and social role transitions.

REFERENCES

Abelson, H.I., and Miller, J.D. A decade of trends in cocaine use in the household population. In: Kozel, N.J., and Adams, E.H., eds. *Cocaine Use in America: Epidemiologic and Clinical Perspectives*. NIDA Research Monograph 61. Rockville, MD: National Institute on Drug Abuse, 1985. pp. 35–49.

Adams, E.H., and Durrel, J. Cocaine: A growing public health problem. In: Grabowski, J., ed. *Cocaine: Pharmacology, Effects and Treatment*. NIDA Research Monograph 50. Rockville, MD: National Institute on Drug Abuse, 1984. pp. 9–14.

Adams, E.H.; Gfroerer, J.C.; and Blanken, A.J. Prevalence, patterns and consequences of cocaine use. In: Brink, C.J., ed. *Cocaine: A Symposium*. Madison, WI: Institute of Drug Abuse, 1985. pp. 37–42.

Anthony, J.C., and Helzer, J.E. Syndromes of drug abuse-dependence. In: Robins, L.N., and Regier, D.E., eds. *Psychiatric Disorders in America*. New York: Free Press, in press.

Anthony, J.C.; Ritter, C.J.; Von Korff, M.R.; Chee, E.N.; and Kramer, M. Descriptive epidemiology of adult cocaine use in four U.S. communities. In: Harris, L.S., ed. *Problems of Drug Dependence, 1985*. Rockville, MD: National Institute on Drug Abuse, 1986. pp. 283–289.

Breslow, N.E., and Day, N.E. *Statistical Methods in Cancer Research: The Analysis of Case Control Studies*. Lyon: International Agency for Research on Cancer, 1980.

Brown, J.W.; Glaser, D.; Waxer, E.; and Geis, G. Turning off: Cessation of marijuana use after college. *Social Problems* 21:527–538, 1974.

Chitwood, D.D. Patterns and consequences of cocaine use. In: Kozel, N.J., and Adams, E.H., eds. *Cocaine Use in America: Epidemiologic and Clinical Perspectives*. NIDA Research Monograph Series 61. Rockville, MD: National Institute on Drug Abuse, 1985. pp. 111–129.

Clayton, R.R. Cocaine use in the United States: In a blizzard or just being snowed? In: Kozel, N.J., and Adams, E.H., eds. *Cocaine Use in America: Epidemiologic and Clinical Perspectives*. NIDA Research Monograph 61. Rockville, MD: National Institute on Drug Abuse, 1985. pp. 8–34.

Eaton, W.W., and Kessler, L.G., eds. *Epidemiologic Field Methods in Psychiatry: The NIMH Epidemiologic Catchment Area Program*. New York: Academic Press, 1985.

Fisher, P.J.; Shapiro, S.; Breakey, W.R.; Anthony, J.C.; Kramer, M. Mental health and social characteristics of the homeless: A survey of mission users. *American Journal of Public Health* 76:519–524, 1986.

Gawin, F.H., and Kleber, H.D. Cocaine use in a treatment population: Patterns and diagnostic distinctions. In: Kozel, N.J., and Adams, E.H., eds. *Cocaine Use in America: Epidemiologic and Clinical Perspectives*. NIDA Research Monograph 61. Rockville, MD: National Institute on Drug Abuse, 1985. pp. 182–192.

Holzer, C.E.; Spitznagel, E.; Jordon, K.B.; Timbers, D.M.; Kessler, L.G.; and Anthony, J.C. Sampling the household population. In: Eaton, W.E., and Kessler, L.G., eds. *Epidemiologic Methods in Psychiatry: The NIMH Epidemiologic Catchment Program*. New York: Academic Press, 1985.

Johnston, L.D.; O'Malley, P.M.; and Bachman, J.G. *National Trends in Drug Use and Related Factors Among American High School Students and Young Adults, 1975–1986*. Washington, DC: Supt. of Docs., U.S. Govt. Print. Off., 1987.

Kandel, D.B.; Murphy, D.; and Karus, D. Cocaine use in young adulthood: Patterns of use and psychological correlates. In: Kozel, N.J., and Adams, E.H., eds. *Cocaine Use in America: Epidemiologic and Clinical Perspectives*. NIDA Research Monograph 61. Rockville, MD: National Institute on Drug Abuse, 1985. pp. 76–110.

Kandel, D.B., and Yamaguchi, K. Job mobility and drug use: An event history analysis. *American Journal of Sociology* 92:836–878, 1987.

Khantzian, E.J. The self-medication hypothesis of addictive disorders: Focus on heroin and cocaine dependence. *American Journal of Psychiatry* 142:1259–1264, 1985.

Khantzian, E.J., and Treece, C. DSM-III psychiatric diagnosis of narcotic addicts: Recent findings. *Archives of General Psychiatry* 42:1067–1071, 1985.

Kozel, N.J.; Crider, R.A.; and Adams, E.H. National surveillance of cocaine use and related health consequences. *Morbidity and Mortality Weekly Report* 31:265–273, 1982.

Nam, C.B., and Powers, M.G. Changes in relative status levels of workers in the United States. *Social Forces* 47:167–170, 1968.

Newcomb, M., and Bentler, P. Cocaine use and psychopathology: Associations among young adults. *International Journal of the Addictions* 22:1167–1188, 1987.

O'Malley, P.M.; Johnston, L.D.; and Bachman, J.G. Cocaine use in American adolescents and young adults. In: Kozel, N.J., and Adams, E.H., eds. *Cocaine Use in America: Epidemiologic and Clinical Perspectives*. NIDA Research Monograph 61. Rockville, MD: National Institute on Drug Abuse, 1985. pp. 50–75.

Ritter, C. Resources, behavior intentions, and drug use: A ten-year national panel analysis. *Social Psychology Quarterly* 51:250–264, 1988.

Robins, L.N.; Helzer, J.E.; Croughan, J.; and Ratcliff, K.A. National Institute of Mental Health Diagnostic Interview Schedule: Its history, characteristics, and validity. *Archives of General Psychiatry* 38:381–389, 1981.

Schesselman, J.J. *Case-Control Studies: Design, Conduct, Analysis*. New York: Oxford University Press, 1982.

Siegel, R.K. New patterns of cocaine use: Changing doses and routes. In: Kozel, N.J., and Adams, E.H., eds. *Cocaine Use in America: Epidemiologic and Clinical Perspectives*. NIDA Research Monograph Series 61. Rockville, MD: National Institute on Drug Abuse, 1985. pp. 204–220.

Siegel, R.K. Changing patterns of cocaine use: Longitudinal observations, consequences and treatment. In: Grabowski, J., ed. *Cocaine: Pharmacology, Effects and Treatment*. NIDA Research Monograph 50. Rockville, MD: National Institute on Drug Abuse, 1984. pp. 92–110.

Single, E.; Kandel, D.B.; and Johnson, B. The reliability of drug use responses in large-scale longitudinal survey. *Journal of Drug Issues* 5:426–443, 1975.

Von Korff, M.R., and Anthony, J.C. The NIMH Diagnostic Interview Schedule modified to record current mental status. *Journal of Affective Disorders* 4:365–371, 1982.

White, H.R. Longitudinal patterns of cocaine use among adolescents. *American Journal of Drug and Alcohol Abuse* 14:1–15, 1988.

Yamaguchi, K., and Kandel, D.B. Dynamic relationships between premarital cohabitation and illicit drug use. *American Sociological Review* 50:530–546, 1985.

ACKNOWLEDGMENTS

Supported in part by grants from the National Institute on Drug Abuse (DA03992) and the National Institute of Mental Health (MH41908, MH33870). One of us (J.C.A.) directed the Epidemiologic Catchment Area household survey work in Baltimore, where M. Kramer was Principal Investigator. PIs at other ECA sites were J.K. Myers (New Haven), L.N. Robins (St. Louis), D. Blazer (Durham), R. Hough and M. Karno (Los Angeles), and D.A. Regier and B.Z. Locke (NIMH). Drs. Susan Schober and Alison M. Trinkoff provided useful comments on earlier drafts of this manuscript. We are grateful to Ms. Jill Schreiber for editorial assistance.

AUTHORS

Christian Ritter, Ph.D.
Department of Sociology
Lowry Hall, Room 120
Kent State University
Kent, OH 44242

James C. Anthony, Ph.D.
Department of Mental Hygiene
The Johns Hopkins University
School of Hygiene and Public Health
615 N. Wolfe Street
Baltimore, MD 21205

Self-Regulation Factors in Cocaine Dependence— A Clinical Perspective

Edward J. Khantzian

Unravelling the etiologic equation in the addictions has important implications for understanding how biology and psychology intersect in governing human behavior. Technologic advances over the past 3 decades have provided breakthroughs in understanding some of the important biologic factors in the equation, the discovery of opiate receptor sites and endorphins being the most recent exciting example. During this same period, extensive clinical work with drug dependent individuals has also provided a basis for understanding some of the psychologic factors that contribute to addictive behavior. A contemporary psychodynamic perspective, complemented by psychiatric diagnostic studies employing standardized diagnostic approaches, has shown that painful feeling states and psychiatric suffering are associated with the addiction and appear to be important etiologic determinants (Rounsaville et al. 1982*a*, 1982*b*; Khantzian 1985; Khantzian and Treece 1985; Deykin et al. 1987).

This chapter focuses and elaborates on psychodynamic and psychiatric factors observed to be important in the development of dependence on drugs, with particular emphasis on cocaine dependence. The approach is based on the assumption that the clinical context and the indepth study of individual cases are valuable in explaining what motivates human behavior, in general, and troubling behaviors such as the addictions, in particular. Ultimately, the explanations that will serve best in solving the etiology of addiction will integrate data derived from the biologic, social, and psychologic perspectives. The aim of this chapter is to delineate more precisely the psychological dimension of cocaine dependence from a psychodynamic perspective with the hope that this approach can shed light on and contribute to an integrated biopsychosocial formulation of cocaine addiction.

PSYCHODYNAMIC THEORIES—OLD AND NEW

Early psychodynamic theory emphasized a topographic model of the mind (i.e., unconscious versus conscious), drive (instinct) psychology, and the symbolic meaning of drugs and did not distinguish among the various classes of drugs. Consistent with early theory, reports by Freud (1905), Abraham (1908), and Rado (1933) focused on satisfaction of libidinal (or pleasure) drives, or, in the case of Glover (1956), aggressive drives. In these early formulations, the use of drugs and associated practices took on important unconscious and subconscious meanings linked to early "fixations" in which an individual might be expressing or attempting to work out unresolved conflicts over sexuality and aggression. Although much of this theory is outdated, these early psychoanalytic formulations were heroic and revolutionary in attempting to go beyond superficial explanations and/or moralistic attitudes to explain the troubling nature of addictive behavior.

Where early psychodynamic theory stressed misguided or repressed drives as the root of addictions, contemporary theory places affect (i.e., feeling) deficits and dysfunction at the heart of addictive disorders. A division of the mind into the unconscious, subconscious, and conscious, with an emphasis on repressive mechanisms, has been supplanted by a view of the mind concerned with feelings, and functions and processes involved in ensuring self-regulation and adaption to reality.

In addition to suffering from deficits in recognizing and regulating affects (feeling life), contemporary psychodynamic studies suggest addicts suffer as well because of vulnerabilities and dysfunction in ego and self structures responsible for regulating and maintaining self-esteem, self-care, and interpersonal relations (Weider and Kaplan 1969; Krystal and Raskin 1970; Milkman and Frosch 1973; Wurmser 1974; Khantzian 1977; Khantzian and Mack 1983; Khantzian 1987). These contemporary psychodynamic formulations of addiction emphasize developmental factors and an adaptive understanding of addiction in which the use of drugs represents an expression of vulnerability and dysfunction in self-regulation; at the same time, it is an attempt at self-correction for these vulnerabilities.

NATURE OF THE DATA

The treatment relationship is a valuable source of information for identifying and understanding the psychologic vulnerabilities of addicts and how such vulnerabilities might motivate a reliance on drugs. With cocaine addicts, for example, the clinical context offers opportunities to explore how the powerful energizing and activating properties of the drug interact with feeling (or affect) states and personality traits and characteristics to make continued or regular use more likely.

A series of diagnostic studies over the past decade, complementing clinical observations, has documented cooccurring psychopathology predominantly involving depression and personality disorder in cocaine abusers (Kleber and Gawin 1984; Gawin and Kleber 1984; Weiss and Mirin 1984, 1986). These studies, not insignificantly and in contrast to studies among opiate addicts, found a disproportionately higher incidence of bipolar type affective disorder, and in the case of the Weiss and Mirin studies, a high incidence of narcissistic and borderline personality disorder. More recently, Weiss et al. (in press) documented a lower but nevertheless substantial incidence of concurrent affective disorder and a higher incidence of antisocial personality disorder.

The main source of data for this report, however, is direct observation and experience with patients in the vis-a-vis context of the patient-therapist relationship, the clinical interview, and group psychotherapy. Such contexts provide unique opportunities to understand the role of state (reactions) and trait (characterologic) factors in susceptibility to a reliance on cocaine.

Empathic appreciation of patients' feeling states and analysis and understanding of characteristic patterns of relating and behavior are part of the bedrock of psychoanalysis and psychoanalytic psychotherapy. These clinical traditions instruct us that a great deal can be learned about what motivates mental life and behavior. Following the nuances of reacting and interacting in treatment relationships allows clinicians to appreciate how personality and feeling states interact and play themselves out, both with the therapist (and with other patients in group therapy) and in the patient's life. These observations allow for inferences about a person's strengths, characteristic ways of coping, and dysfunctions and failure to cope in various aspects of life. They can also provide unique and valuable data for understanding how a powerful feeling-altering drug such as cocaine may be adopted functionally and dysfunctionally in an individual's attempt to cope with internal feeling life and adjustment to external reality.

Luborsky (1984) recently summarized the psychoanalytic traditions behind the technique and principles for psychoanalytic psychotherapy. More importantly, for my purposes here, Luborsky with Woody and associates (Woody et al. 1986) successfully applied these principles to narcotic addicts, demonstrating that they benefit from psychotherapy, depending upon the degree and type of psychopathology present. In their manual for substance abusers, Luborsky et al. (1977) described how core relationship conflicts (i.e., characteristic ways of responding to people) emerge in the treatment relationship and provide valuable clues for understanding the meaning of drug dependence, especially factors that precipitate and maintain it. The relationship themes are apparent in many contexts. The "core" issues or the core conflictual relationship theme (CCRT) appear everywhere in the patient's communication: about the past, about the present, and in the treatment relationship. We have found Luborsky et al.'s approach equally valid and applicable in individual psychotherapy with cocaine addicts in understanding how their feeling states and personality styles contribute to their dependency on cocaine. More recently, we applied these same principles in a NIDA-sponsored relapse prevention program for cocaine addicts. Along lines developed by Luborsky, we described how modified dynamic group therapy (MDGT) for cocaine abusers can activate core themes in which we can learn how certain feeling states and relationship, self-esteem, and self-care problems precipitate and maintain cocaine dependency (Khantzian et al. unpublished).

The following description of the psychodynamic factors found to be important in cocaine dependency is based on clinical observations in individual evaluation sessions and treatment relationships, and in the course of group psychotherapy with substance abusers.

THE SELF-MEDICATION HYPOTHESIS

As a consequence of widespread drug use and abuse in our society over the past 20 years, an increasing number of psychiatric practitioners have treated large numbers of drug abusers in their private practice, in public and private clinics, and in conjunction with self-help programs. Clinical work with such patients has revealed that they experiment with many classes of drugs and often use several drugs simultaneously. However, most patients prefer a particular class of drugs. Exploration of the psychologic makeup of these patients, through clinical evaluations and empirical studies, indicates that they suffer from specific painful feeling states and psychiatric disorders that play a role in determining the class of drug that they choose. Weider and Kaplan (1969) referred to the "drug-of-choice" phenomena, and Milkman and Frosch (1973) talked about the "preferential use of drugs."

In my own work, I originally characterized the differential preference for drugs as the "self-selection" process (Khantzian 1975) and subsequently, as the self-medication hypothesis (Khantzian 1985). My description and formulations were based on a careful evaluation of approximately 500 patients who came to a public methadone maintenance program and to my private practice. I inquired in great detail about all the drugs they had used, the subjective effects they experienced, and the drug they most preferred. In almost every instance, the patients understood what I meant and were able to describe which drug they preferred when I inquired what drug did the most, or was "king drug" for them. A corollary to this finding was that, in a significant percentage of these cases, patients spontaneously offered how drugs other than ones they preferred were often despised or avoided because of their adverse and unwelcome effects.

More recently, I reviewed and summarized clinical and diagnostic findings that supported a self-medication hypothesis of addictive disorders (Khantzian 1985). Although some of the earlier psychoanalysts appreciated the pain-relieving properties of opiates, stimulants, and sedatives, Gerard and Kornetsky (1954, 1955) were among the first to describe systematically how inner-city New York addicts used opiates to overcome painful adolescent anxiety and associated ego and narcissistic pathology. Subsequently, Weider and Kaplan (1969), Krystal and Raskin (1970), Milkman and Frosch (1973), Wurmser (1974), and Khantzian (1974*a*, 1974*b*) produced observations and findings suggesting vulnerabilities and deficits in ego capacities, sense of self, and object relations that cause unbearable psychological suffering and intensely painful affects. Addiction-prone individuals discover that the psychoactive properties of drugs of abuse counter and/or relieve these painful states. Partly as an extension of these psychodynamic studies and partly as a result of the development of standardized diagnostic methods, Weissman et al. (1976), McLellan et al. (1979), Rounsaville et al. (1982*a*, 1982*b*), Khantzian and Treece (1985), and Blatt et al. (1984) documented the cooccurrence of depression, personality disorder, and alcoholism, which supported a self-medication hypothesis of addictive disorders.

Opiates

The pain-relieving properties of opiates are well known, and from this knowledge we interpolate that their appeal must be based on their ability to relieve emotional pain in general. In fact, work with narcotic addicts in methadone programs and in private practice suggests that opiates have appeal because of a much more specific action and effect. A series of reports have revealed that narcotic addicts have lifelong difficulties with traumatic abuse and violence, at first being victims and, subsequently, often becoming perpetrators. Whether victim or perpetrator, they struggle and suffer with acute and chronic states of associated aggressive and rageful feelings that are disruptive and threatening to self and others (Wurmser 1974; Khantzian 1974*a*, 1982; Vereby 1982). Narcotic addicts make the powerful discovery that the distress and threat they experience with their intense aggression is significantly reduced or contained when they first use opiates. Thus, addicts have repeatedly described this antirage, antiaggression action of opiates as "calming—feeling mellow—safe—or, normal for the first time." My experience suggests that the problems with aggression in such individuals are, in part, a function of an excess reservoir of this intense affect—partly constitutional and partly environmental in origin—interacting with psychologic (ego) structures that are underdeveloped or deficient and thus fail to contain such affect. Narcotic addicts find opiates appealing because their antiaggression action mutes uncontrolled aggression and counters the threat of internal psychologic disorganization and external counteraggression from others—not uncommon reactions when such intense feelings and impulses are present (Khantzian 1975, 1985).

Sedative-Hypnotics

The effects of sedative-hypnotics, including alcohol, are opposite to the muting and containing actions of opiates. The psychoanalyst Fenichel (1945) quoted an unknown source to capture the disinhibiting or releasing action of sedatives: "The superego is that part of the mind that is soluble in alcohol." Although this effect may explain the appeal of alcohol as a social lubricant in Western cultures, or why certain tense, neurotically inhibited individuals might prefer alcohol, the appeal for those who become and remain dependent on sedative-hypnotics seems to be more related to deep-seated defenses and fears about human closeness, dependency, and intimacy. Krystal and Raskin (1970) suggested that this class of drugs dissolves exaggerated defenses of denial and splitting and allows the brief and, therefore, safe experience of loving and aggressive feelings, which are otherwise "walled off" in these addicts, leaving them feeling cut off and empty.

Cocaine

Cocaine addicts take advantage of the stimulating and energizing properties of cocaine to counter states of depressive anergia and restlessness, and to augment or compensate for personality factors that govern the individual.

Given the energizing and activating properties of cocaine, it should not be surprising that it appeals to both high-energy and low-energy individuals. In the latter case, cocaine has been considered appealing because it helps to overcome fatigue and depletion states associated with depression (Khantzian 1975) or relieves feelings of boredom and emptiness (Wurmser 1974). For the high-energy, restless personality types, cocaine may be alluring because it leads to increased feelings of assertiveness, self-esteem, and frustration tolerance (Weider and Kaplan 1969) or "augments a hyperactive, restless lifestyle and an exaggerated need for self-sufficiency" (Khantzian 1979, p. 100).

Recently, we considered from a psychiatric/diagnostic perspective the following factors that might predispose an individual to become and remain dependent on cocaine: (1) preexistent chronic depression, (2) cocaine abstinence depression, (3) hyperactive, restless syndrome or attention deficit disorder, and (4) cyclothymic or bipolar illness (Khantzian and Khantzian 1984; Khantzian et al. 1984; Khantzian 1985). A number of recent reports presented empirical findings that support the above speculations and clinical observations (Gawin and Kleber 1984, 1986; Weiss and Mirin 1986; Weiss et al. in press; Kosten et al. 1987).

SECTORS OF PSYCHOLOGICAL VULNERABILITY AND THE APPEAL OF COCAINE

Earlier reports had a tendency to associate or equate drug dependency with severe and significant psychopathology (Weider and Kaplan 1969; Wurmser 1974; Khantzian 1974*a*, 1977, 1980). This emphasis, in my early work, on severe psychopathology as a determinant of drug use was a result of seeing a disproportionate number of heroin addicts in a methadone maintenance program. In more recent years, working with increasing numbers of alcoholics and cocaine addicts seeking treatment, I have found that degrees and sectors of psychological vulnerability are involved rather than global and severe psychiatric disturbance. Degrees of human psychologic distress and suffering interacting with other factors seem to be the important determinants in cocaine's subjective appeal. Notwithstanding this shift in emphasis from psychopathology to suffering, my clinical experience continues to suggest that the more extreme cases (i.e., associated with psychopathology where the suffering is invariably greater) serve as valuable guides in understanding the psychologic underpinnings of drug dependence.

Sectors of vulnerability in personality organization appear to play a part in predisposing some individuals to cocaine dependence. In my experience, however, no one personality type or "addictive personality" is involved that generally predisposes to dependence on drugs or to dependence on cocaine in particular. Although not exactly personality factors, terms such as "sensation seeking" or "stimulus seeking" and "risk taking," described as risk factors in certain populations (Kandel 1980; McAuliffe 1984; McAuliffe et al. 1987), come closer and describe better how a personality trait or predisposition could be influential in certain behaviors and activities that are forerunners of addictive involvement. Sensation seeking, stimulus seeking, and other traits might be particularly important for certain cocaine addicts.

The remainder of this chapter highlights four sectors of psychologic vulnerability—self-regulation vulnerabilities involving affects, self-esteem, self-other relationships, and self-care—and how such vulnerabilities may be important in the development of a dependence on cocaine.

Affects

Feeling life, or affects, appear to be distressing for addicts on at least two counts. They either feel their distress as persistent and unbearable or they do not experience their feeling at all (Khantzian 1979, 1987). In the latter case, terms such as "alexithymia" (Sifneos et al. 1977; Krystal 1982), "dis-affected" (McDougall 1984), and "non-feeling responses" (Sashin 1986) have been coined or adopted to capture this quality in addicts and special populations. These recent conceptualizations have helped to clarify that dysphoria predisposing to addiction may be unpleasant not only because of painful affects such as anxiety, rage, and depression, but that the dysphoria may just as well stem from the fact that feelings may be absent, elusive, or nameless and thus confusing and beyond one's control.

In cocaine addicts, depression or depressive affect has been most frequently identified as a chronic or consistent source of distress that impels individuals to depend on the stimulating and antidepressant action of cocaine (Khantzian and Khantzian 1984; Khantzian 1985; Gawin and Kleber 1986; Weiss and Mirin 1986; Kosten et al. 1987). The ability of cocaine to overcome the fatigue and depletion states associated with acute depression and to activate chronically depressed individuals to overcome their anergia, to complete tasks, and to relate better to others is indeed a powerful short-term antidote to the self-esteem problems associated with these states (Khantzian 1975, 1985; Khantzian and Khantzian 1984). In these cases, self-medication motives seem to play a major part in the initiation and continuation of a dependence on cocaine. Many of these patients predictably and understandably respond to and benefit from the use of tricyclic antidepressant medication (Gawin and Kleber 1984; Rosecan and Nunes 1987).

Not all cocaine addicts suffer with clearly identifiable depression. In fact, earlier estimates that as much as 50 percent of cocaine addicts suffered with depression (Gawin and Kleber 1984; Weiss and Mirin 1986) have recently been reduced to as low as 21 percent (Weiss et al. in press). In their most recent report, Weiss et al. attributed this drop in the rate of depression to changing epidemiology and a corresponding change in the characteristics of patients seeking treatment. In support of this change, they also cited the increase in diagnosis of antisocial personality disorder in their more recent study (16 percent), where in the previous (1984) study sample it was nonexistent.

Although the changing epidemiology could be a sufficient explanation for these shifts in diagnosis, the elusiveness of and confusion around affect experience could also explain why it is hard to identify, specify, or elicit the presence of painful affect, including depressive affect, in many patients and in cohort samples. It awaits further study to determine whether vague feelings of dysphoria or atypical depression, not picked up by diagnostic approaches, might also contribute to seeking out the stimulating or activating properties of cocaine. It certainly is not unusual in clinical practice for patients to complain of feeling bored and empty or to seem devoid of affect. Such a state of being could cause sensation seeking or stimulus seeking and/or explain some of the motives of risk takers. Certainly, the qualities of sensation seeking and risk taking are preferred modes for antisocial characters. They are also notorious for being out of touch with or acting out their feeling life. Along lines proposed by Klein (1975) for borderline personality disorder, perhaps it also holds true that individuals with antisocial personality disorder suffer with "states of dysregulation of affect and activation" and that many such individuals overcome their often hard-to-identify mood and inertia problems with cocaine.

Self-Esteem and Relationships With Others

Cocaine is notorious for producing a sense of well-being within oneself and in relationship to other people. Its energizing action produces a sense of empowerment that can enhance a state of self-sufficiency or it can make contact and involvement with others exhilarating and exciting. Sexually, the user, short term, may also feel increased arousal and potency and a sense of being glamorous and appealing. It should not be surprising, then, that basic aspects of self-esteem and relationships with others are often interwoven in important ways with the fabric of cocaine addiction.

Problems with narcissism, or self-love, are often at the root of the self-esteem problems involved with drug dependence. Kohut and followers (Kohut 1971, 1977; Goldberg 1978; Baker and Baker 1987), in their development of self-psychology, proposed that narcissism evolves or unfolds along certain lines and takes mature (normal) and less mature (disturbed) forms and is evident in certain personality characteristics. Healthy narcissism is basic to emotional health and consists of a subjective sense of well-being, confidence in self-worth and potential, and a balanced valuation of one's importance in relation to other people, groups, and place in the world (Mack 1981; Khantzian and Mack 1989). In clinical work with cocaine addicts, I have been repeatedly impressed that vulnerabilities and deficits around these themes have been particularly important influences in explaining the allure of cocaine. Although a majority of these patients have been very successful and/or high achievers and superficially seem psychologically intact, I have been struck by how fragile their basic sense of self-worth has been. This has been most apparent in exaggerated preoccupation with physical or intellectual prowess, major concerns about performance and achievement, exaggerated needs for acceptance and approval, and vaulting ambitions.

Despite the exaggerated striving and needs, however, cocaine addicts are surprisingly uneven and inconsistent in the ways they express their needs and relate to others. They may alternately be charming, seductive, and passively expectant, or they may act aloof and as if they do not need other people. Their super-sensitivity may be evident in deferential attitudes and attempts to gain approval and acceptance, but they may rapidly shift and become ruthless and demanding in their dealings with others.

Individual and group psychotherapy provide opportunities to observe the characterologic (or characteristic defensive) telltales of these vulnerabilities in self-esteem and in self-other relations. Cocaine addicts have great difficulty in being honest with themselves and others about how driven, ambitious, and needy they are for recognition and acceptance. For many cocaine addicts, high activity levels and an action orientation, augmented by counterdependent attitudes, disguise their dependency needs. For those who are more passive and depressed, postures of helplessness and self-effacement suggest that they are temporarily or more chronically defeated and more obviously struggling with dependency needs. For yet other addicts, disavowal of need and self-sufficiency offer characterologic protection from the realization that one is not all-powerful, perfect, and complete. Such patterns are often startlingly apparent in group therapy interactions with cocaine addicts, with their hyperactivity, self-centeredness, and counterdependence often alternating with reactions of passivity, discouragement, and isolation.

Cocaine effects interact powerfully with the acute and chronic feeling states engendered by the characteristic needs and personality styles of individuals susceptible to cocaine dependence. Their tendency to be hyperactive, restless, and driving can be augmented and sustained by cocaine's energizing properties, thus allowing such people a chemical boost or fuel for this preferred style. However, the extreme measures and standards of performance that such individuals maintain are difficult to constantly achieve. Often, such individuals periodically become depressed or chronically suffer with and/or ward off subclinical or atypical depressive reactions and states. It is not surprising, then, that they find the activating, antidepressant action of cocaine desirable and adaptive on this basis as well.

The diagnostic literature supports these clinical observations; a disproportionately larger percentage of cocaine addicts (compared, for example, to narcotic addicts) suffer with bipolar, cyclothymic, borderline, and narcissistic disorders. All these conditions share a tendency for action, high activity, and rapidly alternating moods, conditions in which the augmenting and/or antidepressant action of cocaine might be desirable.

Finally, consistent with these observations, certain individuals who are driven, hyperactive, emotionally labile, and evidence attentional problems, experience a paradoxical calming response to cocaine much like hyperactive children with attention deficit disorder respond to methylphenidate. In 1983, I reported on such a case involving extreme cocaine dependence that markedly improved with methylphenidate treatment (Khantzian 1983), and Gawin and Kleber (1984), Weiss and Mirin (1984), and Weiss et al. (1985) also identified such a subtype. Although this condition has been identified in only 5 percent of cohorts of cocaine addicts, this interesting finding further supports a self-medication hypothesis of addictive disorders.

Self-Care

Because of the dangerous mishaps and often deadly consequences associated with drug abuse, addicts are often considered to harbor conscious and unconscious self-destructive motives. The highly publicized and untimely deaths of popular athletes and artists suggest that the potential lethal consequence of cocaine use was known by the victims, yet they were not deterred from using it. Are these examples of pleasure instincts overriding survival instincts or, indeed, could this be the "death instinct" (or motive) in action, or are they instinctual at all?

There is little in my experience, nor much in the contemporary psychodynamic literature (Khantzian and Treece 1977), to suggest that these apparent self-destructive behaviors are governed primarily by pleasure instincts or self-destructive drives. Such imputed motives in addicts derive from early and mostly outdated psychoanalytic theory. Evidence suggests that drug effects are sought less to produce pleasure and more to relieve suffering or to induce or enhance states of well-being. Along similar lines, our clinical experience suggests that the self-damaging and lethal aspects of addictive behavior have less to do with self-destructive motives and are more the result of deficits and/or deficiencies in the capacity for self-care. Self-care involves a set of ego functions that are acquired and internalized during childhood from the parents' nurturing and protective functions. Self-care functions serve particular aspects of survival and consist of signal anxiety, reality testing, judgment, control, and the ability to make cause-consequence connections. When optimally developed, the capacity to take care of self ensures that we plan our actions and anticipate events to avoid harm or danger. In adult life, healthy self-care is apparent in appropriate levels of anticipatory affects such as embarrassment, shame, fear, worry, and so forth, when facing potentially harmful or dangerous situations (Khantzian 1980; Khantzian and Mack 1983, 1989).

Although we first discovered and described the self-care vulnerabilities in narcotic addicts (Khantzian 1977), I continue to be impressed that in varying degrees this vulnerability cuts across all substance dependency problems, including alcoholism and cocainism. However, rather than being a capacity that is globally or pathologically impaired, self-care functions in cocaine addicts are more or less established but are subject to lapses or regression in function, or on a more persistent basis, are only marginally present, thus causing these patients to not adequately worry, fear, or consider the potential danger or harm involved in using cocaine. Also, considering how needful, driven, and ambitious cocaine addicts can be, it might also be that priorities about achievement and performance override self-care functions and self-preservation concerns that may be less than optimally developed or established. Furthermore, the defensiveness around the self-esteem and relationship difficulties seen in cocaine addicts causes compensatory posturing, counterdependent, and counterfearful reactions that also interfere with appropriate worry and concerns about self-protection and self-care.

CONCLUSION

This chapter reviews the nature of some psychological vulnerabilities that appear to be important in the development of a dependence on cocaine. Clinical observations and psychiatric diagnostic findings associated with cocaine and other addictions suggest that self-regulation problems involving feeling life, self-other relationships, and self-care cause subjective states of distress and behavioral difficulties. The combination of distress and behavior problems leaves people who suffer from such vulnerabilities at greater risk for seeking out and succumbing to the powerful psychotropic effects of cocaine.

This report is not concerned with the issue of the degree or mechanism of interaction with other etiologic influences such as biologic (i.e., genetic and neurobiologic) and sociocultural (i.e., setting, drug availability, environmental stressors) factors. My own experience has led me to conclude that the psychologic vulnerabilities delineated in this chapter are important determinants in the development of cocaine dependence in patients seen in a clinical context. It remains unclear whether findings in clinical populations of cocaine addicts are unique to them, or whether there may be implications for understanding cocaine use and abuse in nonclinical populations. For heuristic purposes, I would conclude that psychologic factors, as well as social and biologic factors to some degree, play a role in all instances of cocaine abuse. The psychologic factors reviewed in this chapter are on a continuum and exercise a greater degree of influence in some cases than in others.

REFERENCES

Abraham, K. The psychological relation between sexuality and alcoholism. (1908). In: *Selected Papers of Karl Abraham*. New York: Basic Books, 1960.

Baker, H.S., and Baker, M.N. Heinz Kohut's self psychology: An overview. *American Journal of Psychiatry* 144:1–9, 1987.

Blatt, S.J.; Berman, W.; Bloom-Feshback, S.; Sugarman, A.; Wilber, C.; and Kleber, H. Psychological assessment of psychopathology in opiate addiction. *Journal of Nervous and Mental Disease* 172:156–165, 1984.

Deykin, E.Y.; Levy, J.D.; and Wells, V. Adolescent depression, alcohol and drug abuse. *American Journal of Public Health* 77:178–182, 1987.

Fenichel, O. *The Psychoanalytic Theory of Neurosis*. New York: Norton, 1945.

Freud, S. Three essays on the theory of sexuality. *S.E.* 7. London: Hogarth Press, 1905.

Gawin, F.H., and Kleber, H.D. Cocaine abuse treatment. *Archives of General Psychiatry* 41:903–908, 1984.

Gawin, F.H., and Kleber, H.D. Abstinence symptomatology and psychiatric diagnosis in cocaine abusers. *Archives of General Psychiatry* 43:107–113, 1986.

Gerard, D.L., and Kornetsky, C. Adolescent opiate addiction: A case study. *Psychiatric Quarterly* 28:367–380, 1954.

Gerard, D.L., and Kornetsky, C. Adolescent opiate addiction: A study of control and addict subjects. *Psychiatric Quarterly* 29:457–486, 1955.

Glover, E. On the etiology of drug addiction. In: *On the Early Development of Mind*. New York: International Universities Press, 1956.

Goldberg, A., ed. *The Psychology of the Self*. New York: International Universities Press, 1978.

Kandel, D.B. Developmental stages in adolescent drug involvement. In: Lettieri, D.J.; Sayers, M.; and Wallenstein, H.W., eds. *Theories of Addiction*. National Institute on Drug Abuse Research Monograph No. 30. DHHS Pub. No. (ADM) 80–967. Washington, DC: Supt. of Docs., U.S. Govt. Print. Off., 1980.

Khantzian, E.J. Opiate addiction: A critique of theory and some implications for treatment. *American Journal of Psychotherapy* 28:59–70, 1974*a*.

Khantzian, E.J. Heroin use as an attempt to cope: Clinical observations. *American Journal of Psychiatry* 131:160–164, 1974*b*.

Khantzian, E.J. Self selection and progression in drug dependence. *Psychiatry Digest* (Original article; by invitation) 10:19–22, 1975.

Khantzian, E.J. The ego, the self and opiate addiction: Theoretical and treatment considerations. In: Blaine, J.D., and Julius, D.A., eds. *Psychodynamics of Drug Dependence*. National Institute on Drug Abuse Research Monograph No. 12. DHEW Pub. No. (ADM)77–470. Washington, DC: Supt. of Docs., U.S. Govt. Print. Off., 1977. pp. 101–107. Also in *International Review of Psychoanalysis* 5:189–198, 1978.

Khantzian, E.J. Impulse problems in addiction: Cause and effect relationships. In: Wishnie, H., ed. *Working With the Impulsive Person*. New York: Plenum, 1979. pp. 97–112.

Khantzian, E.J. An ego-self theory of substance dependence. In: Lettieri, D.J.; Sayers, M.; and Wallenstein, H.W., eds. *Theories of Addiction*. National Institute on Drug Abuse Research Monograph No. 30. DHHS Pub. No. (ADM)80–967. Washington, DC: Supt. of Docs., U.S. Govt. Print. Off., 1980. pp. 29–33.

Khantzian, E.J. Psychological (structural) vulnerabilities and the specific appeal of narcotics. *Annals of the New York Academy of Sciences* 398:24–32, 1982.

Khantzian, E.J. An extreme case of cocaine dependence and marked improvement with methylphenidate treatment. *American Journal of Psychiatry* 140(6):484–485, 1983.

Khantzian, E.J. The self-medication hypothesis of addictive disorders. *American Journal of Psychiatry* (Special Article) 142(11):1259–1264, 1985.

Khantzian, E.J. A clinical perspective of the cause-consequence controversy in alcoholic and addictive suffering. *Journal of the American Academy of Psychoanalysis* 15(4):521–537, 1987.

Khantzian, E.J., and Khantzian, N.J. Cocaine addiction: Is there a psychological predisposition? *Psychiatric Annals* 14(10):753–759, 1984.

Khantzian, E.J., and Mack, J.E. Self-preservation and the care of the self—ego instincts reconsidered. *Psychoanalytic Study of the Child* 38:209–232, 1983.

Khantzian, E.J., and Mack, J.E. A.A. and contemporary psychodynamic theory. In: Galanter, M., ed. *Recent Developments in Alcoholism*, Vol. 7. New York: Plenum, 1989. pp. 67–89.

Khantzian, E.J., and Treece, C. Psychodynamics of drug dependence: An overview. In: Blaine, J.D., and Julius, D.A., eds. *Psychodynamics of Drug Dependence*. National Institute on Drug Abuse Research Monograph No. 12. DHEW Pub. No. (ADM)77–470. Washington, DC: Supt. of Docs., U.S. Govt. Print. Off., 1977. pp. 11–25.

Khantzian, E.J., and Treece, C. DSM-III psychiatric diagnosis of narcotic addicts: Recent findings. *Archives of General Psychiatry* 42:1067–1071, 1985.

Khantzian, E.J.; Gawin, F.; Kleber, H.D.; and Riordan, C.E. Methylphenidate treatment of cocaine dependence—A preliminary report. *Journal of Substance Abuse Treatment* 1:107–112, 1984.

Khantzian, E.J.; Halliday, K.; and McAuliffe, W.E. "Modified Dynamic Group Therapy for Substance Abusers (MDGT): A Manual." Unpublished.

Kleber, H.E., and Gawin, F.H. Cocaine abuse: A review of current and experimental treatments. In: Grabowski, J., ed. *Cocaine: Pharmacology Effects and Treatment of Abuse*. Washington, DC: National Institute on Drug Abuse, 1984. pp. 11–129.

Klein, D.F. Psychopharmacology and the borderline patient. In: *Borderline States in Psychiatry*. New York: Grune & Stratton, 1975.

Kohut, H. *The Analysis of the Self*. New York: International Universities Press, 1971.

Kohut, H. *The Restoration of the Self*. New York: International Universities Press, 1977.

Kosten, T.R.; Rounsaville, B.J.; and Kleber, H.D. A 2.5 year follow-up of cocaine use among treated opioid addicts. *Archives of General Psychiatry* 44:281–285, 1987.

Krystal, H. Alexithymia and the effectiveness of psychoanalytic treatment. *International Journal of Psychoanalytic Psychotherapy* 9:353–378, 1982.

Krystal, H., and Raskin, H.A. *Drug Dependence: Aspects of Ego Functions*. Detroit: Wayne State University Press, 1970.

Luborsky, L. *Principles of Psychoanalytic Psychotherapy—A Manual for Supportive-Expressive Treatment*. New York: Basic Books, 1984.

Luborsky, L.; Woody, G.E.; Holey, A.; and Velleco, A. "Treatment Manual for Supportive-Expressive Psychoanalytically Oriented Psychotherapy: Special Adaptation for Treatment of Drug Dependence." Unpublished manual.

Mack, J.E. Alcoholism, A.A. and the governance of the self. In: Bean, M.H., and Zinberg, N.E., eds. *Dynamic Approaches to the Understanding and Treatment of Alcoholism*. New York: Free Press, 1981. pp. 128–162.

McAuliffe, W.E. Nontherapeutic opiate addiction in health professionals: A new form of impairment. *American Journal of Drug and Alcohol Abuse* 10(1):1–22, 1984.

McAuliffe, W.E.; Santangelo, S.; Magnunson, E.; Sobol, A.; Rohman, M.; and Weissman, J. Risk factors of drug impairment in random samples of physicians and medical students. *International Journal of the Addictions* 22(9):825–841, 1987.

McDougall, J. The 'dis-affected' patient: Reflections on affect pathology. *Psychoanalytic Quarterly* 53:386–409, 1984.

McLellan, A.T.; Woody, G.E.; and O'Brien, C.P. Development of psychiatric illness in drug abusers. *New England Journal of Medicine* 201:1310–1314, 1979.

Milkman, H., and Frosch, W.A. On the preferential abuse of heroin and amphetamine. *Journal of Nervous and Mental Disease* 156:242–248, 1973.

Rado, S. The psychoanalysis of pharmacothymia. *Psychoanalytic Quarterly* 2:1–23, 1933.

Rosecan, J.S., and Nunes, E.V. Pharmacological management of cocaine abuse. In: Spitz, H.I., and Rosecan, J.S., eds. *Cocaine Abuse: New Directions in Treatment and Research*. New York: Brunner Mazel, 1987.

Rounsaville, B.J.; Weissman, M.M.; Crits-Cristoph, K.; Wilbur, C.; and Kleber, H. Diagnosis and symptoms of depression in opiate addicts: Course and relationship to treatment outcome. *Archives of General Psychiatry* 39:151–156, 1982*a*.

Rounsaville, B.J.; Weissman, M.M.; Kleber, H.; and Wilber, C. Heterogeneity of psychiatric diagnosis in treated opiate addicts. *Archives of General Psychiatry* 39:161–166, 1982*b*.

Sashin, J.I. "The Relation Between Fantasy and the Ability To Feel Affect." Unpublished paper presented at Grand Rounds, The Cambridge Hospital, Cambridge, MA, November 5, 1986.

Sifneos, P.; Apfel-Savitz, R.; and Frank, F. The phenomenon of "alexithymia." *Psychotherapy Psychosomatics* 28:47–57, 1977.

Vereby, K., ed. *Opioids in Mental Illness: Theories, Clinical Observations, and Treatment Possibilities*. Vol. 398. New York: Annals of the New York Academy of Sciences, 1982.

Weider, H., and Kaplan, E. Drug use in adolescents. *Psychoanalytic Study of the Child* 24:399–431, 1969.

Weiss, R.D., and Mirin, S.M. Drug, host and environmental factors in the development of chronic cocaine abuse. In: Mirin, S.M., ed. *Substance Abuse and Psychotherapy*. Washington, DC: American Psychiatric Association Press, 1984. pp. 42–55.

Weiss, R.D., and Mirin, S.M. Subtypes of cocaine abusers. *Psychiatric Clinics of North America* 9:491–501, 1986.

Weiss, R.D.; Pope, H.G.; and Mirin, S.M. Treatment of chronic cocaine abuse and attention deficit disorder, residual type with magnesium pemoline. *Drug and Alcohol Dependence* 15:69–72, 1985.

Weiss, R.D.; Mirin, S.M.; Griffin, M.L.; and Michaels, J.L. Psychopathology in cocaine abusers: Changing trends. *Journal of Nervous and Mental Disease* 176(12):719–725, 1988.

Weissman, M.M.; Slobetz, F.; Prusoff, B.; Mezritz, M.; and Howard, P. Clinical depression among narcotic addicts maintained on methadone in the community. *American Journal of Psychiatry* 133:1434–1438, 1976.

Woody, G.E.; McLellan, A.T.; Luborsky, L.; and O'Brien, C.P. Psychotherapy for substance abuse. In: Mirin, S.M., ed. *The Psychiatric Clinics of North America* 9:547–562, 1986.

Wurmser, L. Psychoanalytic considerations of the etiology of compulsive drug use. *Journal of the American Psychoanalytic Association* 22:820–843, 1974.

AUTHOR

Edward J. Khantzian, M.D.
Associate Professor of Psychiatry
Harvard Medical School
The Cambridge Hospital
1493 Cambridge Street
Cambridge, MA 02139

Psychiatric Disorders in Treatment-Entering Cocaine Abusers

Bruce Rounsaville and Kathleen Carroll

Using infectious disease terminology, epidemiological approaches to cocaine use and abuse can focus on many levels at which the agent (cocaine) is dispersed, comes into contact with the host (cocaine user/abuser), and leads the host to be counted by various monitoring sources (surveys of households, schools, or public places; surveillance of cocaine-distribution networks; arrests; seeking treatment for cocaine-related medical problems; seeking treatment for cocaine-using behaviors; cocaine-related deaths). In this chapter, we present preliminary findings from a study that derives data from one of these sources: cocaine abusers entering an inpatient or outpatient drug treatment program.

The major aims of this study are to evaluate the rates and clinical significance of coexistent psychiatric disorders in treatment-entering cocaine abusers and to begin to assess evidence for familial transmission of disorders in the biological relatives of this sample. Because these findings appear in a volume presenting epidemiological data derived from a strikingly diverse set of studies, we begin with a general discussion of the rationale for studying (a) treatment seekers and (b) psychiatric disorders.

WHY STUDY TREATMENT SEEKERS?

Before discussing the advantages of studying treatment-seeking cocaine abusers, it is important to enumerate some of the limitations of this kind of sample. These relate to generalizability of findings and the scope of research questions that can be addressed from a clinical population.

Generalizing on the basis of findings derived from treated samples is likely to be affected by several important, widely recognized biases. The first bias is in the severity of substance use and/or substance-related problems, with clinical groups representing the more severe end of the spectrum. For example, a landmark finding in the epidemiology of drug abuse by Robins and associates (1974; Robins 1978) changed prevailing ideas about the long-term prognosis of heroin addiction. While previous longitudinal studies of treated heroin addicts showed that the great majority had resumed heroin use within a year following discharge from treatment, their non-treatment-seeking sample of veterans who had become addicted to heroin in Vietnam showed that fewer than 10 percent had resumed heroin use during the 3 years after being detoxified. This finding is of tremendous clinical and theoretical importance because it suggests that factors other than heroin-induced changes in opioid receptors (Dole and Nyswander 1967) are related to addicts' long-term vulnerability to relapse.

A number of other studies of nonclinical populations point to the relatively high severity of drug abuse in treatment-seeking groups compared with unselected drug users and abusers in the community. Surveys by Robins et al. of young black men in the community (Robins et al. 1968) and by O'Donnell et al. (1976) demonstrated that a substantial proportion of those reporting past regular use of even "hard" drugs like heroin did not report having sought treatment and did report ceasing regular use without treatment. The Epidemiologic Catchment Area (ECA) (Myers et al. 1984; Robins et al. 1984) and National Household Survey on Drug Abuse (Abelson and Miller 1985) found that most regular users of illicit drugs reported no contact with substance abuse treatment systems. From the treatment-seeking samples, the average heroin-abusing patient reported around 4 years of regular use before first admission into a substance abuse program (Robins 1980). These findings converge to suggest that treatment-seeking drug abusers are a self-selected minority of users who have relatively longstanding use and a comparatively poor prognosis for sustained abstinence.

A second bias is a tendency for treatment-seeking drug abusers to have more than one disorder. While this bias has been long noted (Berkson 1946) for medical disorders, studies of opioid addicts (Rounsaville and Kleber 1985*a*) and alcoholics (Jaffe and Ciraulo 1986; Woodruff et al. 1973) extend this finding to coexistent psychiatric disorders in treated versus untreated substance abusers. These findings are particularly important in evaluating the results of the current study and comparing them to those of Anthony and Petronis (this volume), who evaluated psychiatric disorders in community cocaine users, most of whom did not meet diagnostic criteria for cocaine dependence or abuse.

The types of topics that can be fruitfully studied in treatment-seeking drug abusers are also limited. Studies of temporal trends in use of different substances are best done in community samples because of the lag time between first use of substances and occurrence of sufficient problems to seek treatment. This is illustrated in current cocaine abuse epidemiology: indices of casualties and treatment-seeking related to cocaine continued to rise in the late 1980s, while indices from O'Malley and associates' high school senior survey indicated a leveling off or decrease in cocaine use in the same period (O'Malley et al. this volume; Colliver 1987; NIDA 1987).

Studies attempting to document the rates of cocaine-related medical, psychological, or social consequences are best conducted in a community setting where a full spectrum of consequences can be observed. Studies of how some individuals manage to use illicit drugs without severe consequences or of how drug abusers are able to curtail their drug use without treatment cannot take place in a treatment environment. Studies of factors related to treatment seeking or of barriers to treatment seeking cannot take place in a setting where all subjects are receiving treatment. Similarly, studies of factors related to progression of drug involvement from mild to severe cannot take place due to the truncated range of problems noted in treatment-seeking samples.

The limited variability in drug use severity in a treated population may give the mistaken impression that severity is a relatively unimportant factor in treatment outcome. This has been an issue in the body of research attempting to evaluate the generalizability of prognostic significance for the drug-dependence syndrome from alcohol to other drugs of abuse (Rounsaville et al. 1987; Edwards et al. 1981; Skinner and Goldberg 1986; Kosten et al. 1987*b*; Babor et al. in press). While severity of alcohol dependence has been consistently shown to be related to treatment outcome (Hodgson 1980; Hesselbrock et al. 1983; Foy et al. 1984; Orford et al. 1976), severity of opioid dependence has not (Babor et al. in press; McLellan et al. 1981, 1983; Rounsaville et al. 1982*a*), and other factors such as coexistent psychopathology have been better predictors in the opioid-dependent group. This negative finding may be related to the uniformly high degree of dependence noted in treatment-seeking opioid addicts compared with the variable range of dependence seen in treated alcoholics.

Given these limitations, what are the strengths of this type of sample? A first major strength in studying treated groups is feasibility. Given that relatively severe abuse or dependence on cocaine or opiates appears to take place in less than 1 percent of the adult population, studies that require large samples must screen very large numbers of community members to detect the population of interest. Studies of such large numbers are typically severely limited in the amount of subject burden that can be imposed on community participants. Hence, extensive testing is usually precluded, and topics cannot be addressed in as much depth as intensive studies of highly motivated clinical groups. The use of comparatively small numbers of clinical subjects allows greater flexibility in study design and instrumentation because such studies can be completed and replicated more rapidly than large community surveys.

A second major strength of epidemiological research on treatment samples is that information gathered can be used to guide treatment even if it is not generalizable beyond the treatment setting. Surveys of treatment-seeking cocaine abusers can alert clinicians to the types of problems they are likely to encounter with this group, the factors related to good or poor prognosis in treatment, and patient characteristics that can be used in matching patients to the program that is likely to be optimally helpful. Beyond addressing questions directly related to treatment issues, surveys and case control studies of treated samples can be valuable for studying more general aspects of cocaine dependence, as long as investigators recognize that generalizability may be limited to more severe cases. Hence, studies of patterns and consequences of cocaine abuse, biological and other markers of cocaine abusers, the comparative assets of varying methods for detecting and measuring cocaine use and abuse, the relationship between patterns of use and consequences, the familial and other risk factors for development and progression of drug use disorders, and the relationship of cocaine abuse to use of other substances are among the many topics of current interest in the epidemiology of cocaine abuse that can be addressed within treated samples.

WHY STUDY PSYCHIATRIC DISORDERS IN COCAINE ABUSERS?

The primary goal of studying rates of psychiatric disorders in different types of substance abusers is to provide information that might guide development of more effective treatment programs. Studies of non-drug-abusing patient groups have demonstrated the efficacy of both psychological and pharmacological treatments for a number of psychiatric disorders including major depression, bipolar disorders, schizophrenia, and a variety of anxiety disorders including phobia, panic disorder, and obsessive-compulsive disorder. If a substantial proportion of treatment-seeking cocaine abusers have these disorders, then provision of treatments that have been useful in non-cocaine abusers is likely to be beneficial not only in controlling psychiatric symptoms but also in facilitating reduction or cessation of illicit drug abuse.

Research of this kind has become increasingly important because of advances in methods used to define and assess psychopathology. While clinicians have long asserted that many substance abusers display clinically significant psychopathology, the impetus for assessing specific psychiatric disorders in this group has been small because of poor reliability of diagnostic methods (Spitzer and Fleiss 1974; Beck et al. 1962) and the unavailability of demonstrably effective treatments targeted at specific disorders such as depression, mania, or schizophrenia.

While numerous studies in the 1960s and early 1970s assessed psychopathology in substance abusers using personality and symptom-rating scales, the findings had limited clinical relevance because symptoms assessed were not organized into treatable syndromes with a defined cluster of clinically significant symptoms, of duration sufficient to warrant attention, and with specification of exclusion criteria. For example, an elevated score for depressive symptoms may be (a) a transient reaction to acute stress or an acute effect of ingesting or withdrawing from psychoactive substances, (b) an associated feature of a nonaffective psychiatric disorder such as schizophrenia, or (c) an indication of a current depression syndrome that may respond to antidepressant pharmacotherapy or psychotherapy. In contrast, a diagnosis of major depression denotes a cluster of depressive symptoms of sufficient severity and duration to warrant clinical attention.

Methods for reliably diagnosing psychiatric disorders include use of specified and operationalized diagnostic criteria (American Psychiatric Association 1980, 1987; Spitzer et al. 1978; Feighner et al. 1972) and structured interview guides to improve consistency in eliciting diagnostic information (Endicott and Spitzer 1978; Spitzer and Williams 1985; Robins et al. 1981*a*, 1981*b*). These were not available until the middle to late 1970s. At that time, a number of studies were undertaken to evaluate rates of psychiatric disorders in substance-abusing populations including opioid addicts and alcoholics. Results of this work suggested the clinical significance of psychopathology in opioid addicts (Rounsaville et al. 1982; Khantzian and Treece 1985) and alcoholics (Schuckit 1985; Powell et al. 1982; Hesselbrock et al. 1985), as findings from different investigations repeatedly showed that rates of psychiatric disorders in treated substance abusers exceeded community rates of major depression, anxiety disorders, antisocial personality, and nontargeted substance abuse (e.g., alcoholism in opioid addicts, opioid abuse in alcoholics).

Followup studies of opioid addicts (Rounsaville et al. 1982*a*, 1986) and alcoholics (Rounsaville et al. 1987; Schuckit 1985*a*; Penick et al. 1984) have demonstrated that coexistent psychiatric disorders are associated with poorer treatment outcome. Clinical trials of psychotherapy (Rounsaville and Kleber 1985*b*) and antidepressant pharmacotherapy (Rounsaville et al. 1985*a*) have generally shown these treatment approaches to be beneficial for opioid addicts with concurrent psychiatric disorders, while studies of treatments targeted at psychiatric disorders in alcoholics have been less frequently undertaken and results have been equivocal (Kranzler and Liebowitz 1988).

While studies of psychiatric disorders in opioid addicts and alcoholics suggest their clinical importance, a similar body of findings is not available for cocaine abusers, largely because clinical investigators saw comparatively few treatment-seeking, severely impaired users until the early to middle 1980s, several years after rates of use in the community had risen dramatically and leveled off (see chapters by O'Malley et al. and Rouse this volume). The separate study of patients who are primary abusers of different types of substances is of value because the different pharmacological effects of cocaine, heroin, and alcohol may (a) appeal to different individuals who are attempting to treat different types of psychopathology (see Khantzian chapter) or (b) induce different types of psychopathology.

Findings available at the time of this study demonstrated elevated rates of affective disorders, alcoholism, and antisocial personality in small treatment samples of cocaine abusers (Gawin and Kleber 1985, 1986; Weiss et al. 1986). The aims of this study were to replicate and extend these preliminary findings by examining psychiatric disorders, addictive behaviors, and family psychiatric history in cocaine abusers entering inpatient and outpatient treatment. Findings will be used to assess the rates of psychiatric disorders in cocaine-abusing inpatients and outpatients compared with rates derived from community samples, to assess clinical and demographic features associated with psychiatric disorders in treated cocaine abusers, to evaluate the utility of different techniques for diagnosing psychopathology in cocaine abusers, to evaluate the predictive significance of psychiatric disorders in cocaine abusers through a 1-year followup reevaluation, and to compare the risk and familial patterns of addictive behaviors and psychiatric disorders in the first-degree relatives of cocaine abusers using proband-reported family history, with similar data obtained from probands who are opioid addicts and normals with no psychiatric disorders. In this study, we intend to interview 300 treatment-entering cocaine abusers, evenly divided between an outpatient and an inpatient setting. The study is currently in the data collection phase. This preliminary report focuses on (a) rates of psychiatric disorders, (b) demographic features associated with psychiatric disorders, and (c) overlap among disorders in the first 149 subjects.

METHOD

Subjects

Subjects were adults (>18 years old) seeking treatment for cocaine abuse at an outpatient cocaine clinic (n=98) or an inpatient drug abuse unit within a psychiatric hospital (n=51) in southern Connecticut. In addition to seeking treatment for cocaine abuse, subjects were required to meet current DSM–III–R criteria for cocaine dependence (American Psychiatric Association 1987).

Because we were interested in the types of psychiatric disorders that affect individuals whose main drug of abuse is cocaine, and because we had already evaluated psychiatric diagnoses in a sample of heroin addicts who abused cocaine as a secondary drug (Kosten et al. 1986, 1987*a*), we decided to exclude treatment seekers who had a history of heroin dependence that preceded the onset of cocaine abuse. Also, this group was unlikely to represent the most common pathway to cocaine abuse, as rates of heroin use in the community were far lower than rates of cocaine use (Abelson and Miller 1985).

We did not exclude subjects who had abused drugs other than heroin prior to the onset of cocaine use because findings from surveys of general populations have indicated that initial use and abuse of psychoactive substances typically follows a graded sequence, with initial use of licit substances such as alcohol and tobacco occurring prior to "gateway" illicit substances such as marijuana and hashish, which are then followed by use of harder substances such as barbiturates, amphetamine, cocaine, and opioids (Kandel 1975, 1978). Because of this typical sequence, a sample of cocaine abusers who did not also meet criteria for past dependence on some other substance would be very small and unrepresentative.

We attempted to interview a consecutive sample of patients seeking treatment for cocaine abuse at the inpatient and outpatient settings. Interviewing took place between June 1986 and September 1987. At the outpatient setting, 138 patients reporting cocaine use were screened; 20 failed to meet criteria, usually due to heroin use; 118 were eligible and 98 were interviewed, with 20 refusing to participate in the study or being unavailable for a research interview. At the inpatient setting, 102 patients reporting cocaine use were screened; 34 failed to meet criteria, 68 were eligible, and 51 were interviewed, with 17 refusing to participate in the study or being unavailable for a research interview.

Diagnostic Techniques

Information for making diagnostic judgments was collected with the Schedule for Affective Disorders and Schizophrenia—Lifetime Version (SADS–L) (Endicott and Spitzer 1978) and classified using Research Diagnostic Criteria (RDC) (Spitzer et al. 1978). Diagnoses on the RDC were made for both current (point prevalence rates) and lifetime (lifetime prevalence). We used this system rather than DSM–III or DSM–III–R in order to closely compare rates of disorders in cocaine abusers and their relatives to data already gathered on opioid addicts in a study that also used the SADS/RDC system. We did supplement the SADS–L interview with numerous questions about psychoactive substance use disorders to determine if subjects met criteria for substance use disorders according to DSM–III–R criteria.

We gave considerable attention to the need to determine whether psychiatric symptoms elicited using the SADS–L were drug related in a trivial and strictly pharmacological sense. Laboratory studies of stimulant (amphetamine, cocaine) administration in humans have demonstrated that large doses of these agents have powerful acute effects that can mimic symptoms of paranoia, mania, or anxiety disorders and protracted effects that can mimic depression or anxiety disorders (Gawin and Ellinwood 1988). Such symptoms, while of short-term clinical interest, were unlikely to tell us about enduring psychiatric characteristics of cocaine abusers and would probably resolve with cocaine abstinence of relatively brief duration (5–10 days).

Several options have been suggested for distinguishing clinically significant, enduring psychiatric syndromes from transient, drug-induced symptoms. The first approach was used by the Diagnostic Interview Schedule (DIS), which was the instrument for the ECA study reported on by Anthony and Petronis in this volume. Every time a subject answered positively to an inquiry about a psychiatric symptom (e.g., depression), a followup question asked whether this occurred only in relation to use of psychoactive drugs. Being related to drug use was commonly inferred if the symptom took place during a period of regular use of a psychoactive substance. Hence, this rule tended to paradoxically protect chronic substance abusers from receiving a diagnosis of a psychiatric disorder, even if these substance abusers reported quite severe symptoms. Of course, this system allowed diagnosis of psychiatric disorders if these preceded the onset of cocaine abuse or other regular substance use and if these disorders occurred during a sustained drug-free period. However, many subjects had regularly used drugs over many years, extending from late adolescence into young and even middle adulthood. Hence, episodes of psychiatric disorders during this long period might be excluded using this system.

To address the problem of transient, substance-induced state effects while also allowing diagnosis of more enduring syndromes during periods of steady-state use, our group developed the following guidelines for allowing symptoms elicited to be considered as part of a psychiatric disorder (Rounsaville in press). For individuals who used psychoactive substances regularly, psychiatric symptoms elicited were counted unless these symptoms only appeared during a period of marked change (either a marked increase or a marked decrease) in amounts of substances taken. The exceptions to this general rule were psychotic symptoms that occurred during use of PCP or hallucinogens and paranoid, anxiety, and depression symptoms that occurred during regular heavy use of stimulants (amphetamine and cocaine). For cocaine abusers, we included depression, anxiety, or paranoid symptoms as part of a syndrome diagnosis only if these symptoms persisted at least 10 days beyond last use of cocaine. We also recorded the symptoms and syndromes if they occurred during heavy cocaine abuse but do not report these findings in this chapter.

RESULTS

Demographic Characteristics

As shown in table 1, cocaine abusers in our sample were predominantly male (67 percent), in the 18–35 age range (88 percent), white (66 percent), with a high school or lower educational level (71 percent), and single (57 percent).

Current Rates of Psychiatric Disorders in Cocaine Abusers

In table 2, we present current rates of psychiatric disorders in cocaine abusers in our sample and provide rates from two previously published studies of other populations to place the current findings in context: rates of RDC diagnoses made in treatment-seeking opioid addicts in New Haven (Rounsaville et al. 1982*b*), and rates of DSM–III diagnoses made in the New Haven sample of the ECA study (Robins et al. 1984; Myers et al. 1984). Rates of current disorders in cocaine abusers were not substantially higher than those for a general New Haven community sample except in the category of alcoholism, in which the current rate was 24.2 percent while the community rate was 4.8 percent. Most notably, the high rate of current depression noted in opioid addicts, 23.8 percent, was not seen in cocaine abusers. However, most of the cocaine abusers in

TABLE 1. *Demographic characteristics of treatment-seeking cocaine abusers (n=149)*

Characteristics	Percent
Sex	
Male	67
Female	33
Age	
18–24	39
25–35	49
36–54	12
Race	
White	66
Nonwhite	34
Education level	
Less than high school	29
High school	42
Some college	29
Marital status	
Single	57
Married	27
Divorced/widowed	16

TABLE 2. *Prevalence of current psychiatric disorders in cocaine abusers, opioid addicts, and the New Haven community (in percents)*

Diagnosis	Cocaine abusers (n=149) RDC	Opioid addicts (n=533) RDC	New Haven community (ECA) (n=3058) DSM–III
Major depression	4.7	23.8	3.5
Bipolar I (mania)	0.0	0.0	0.8
Schizophrenia	0.0	0.2	1.1
Panic	0.0		
Generalized anxiety	4.0	0.9	
Phobia	8.7	9.2	5.9
Obsessive compulsive	0.0	1.3	1.4
Alcoholism	24.2	13.7	4.8

this sample had not been cocaine free for 10 days at the time of evaluation and therefore could not meet our criteria for major depression. A similar requirement for persistence of depression into a 10-day drug-free period was not made for opioid addicts.

Lifetime Rates of Psychiatric Disorders in Cocaine Abusers

We present lifetime rates of psychiatric disorders in cocaine abusers, treatment-seeking opioid addicts, and the New Haven sample from the ECA study in table 3. Rates for cocaine abusers markedly exceeded those in the community for major depression (cocaine 31.5 percent, ECA 6.7 percent), antisocial personality (cocaine 34.9 percent, ECA 2.1 percent), and alcoholism (cocaine 63.8 percent, ECA 15 percent). Rates of other tabulated disorders including bipolar I, schizophrenia, and phobia appeared comparable to ECA rates. It is noteworthy that elevated rates appeared in the same categories for cocaine abusers as for opioid addicts. However, cocaine abusers had somewhat lower rates of major depression (cocaine 31.5 percent, opioid 53.9 percent) and higher rates of alcoholism (cocaine 63.8 percent, opioid 34.5 percent). For major depression and for alcoholism, we also computed the rates at which these diagnoses preceded cocaine abuse. Major depression preceded first cocaine abuse in only 12.7 percent of subjects, while 31.5 percent

TABLE 3. *Lifetime prevalence of psychiatric disorders in cocaine abusers, opioid addicts, and community*

Diagnosis	Cocaine abusers (n=149) RDC	Opioid addicts (n=201) RDC	New Haven community (ECA) (n=3058) DSM–III
Major depression	31.5	53.9	6.7
Major depression (preceded drug abuse)	12.7	4.9	
Bipolar I (mania)	3.4	0.6	1.1
Schizophrenia	0.7	0.8	1.9
Phobia	11.4	9.6	7.8
Antisocial personality	34.9	26.5	2.1
Alcoholism	63.8	34.5	15.0
Alcoholism (preceded drug abuse)	14.1	22.6	

met criteria sometime in their lives. For alcoholism, this diagnosis preceded cocaine abuse in only 14.1 percent, while 63.8 percent met criteria sometime in their lives.

Demographic Correlates of Psychiatric Disorders in Cocaine Abusers

In table 4, we display lifetime rates of the major diagnostic categories by treatment setting in which subjects were evaluated and by demographic characteristics. The differences in the prevalence rates by these characteristics were as follows:

- *Inpatient/outpatient*. The overall rates of disorders for inpatient and outpatient treatment seekers were comparable except for alcoholism, which occurred more frequently in the outpatient sample.
- *Sex*. Males had higher rates of alcoholism and antisocial personality.
- *Race*. Whites had higher rates of major depression and of alcoholism.
- *Age*. Older cocaine abusers had higher rates of any anxiety disorder.
- *Education*. No differences were found in rates of disorders in those cocaine abusers with high school or less education compared with those with some college or above.

Multiple Diagnoses

Diagnoses by RDC are not mutually exclusive, and multiple diagnoses were common in our sample. The degree of overlap between types of RDC diagnoses is given in table 5, which shows the lifetime prevalence of psychiatric diagnoses by the presence of other lifetime diagnoses. The analysis was done on the basis of 2 x 2 contingency tables (diagnosis A[no-yes] versus diagnosis B[no-yes]), and the significance of the associations was calculated using the χ^2 statistic. The relationship of major depression and alcoholism was significantly higher than might be expected. Thirty-six subjects met criteria for both major depression and alcoholism, comprising 76.6 percent of the depressives and 37.9 percent of the alcoholics. Major depression was also significantly associated with all other diagnostic categories listed, including antisocial personality, any anxiety disorder, and bipolar I. The only other significant association was between any anxiety disorder and bipolar I.

TABLE 4. *Lifetime prevalence of psychiatric disorders in cocaine abusers by treatment setting and demographic characteristics (in percents)*

Diagnosis	Inpatient n=98	Outpatient n=51	Male n=100	Female n=49	White n=83	Nonwhite n=66	29 and under n=101	30 and over n=48	Less than high school n=43	College n=106
Major depression	28.6	37.3	31.0	32.7	35.5	22.7*	32.7	29.2	37.6	31.1
Alcoholism	59.2	72.6*	72.0	46.9*	72.3	53.0*	65.4	60.4	65.1	63.2
Any anxiety	19.4	19.6	18.0	22.5	16.9	22.7	15.8	27.1*	23.3	17.9
Bipolar I	3.0	3.9	2.0	6.1	3.6	3.0	4.0	2.1	4.7	2.8
Schizophrenia	1.0	0.0	1.0	0.0	1.2	0.0	0.0	2.1	0.0	0.9
Antisocial	34.7	35.3	40.0	24.5*	33.7	36.4	34.7	35.4	39.5	33.0

* $p<.05$ as analyzed by χ^2.

TABLE 5. *Lifetime prevalence of psychiatric diagnoses by history of other diagnoses in cocaine abusers (in percents)*

Concurrent diagnosis	Cocaine abusers with history of diagnosis					
	Total sample	Major depression	Alcoholism	Antisocial personality	Any anxiety	Bipolar
(N)	(149)	(47)	(95)	(52)	(29)	(5)
Major depression	31.5	—	37.9*	42.3*	58.6**	100.00**
Alcoholism	63.8	76.6*	—	71.2	65.5	80.0
Antisocial	34.9	46.8*	39.0	—	44.8	20.0
Any anxiety	19.5	36.2**	20.0	25.0	—	60.0*
Bipolar	3.4	10.6**	4.2	1.9	10.3*	—

* $p<.05$.
** $p<.001$.

DISCUSSION

Overall Rates of Disorders

The results of the current study now add to a growing body of findings suggesting that psychiatric disorders are more commonly diagnosed in treatment-seeking drug abusers than in the general community. In common with other studies of cocaine abusers (Gawin and Kleber 1985, 1986; Weiss et al. 1986) and with studies of opioid addicts (Rounsaville et al. 1982*b*; Khantzian and Treece 1985) and alcoholics (Hesselbrock et al. 1985; Powell et al. 1982; Schuckit 1985*a*), the particular diagnostic categories in which high lifetime rates were diagnosed were major depression, antisocial personality, and alcoholism. Moreover, also in common with these other studies, treatment-seeking cocaine abusers did not have excessive rates of mania or schizophrenia when compared with community samples.

While opioid addicts, alcoholics, and cocaine abusers appear to share the same pattern of disorders that exceed community rates, cocaine abusers in this and other samples appear to differ substantially from opioid addicts by having lower rates of major depression and higher rates of alcoholism. The current study is consistent with other samples in suggesting that, in contrast to opioid addicts, depressive disorders are not a substantial feature of the clinical picture in the majority of cocaine abusers. This may reflect (a) differences in the characteristics of those who become opioid addicts (Blatt et al. 1984*a*, 1984*b*), with affective disordered patients wishing to self-treat with more soothing, narcotizing agents, (b) differences in the affective symptoms induced by chronic use of opioids versus cocaine, or (c) differences in the diagnostic criteria by which cocaine abusers, but not opioid addicts, are required to have depressive symptoms extend 10 days beyond last drug use. We are clinically impressed with the first possibility, as cocaine abusers as a group have been less likely to discuss depressive moods in psychotherapeutic treatment settings (Rounsaville et al. 1985*b*). For the second, heroin seems less likely than cocaine to induce dysphoria, given the frequency of depressive symptoms seen during the postcocaine "crash" (Gawin and Ellinwood 1988). The final possibility—that differences in rates are due to diagnostic decision rules—has real merit, but detailed exploration of this issue is beyond the scope of this preliminary report.

The finding that rates of alcoholism are almost twice as high in cocaine abusers as in heroin abusers is striking. However, only 14.1 percent of the cocaine abusers were alcoholic before abusing cocaine, while 22.6 percent of the opioid addicts were alcoholic before abusing opioids.

Combined with clinical observations that many cocaine abusers use alcohol or other sedating drugs to reduce anxiety symptoms induced by excessive cocaine use (Gawin and Ellinwood 1988), it appears that much of the alcoholism in cocaine abusers is directly attributable and linked to binge cocaine use, while most of the alcoholism in opioid addicts preceded their use of opioids.

Demographic Treatment-Seeking Correlates of Psychiatric Disorders

We expected rates of coexistent psychiatric disorders to be generally higher in the inpatient setting, with an underlying pattern of those with more severe and complex problems requiring more intensive treatment. This pattern, in fact, did not hold; rates of disorders were largely comparable in the inpatient and outpatient settings, with a trend toward higher rates among outpatients and significantly higher rates of alcoholism in outpatients. This finding suggests that choice of inpatient versus outpatient treatment depends on factors other than coexistent disorders, such as severity of cocaine abuse or ability to afford inpatient treatment.

We anticipated that, as with opioid addicts and alcoholics, demographic correlates of psychiatric disorders would follow the patterns noted in community samples (e.g., ECA, New Haven community survey) with, for example, female excess of major depression and male excess of alcoholism and antisocial personality. This was largely upheld, with two exceptions: male and female cocaine abusers reported comparable rates of major depression, and white cocaine abusers reported higher rates of alcoholism than nonwhites. The lack of sex differences in rates of depression suggests that either cocaine-abusing males are differentially at risk in comparison to the females or that the females are differentially protected from depression compared with the males. This finding will be explored in greater detail in the full sample. The higher rates of alcoholism among the white cocaine abusers most likely relate to ethnic differences in choice of class of sedative drug used to reduce cocaine-induced anxiety. For whites, the sedative of choice appears to be alcohol, with almost three-fourths meeting RDC criteria for alcoholism. For blacks, the lower rates of alcoholism may be accounted for by differentially higher rates of cocaine-related sedative/hypnotic or heroin abuse.

Multiple Diagnoses in Cocaine Abusers

In common with findings of Boyd et al. (1984) using ECA data and our previous findings with opioid addicts, we found that among cocaine abusers, having any given psychiatric disorder tended to increase the likelihood of having any other disorder. In cocaine abusers, this was most striking with major depression, which was significantly associated with all other major classes of disorders. This pattern may be part of a general tendency for mood disturbances to be relatively lower on a hierarchy of psychiatric symptoms than other classes, such as obsessional rituals or psychotic symptoms (Stuart 1981). From a clinical standpoint, this association is important because major depression is among the most treatable of psychiatric disorders, with the majority of patients responding to psychotheraphy or pharmacotherapy after a comparatively brief course of treatment (Weissman et al. 1987). In addition, the presence of a depressive syndrome may motivate people to engage in treatment to relieve dysphoric symptoms. The association between antisocial personality and major depression is particularly noteworthy. It contradicts the classic picture of antisocial personality as having a high degree of defensiveness and relative invulnerability to depression. Moreover, Woody and associates (1985) have shown that, while antisocial opioid addicts have a generally poor prognosis in treatment, those with antisocial personality in combination with major depression have a comparatively good prognosis if given professional psychotherapy. In our study, this would comprise 42 percent of the cocaine abusers who met diagnostic criteria for antisocial personality (i.e., approximately one-sixth of the total clinic population).

Comparison to Other Reports in This Volume

The comparatively high rates of psychiatric disorders in treatment-seeking cocaine abusers may seem to contrast somewhat with the findings reported by Anthony and Petronis and by Ritter and Anthony in this volume. To place the differences in context, it is important to note the major differences in (a) the sample being studied, (b) the timeframe of the diagnoses, and (c) the definition of cocaine use/abuse. In the current study, treatment-seeking individuals who had relatively severe syndromes of cocaine dependence were evaluated for rates of disorders that they might have developed over the course of their entire adult lives. Anthony and Petronis attempted to determine from a community sample whether cocaine use was associated with the onset of depression or anxiety syndromes during a comparatively brief period between the first and second wave interviews of the ECA studies. Hence, while both studies support the generalization that cocaine use or abuse is associated with disturbance in mood and/or level of anxiety, the absolute rates are very different, with the community rates being substantially lower than those seen in a treatment-seeking sample of chronic cocaine abusers.

Treatment Implications

A major advantage of using a syndrome approach to diagnosing psychopathology is that the disorders so described are generally thought to be at a clinically significant level of severity and to be associated with standard treatment regimens. In the current study, the disorders diagnosed most frequently were major depression, alcoholism, and antisocial personality. If psychiatric diagnosis were to become a routine part of clinical assessment of treatment-seeking cocaine abusers, what implications might arise from detecting these disorders?

Major depression was seen in nearly one-third of our sample, although current rates of major depression were only 4 percent. This low current rate of depression was most likely related to our exclusion of this diagnosis in cocaine abusers who had not had at least 10 days of abstinence from cocaine. As noted above, major depression in non-drug-abusing populations is highly treatable (Weissman et al. 1987). In opioid addicts, major depression is associated with a poorer prognosis (Rounsaville et al. 1982*c*, 1986), and several studies have suggested that depression in opioid addicts responds well to treatment with tricyclic antidepressants (Rounsaville et al. 1985*b*). For cocaine abusers, depressive symptoms appear to be nearly universal in the early phases of abstinence.

Our research group has conducted a series of clinical studies evaluating a tricyclic antidepressant, desipramine, as treatment for ambulatory cocaine abusers with or without a current or lifetime diagnosis of major depression. In this mixed group, open and double-blind trials have suggested the superiority of desipramine over placebo and comparison pharmacotherapies in reducing relapse to cocaine use and cocaine craving, with no differential effectiveness in those who have a past or current depressive disorder. Hence, from a clinical perspective, the dysphoric effects of cocaine use and its early withdrawal may be so pronounced that they override previous individual differences in vulnerability to depression. Thus, use of an antidepressant pharmacotherapy may be indicated even in those cocaine abusers who do not meet diagnostic criteria for major depression. The significance of this coexistent diagnosis in cocaine abusers may be more related to the initiation of cocaine use in this group (Deykin et al. 1987) or to the long-term prognosis following the first 6–8 weeks of abstinence. We will attempt to evaluate this issue in a 1-year followup that is included in the current study.

Alcoholism was by far the most commonly diagnosed disorder, occurring in nearly one-fourth of our sample. This implies that clinicians should be particularly alert to the presence of alcoholism in treatment-seeking cocaine abusers because, while cocaine's withdrawal syndrome does not require any special pharmacological intervention, the alcohol withdrawal syndrome is a medically significant event requiring pharmacologically assisted monitoring to prevent the onset of seizures and/or delirium tremens.

We have hypothesized that most of the alcoholism seen in cocaine abusers is directly attributable to their need to manage anxiety symptoms associated with cocaine binges. Notably, only 12 percent of the sample had alcoholism preceding cocaine abuse. If this is true, then after managing initial withdrawal from alcohol, many cocaine abusers may not require special treatment aimed at their alcoholism as long as their cocaine use is curtailed. However, our cross-sectional findings cannot rule out the possibility that alcoholism initially induced by excessive cocaine use may endure after cocaine use is curtailed. Again, this issue is best addressed in a longitudinal design and will be assessed in a 1-year followup study of the current sample.

Drug abusers with antisocial personality require more clinical attention and ingenuity. While Woody et al. (1985) have shown that antisocial opioid addicts with major depression had a comparatively favorable outcome with psychotherapy and methadone maintenance, antisocial addicts without depression had a poor prognosis. In the current sample of cocaine abusers, 42 percent of those with antisocial personality also met criteria for major depression. However, that leaves a majority who did not.

Followup studies of alcoholics (Rounsaville et al. 1987; Schuckit 1985*a*) and heroin addicts (Rounsaville et al. 1986) concur in suggesting that antisocial substance abusers have a poorer prognosis. However, no treatments have been demonstrated to be effective for antisocial personality with or without concurrent substance abuse. Structured, limit-setting approaches such as those practiced in therapeutic communities are designed to counter antisocial tendencies of drug abusers, and graduates of these programs have been shown to display more socially acceptable personality traits (DeLeon 1984; DeLeon and Jainchill 1981). However, lengthy residential treatment is not a feasible choice for the majority of antisocial drug abusers, and even this alternative has never been evaluated for efficacy using an experimental design. Ambulatory treatment approaches for this large group of substance abusers are urgently needed.

Directions for Future Research

Given the clinical nature of this work, the next logical step is to evaluate the treatment implications of the high rates of psychiatric disorders in cocaine abusers by evaluating their prognostic significance and assessing the efficacy of treatment approaches aimed at diagnostic subgroups.

A second general research direction involves an attempt to understand the relationship between psychiatric disorders and cocaine abuse. Meyer (1986) has described six paradigmatic mechanisms whereby psychiatric disorders and substance use disorders might be noted in the same individual. One productive approach has been to evaluate whether disorders often seen together are conjointly or independently transmitted in families (Weissman et al. 1986). This strategy has been more widely used with psychiatric disorders such as antisocial personality and hysteria (Cloninger et al. 1975, 1978). However, recent studies have addressed psychopathology and substance use disorders, most notably depression with alcoholism (Merikangas et al. 1985; Schuckit 1986).

A second approach to evaluation of the relationship of drug abuse and psychopathology would be to assess the natural development of these two disorders by following a cohort of individuals throughout the periods of risk. However, given the comparatively low population prevalence of individual substance use disorders and of individual psychiatric disorders, very large samples would be needed. A more feasible design involves longitudinal study of individuals who are at high risk for developing substance use disorders, such as the children of substance-abusing parents. While this approach has been used to study alcoholism (Schuckit 1985*b*), it has not been applied to abuse of other classes of substances. We are currently designing a project to evaluate children of opioid abusers and of cocaine abusers, who will be contrasted with children of alcoholics and of normals in order to assess the specificity of vulnerability to abuse of different substances and the relationship between the onset of psychopathology and substance use disorders in these different cohorts.

REFERENCES

Abelson, H.I., and Miller, J.D. A decade of trends in cocaine use in the household population. In: Adams, E.H., and Kozel, N.J., eds. *Cocaine Use in America: Epidemiologic and Clinical Perspectives.* NIDA Research Monograph No. 61. Washington, DC: Supt. of Docs., U.S. Govt. Print. Off., 1985. pp. 35–49.

American Psychiatric Association. *Diagnostic and Statistical Manual, Third Edition (DSM–III).* Washington, DC: American Psychiatric Association Press, 1980.

American Psychiatric Association. *Diagnostic and Statistical Manual, Third Edition, Revised (DSM–III–R)*. Washington, DC: American Psychiatric Association Press, 1987.

Babor, T.F.; Cooney, N.L.; Hubbard, R.; Jaffe, J.H.; Kosten, T.R.; Lauerman, R.J.; McLellan, A.T.; Rankin, H.; Rounsaville, B.J.; and Skinner, H.A. The syndrome concept of alcohol and drug dependence: Results of the secondary analysis project. In: Harris, L., ed. *Problems of Drug Dependence: 1987*. NIDA Research Monograph, in press.

Beck, A.T.; Ward, C.H.; Mendelson, M.; Mock, J.E.; and Ergaugh, J.K. Reliability of psychiatric diagnosis: A study of consistency in clinical judgments and ratings. *American Journal of Psychiatry* 119:351, 1962.

Berkson, J. Limitations on the application of the four-fold table analysis to hospital data. *Biometrics* 2:47–53, 1946.

Blatt, S.; Berman, W.; Bloom-Feshbach, S.; Sugarman, A.; Wilber, C.; and Kleber, H. Psychological assessment of psychopathology in opiate addicts. *Journal of Nervous and Mental Disorders* 172:156–165, 1984*a*.

Blatt, S.; Rounsaville, B.J.; Eyre, S.; and Wilber, C. The psychodynamics of opiate addiction. *Journal of Nervous and Mental Disorders* 172:342–352, 1984*b*.

Boyd, J.H.; Burke, J.D.; Gruenberg, E.; Holzer, C.E.; Rae, D.S.; George, L.K.; Karno, M.; Stoltzman, R.; McEvoy, M.A.; and Nestadt, G. Exclusion criteria of DSM-III: A study of co-occurrence of hierarchy-free syndromes. *Archives of General Psychiatry* 41:983–989, 1984.

Cloninger, C.R.; Reich, T.; and Guze, S.B. The multifactorial model of disease transmission. III: The familial relationship between sociopathy and hysteria (Briquet's syndrome). *British Journal of Psychiatry* 127:23–32, 1975.

Cloninger, C.R.; Christiansen, K.O.; Reich, T.; and Gottesman, I.I. Implications of sex differences in the prevalence of antisocial personality, alcoholism, and criminality for models of familial transmission. *Archives of General Psychiatry* 35:941–951, 1978.

DeLeon, G., and Jainchill, N. Male and female drug abusers: Social and psychological status 2 years after treatment in a therapeutic community. *American Journal of Drug and Alcohol Abuse* 4:382, 1981.

DeLeon, G. *The Therapeutic Community: Study of Effectiveness*. Treatment Research Monograph Series. Washington, DC: National Institute on Drug Abuse, 1984.

Deykin, E.; Levy, J.; and Wells, V. Adolescent depression, alcohol and drug abuse. *American Journal of Public Health* 77:178–182, 1987.

Dole, V.P., and Nyswander, M.E. Addiction: A metabolic disease. *Archives of Internal Medicine* 120:19–24, 1967.

Edwards, G.; Arif, A.; and Hodgson, R. Nomenclature and classification of drug and alcohol related problems. *Bulletin of WHO* 59:225–242, 1981.

Endicott, J., and Spitzer, R.L. A diagnostic interview: The schedule for affective disorders and schizophrenia. *Archives of General Psychiatry* 37:837, 1978.

Feighner, J.P.; Robins, E.; and Guze, S.B. Diagnostic criteria for use in psychiatric research. *Archives of General Psychiatry* 26:57, 1972.

Foy, D.W.; Nunn, L.B.; and Rychtarik, R.G. Broad-spectrum behavioral treatment for chronic alcoholics: Effects of training controlled drinking skills. *Journal of Consulting and Clinical Psychology* 52:218–230, 1984.

Gawin, F.H., and Ellinwood, E.H. Cocaine and other stimulants. *New England Journal of Medicine* 318(18):1173–1182, 1988.

Gawin, F.H., and Kleber, H.D. Cocaine abuse in a treatment population: Patterns and diagnostic distractions. In: Adams, E.H., and Kozel, N.J., eds. *Cocaine*

Use in America: Epidemiologic and Clinical Perspectives. NIDA Research Monograph Series, Vol. 61. Washington, DC: Supt. of Docs., U.S. Govt. Print. Off., 1985. pp. 182–192.

Gawin, F.H., and Kleber, H.D. Abstinence symptomatology and psychiatric diagnosis in chronic cocaine abusers. *Archives of General Psychiatry* 43:107–113, 1986.

Hesselbrock, M.; Babor, T.F.; Hesselbrock, V.; et al. Never believe an alcoholic? On the validity of self-report measures of alcohol dependence and related constructs. *International Journal of Addictions* 18:593–609, 1983.

Hesselbrock, M.N.; Meyer, R.E.; and Keener, J.J. Psychopathology in hospitalized alcoholics. *Archives of General Psychiatry* 42:1050–1055, 1985.

Hodgson, R.J. Treatment strategies for the early problem drinker. In: Edwards, G., and Grant, M., eds. *Alcoholism Treatment in Transition*. Baltimore: University Park Press, 1980.

Jaffe, J.H., and Ciraulo, D.A. Alcoholism and depression. In: Meyer, R.E., ed. *Psychopathology and Addictive Disorders*. New York: Guilford Press, 1986. pp. 293–319.

Kandel, D.B. Stages in adolescent involvement in drug use. *Science* 190:912–914, 1975.

Kandel, D.B. Convergences in prospective longitudinal surveys of drug use in normal populations. In: Kandel, D.B., ed. *Longitudinal Research on Drug Use*. Washington, DC: Hemisphere, 1978. pp. 3–40.

Khantzian, E.J., and Treece, C. DSM-III diagnosis of narcotic addicts: Recent findings. *Archives of General Psychiatry* 42:1067–1071, 1985.

Kosten, T.R.; Gawin, F.; Rounsaville, B.J.; and Kleber, H.D. Cocaine abuse among opioid addicts: Demographic and diagnostic factors in treatment. *American Journal of Drug and Alcohol Abuse* 12:1–16, 1986.

Kosten, T.R.; Rounsaville, B.J.; and Kleber, H.D. A 2.5 year follow-up of cocaine use among treated opioid addicts: Have our treatments helped? *Archives of General Psychiatry* 44:281–284, 1987*a*.

Kosten, T.R.; Rounsaville, B.J.; Babor, T.; Spitzer, R.L.; and Williams, J.B.W. Substance use disorders in DSM–III–R: Evidence for the drug dependence syndrome across different abused substances. *British Journal of Psychiatry* 151:834–843, 1987*b*.

Kranzler, H.R., and Liebowitz, N. Depression and anxiety in substance abuse: Clinical implications. In: Frazier, S., ed. *Depression and Anxiety*. New York: Medical Clinics of North America, 1988.

McLellan, A.T.; O'Brien, C.P.; Luborsky, L.; and Woody, G.E. Are the "addiction-related" problems of substance abusers really related? *Journal of Nervous and Mental Disorders* 169:232–239, 1981.

McLellan, A.T.; Luborsky, L.; Woody, G.E.; et al. Predicting response to alcohol and drug abuse treatments: Role of psychiatric severity. *Archives of General Psychiatry* 40:620–625, 1983.

Merikangas, K.R.; Weissman, M.M.; Prusoff, B.A.; Pauls, D.L.; and Leckman, J.F. Depressives with secondary alcoholism: Psychiatric disorders in offspring. *Journal of Studies on Alcoholism* 46:194–204, 1985.

Meyer, R.E. How to understand the relationship between psychopathology and addictive disorders: Another example of the chicken and the egg. In: Meyer, R.E., ed. *Psychopathology and Addictive Disorders*. New York: Guilford Press, 1986. pp. 3–16.

Myers, J.K.; Weissman, M.M.; Tischler, G.L., et al. Six-month prevalence of psychiatric disorders in three communities. *Archives of General Psychiatry* 41:959–967, 1984.

National Institute on Drug Abuse. *Cocaine Client Admissions 1976–1985*. Pub. No. DHHS (ADM)87–1528. Washington, DC: Supt. of Docs., U.S. Govt. Print. Off., 1987.

National Institute on Drug Abuse. *Decade of Dawn: Cocaine Related Cases, 1976–1985*, by Colliver, J.A. Washington, DC: Supt. of Docs., U.S. Govt. Print. Off., 1987.

O'Donnell, J.A.; Voss, H.L.; Clayton, R.R.; Slatin, G.T.; and Room, R.G.W. *Young Men and Drugs: A Nationwide Survey*. NIDA Research Monograph No. 5. Washington, DC: Supt. of Docs., U.S. Govt. Print. Off., 1976.

Orford, J.; Oppenheimer, E.; and Edwards, G. Abstinence or control: The outcome for excessive drinkers two years after the consultation. *Behavioral Research and Therapy* 14:409–418, 1976.

Penick, E.C.; Powell, B.J.; Othmer, E.; Bingham, S.F.; Rice, A.S.; and Liese, B.S. Subtyping alcoholics by co-existing psychiatric syndromes: Course, family history, outcome. In: Goodwin, D.W.; Van Dusen, R.T.; and Mendick, S.A., eds. *Longitudinal Research in Alcoholism*. Hingham, MA: Kluwer-Nijhoff, 1984.

Powell, B.J.; Penick, E.C.; Othmer, E.; Bingham, S.F.; and Rice, A.S. Prevalence of additional psychiatric syndromes among male alcoholics. *Journal of Clinical Psychiatry* 43:404–407, 1982.

Robins, L.N. The interaction of setting and predisposition in explaining novel behavior: Drug initiations before, in and after Vietnam. In: Kandel, D.B., ed. *Longitudinal Research on Drug Use*. Washington, DC: Hemisphere, 1978.

Robins, L.N. Addicts careers. In: Dupont, R.I.; Goldstein, A.; and O'Donnell, J., eds. *Handbook on Drug Abuse*. Rockville, MD: National Institute on Drug Abuse, 1980. pp. 325–336.

Robins, L.N.; Murphy, G.E.; and Breckenridge, M.B. Drinking behavior of young Negro men. *Quarterly Journal on Studies of Alcohol* 29:657–684, 1968.

Robins, L.N.; Davis, D.H.; and Nurco, D.N. How permanent was Vietnam drug addiction? *American Journal of Public Health* 64(suppl):38–43, 1974.

Robins, L.N.; Helzer, J.E.; Croughan, J.; Williams, J.B.W.; and Spitzer, R.L. *NIMH Diagnostic Interview Schedule*, Version III. St. Louis: Washington University School of Medicine, 1981*a*.

Robins, L.N.; Helzer, J.E.; Croughan, J.; and Ratcliff, K.S. National Institute of Mental Health Diagnostic Interview Schedule: Its history, characteristics, and validity. *Archives of General Psychiatry* 39:381–389, 1981*b*.

Robins, L.N.; Helzer, J.E.; Weissman, M.M.; Orvaschel, H.; Gruenberg, E.; Burke, J.D.; and Regier, D.A. Prevalence of specific psychiatric disorders in three states. *Archives of General Psychiatry* 41:949–958, 1984.

Rounsaville, B.J. Clinical assessment of drug abusers. In: Karasu, T.B., ed. *Treatments of Psychiatric Disorders*. Washington, DC: American Psychiatric Association Press, 11:1183–1191, 1989.

Rounsaville, B.J., and Kleber, H.D. Untreated opiate addicts: How do they differ from those seeking treatment? *Archives of General Psychiatry* 42:1072–1077, 1985*a*.

Rounsaville, B.J., and Kleber, H.D. Psychotheraphy/counseling for opiate addicts: Strategies for use in different treatment settings. *International Journal of Addictions* 20(6&7):869–896, 1985*b*.

Rounsaville, B.J.; Tierney, T.; Crits-Christoph, K.; Weissman, M.M.: and Kleber, H.D. Predictors of treatment outcome in opiate addicts: Evidence for the multidimensionality of addicts' problems. *Comprehensive Psychiatry* 23:462–478, 1982*a*.

Rounsaville, B.J.; Weissman, M.M.; Kleber, H.D.; and Wilber, C.H. Heterogeneity of psychiatric diagnosis in treated opiate addicts. *Archives of General Psychiatry* 39:161–166, 1982*b*.

Rounsaville, B.J.; Weissman, M.M.; Wilber, C.H.; Crits-Christoph, K.; and Kleber, H.D. Diagnosis and symptoms of depression in opiate addicts: Course and relationship to treatment outcome. *Archives of General Psychiatry* 39:151–156, 1982*c*.

Rounsaville, B.J.; Gawin, F.H.; and Kleber, H.D. Interpersonal Psychotheraphy (IPT) adapted for ambulatory cocaine abusers. *American Journal of Drug and Alcohol Abuse* 11:171–191, 1985*a*.

Rounsaville, B.J.; Kosten, T.R.; Weissman, M.M.; and Kleber, H.D. *Evaluating and Treating Depressive Disorders in Opiate Addicts*. Treatment Research Monograph. Rockville, MD: National Institute on Drug Abuse, 1985*b*.

Rounsaville, B.J.; Kosten, T.R.; Weissman, M.M.; and Kleber, H.D. Prognostic significance of psychiatric disorders in treated opiate addicts. *Archives of General Psychiatry* 43:739–745, 1986.

Rounsaville, B.J.; Dolinsky, Z.S.; Babor, T.F.; and Meyer, R. Psychopathology as a predictor of treatment outcomes in alcoholics. *Archives of General Psychiatry* 44:505–513, 1987.

Schuckit, M.A. The clinical implications of primary diagnostic groups among alcoholics. *Archives of General Psychiatry* 42:1043–1049, 1985*a*.

Schuckit, M.A. Studies of populations at high risk for alcoholism. *Psychiatric Development* 3:31–64, 1985*b*.

Schuckit, M.A. Genetic and clinical implications of alcoholism and affective disorder. *American Journal of Psychiatry* 143:140–147, 1986.

Skinner, H.A., and Goldberg, A.E. Evidence for a drug dependence syndrome among narcotic users. *British Journal of the Addictions* 81:479–484, 1986.

Spitzer, R.L., and Fleiss, J.L. A re-analysis of the reliability of psychiatric diagnosis. *British Journal of Psychiatry* 125:341, 1974.

Spitzer, R.L., and Williams, J.B.W. *Structured Clinical Interview for DSM–III—Patient Version (SCID–P)*. New York: New York State Psychiatric Institute, May 1985.

Spitzer, R.L.; Endicott, J.; and Robins, E. Research Diagnostic Criteria: Rationale and reliability. *Archives of General Psychiatry* 35:773–782, 1978.

Stuart, E. Hierarchical patterns in the distribution of psychiatric symptoms. *Psychological Medicine* 11:783–794, 1981.

Weiss, R.D.; Mirin, S.M.; Michael, J.L.; and Sollogub, A.C. Psychopathology in chronic cocaine abusers. *American Journal of Drug and Alcohol Abuse* 12:17–29, 1986.

Weissman, M.M.; Merikangas, K.R.; Joh, K.; Wickramarantne, P.; Prusoff, B.A.; and Kidd, K.K. Family-genetic studies of psychiatric disorders: Developing technologies. *Archives of General Psychiatry* 43:1104–1116, 1986.

Weissman, M.M.; Jarrett, R.B.; and Rush, J.A. Psychotherapy and its relevance to the pharmacotherapy of depression: A decade later (1976–1985). In: Meltzer, H.Y., ed. *Psychopharmacology: A Third Generation of Progress*. New York: Raven Press, 1987. pp. 1059–1069.

Woodruff, R.A.; Guze, S.B.; and Clayton, P.J. Alcoholics who see a psychiatrist compared with those who do not. *Quarterly Journal on Studies of Alcohol* 34:1162–1171, 1973.

Woody, G.E.; McLellan, A.T.; Luborsky, L.; and O'Brien, C.P. Sociopathy and psychotherapy outcome. *Archives of General Psychiatry* 42:1081–1086, 1985.

ACKNOWLEDGMENTS

Support for this work was provided by grants from the National Institute on Drug Abuse including Center Grant #P50–DA04060, R01–DA04299, R01–DA04029, and Research Career Development Awards DA00089 to BJR.

AUTHORS

Bruce J. Rounsaville, M.D.
Kathleen Carroll, Ph.D.

Department of Psychiatry
Yale University
School of Medicine
27 Sylvan Avenue
New Haven, CT 06519

Risk of Cocaine Abuse and Dependence

Edgar H. Adams and Joseph Gfroerer

Since 1974, the prevalence of cocaine use in the United States has increased fourfold, and consequences associated with cocaine use have increased more than 1,000 percent. In 1987, more than 45,000 cases associated with cocaine use were reported to the Drug Abuse Warning Network (DAWN).

While the increase in the prevalence and consequences of cocaine use have been well documented (Kozel et al. 1982; Adams and Durell 1984; Adams et al. 1986), questions persist about the number of dependent persons ("addicts"), the number of cocaine abusers, and the problems reported by cocaine users. Although cocaine has been called one of the most reinforcing of all drugs, the Diagnostic and Statistical Manual of Mental Disorders (DSM–III) (APA 1980) does not have a classification for cocaine dependence. The criteria for dependence require that a drug produce tolerance or withdrawal; cocaine was thought to produce only transitory withdrawal symptoms after cessation or reduction of cocaine use. Also, tolerance was absent. In fact, some studies have produced evidence suggesting that sensitization rather than tolerance might occur (Post 1977).

DSM–III does provide a classification of amphetamine dependence. Cocaine and amphetamine intoxication produce similar clinical pictures, distinguishable only by the presence of cocaine metabolites in the urine or cocaine in plasma (DSM–III). These similarities have been noted in animal studies, controlled human studies, and epidemiologic studies (Kramer et al. 1967; Deneau et al. 1969; Johanson et al. 1976; Fischman and Schuster 1980; Johanson and Uhlenhuth 1980).

Although various studies have provided evidence for either sensitization or tolerance, Wolverton et al. (1978) demonstrated that rats became tolerant to cocaine and d-amphetamines as measured by decreases in milk intake. Cross-tolerance between the two drugs was also demonstrated (Wolverton et al. 1978).

Studies by Fischman and Schuster in human volunteers suggest that acute tolerance to the subjective effects of cocaine may occur (Fischman and Schuster 1980, 1982; Fischman et al. 1985). Acute tolerance has also been demonstrated for the cardiovascular effects of cocaine (Fischman and Schuster 1980; Fischman et al. 1985).

Tolerance or decreased sensitivity to the euphoric effects of cocaine during binges has been reported by Gawin and Kleber (1986). The subjects in this study were unable to reach the same levels of euphoria achieved on the first doses regardless of the size of the dose employed. Studies of amphetamines also suggest that chronic administration produces tolerance to the euphoric effects (Gunne 1977).

Data on the proportion of the cocaine-using population reporting specific cocaine-associated problems were obtained as part of the Epidemiology Catchment Area (ECA) project (Anthony et al. 1986). In this study, the symptom most often reported by those who had used cocaine six or more times was perceived tolerance. Also, Gawin and Kleber (1986) described a withdrawal syndrome associated with cocaine abuse.

Because of the similarities between the effects of cocaine and amphetamine, the evidence for tolerance associated with cocaine, and the description of the withdrawal syndrome in humans, self-reports of either tolerance or withdrawal in the 1985 National Household Survey on Drug Abuse (NHSDA) were used to estimate cocaine dependence.

METHOD

Data for this study were obtained from preliminary files of the 1985 NHSDA. It was the largest of the national surveys conducted, with completed interviews from 8,038 respondents. Among the changes in the 1985 survey was the inclusion of questions on drug problems and also self-reported dependence measures.

Since more than 90 percent of past-year cocaine users are over the age of 18 and the factors to be studied, such as marital status, are more appropriate to the adult population, the study was restricted to adults 18–54. The analysis was based on 435 adults who had used cocaine during the year prior to interview.

The questions on dependency in the NHSDA were essentially a subset of the Diagnostic Interview Schedule (DIS) (Robins et al. 1981). The algorithm used in the DIS to estimate abuse or dependence was as follows:

Abuse = Yes on "Tried to cut down" or health problems or emotional, psychological problems plus a Yes on social problems

Dependence = Yes on tolerance or withdrawal

While the NHSDA and the DIS used the same questions necessary to meet the dependence criteria, they differed in the way they collected the data necessary to meet the criteria for abuse; thus, the primary analysis in this study was based on dependence. The NHSDA questions measured the respondents' perception that they might be using too much cocaine and therefore need to cut down, while the DIS measured failed attempts to cut down. As might be expected, there was a substantial difference between these proportions (20.7 percent in the NHSDA versus 4.2 percent in the ECA). It should be noted that the criteria for abuse required the presence of social problems plus one or more additional problems, one of which was "tried to cut down."

The independent variables were selected from the NHSDA based upon previous research and a review of the distribution of each of the proposed variables. The variables used in the regression analysis on cocaine dependence included age, race/ethnicity, education, income, marital status, number of moves in the past 5 years, frequency of cocaine use in the past year, route of administration, number of times cocaine used in lifetime, and years of cocaine use. Odds ratios, an estimate of the relative risk, were computed by logistic regression using the LOGIST procedure in SAS (Harrell 1983).

RESULTS

Approximately 17 percent of the past-year cocaine users reported one or more problems associated with their cocaine use. The problems reported most often—feeling nervous and anxious, feeling irritable and upset, skipping four or more meals, becoming depressed—are often associated with cocaine use (table 1). In contrast, driving unsafely was often attributed to alcohol. The response categories were grouped to match the DIS algorithm for abuse.

The distribution of self-reported dependency measures indicated that trying to cut down and needing larger amounts to get the same effect (tolerance) were reported more than other problems (table 2). Withdrawal symptoms were reported by 4 percent of the population.

Of the 435 past-year cocaine users, 43 males and 21 females, for a total of 64, met the criteria for cocaine dependence. The application of

TABLE 1. *Distribution of reported problems among past-year cocaine users aged 18–54*

Problem	Percent
Became depressed or lost interest in things	1.1
Felt completely alone and isolated	1.8
Had trouble at school or on the job	0.5
Drove unsafely	2.6
At times, I could not remember what happened to me	1.1
Felt completely alone and isolated	1.8
Felt very nervous and anxious	10.4
Had health problems	1.6
Found it difficult to think clearly	2.2
Had serious money problems	3.3
Felt irritable and upset	6.2
Got less work done than usual at school or on the job	1.3
Felt suspicious and distrustful of people	1.8
Had trouble with the police	0.7
Skipped four or more regular meals in a row	5.4
Found it harder to handle my problems	2.2
Had to get emergency medical help	0.5

Source: 1985 National Household Survey on Drug Abuse.
n = 435.

TABLE 2. *Distribution of dependency measures among past-year cocaine users aged 18–54*

Measure	Percent
Tried to cut down	20.7
Needed larger amounts	13.0
Used daily 2 or more weeks	11.3
Felt dependent	6.4
Withdrawal symptoms	4.4

Source: 1985 National Household Survey on Drug Abuse.
n = 435.

sampling weights resulted in the following estimate. Almost 9,760,000 of the U.S. household population used cocaine at least once in the past year, and more than 1.6 million met the criteria for DSM–III diagnosis of either abuse, dependence, or combined abuse and dependence. The majority, approximately 1,360,000, met the criteria for cocaine dependence (table 3).

The results of the logistic regression for males indicated that only four variables had odds ratios where the lower limit of the confidence interval was greater than one. Two lifestyle variables were associated with an elevated risk of dependence. Being single, that is, never married or divorced/separated, and having moved two or more times in the past 5 years had odds ratios of 3.3 and 2.87, respectively. However, the strongest associations were found in the cocaine use variables of "cocaine use 12 or more times in the past year" and "50 or more times in a lifetime." No association between dependency and route of administration appeared in this model. This may be because the intravenous and smoking routes of administration are most often associated with the compulsive or frequent use of cocaine and a contribution was already accounted for by the frequency of use variable (table 4).

TABLE 3. *Distribution of cocaine abuse, dependence, and abuse and dependence among male and female past-year cocaine users aged 18–54*

Sex	None	Abuse	Dependency	Abuse and dependency
Male				
Population estimate in 1,000s	5,103	110	737	230
%	82.54	1.79	11.95	3.72
Female				
Population estimate in 1,000s	3,017	168	280	112
%	84.34	4.69	7.84	3.13
Total				
Population estimate in 1,000s	8,120	278	1,019	342
%	83.2	2.85	10.44	3.51

Source: 1985 National Household Survey on Drug Abuse.
n = 435.

TABLE 4. *Results of logistic regression on cocaine dependence among male past-year cocaine users aged 18–54*

Independent variable	Odds ratio	95% CI
Age (vs. 35–54 years)		
18–20	5.04	0.43–58.36
21–25	2.61	0.35–19.67
26–34	5.41	0.86–34.06
At least some college vs. no college	0.76	0.28–2.06
Income ≥$20,000 vs. <$20,000	1.86	0.60–4.93
Single vs. married or living as married	3.3	1.02–10.57
Black vs. white	0.55	0.09–3.43
Hispanic vs. white	3.54	0.58–21.32
Relocated ≥2 times vs. <2 times	2.87	1.05–7.85
Cocaine frequency ≥12 times 1 year vs. <12 times	3.43	1.40–8.41
Cocaine IV vs. not IV	2.44	0.67–8.8
Cocaine freebase vs. not freebase	1.30	0.49–3.46
Cocaine ≥50 times in lifetime vs. <50 times in lifetime	7.24	2.44–21.54
Cocaine used ≥5 years vs. <5 years	1.71	0.46–6.32

Source: 1985 National Household Survey on Drug Abuse.

Among females, only the odds ratios associated with cocaine use had confidence intervals with the lower range above 1. In this model, intravenous use of cocaine was strongly associated with cocaine dependence, as was the use of cocaine for 5 or more years (table 5).

DISCUSSION

Cocaine is known as one of the most reinforcing, if not *the* most reinforcing drug. Yet, among past-year cocaine users, only 17 percent reported any problems related to cocaine, and only 29 percent reported at least one item from the dependency scale. A number of factors may explain this. One is that among past-year cocaine users, only 47 percent used cocaine six or more times in the past year. Another is that those who are self-medicating may not associate their problems with cocaine use since they may view their use in a positive light. Smart et al. (1984) noted that about a quarter of the users in their sample said cocaine had a positive

TABLE 5. *Results of logistic regression on cocaine dependence among female past-year cocaine users aged 18–54*

Independent variable	Odds ratio	95% CI
Age (vs. 35–54 years)		
18–20	0.15	0.006–3.96
21–25	0.38	0.05–2.81
26–34	0.09	0.009–0.84
At least some college vs. no college	4.31	0.82–22.65
Income ≥$20,000 vs. <$20,000	1.51	0.35–6.55
Single vs. married or living as married	1.40	0.33–6.05
Black vs. white	5.53	0.75–40.85
Hispanic vs. white	0.83	0.25–2.77
Relocated ≥2 time vs. <2 times	2.08	0.52–8.25
Cocaine frequency ≥12 times 1 year vs. <12 times	3.10	0.51–19.0
Cocaine IV vs. not IV	18.80	1.91–185.12
Cocaine freebase vs. not freebase	0.16	0.02–1.12
Cocaine ≥50 times in lifetime vs. <50 times in lifetime	4.22	0.76–23.34
Cocaine used ≥5 years vs. <5 years	6.23	1.19–32.79

Source: 1985 National Household Survey on Drug Abuse.

impact on their lives, so it may take several years before the problems related to cocaine use become significant to the cocaine user. For example, the median waiting time from first use to entry into treatment is about 4 years (Adams and Kozel 1985). In this study, more than half of past-year cocaine users had used cocaine 4 years or less. Increases in the frequency of cocaine use have been found to occur over time (Chitwood 1985; O'Malley et al. 1985). Therefore, it is likely that cocaine-related problems can be expected to increase substantially if the cocaine use in this population persists.

Population estimates indicated that more than a million people met the criteria for dependency (self-reported tolerance or withdrawal). In males, the factors associated with dependence included being unmarried or divorced/separated and relocating two or more times in the past 5 years. Studies of treated populations have also reported a high proportion of divorced persons (Schnoll et al. 1985; Ives et al. 1987).

Older age, i.e., 26 to 34 years, appears to be protective in women. Although similar proportions of men and women (46 percent versus 44 percent) were in this age group, a smaller proportion of women were dependent (7.9 percent versus 21.6 percent). In this regard, women were likely to have used for a shorter period of time than men had. More than half of the men (52 percent) and only slightly more than one-third (36 percent) of the women had used cocaine 5 or more years. This implies that an increasing proportion of women may become cocaine dependent in the future if their cocaine use continues.

In clinical studies, dosage escalation and increased frequency of use are the most important determinants of abuse (Schnoll et al. 1985; Gawin and Kleber 1985). These studies also had a high proportion of intravenous users and freebase users. In our study, male freebase users were more likely to be diagnosed as dependent, but the odds ratio was not significant. This may be due to the fact that the intravenous and smoking routes are associated with increased frequency of use. Increased frequency of use, i.e., the use of cocaine 12 or more times in the past year, was associated with dependence even after controlling for freebasing and intravenous use.

Among females, an elevated risk of cocaine dependence was confined to the cocaine use variables, intravenous use, and use 5 or more years. A relatively high proportion of male and female intravenous and freebase users were dependent, but the small sample sizes affected the significance tests. Although Van Dyke and Byck (1982) suggested that intranasal use of cocaine was relatively safe compared to administration via intravenous and smoking routes, these data suggest that frequency of use and length of use are the important criteria regardless of the route of administration.

REFERENCES

Adams, E.H., and Kozel, N.J. Cocaine use in America: Introduction and overview. In: Kozel, N.J., and Adams, E.H., eds. *Cocaine Use in America: Epidemiologic and Clinical Perspectives*. NIDA Research Monograph 61. Washington, DC: Supt. of Docs., U.S. Govt. Print. Off., 1985.

Adams, E.H., and Durell, J. Cocaine: A growing public health problem. In: Grabowski, J., ed. *Cocaine: Pharmacology, Effects, and Treatment of Abuse*. National Institute on Drug Abuse Research Monograph 50. DHHS Pub. No. (ADM)84–1326. Washington, DC: Supt. of Docs., U.S. Govt. Print. Off., 1984. pp. 9–14.

Adams, E.H.; Gfroerer, J.D.; Rouse, B.A.; and Kozel, N.J. Trends in prevalence and consequences of cocaine use. *Cocaine, Pharmacology, Addiction and Therapy, Advances in Alcohol and Substance Abuse* 6(2):49–72, Winter 1986 [special issue].

American Psychiatric Association. *Diagnostic and Statistical Manual of Mental Disorders (DSM–III)*. Washington, DC: the Association, 1980.

Anthony, J.C.; Ritter, C.J.; Von Korff, M.R.; Chee, E.M.; and Kramer, M. Descriptive epidemiology of adult cocaine use in four U.S. communities. In: Harris, L.S., ed. *Problems of Drug Dependence, 1985*. National Institute on Drug Abuse Research Monograph 67. DHHS Pub. No. (ADM)86–1448. Washington, DC: Supt. of Docs., U.S. Govt. Print. Off., 1986. pp. 283–289.

Chitwood, D.D. Patterns and consequences of cocaine use. In: Kozel, N.J., and Adams, E.H., eds. *Cocaine Use in America: Epidemiologic and Clinical Perspectives*. National Institute on Drug Abuse Research Monograph 61. DHHS Pub. No. (ADM)85–1414. Washington, DC: Supt. of Docs., U.S. Govt. Print. Off., 1985. pp. 111–129.

Deneau, G.; Yanagita, T.; and Seevers, M.H. Self-administration of psychoactive substances by the monkey. *Psychopharmacologia* (Berlin) 16:30–48, 1969.

Fischman, M.W., and Schuster, C.R. Experimental investigations of the actions of cocaine in humans. In: Jeri, F.R., ed. *Cocaine, 1980*. Lima, Peru: Pacific Press, 1980.

Fischman, M.W., and Schuster, C.R. Cocaine self-administration in humans. *Federal Proceedings* 41:241–246, 1982.

Fischman, M.W.; Schuster, C.R.; Javaid, J.; Hatano, Y.; and Davis, J. Acute tolerance development to the cardiovascular and subjective effects of cocaine. *Journal of Pharmacology and Experimental Therapeutics* 235(3):677–682, 1985.

Gawin, F.H., and Kleber, H.D. Cocaine use in a treatment population: Patterns and diagnostic distinctions. In: Kozel, N.J., and Adams, E.H., eds. *Cocaine Use in America: Epidemiologic and Clinical Perspectives*. National Institute on Drug Abuse Research Monograph 61. DHHS Pub. No. (ADM)85–1414. Washington, DC: Supt. of Docs., U.S. Govt. Print. Off., 1985. pp. 182–192.

Gawin, F.H., and Kleber, H.D. Abstinence symptomatology and psychiatric diagnosis in cocaine abusers: Clinical observations. *Archives of General Psychiatry* 43:107–113, 1986.

Gunne, I.M. Effects of amphetamines in humans. In: Martin, W.R., ed. *Drug Addiction II: Amphetamine, Psychotogen, and Marihuana Dependence*. Berlin: Springer-Verlag, 1977. pp. 247–276.

Harrell, F.E. The LOGIST procedure in SAS Institute, Inc. *SUGI Supplemental Library Users Guide,* 1983 Edition. Cary, NC: SAS Institute, 1983.

Ives, T.J.; Bentz, E.J.; and Gwyther, R.E. Drug-related admissions to a family medicine inpatient service. *Archives of Internal Medicine* 147(6):1117–1120, 1987.

Johanson, C.E.; Balster, R.L.; and Bonese, K. Self-administration of psychomotor stimulant drugs: The effects of unlimited access. *Pharmacology and Biochemical Behavior* 4:45–51, 1976.

Johanson, C.E., and Uhlenhuth, E.H. Drug preference and mood in humans: d-Amphetamine. *Psychopharmacology* 71:275–279, 1980.

Kozel, N.J.; Crider, R.A.; and Adams, E.H. National surveillance of cocaine use and related health consequences. *Morbidity and Mortality Weekly Report* 31:265–273, 1982.

Kramer, J.C.; Fischman, V.S.; and Littlefield, D.C. Amphetamine abuse: Patterns and effects of high doses taken intravenously. *JAMA* 201:305–309, 1967.

O'Malley, P.M.; Johnston, L.D.; and Bachman, J.G. Cocaine use among American adolescents and young adults. In: Kozel, N.J., and Adams, E.H., eds. *Cocaine Use in America: Epidemiologic and Clinical Perspectives*. National

Institute on Drug Abuse Research Monograph 61. DHHS Pub. No. (ADM)85–1414. Washington, DC: Supt. of Docs., U.S. Govt. Print. Off., 1985. pp. 50–75.

Post, R.M. Progressive changes in behavior and seizures following chronic cocaine administration: Relationship to kindling and psychosis. In: Ellinwood, E.H., and Kilbey, M.M., eds. *Cocaine and Other Stimulants*. (Vol. 21. *Advances in Behavioral Biology*. New York: Plenum Press, 1977. pp. 353–372.

Robins, L.N.; Helzer, J.E.; and Croughhan, J. NIMH Diagnostic Interview Schedule. Its history, characteristics, and validity. *Archives of General Psychiatry* 38:387–389, 1981.

Schnoll, S.H.; Karrigan, J.; Kitchen, S.B.; Daghestani, A.; and Hansen, T. Characteristics of cocaine abusers presenting for treatment. In: Kozel, N.J., and Adams, E.H., eds. *Cocaine Use in America: Epidemiologic and Clinical Perspectives*. National Institute on Drug Abuse Research Monograph 61. DHHS Pub. No. (ADM)85–1414. Washington, DC: Supt. of Docs., U.S. Govt. Print. Off., 1985. pp. 171–181.

Smart, R.G.; Erickson, P.G.; Adlaf, E.M.; and Murray, G.F. *Preliminary Report on a Study of Adult Cocaine Users: Patterns, Problems and Perspectives*. Toronto, Ontario: Alcoholism and Drug Addiction Research Foundation, 1984.

Van Dyke, C., and Byck, R. Cocaine. *Scientific American* 246(3):128–141, 1982.

Woolverton, W.L.; Kandel, D.; and Schuster, C.R. Tolerance and cross-tolerance to cocaine and d-amphetamine. *Journal of Pharmacology and Experimental Therapeutics* 205(3):525–535, 1978.

AUTHORS

Edgar A. Adams, Sc.D.
Joseph Gfroerer

Division of Epidemiology and Prevention Research
National Institute on Drug Abuse
5600 Fishers Lane
Rockville, MD 20857

Crack-Cocaine in Miami

James A. Inciardi

How many of us can remember the more newsworthy events of 1986? There were many, with some standing out more prominently than others. Perhaps most notably, although the number of Americans smoking, snorting, swallowing, sniffing, shooting, or otherwise ingesting one drug or another had not changed dramatically that year, the national media fully discovered crack-cocaine in the late spring of 1986. For *Newsweek*, crack became the biggest story since Vietnam and the fall of the Nixon presidency; other media giants compared the spread of crack with the plagues of medieval Europe. By the end of 1986, the major dailies and weekly news magazines had served the Nation more than one thousand stories in which crack figured prominently. Not to be outdone, network television offered hundreds of reports on drug abuse, capped by CBS's *48 Hours on Crack Street,* a prime-time presentation that became one of the highest rated documentaries in the history of television.

For the majority of us working in the drug field, crack was not a particularly new drug. Many of us had been hearing about it for years. In fact, a number of us remembered its introduction almost two decades ago. And importantly, while the media was taking credit for the discovery of crack as the new "flavor-of-the-month" drug, a few of us had long since initiated systematic study of the drug.

Within the context of these opening remarks and observations, my intention here is to briefly review the nature and history of crack-cocaine, followed by a preliminary analysis of crack use among a cohort of juvenile drug users in Miami, Florida.

CRACK-RELATED COCA PRODUCTS

Before embarking on any meaningful discussion of the nature and history of crack-cocaine, two other derivatives of coca must be described first. The first is coca paste, and the second is freebase cocaine.

Common in the drug-using communities of Colombia, Bolivia, Venezuela, Ecuador, Peru, and Brazil is the use of *coca paste*, known to most South Americans as "basuco," "susuko," "pasta basica de cocina," or just simply "pasta" (Jeri 1984). Coca paste is an intermediate product in the processing of the coca leaf into cocaine.

In the initial stages of coca processing, the leaves are pulverized, soaked in alcohol mixed with benzol or gasoline, and shaken. This mixture is drained, sulfuric acid is added, and the solution is shaken again. Next, a precipitate is formed by adding sodium carbonate to the solution. When this is washed with kerosene and chilled, crystals of crude cocaine in the form of cocaine base and cocaine sulfate, or coca paste, are left behind. While the cocaine content of leaves is relatively low—0.5 to 1 percent by weight—paste has a cocaine concentration ranging up to 90 percent, but more commonly about 40 percent.

Coca paste is typically smoked straight, or in cigarettes mixed with either tobacco or marijuana. The practice became popular in South America in the early 1970s. Paste was readily available, inexpensive, had a high cocaine content, and was absorbed quickly when smoked. As the phenomenon was studied, however, it was quickly realized that paste smoking was far more serious than any other form of cocaine use. In addition to cocaine, paste contains traces of all the chemicals used to initially process the coca leaves—kerosene, sulfuric acid, methanol, benzoic acid, and the oxidized products of these solvents, plus any number of other alkaloids that are present in the coca leaf (Almeida 1978). One analysis undertaken in Colombia in 1986 found, in addition to all of these chemicals, traces of brick dust, leaded gasoline, ether, and various talcs (Bogota *El Tiempo* 1986).

By contrast, freebase cocaine is a different chemical product than either coca paste or cocaine itself. In the process of freebasing, street cocaine—which is usually in the form of a hydrochloride salt—is treated with a liquid base to remove the hydrochloric acid. The *free* cocaine, or cocaine *base* (and hence the name "freebase"), is then dissolved in a solvent such as ether, from which the purified cocaine is crystallized. These crystals are then crushed and used in a special glass pipe. Smoking freebase cocaine provides a more potent rush and a powerful high comparable to intravenous injection of cocaine hydrochloride.

CRACK-COCAINE

Contrary to popular belief, crack is not a new substance, first having been reported in the literature during the early 1970s (Anonymous 1972).

At that time, however, knowledge of crack, known then as "base" or "rock," seemed to be restricted to segments of cocaine's freebasing subculture. Crack is processed from cocaine hydrochloride by adding ammonia or baking soda (sodium bicarbonate) and water, and heating it to remove the hydrochloride. The result is a pebble-sized crystalline form of cocaine base.

Contrary to another popular belief, crack is neither "freebase cocaine" nor "purified cocaine." Part of the confusion about what crack actually is comes from the different ways that the word "freebase" is used in the drug community. "Freebase" (the noun) is a drug, a cocaine product converted to the base state from cocaine hydrochloride after adulterants have been chemically removed. Crack is converted to the base state *without* removing the adulterants. "Freebasing" (the act) means to inhale vapors of cocaine base, of which crack is but one form. Finally, crack is not purified cocaine because when it is processed the baking soda remains as a salt and can reduce the purity of 90 percent cocaine hydrochloride to as low as 40 percent cocaine. Informants in the Miami drug subculture indicate that the purity of crack ranges from 40 to 80 percent and generally contains portions of the filler and impurities found in the original cocaine hydrochloride, along with some of the sodium bicarbonate from the processing. A few samples of crack have been found to bottom out in the 5 to 10 percent purity range, but these were typically the result of improper processing by youths unskilled in the techniques of crack production.

The rediscovery of crack during the early 1980s seemed to occur simultaneously on the East and West Coasts. The Colombian government's attempts to reduce the amount of illicit cocaine production within its borders, apparently, at least for a time, successfully restricted the amount of ether available for transforming coca paste into cocaine hydrochloride. The result was the diversion of coca paste from Colombia, through Central America and the Caribbean, into South Florida for conversion into cocaine. Spillage from shipments through the Caribbean corridor acquainted local island populations with coca paste smoking, which developed into the forerunner of crack-cocaine in 1980 (Hall 1986; Inciardi 1987). Known as "baking-soda base," "base-rock," "gravel," and "roxanne," the prototype was a smokable product composed of coca paste, baking soda, water, and rum. Immigrants from Jamaica, Trinidad, and locations along the Leeward and Windward Islands chain introduced the crack prototype to Caribbean inner-city populations in Miami and New York, where it was ultimately produced from cocaine hydrochloride rather than coca paste (Inciardi 1987).

At about the same time, apparently, a Los Angeles basement chemist rediscovered the rock variety of baking-soda cocaine; it was initially referred to as "cocaine rock" (*U. S. News & World Report* 1985). It was an immediate success, as was the East Coast type, and for a variety of reasons. First, it could be smoked rather than snorted. When cocaine is smoked, it is more rapidly absorbed and reportedly crosses the blood-brain barrier within 6 seconds—hence, an almost instantaneous high. Second, it was cheap. While a gram of cocaine for snorting may cost $60 or more depending on its purity, the same gram can be transformed into anywhere from 5 to 30 "rocks." For the user, this meant that individual rocks could be purchased for as little as $2, $5, $10, or $20. For the seller, $60 worth of cocaine hydrochloride (purchased wholesale for $30–40) could generate as much as $150 when sold as rocks. Third, it was easily hidden and transportable, and when hawked in small glass vials, it could be readily scrutinized by potential buyers.

CRACK-COCAINE IN MIAMI

Already aware of the presence of crack in Miami when designing a data collection instrument for a new NIDA-funded study of drug use and delinquency in late 1985, crack was added to the drug history section of the interview schedule. The focus of the research was not crack per se, but rather, the drug-taking and drug-seeking behaviors of Miami street youth who were heavily involved in both drug use and criminal activity.

The youths recruited for the study were obtained through standard "snowball sampling" techniques (Inciardi 1986), and of the first 308 interviewed during 1986, 95.5 percent reported having used crack at least once, and 87.3 percent reported "regular use."[1] Given this high prevalence and incidence of crack use, additional funds were secured from NIDA to further study crack use within the balance of the youths to be interviewed. Ultimately, supplementary crack data were collected on 254 youths. What is reported here reflects a preliminary analysis of a data subset—youthful crack use and the nexus of crack use and involvement in crack distribution.

Of the 254 youths, 85 percent were male and 15 percent were female; 39.4 percent were black, 43.3 percent were white, and 17.3 percent were Hispanic; they ranged in age from 12 to 17 years, with a mean of 14.7. Some 96.9 percent of these youths (n=246) had tried crack, 84.3 percent had used it on a regular basis, 95.3 percent had used the drug during the 90-day period prior to interview, and 54.7 percent were using crack daily.

Given the media blitz on crack during 1986, it certainly appeared that the major dailies, news magazines, and television networks had become pushers in their own right. Coverage of the "horrors" of crack seemed to be feeding more coverage, to a point where some observers were suggesting that if there were indeed a crack epidemic, the media had caused it (Gladwell 1986; Weisman 1986).

The first mention of crack by name in the major media occurred on November 17, 1985, in a short article buried on page B12 of the *New York Times*. This was followed by a page-1 story on November 29, 1985, also in the *New York Times*. By contrast, over half of the Miami youths interviewed were already aware of crack almost a full year prior to the first *Times* article (table 1), and almost three-fourths were conscious of the presence of the drug on the streets of Miami by the time of the initial media blitz. In addition, almost two-thirds of the 246 youths who tried crack did so prior to the appearance of the first *New York Times* article. Important, too, was the fact that only 2 percent of these youths reported having first heard about crack through the media, while the rest had been told about it by friends or drug dealers.

TABLE 1. *Dates of first knowledge and first use of crack*

	Number	Percent
When did you first hear about crack?	254	100.0
November 1982-December 1983	70	27.6
January-December 1984	79	31.1
January-December 1985	33	13.0
December 1985-February 1987	72	28.3
When did you first try crack?	246	100.0
By December 1984	126	51.2
January-November 15, 1985	42	17.1
December 1985-February 1987	77	31.3
No data	1	.4

DOING CRACK

Crack appears in various shapes, sizes, and colors on the Miami street scene. "Crumbs" have a maximum length or diameter of .25"; "pebbles" and "rocks" are up to .3" and .5"; "chunks" are .7" to 1.0"; "big rocks" are in excess of 1"; and "twigs" and "splinters" come in various lengths and thicknesses. Prices vary, depending on size and cocaine content.

There seems to be no typical device for smoking crack in the Miami youth drug scene. The most efficient way, however, is with a crack pipe—a glass pipe with a small hole at the top and a long stem coming from the bowl. The crack is placed on a piece of wire mesh that covers the hole. A flame, from either a cigarette lighter or small blow torch, is applied directly to the crack. As the drug melts, its vapors are inhaled through the pipe. Some users place water or rum in specially designed pipes to cool the crack vapors. And while glass crack pipes of all sizes and shapes are seen, common too are home-made contraptions—soda cans, tin boxes, and bottles fashioned into bulky crack pipes.

Although crack is a drug of rapid onset and short duration, usually about 5 minutes, most of the 246 youths in this study who used crack reported considerably longer highs (10 to 20 minutes). Upon further inquiry, however, it became clear these differences were related to the size and purity of the crack being used, and hence, the length of the overall smoking experience.

The majority of the users (57.3 percent) indicated that after their first experience with crack, they felt fine. Some 19.9 percent, however, experienced the "cocaine blues" (depression and craving); 20.7 percent had physical problems (nausea, headache, the jitters, or overdose); and 2 percent experienced both psychological and physical problems. In addition, at some time during the course of their crack-using careers, 40.2 percent experienced an adverse reaction to the drug, and 8.9 percent ended up in a hospital emergency room for overdose treatment.

CRACK VERSUS COCAINE AND OTHER DRUGS

All of the members of this subsample were asked: "Which do you like better—crack or cocaine?" Not unexpectedly, of those who had tried crack, 75.2 percent preferred crack, 20.3 percent preferred cocaine, and 4.5 percent had no preference. Of the 185 youths who preferred crack, the main reason involved the drug's rapid onset and seemingly greater potency, followed by its ready availability, low cost, and ease of concealment. Those who preferred cocaine typically expressed dissatisfaction with crack's extremely short high.

Interestingly, 242 youths were "current users"[2] of crack at the time of interview, and of these, two-thirds (67.7 percent) often used crack when already high on some other drug. In 92.6 percent of the cases, the other drug was marijuana and/or alcohol. However, only 1.2 percent (n=3) of these current users ever mixed crack with another drug. The drugs, in these few cases, were heroin, coca paste, and PCP—combinations known in the Miami street scene as "space base."

Of the current users of crack, some 55.8 percent reported that they now used cocaine less often, and 6.6 percent reported the diminished use of some other drug (typically in conjunction with cocaine, such as a heroin/cocaine speedball). By contrast, some 37.5 percent reported that their use of crack had not altered their intake of other drugs.

CRACK USE AND DISTRIBUTION

Of the 254 youths under analysis here, all but 50 (19.7 percent) had some type of involvement in the crack business (table 2). The 20 subjects designated as having "minor" involvement sold the drug only to their friends, served as a lookout for dealers, or steered customers to one of Miami's 700 known crack houses. A "dealer" was anyone involved directly in the retail sale of crack, and a "dealer+" not only sold the drug, but manufactured or smuggled it as well.

TABLE 2. *Crack business involvement*

Level of involvement	Total (n=254)	Sample %	Any involvement (n=204) %	All dealers (n=184) %
None	50	19.7		
Minor	20	7.9	9.8	
Dealer	139	54.7	68.1	75.5
Dealer+	45	17.7	22.1	24.5

By examining other aspects of crack use within the context of these four levels of involvement in the crack business in Miami, it quickly became clear that the extent to which individuals are tied to the crack distribution network is directly related to the extent of their use of the drug. For example, and not surprisingly, the more people are meshed in the crack business, the more aware they are of where the drug can be purchased (table 3). Those with no involvement in the crack business knew of a median of only 2.5 locations where crack could likely be purchased. This figure increased to 4.5 for those with minor involvement, 18.0 for anyone designated as a dealer, and 20 for those in the dealer+ category.

TABLE 3. *Known places to buy crack in miami*

Number of places	Crack business involvement None (n=50)	Minor (n=20)	Dealer (n=139)	Dealer+ (n=45)	Total (n=254)
			Percentages		
50 or more	0.0	5.0	17.3	13.3	12.2
20 to 45	4.0	5.0	31.7	42.2	26.0
7 to 18	16.0	15.0	28.8	35.6	26.4
3 to 6	30.0	65.0	19.4	8.9	23.2
0 to 2	50.0	10.0	2.9	0.0	12.2
Median	2.5	4.5	18.0	20.0	13.0
			Cumulative percentages		
50 or more	0.0	5.0	17.3	13.3	12.2
20 to 45	4.0	10.0	48.9	55.6	38.2
7 to 18	20.0	25.0	77.7	91.1	64.6
3 to 6	50.0	90.0	97.1	100.0	87.8
1 or 2	92.0	100.0	100.0	100.0	98.4

A similar pattern was also apparent with regard to the amount spent on crack (table 4). For example, of the 242 youths designated as current users of crack, the amount of money spent on the drug over a 90-day period reflects a considerable range. Those in the dealer and dealer+ groups, in spite of their intimate connections with the crack marketplace, nevertheless spent the most on the drug. As one 17-year-old dealer-manufacturer explained in 1987:

> Oh, sure, I got plenty access to the stuff, and I do a pretty hot good business, but ya can't be just takin' it all for yourself. Then there'd be no business.
>
> Figure it out this way. There's this dealer on 112th Avenue that knows that I never mess up the money, so he'll front me with about an ounce of pretty good stuff. Maybe I'll owe him about $600 for the ounce, maybe $800–900, it depends on a lot of things. Then I make up a mess of crack—sell half and use half myself. I do that maybe once/twice a week, so altogether my crack costs me a hundred a day.

By contrast, youths with only minor involvement in the crack trade spent considerably less on the drug—a median of $225 over the 90-day period

TABLE 4. *Money spent on crack during the 90 days prior to interview*

Money spent for own use	None (n=38)	Minor (n=20)	Dealer (n=139)	Dealer+ (n=45)	Total (n=242)
	Crack business involvement				
	Cumulative percentage				
$3100+	0.0	0.0	13.7	28.9	13.2
2000+	2.6	0.0	51.8	71.1	43.4
1000+	2.6	0.0	69.8	95.6	58.3
275+	18.4	30.0	79.9	97.8	69.4
100+	47.4	75.0	95.0	100.0	86.8
12+	97.4	100.0	100.0	100.0	99.6
No $ spent	2.6	0.0	0.0	0.0	0.4
Median spent	$75	$225	$2000	$2500	$1750

or the equivalent of less than $20 per week. Those with no crack business involvement spent even less on the drug.

CRACK AND CRIME

Although the purpose of this study was not an analysis of the relationship between crack use and crime, a few observations can be made nevertheless. To begin with, all respondents were asked how they got their crack. Most had numerous avenues for obtaining the drug, and the range of answers was interesting. Many involved illegal activities. For example:

exchange for other drug(s)	25.6	percent
exchange for stolen goods	85.1	
pay/bonus for drug sales	87.2	
pay/bonus for sex	15.7	
buy from friend/relative	61.9	
buy from crack-only dealer	73.6	
buy from cocaine-also dealer	96.7	
buy from heroin-also dealer	84.7	
theft/robbery of dealer	55.0	
theft/robbery of other person	18.6	
making crack	11.1	
free from friend/relative	87.2	

Of the current users of crack, most reported higher levels of criminality as the result of crack use: 16.5 percent indicated less crime, 67.8 percent indicated more crime, and 15.7 percent indicated no change (table 5). Within the context of involvement in the crack business, it would appear that within this population of youths, crack use intensified criminal behavior. On the whole, 64 percent of these current users of crack reported increased drug sales, while considerably smaller proportions

TABLE 5. *Less/more crime as the result of crack use (in percentages)*

	Crack business involvement				
Criminal activity	None (n=38)	Minor (n=20)	Dealer (n=139)	Dealer+ (n=45)	Total (n=242)
Less crime?					
No, none	100.0	95.0	84.2	66.7	84.3
Less theft	0.0	5.0	8.6	24.4	9.9
Less robbery, or less theft and robbery	0.0	0.0	6.5	8.9	5.4
Less prostitution	0.0	0.0	0.7	0.0	0.4
More crime?					
No, none	78.9	70.0	23.0	4.4	32.2
More drug sales only	15.8	10.0	30.2	48.9	29.8
Yes, other crimes	5.3	20.0	46.8	46.7	38.0
More drug sales?					
No	81.6	75.0	27.3	6.7	36.0
Yes	18.4	25.0	72.7	93.3	64.0
More other petty crime?					
No	94.7	80.0	54.7	57.8	63.6
Yes, prostitution only	0.0	0.0	5.8	2.2	3.7
Yes, both prostitution and property	0.0	0.0	6.5	2.2	4.1
Yes, petty theft and/or stolen goods only	5.3	20.0	33.1	37.8	28.5
More serious crime?					
No	97.4	100.0	79.9	73.3	83.1
Yes, burglary only	0.0	0.0	11.5	20.0	10.3
Yes, both burglary and robbery	2.6	0.0	7.2	4.4	5.4
Yes, robbery only	0.0	0.0	1.4	2.2	1.2

reported increased activity in the areas of prostitution, burglary, robbery, and petty theft. And within the context of crack business involvement, increased criminality was even more pronounced.

DISCUSSION

Although these data are only preliminary and reflect but a subset of a considerably larger and more comprehensive study, a number of conclusions might nevertheless be drawn.

- Whereas the media did not begin focusing on crack as the newest drug of abuse until late 1985, crack-cocaine likely arrived in Miami in 1981, and a few members of this sample of youths were aware of the drug as early as late 1982. Furthermore, more than half of these juveniles had used crack a full year prior to its attracting the attention of the national media.

- Although national surveys have documented that the prevalence of the recent use of crack is low within the general population (Rouse this volume) as well as within samples of high school seniors, college students, and young adults (O'Malley et al. this volume), that does not appear to be the case in this population. Of the 254 Miami youths interviewed here, all had the opportunity to try crack, and 96.9 percent (n=246) did so. Moreover, 84.3 percent reported the regular use of crack at the time of interview, and 54.7 percent admitted to daily use. This suggests that while antidrug messages have been having an impact on mainstream America, they are either not reaching, not being heard, or not being listened to in the juvenile street community.

- Within this population of juvenile drug users, crack is unquestionably a drug of preference. Of those who tried crack, three-fourths preferred the drug to cocaine. This remained so despite a relatively high proportion of youths having complications with crack use. Some 40.2 percent of these youths experienced some type of adverse reaction to crack, and of these, 22 percent received hospital emergency room treatment for a crack overdose.

- Perhaps most important in these data is the clear relationship between the use of crack and involvement in the crack business. That is, when grouping crack users in terms of their relative association with the crack trade in Miami, the higher the association the greater the crack use.

FOOTNOTES

1. "Regular use" is defined here as use for 3 or more days a week for at least 4 consecutive weeks at any time during a person's drug-using career.
2. "Current use" is defined here as any use during the 90 days prior to the interview.

REFERENCES

Almeida, M. Contrabucion al estudio de la historia natural de la dependencia a la pasta basica de cocaina. *Revista de Neuro-Psiquiatria* 41:44–45, 1978.

Anonymous. *The Gourmet Cokebook: A Complete Guide to Cocaine*. White Mountain Press, 1972. Cited by Schatzman, M.; Sabbadini, A.; and Forti, L. Coca and cocaine. *Journal of Psychedelic Drugs* 8:95–128, Apr.-June 1976.

Bogota *El Tiempo*, June 19, 1986, p. 2–D.

Gladwell, M. A new addiction to an old story. *The Washington Times Insight* Oct. 27:8–12, 1986.

Hall, J. N. Hurricane crack. *Street Pharmacologist* 10:1–2, Sept. 1986.

Inciardi, J. A. *The War on Drugs: Heroin, Cocaine, Crime and Public Policy*. Palo Alto, CA: Mayfield, 1986.

Inciardi, J. A. Beyond cocaine: Basuco, crack, and other coca products. *Contemporary Drug Problems* Fall:461–492, 1987.

Jeri, F. R. Coca-paste smoking in some Latin American countries: A severe and unabated form of addiction. *Bulletin on Narcotics* Apr.-June:15–31, 1984.

U. S. News & World Report, February 11, 1985, p. 33.

Weisman, A. P. I was a drug-hype junkie. *The New Republic* October 6:14–17, 1986.

ACKNOWLEDGMENTS

This research was funded by grant number 1–R01–DOA–1827 from the National Institute on Drug Abuse.

AUTHOR

James A. Inciardi, Ph.D.
Division of Criminal Justice
University of Delaware
Newark, DE 19716

Descriptive Epidemiology of International Cocaine Trafficking

Michael Montagne

While the smuggling of contraband goods is a centuries-old phenomenon, trafficking in drugs is, with a few exceptions, an activity of the industrialized 20th century. The use of a variety of psychoactive substances was a common, everyday occurrence in the United States until legislation, beginning with the Pure Food and Drug Act of 1906, instituted controls to regulate them. Throughout the 20th century, a number of national and international laws and treaties have been developed in an attempt to prevent or limit the use of dangerous drugs.

Drug trafficking on an international scale arguably began during the 19th century with the smuggling of opium from India into China. Attempts by the Chinese emperor to suppress this activity resulted in the two Opium Wars, 1839–42 and 1853–60 (Solomon 1978). Around the turn of the century, during the height of the patent medicine era, there was a great deal of intrastate and interstate trafficking in medicinals, especially in the United States. As a result of the actual, or perceived, high levels of use of psychoactive substances, a number of governments began to place restrictions on the manufacture, distribution, or use of these drugs. The first attempt at worldwide drug use control occurred at the Shanghai Opium Convention of 1909 (Henman et al. 1985). A number of similar conventions and commissions met during the 1910s and 1920s. Efforts to respond to increased drug use focused on the distribution of these drugs; specific strategies were first codified at the International Opium Convention at the Hague in 1912 (Renborg 1947).

The International Opium Convention at Geneva in 1925 developed a treaty to monitor and regulate the international trade in narcotic drugs. The Permanent Control Board was created and defined as part of the League of Nations at the Convention to Limit the Manufacture and Regulate the Distribution of Narcotic Drugs in Geneva in 1931 (Cusack 1986). This Board was actually implemented in 1935 as the Permanent Central

Opium Board (PCOB). It was the first systematic attempt at a detailed supervision and accounting of the international narcotic trade (Renborg 1947). In the United States, control efforts were legislated by the Harrison Narcotics Act of 1914. But it wasn't until the early 1930s that the Federal Bureau of Narcotics decided that drug trafficking had to be attacked on an international level, since it was assumed that most illicit drugs entering the country were of foreign origin (Warner 1983). Most of these early efforts focused on the opiates.

Efforts to control the international distribution of coca and cocaine began in the early 1920s. International conventions shifted much of their attention from opium to coca and cocaine, especially the Convention at Geneva in 1925 (Chatterjee 1981). In the United States, the Harrison Narcotics Act (1914), and a series of amendments in succeeding years, reduced licit cocaine use to surgical situations, and suppressed or removed remaining amounts from the marketplace through registration, revenue measures, and importation quotas (Wisotsky 1983). Prior to 1950, no country was required by any treaty or agreement to regulate or restrict the cultivation of narcotic plants such as coca bushes. The United Nations' Single Convention on Narcotic Drugs in 1961 declared that chewing coca leaves was considered to be abuse of a drug, and it recommended that all chewing (by native groups in South America) must be abolished in 25 years (U.N. Commission 1966). The Single Convention also limited coca cultivation to that amount needed for scientific and pharmaceutical purposes, required the destruction of illegally grown coca bushes and those growing wild, and obligated countries to campaign against drug trafficking (Wisotsky 1983).

THE NATURE OF THE AVAILABLE DATA

The most commonly used definition, nationally and internationally, of drug trafficking refers to it as "the cultivation, production, processing, transportation, distribution or sale of drugs" (President's Commission 1986, p. 5). The term "drugs" refers to illicit substances, controlled substance analogs, and drugs diverted from the licit market for illicit use. From a slightly different perspective, the illicit cocaine industry has been described as consisting of four functional phases: cultivation and production, export (smuggling), distribution in the consumer country, and the processing of money (Wisotsky 1983). These four activities comprise the phenomenon of trafficking. It should also be realized that illicit cocaine production and distribution can be influenced by economic, political, sociocultural, legal, geographical, meteorological, and many other factors.

The PCOB was the first group organized to collect data and to analyze the international flow of narcotic drugs, including coca and cocaine (U.N. Permanent Central Narcotics Board [PCNB] 1966). This Board provided annual estimates of the need for licit narcotic drugs for each country. The estimate was based upon the amount required for medicinal consumption, amounts in reserve stocks, and the amount needed for manufacturing processes. The PCOB issued these reports for each year from 1932 to 1968, the last 7 years under the name of the Permanent Central Narcotics Board (U.N. Commission 1966). Retrospective analyses of some of these estimates, compared to actual production amounts, indicated a consistent overestimation of production levels by most countries. These overestimates were, on average, around 65 percent greater than the amounts of coca and cocaine that were actually produced (U.N. Commission 1962, 1966; U.N. PCNB 1966). The United Nations' Single Convention on Narcotic Drugs (1961) reorganized the PCOB and established the International Narcotics Control Board (INCB) to administer a statistical control system and to estimate the worldwide distribution and use of narcotics (U.N. 1987*a*, 1987*b*). The INCB became active in 1968, and it generates annual summary reports (U.N. INCB 1968–81*a*), as well as annual estimates of the world's requirements of narcotic drugs (U.N. INCB 1968–81*b*). These latter reports provide estimates of coca and cocaine cultivation and production, licit coca leaf and cocaine consumption, exports and imports of licit cocaine, and seizure data for each participating country.

The U. S. Treasury Department's Bureau of Narcotics (1943–61) collected some data on coca and cocaine throughout the middle part of this century. Until the late 1960s, they were the primary source of information in the United States on the traffic in narcotics. The U.S. State Department's Bureau of International Narcotics Matters (INM) attempts to reduce cocaine importation through control of coca production at its source (DiCarlo 1982). The INM collects data on cultivation and production, mostly through its regional offices, Narcotics Assistance Units (NAU), which are located in producer countries.

The National Narcotics Intelligence Consumers Committee (NNICC) was established in the United States in 1978 (Federal Strategy 1983). NNICC is a collection of agencies in the enforcement and intelligence communities (e.g., U.S. Coast Guard and Customs Service, Federal Bureau of Investigation, Internal Revenue Service, Drug Enforcement Administration (DEA), National Institute on Drug Abuse, Departments of State and Defense, and the White House) that combine their resources to produce annual estimates of trafficking activity based on the amount of money in the traffic, the number of users, seizure data, and estimates of cultivation and production (Monastero 1985; U.S. Congress OTA 1987). These estimates of illicit production and consumption are published annually as the *Narcotics Intelligence Estimate* (NNICC 1979, 1980, 1981*a*, 1982, 1983, 1984, 1985*a*, 1986).

These estimates of the total amount of drug trafficking are not subjected to retrospective validation. Statistical sampling techniques are not employed by any agency or group in analyzing the level of drug trafficking or in determining the effectiveness of drug control efforts. In addition, some estimates used in calculations are out of date, data concerning price and purity is insufficient, background data used to develop the estimates are not published, and the whole "methodology has been criticized as 'analysis by negotiation' with final estimates resulting from a bargaining process among the member agencies" (President's Commission 1986, p. 343). NNICC itself has stated that "because of gaps in some of the data used to derive the estimates, there is a high degree of uncertainty to the resulting estimates" (1984, p. i).

Internal estimates of coca leaf cultivation and production are made by a variety of governmental agencies in the producer countries, such as Ministries of Agriculture, the Interior, and Taxation (Agreda 1986; Henman et al. 1985; Jeri 1980; Kline 1987). Estimates have also been made, on an irregular basis, by research centers, independent scholars, agronomists, and investigative reporters (Antonil 1978; Craig 1983; Healy 1986; Strug 1986).

Seizure data are collected and analyzed differently by the various U.S. agencies involved as indicators of trafficking activity. The El Paso Intelligence Center (EPIC) is the repository for these data, but they rarely identify the agency responsible for individual seizures (U.S. Congress OTA 1987). Data on drug prices and purity levels are collected by DEA, and these represent another indicator of trafficking activities (U.S. DEA 1987*a*). Other types of data also used on occasion to estimate the level of drug trafficking include data on emergency room incidents (Drug Abuse Warning Network) and treatment admissions, identification of clandestine labs, arrests and convictions of drug traffickers, and forfeitures of assets.

The trafficking situation can also be viewed from the demand side (i.e., consumption instead of production), with a focus on illicit importation. Estimates of illicit cocaine importation are calculated in two different ways (NNICC 1987; Wisotsky 1983). A production-based estimate is calculated by multiplying the total number of hectares (1 hectare=2.47 acres) under cultivation by the average number of kilograms of coca leaf that a single hectare yields (the values used range from 800 to 1,200 kg/hectare, depending upon the region where it was cultivated). The total amount of coca leaf produced is numerically reduced by subtracting the amount of leaf needed for domestic chewing, licit pharmaceutical manufacturing, and other legal uses.

This combined amount of licit production is often referred to as the accountable stock. The remaining amount is the potential unaccountable stock, which is basically available for illicit processing and distribution. The value of this amount of coca leaf is converted into the amount of cocaine that could be theoretically produced. (On average, 200 kg of coca leaf will yield 1 kg of coca paste, and 2.5 kg coca paste will yield 1 kg of cocaine.) The value for the estimated maximum amount of cocaine that could be potentially produced is further reduced by subtracting the amount of cocaine that is seized or lost/stolen in transit and the amount of cocaine that is not converted due to inefficient production, spoilage, and other problems in the manufacturing process. The remainder (in metric tons) represents the amount of illicit cocaine available for consumption.

The consumption-based approach to calculating illicit importation also starts from the demand side (NNICC 1987; Wisotsky 1983). The annual number of cocaine users (based on a variety of surveys) is broken down by pattern of use; the latter variable represents an estimate of how much is consumed per session (i.e., dose) and how many sessions occur each year (i.e., frequency) for each person. Within each category, the number of users is multiplied by the average amount consumed annually, with an adjustment for the purity of the product being consumed. All the categories are summed, and the result is an estimate of the quantity of cocaine consumed (in metric tons) for that given year, and thus the amount of cocaine that must have been imported.

There are a number of serious obstacles to attempts to establish precisely the amount of coca leaf that is produced annually. Until just recently, the total number of hectares under cultivation, or the amount produced, was not known. The most accurate figures came from that part of the total production that came onto the market after payment of an official tax (Granier-Doyeux 1962). Aerial surveillance is limited and haphazard, and until such surveys improve, confidence in estimates generated from them is very low (Taylor 1985). Successful interdiction efforts sometimes result in a reassessment of many estimates of the degree of trafficking as being too conservative. New or revised information on the amount of coca leaf used for domestic chewing, amounts of cocaine seized in transit or at clandestine labs, and other related figures suggest that cultivation and production rates are much greater than what is currently reported (U.S. House CFA 1986*d*). The U.S. Office of Technology Assessment has recently reported that "data on drug smuggling, the trafficking system, and interdiction activities are inadequate for effective planning and management" (U.S. Congress OTA 1987, p. 3).

SOURCES OF SUPPLY

Coca refers to two distinct but closely related species of the genus *Erythroxylum*, with a number of varieties in each (Plowman 1986). Once established, a coca bush will yield its first harvest in 1 to 2 years, sometimes as early as 6 months. Maximum productivity is reached in 3 to 5 years, and the plants can remain productive for 40 to 50 years. Coca is harvested from the bushes three or four times a year, and in some instances, as often as six times a year. Cultivation is essentially a continuous, year-round activity. The coca yield per hectare varies considerably, from 260 kg/hectare in parts of Bolivia to 1,200 kg/hectare in parts of Peru (Plowman 1986). Cultivation of coca represents a long historical and cultural tradition in many South American countries, particularly those of the Andean region (Antonil 1978; Pacini and Franquemont 1986; Walker 1981).

From the late 19th century until the Second World War, a number of countries outside of South America were involved in the cultivation of coca (see table 1), including Indonesia, India, the West Indies, Puerto Rico, and Australia. A significant increase in the cultivation of coca began after the Second World War (Cusack 1986). The U.N.'s INCB has reported that extensive coca bush cultivation and overproduction of coca began in Peru and Bolivia in the early 1970s (U.N. INCB 1968–81*a*). Around 1971, the production of cocaine for illicit markets began to increase (U.N. INCB 1971). In the late 1970s, the INCB (1978) reported that overproduction had been occurring for decades. And in the 1980s, the INCB (1981) noted that both cultivation of coca and production of cocaine had risen dramatically.

Peru and Bolivia are the only two countries currently authorized under international agreements to grow coca legally for the pharmaceutical market. These two countries are also the source of most of the illicit coca leaves and paste used in making cocaine. Processing of coca into cocaine occurs mostly in Colombia. The growth of processing in and distribution through Colombia increased greatly in a period of only a few years during the early 1980s. Clandestine labs are commonplace throughout the country (Craig 1983). Conversion laboratories have been constructed more recently in Brazil, Venezuela, some Central American

TABLE 1. *Countries where coca leaf is cultivated*

19th century to early 1960s	Current	Potential
Indonesia (Java)	Peru	Indonesia
India	Bolivia	Ceylon
Ceylon (Sri Lanka)	Colombia	Philippines
Cameroon	Ecuador	Chile
Zanzibar (Tanzania)	Brazil	Guyana
Australia	Argentina	Madagascar
West Indies	Paraguay	Appalachia (U.S.)
Puerto Rico	Venezuela	
	Panama	
	Mexico	
	Hawaii (U.S.)	

Sources: Chopra and Chopra 1958; Erickson et al. 1987; Henman et al. 1985; U.N. Commission 1962; Walker 1981; NNICC 1984, 1987; President's Commission 1984; U.S. House CFA 1984*b*, 1985, 1987*c*; U.S. House SCNAC 1978*b*, 1980, 1984; Brecher 1986; Taylor 1985.

countries, and some islands of the Caribbean (President's Commission 1986). Recent cultivation has begun, or has increased, in Colombia, Ecuador, Brazil, Venezuela, and other South American countries, as well as in Mexico and Hawaii. On the basis of a past history of cultivation activities, or current favorable conditions, coca cultivation could also begin in a number of other regions around the world (see table 1). Coca cultivation has already been noted in the Philippines, Indonesia, and Madagascar.

It was recognized in the late 1970s that Colombia and Bolivia, and other South American countries as well, had a great potential for expanding both their cultivation and production of coca and cocaine. The great increase in illicit cultivation in Peru and Bolivia began around 1971–72, and in Colombia in the late 1970s (NNICC 1985*b*; U.S. House SCNAC 1984). The annual cultivation and eradication of coca bushes in Peru, Bolivia, and Colombia for 1979 to 1986 is presented in table 2. It has been reported that greater amounts of coca are being cultivated in Bolivia, perhaps as much as 42,000–53,000 hectares (U.S. House CFA 1987*b*). Craig (1983) suggested that Colombia has been cultivating more than 30,000 hectares since at least 1979. Coca cultivation has also occurred in Ecuador, with 1,000–2,000 hectares in 1986 and over 2,000 hectares in 1987 (U.S. House CFA 1987*c*), though perhaps as much as half the crop is eradicated each year (NNICC 1987).

TABLE 2. *Coca leaf cultivation and eradication in South America (in hectares)*

	1979	1980	1981	1982	1983	1984	1985	1986
Peru								
Cult.	30,000	50,000	50,000	50,000	60,000	60,000	70,000	110,000
Erad.	—	—	0	0	680	3,180	5,350	2,675
Bolivia								
Cult.	25,000	35,000	35,000	35,000	40,000	55,000	38,000	38,000
Erad.	—	—	0	85	0	2,000	30	135
Colombia								
Cult.	3,000	3,000	2,900	5,000	13,000	15,000	18,000	18,000
Erad.	—	—	400	1,970	2,000	3,414	2,000	760

(1 hectare=2.47 acres)

Sources: U.N. INCB 1968-81*a*; Jeri 1980; NNICC 1981*b*, 1985*b*, 1987; President's Commission 1984; U.S. House CFA 1984*a*, 1984*b*, 1986*b*; 1986*c*, 1987*a*, 1987*b*.

Estimates of the amount of coca leaf under cultivation vary greatly, depending upon the source of the data (table 3). It is important to note that internal or domestic estimates and estimates made by independent (nongovernmental) groups tend to be higher than those provided by

TABLE 3. *Differences in estimates of coca leaf cultivation (in thousands of hectares)*

	1984	1985	1986
Peru			
NNICC	60	70	95–120
Ministry of Interior	135	120–200	100–183
Colombia			
NNICC	9		
Colombian researchers	50		
Bolivia			
NNICC	55	55	35
U.S. DEA	81		
U.S. INM	35	35	35
U.S. INM (La Paz)			60
Ministry of Agriculture			100
CERES (Bolivia)	152	171	
Internal estimate (Kline)		200	200

(1 hectare = 2.47 acres)

Sources: Agreda 1986; A Condor Strikes 1986; Healy 1986; Kline 1987; NNICC 1984; U.S. House CFA 1984*a*, 1985, 1986*b*, 1987*a*, 1987*b*; U.S. House CJ 1984.

governmental agencies. Also, estimates from the late 1970s and early 1980s were revised in 1984–85, making it look like a dramatic increase in cultivation had occurred, when a slower, more constant rate of increase might actually have been occurring (Henman et al. 1985).

The worldwide production of coca leaf is presented in table 4. The wide range of values is due to the differences in estimates by different groups.

TABLE 4. *Worldwide coca leaf production (in metric tons)*

1963–69 average	13,514 (S.D.=859)
1970–77 average	16,063 (S.D.=1,330)
1978	19,500
1979	25,000
1980	25,230
1981	120,000
1982	135,000
1983	135,000–150,000
1984	135,000–270,000
1985	125,000–137,000
1986	152,000–188,000

(500 kg coca leaf = 1 kg cocaine)

Sources: Cohen 1984; NNICC 1984, 1987; U.N. INCB 1968-81*b*; U.S. House CFA 1984*a*.

The yield of cultivated coca also varies considerably by country. Worldwide coca leaf production is currently estimated to be 8 to 10 times greater than the current level of worldwide illicit consumption of cocaine (U.S. House SCNAC 1987). The annual worldwide *licit* consumption of cocaine (table 5) is so small that it is given in kilograms instead of metric tons (500 kg of coca leaf can produce 1 kg of cocaine; 1 metric

TABLE 5. *Worldwide licit cocaine consumption (in kilograms)*

1906	9,524
1932–39 average	1,625 (S.D.=283)
1946–49 average	1,702 (S.D.=265)
1950–59 average	1,964 (S.D.=512)
1960–69 average	2,689 (S.D.=226)
1970–79 average	2,529 (S.D.=441)
1980	1,644
1981	1,441

Sources: U.N. INCB, 1968-81*b*; Walker 1981; Wisotsky 1983.

TABLE 6. *Licit coca leaf consumption in South America (in metric tons)*

	1960–69 average	1977	1985
Peru	8,480 (S.D.=299)	7,183	54,000
Bolivia	4,473 (S.D.=938)	8–12,000	16,000
Colombia	—	—	4,000
Argentina	97 (S.D.=42)	0	0

Sources: Pacini and Franquemont 1986; Kline 1987; Phillips and Wynne 1980; U.N. INCB 1968-81*b*; U.S. House CFA 1984*b*, 1986*d*; U.S. House CJ 1984.

ton=1,000 kg). The annual licit consumption of coca leaf in South American countries (table 6) has increased steadily. And while some countries, like Argentina, have successfully abolished most coca chewing, other countries, like Colombia, have seen a renewed interest in it. The annual *illicit* importation of cocaine, based on production and consumption estimates, is presented in table 7.

TABLE 7. *Estimated illicit cocaine importation: United States, Canada, and Europe (in metric tons)*

	1979	1980	1981	1982	1983	1984	1985	1986	1987
United States									
Production-based	25–31	35–50	40–65	45–70	54–71	71–137	110–145		
Consumption-based	30	40–48	35–45	45–54	50–61	85	100	150	178
Canada and Europe									
Consumption-based	5	5-8	12			20	20-30		

Sources: NNICC 1981*b*, 1985*b*, 1987; U.S. DEA 1987*b*; U.S. House SCNAC 1987.

Technological and other developments have had an impact on cultivation, both new and old. The building of the Pan-American Highway in the Andean region greatly facilitated transport, and many new plantations were started (Healy 1986; Inciardi 1987). The cultivation of coca can shift in response to both natural and manmade barriers or disruptions. Severe flood and drought conditions in Bolivia in the early 1980s (especially a major drought in 1982–83) greatly reduced the production of coca leaves for some time (Healy 1986; U.S. House SCNAC 1984). Agricultural reforms in the 1950s in many South American countries released peasant growers from large estates and their owners, and coca cultivation was then begun by many small growers (Henman et al. 1985). Crop eradication and substitution programs will also shift coca fields to other areas. The U.N.'s Single Convention on Narcotic Drugs states that both the producer and the transit nations have the primary responsibility for controlling coca production within their borders.

While an estimated 90 percent of the illicit drugs, and perhaps all of the cocaine, that are consumed in the United States are produced in other countries (Federal Strategy 1983), it is important to realize that coca could be grown in some parts of this country. The mountainous region of the Appalachian chain is conducive to the cultivation of coca (Brecher 1986). Cocaine could also be synthesized in this country from precursor chemicals. The production of synthetic cocaine is a well-defined process that has not been greatly improved upon since it was developed in 1923. It involves four steps and gives an overall yield of 60 percent (Archer and Hawks 1976). This process employs easily available starting materials and equipment, though the steps involved have been described by medicinal chemists as being very tedious.

DISTRIBUTION AND TRANSSHIPMENT CHANNELS

In the 1970s, cocaine was illegally imported into the United States through at least three major routes (Phillips and Wynne 1980). One route originated in Peru, with transshipment through Ecuador and Panama and into Mexico, where the cocaine was smuggled into the United States, primarily into Texas. A second route originated in Chile with processed cocaine; the ultimate destinations were cities on the Pacific coast. The third route started in Bolivia, with transshipment through the Caribbean and into Miami and New York. In the 1970s, the cocaine trade was not the prerogative of any one organized crime group, as was the case with heroin trafficking. This has, perhaps, changed in the 1980s.

The major transshipment countries for cocaine traffic in the 1950s through the 1980s are presented in table 8. An estimated 60–70 percent

TABLE 8. *Coca leaf and cocaine transshipment countries*

1950s	1970s	1980s (early)	1980s (late)	
Colombia	Colombia	Colombia	*For United States:*	*For Europe:*
Chile	Panama	Panama	Colombia	Austria
Ecuador	Ecuador	Bahamas	Jamaica	Italy
Paraguay	Chile	Nicaragua	Bahamas	Spain
	Costa Rica	Cuba	Haiti/Dominican Rep.	West Germany
	Cuba	Trinidad/Tobago	Eastern Caribbean	
	Hawaii (U.S.)	Costa Rica	Panama	*For Asia:*
	Guam (U.S.)	Ecuador	Belize	Bali
	Tahiti	Venezuela	Guatemala	Indonesia
		Mexico	Mexico	
		Hawaii (U.S.)	South America	

Sources: Allen 1987; Cocaine Trafficking 1982; Colombia 1982; Erickson et al. 1987; Henman et al. 1985; NNICC 1987; President's Commission 1984; U.N. INCB 1968-81*a*; U.S. House CFA 1982, 1984*b*, 1986*a*, 1986*b*, 1987*a*, 1987*c*; U.S. House SCNAC 1978*a*, 1978*b*, 1980, 1984, 1987; Walker 1981.

of the cocaine that currently enters the United States is shipped through the Caribbean islands (U.S. House CFA 1987*d*), and perhaps as much as 50 percent of all the cocaine is transshipped through the Bahamas (U.S. House CFA 1987*e*).

In the 1950s and 1960s, Miami was the center of cocaine smuggling due primarily to the growth of the Cuban community. By the 1970s, the center had shifted to New York, and most smugglers were of Colombian and Chilean origin (Phillips and Wynne 1980; President's Commission 1986). In the 1980s, the influx of Bahamians and Jamaicans have again shifted the smuggling routes through their native countries and to points in the United States where they have settled. The epidemiologic notion of a "contagion" might be applicable here, since cocaine trafficking routes often seem to follow the settlement of immigrants, and particularly migrant laborers, in a specific area. This is especially noticeable in many rural areas, where cocaine use and trafficking were negligible before the recent growth of migrant workforces.

Shifts in the flow of cocaine through smuggling activities have occurred on a regular basis. Law enforcement experience has shown, historically, that traffickers seek the transit routes of least resistance, where enforcement efforts are not taking place (U.S. House CFA 1985). For instance, in the 1980s, most of the cocaine entering the United States came through Florida (70–80 percent) and the other Gulf Coast States

(U.S. House CGO 1985). Recent interdiction efforts in Florida (e.g., South Florida Task Force) have resulted in a partial shifting of these cocaine trafficking activities to the West Coast (President's Commission 1986). This shifting phenomenon has been most notable in the Caribbean, with trafficking routes changing from one island group to another depending on the presence of law enforcement agents and interdiction activities.

In the 1970s, Bolivian coca was processed extensively in Chile and Brazil, while Peruvian coca was refined in Colombia and Ecuador. In the late 1970s, around 50 percent of the illicit cocaine entering the United States came from Colombia (NNICC 1980); in 1982, 70 percent was processed in and distributed from Colombia (DiCarlo 1982; U.S. House SCNAC 1984). More recent estimates place that figure closer to 80 percent, with another 15 percent coming from Bolivia (NNICC 1987). In 1984, U.S. officials estimated that 10–20 percent of the cocaine entering the United States came from Mexico (U.S. House SCNAC 1984). The cocaine transit industry in Mexico came about as a result of opium and marijuana eradication programs in the mid-1970s, and more recently as a result of interdiction efforts in Florida and the Caribbean (U.S. Congress OTA 1987).

Worldwide seizures of coca leaf and cocaine are presented in table 9. An often-used seizure statistic was that approximately 5 percent (anywhere from 3 to 12 percent) of the cocaine destined for the United States was intercepted en route (U.S. House SCNAC 1978*a*). The South Florida Task Force estimated that it seized about 10 percent of the cocaine that entered the United States, but that this was a general figure for "getting some, but not getting a lot" (U.S. House CGO 1985). The U.S. DEA now estimates that 20–25 percent of the cocaine is seized en route (U.S. House CFA 1987*d*). This is based on the lower estimates of production, which points out the importance of quality denominator data. Seizure statistics in 1984 indicated that most cocaine smuggling into the United States occurred by private aircraft (62 percent), commercial air travel (18 percent), and private vessels (11 percent) (President's Commission 1986). By 1986, private aircraft represented the primary means of transport, and private vessels had become more popular (25 percent) (NNICC 1987).

Canadian officials estimate that over half the cocaine entering their country in 1983 came from Colombia (Stamler et al. 1984). Most of the cocaine smuggled into Canada in the early 1980s was by commercial air transport (75 percent) and the rest by land. The Canadians have noted that as law enforcement efforts increase and become effective in one

TABLE 9. *Worldwide seizures of coca leaf and cocaine*

	1960-69	1970	1971	1972	1973	1974
Coca Leaf (metric tons)	22.4 (S.D.=1.1)	13.7	—	21.4	20.0	8.2
Cocaine (kilograms)	98 (S.D.=50)	347	403	489	1,053	1,383

	1975	1976	1977	1978	1979	1980
Coca Leaf (metric tons)	9.0	—	24.7	27.9	—	10.6
Cocaine (kilograms)	2,356	1,464	3,898	6,884	2,440	2,151*

	1981	1982	1983	1984	1985	1986
Coca Leaf (metric tons)	—	—	20	21	—	—
Cocaine (kilograms)	—	5,240*	8,000*	15,000*	18,000*	23,819*

*Data from United States only.

Sources: Cusack 1986; NNICC 1987; President's Commission 1986; U.N. INCB 1968–81*b*; U.S. House CFA 1984*a*, 1984*b*, 1987*d*; U.S. House CGO 1985; U.S. House SCNAC 1978*a*, 1980.

area, traffickers shift their illicit distribution to other geographical areas. Transshipment of cocaine to Canada is primarily through Colombia and other South American countries. But more recently, trafficking routes have been established through Mexico and other Central American countries and the Caribbean islands, which in the early 1980s were transshipment points for 20 percent of the cocaine that entered Canada (Stamler et al. 1984).

Transit countries for Europe include France, the primary point of entry in the early 1980s, West Germany, Spain, and Italy (Cocaine Trafficking 1982; U.S. House CFA 1986*b*). A recently reported case presents an interesting variation. In March 1988, U.S. law enforcement officials broke an organized crime distribution network that was sending cocaine from the United States to Italy (Sicily) in exchange for heroin, due to the glut of cocaine in the U.S. market. Virtually any user nation has the potential for becoming a transshipment, or even a processing, country.

THE SOCIAL PHENOMENON OF TRAFFICKING NETWORKS

Until the 1950s, most of the cocaine smuggled out of South American countries was done so by individuals using simple, and mostly commercial, modes of transportation in crossing a border (Granier-Doyeux 1962). The use of organized groups, high-technology equipment and transportation methods, and clandestine facilities to move large amounts of the drug was a rare occurrence. Most individuals, especially in the 1970s, just traveled to Colombia, Bolivia, or another South American country and picked up small amounts of cocaine for personal use or for a small network of friends. A few adventurous individuals made an occupation of it. This early tradition of free-spirited smugglers has largely died out, while organized networks of traffickers have become the norm (Wisotsky 1983). These networks are more vertically integrated than the organizations that traffic in heroin or marijuana, and they can also be geographically dispersed (U.S. Congress OTA 1987).

The use of cocaine increased throughout the 1920s, but with legislative controls in the 1930s, its use declined considerably. Consumption began to increase a bit in the 1950s, primarily the use of coca in South America. The amount of cocaine reaching the United States began to increase considerably around 1971–72, and it increased steadily throughout the 1970s. Some have argued that the increased use of cocaine in the past 15 years is due to controls placed on other stimulant drugs, such as the amphetamines (Inciardi 1987; Wisotsky 1983).

Colombia has been the primary focus of distribution, both geographically (centrally located on transportation routes) and topographically (many forested areas for concealment and open land, especially along the northern coast, for building airstrips). It has also been noted organizationally that the Colombians are world-renowned smugglers (Monastero 1985). The processing and distribution of cocaine are now controlled by at least 12 major cocaine cartels in Colombia (U.S. Congress OTA 1987). These groups are also responsible for the initiation of coca cultivation in Colombia in the late 1970s. Their sophisticated networks assure that up to 90 percent of the illicit cocaine they export reaches their foreign destinations (Craig 1983; Stamler et al. 1984). Bolivian authorities in the late 1970s estimated that 80 percent of the coca leaves produced in that country went to the illicit foreign market (Phillips and Wynne 1980).

Trafficking activities have also shifted from marijuana to almost exclusively cocaine in some countries (Allen 1987). The growing of both cannabis and coca continues, but the real supply efforts have focused on cocaine, primarily due to a much greater price-to-volume ratio (higher prices and smaller amounts to transport). Those who were already growing coca are greatly expanding their operations. Unstable political and economic conditions in Central and South American countries have created ideal environments for the development of an illicit drug trade. As a result of these conditions and shifts in the patterns of the illicit international trade, many of these countries have emerged as both sources and transit points in the supply of drugs to the United States (Solomon 1979).

Trafficking routes shift constantly in response to the discovery and destruction of clandestine processing labs, interdiction activities at borders, surveillance efforts, and other activities (Taylor 1985; Wisotsky 1983). Recent evidence suggests that clandestine processing labs are now operational in many parts of Florida and throughout the United States. The international cocaine trade has reached a point where it is becoming difficult to separate the source countries from the processing and transit countries from the consumer countries. Cocaine use has become more popular in Europe and parts of the Middle East, and even in some African countries (e.g., Nigeria). Transshipment countries for the European market have changed due to changes in law enforcement efforts, patterns of travel, and demand for the drug (Cocaine Trafficking 1982). Most consumer countries in Europe are also transit countries.

STRATEGIES FOR CONTROLLING COCAINE TRAFFICKING

One approach for controlling cocaine trafficking is to focus on the source of supply and attempt to reduce or eliminate production. A number of problems have prevented the successful implementation of this approach, including frequent changes in local governments, local populations in countries with weak economies that are heavily dependent upon coca trafficking for their primary source of income, governments that are indifferent to U.S. interests or believe that the drug "abuse" problem is an issue of demand (i.e., U.S. users have created the cocaine trade), the traditional chewing of coca leaf that must allow for continued cultivation, and, of course, local involvement in the trade (DiCarlo 1982).

The other approach focuses on reducing demand for the drug. This approach uses strategies such as increased domestic law enforcement, education and prevention programs, increased availability of treatment programs and facilities, and even drug-testing programs. It is important to note, however, that the shifting phenomenon seen in the trafficking of drugs from the supply side can also occur if demand is altered. If demand were reduced in a given country, the use of cocaine could increase dramatically elsewhere. This would certainly occur if the issue of extensive cultivation and overproduction is not addressed, and the supply of cocaine continues to escalate at a high rate.

All phases of illicit cocaine trafficking appear to have expanded greatly since the early 1980s, and this illicit industry shows no signs of diminishing despite levels of coca leaf and cocaine production that far exceed current consumer demand (President's Commission 1986). A recent report by the U.S. Office of Technology Assessment concluded that "there is no clear correlation between the level of expenditures or effort devoted to interdiction and the long-term availability of illegally imported drugs in the domestic market" (U.S. Congress OTA 1987, p. 3). The report also noted that no single technology can limit or prevent the illicit drug trade and that new technological developments have only a temporary benefit, since drug traffickers seem to act quickly and successfully to neutralize their effectiveness. In addition, many technological advances are adopted by the traffickers themselves, oftentimes in advance of law enforcement agencies.

This descriptive analysis of the nature and extent of cocaine trafficking suggests that the quality and availability of data and specific information are quite limited. The validity and reliability of the data that are collected are not well known. One of the greatest needs in this area of research is for valid and reliable denominator data. Such information would include precise measurements (or estimates that are continually validated in a retrospective manner) of the total amount of coca that is cultivated, the amount of extracted coca paste and cocaine that is availiable for transshipment, the amount of cocaine that is present in user countries, and related data that would give meaning to numerator statistics (e.g., amounts consumed or seized). Any analysis of supply-reduction or demand-reduction activities would require this type of quality data to evaluate their effectiveness.

The epidemiology of international cocaine trafficking certainly needs to be studied in greater detail. Epidemiologic surveillance requires a data collection system based on controlled measurements (Anthony 1983; Anthony and Trinkoff 1986; Josephson and Carroll 1974). Although existing data sources are valuable in providing some information, they have limitations, including a dependence on drug enforcement decisions and drug control legislation (which can introduce a bias), the nature of reporting efforts leading to over- or underreporting (especially when prevalence of use is low), the lack of research designs and sampling techniques for measuring the effectiveness of specific strategies, the different procedures for calculating estimates, the lack of denominator data, and the lack of independent assessment (i.e., by indigenous research groups or organizations other than law enforcement agencies) in the systematic collection of information (Anthony and Trinkoff 1986). These limitations need to be addressed and corrected so that the value of the epidemiologic approach in studying cocaine trafficking can be realized.

REFERENCES

A condor strikes the snowbirds of Peru. *Newsweek* 108:23, August 18, 1986.

Agreda, R.F. Drug abuse problems in countries of the Andean subregion. *Bulletin on Narcotics* 38:27–36, Jan.-June 1986.

Allen, D., ed. *The Cocaine Crisis*. New York: Plenum Press, 1987.

Anthony, J.C. The regulation of dangerous psychoactive drugs. In: Morgan, J.P., and Kagan, D.V., eds. *Society and Medication: Conflicting Signals for Prescribers and Patients*. Lexington, MA: Lexington Books, 1983. pp. 163–180.

Anthony, J.C., and Trinkoff, A.M. Epidemiologic issues pertinent to international regulation of 28 stimulant-hallucinogenic drugs. *Drug and Alcohol Dependency* 17:193–211, 1986.

Antonil. *Mama Coca*. London: Hassle Free Press, 1978.

Archer, S., and Hawks, R.L. The chemistry of cocaine and its derivatives. In: Mulé, S.J., ed. *Cocaine: Chemical, Biological, Clinical, Social, and Treatment Aspects.* Cleveland, OH: CRC Press, 1976. pp. 15–32.

Brecher, E.M. Drug laws and drug law enforcement: A review and evaluation based on 111 years of experience. *Drugs & Society* 1:1–27, 1986.

Chatterjee, S.K. *Legal Aspects of International Drug Control*. The Hague, Netherlands: Martinus Nijhoff, 1981.

Chopra, I.C., and Chopra, R.N. The cocaine problem in India. *Bulletin on Narcotics* 10:12–24, Apr.-June 1958.

Cocaine trafficking trends in Europe. *Drug Enforcement* Fall:21–22, 1982.

Cohen, S. Recent developments in the abuse of cocaine. *Bulletin on Narcotics* 36:3–14, Apr.-June 1984.

Colombia: South America's cocaine cornucopia. *Drug Enforcement* Fall:23–24, 1982.

Craig, R.B. Domestic implications of illicit Colombian drug production and trafficking. *Journal of Inter-American Studies and World Affairs* 25:325–350, 1983.

Cusack, J.T. The international narcotics control system: Coca and cocaine. In: Pacini, D., and Franquemont, C., eds. *Coca and Cocaine*. Cultural Survival Report #23. Cambridge, MA: Cultural Survival, 1986. pp. 65–71.

DiCarlo, D.L. International initiatives to control coca production and cocaine trafficking. *Drug Enforcement* Fall:6–9, 1982.

Erickson, P.G.; Adlaf, E.M.; Murray, G.F.; and Smart, R.G. *The Steel Drug: Cocaine in Perspective*. Lexington, MA: Lexington Books, 1987.

The federal strategy. *Drug Enforcement* Spring:10–14, 1983.

Granier-Doyeux, M. Some sociological aspects of the problem of cocaism. *Bulletin on Narcotics* 14:1–16, Oct.-Dec. 1962.

Healy, K. The boom within the crisis: Some recent effects of foreign cocaine markets on Bolivian rural society and economy. In: Pacini, D., and Franquemont,

C., eds. *Coca and Cocaine*. Cultural Survival Report #23. Cambridge, MA: Cultural Survival, 1986. pp. 101–143.

Henman, A.; Lewis, R.; and Malyon, T. *Big Deal: The Politics of the Illicit Drug Business*. London: Pluto Press, 1985.

Inciardi, J.A. Beyond cocaine: Basuco, crack and other coca products. *Contemporary Drug Problems* 14:461–492, 1987.

Jeri, F.R., ed. *Cocaine 1980*. Lima, Peru: Pacific Press, 1980.

Josephson, E., and Carroll, E., eds. *Drug Use: Epidemiological and Sociological Approaches*. Washington, DC: Hemisphere, 1974.

Kline, D. How to lose the coke war. *Atlantic* 259:22–27, 1987.

Monastero, F.V. Controlling the supply of cocaine: The law enforcement response. In: Brink, C., ed. *Cocaine: A Symposium*. Madison, WI: Wisconsin Institute on Drug Abuse, 1985. pp.13–15.

National Narcotics Intelligence Consumers Committee. *Narcotics Intelligence Estimate, 1978*. Washington, DC: Supt. of Docs., U.S. Govt. Print. Off., 1979.

National Narcotics Intelligence Consumers Committee. *Narcotics Intelligence Estimate, 1979*. Washington, DC: Supt. of Docs., U.S. Govt. Print. Off., 1980.

National Narcotics Intelligence Consumers Committee. *Narcotics Intelligence Estimate, 1980*. Washington, DC: Supt. of Docs., U.S. Govt. Print. Off., 1981*a*.

National Narcotics Intelligence Consumers Committee. *The Supply of Drugs to the U.S. Illicit Market from Foreign and Domestic Sources in 1979 (with projections for 1980–1983)*. Washington, DC: Supt. of Docs., U.S. Govt. Print. Off., 1981*b*.

National Narcotics Intelligence Consumers Committee. *Narcotics Intelligence Estimate, 1981*. Washington, DC: Supt. of Docs., U.S. Govt. Print. Off., 1982.

National Narcotics Intelligence Consumers Committee. *Narcotics Intelligence Estimate, 1982*. Washington, DC: Supt. of Docs., U.S. Govt. Print. Off., 1983.

National Narcotics Intelligence Consumers Committee. *Narcotics Intelligence Estimate, 1983*. Washington, DC: Supt. of Docs., U.S. Govt. Print. Off., 1984.

National Narcotics Intelligence Consumers Committee. *Narcotics Intelligence Estimate, 1984*. Washington, DC: Supt. of Docs., U.S. Govt. Print. Off., 1985*a*.

National Narcotics Intelligence Consumers Committee. *The Supply of Drugs to the U.S. Illicit Market from Foreign and Domestic Sources in 1980 (with projections thru 1984)*. Washington, DC: Supt. of Docs., U.S. Govt. Print. Off., 1985*b*.

National Narcotics Intelligence Consumers Committee. *Narcotics Intelligence Estimate, 1985*. Washington, DC: Supt. of Docs., U.S. Govt. Print. Off., 1986.

National Narcotics Intelligence Consumers Committee. *The Supply of Illicit Drugs to the United States from Foreign and Domestic Sources in 1985 and 1986 (with near term projections)*. Washington, DC: Supt. of Docs., U.S. Govt. Print. Off., 1987.

Pacini, D., and Franquemont, C., eds. *Coca and Cocaine*. Cultural Survival Report #23. Cambridge, MA: Cultural Survival, 1986.

Phillips, J.L., and Wynne, R.W. *Cocaine: The Mystique and the Reality*. New York: Avon, 1980.

Plowman, T. Coca chewing and the botanical origins of coca (*Erythroxylum Spp.*) in South America. In: Pacini, D., and Franquemont, C., eds. *Coca and Cocaine*. Cultural Survival Report #23. Cambridge, MA: Cultural Survival, 1986. pp. 5–33.

President's Commission on Organized Crime. *Organized Crime and Cocaine Trafficking*. Washington, DC: Supt. of Docs., U.S. Govt. Print. Off., 1984.

President's Commission on Organized Crime. *America's Habit: Drug Abuse, Drug Trafficking and Organized Crime*. Washington, DC: Supt. of Docs., U.S. Govt. Print. Off., 1986.

Renborg, B.A. *International Drug Control*. Washington, DC: Carnegie Endowment for International Peace, 1947.

Solomon, R. The evolution of opiate use in China: The origins of the illicit international trade. *Journal of Psychedelic Drugs* 10:43–49, 1978.

Solomon, R. The development and politics of the Latin American heroin market. *Journal of Drug Issues* 9:349–369, 1979.

Stamler, R.T.; Fahlman, R.C.; and Keele, S.A. Illicit traffic and abuse of cocaine in Canada. *Bulletin on Narcotics* 36:45–55, Apr.-June 1984.

Strug, D.L. The foreign politics of cocaine: Comments on a plan to eradicate the coca leaf in Peru. In: Pacini, D., and Franquemont, D., eds. *Coca and Cocaine*. Cultural Survival Report #23. Cambridge, MA: Cultural Survival, 1986. pp. 73–88.

Taylor, C.D. International consequences of the U.S. demand for cocaine. In: Brink, C., ed. *Cocaine: A Symposium*. Madison, WI: Wisconsin Institute on Drug Abuse, 1985. pp. 4–6.

United Nations. *The United Nations and Drug Abuse Control*. New York: United Nations, 1987*a*.

United Nations. *Report on the International Conference on Drug Abuse and Illicit Trafficking*. New York: United Nations, 1987*b*.

United Nations Commission on Narcotic Drugs. Ten years of the coca monopoly in Peru. *Bulletin on Narcotics* 14:9–17, Jan.-March, 1962.

United Nations Commission on Narcotic Drugs. Twenty years of narcotics control under the United Nations. *Bulletin on Narcotics* 18:1–67, Jan.-March, 1966.

United Nations International Narcotics Control Board. *I.N.C.B. Reports*. New York: United Nations, 1968–1981*a*.

United Nations International Narcotics Control Board. *Estimated World Requirements of Narcotic Drugs*. New York: United Nations, 1968–1981*b*.

United Nations Permanent Central Narcotics Board. Work of the PCNB in 1965. *Bulletin on Narcotics* 18:43–48, Apr.-June 1966.

U.S. Congressional Office of Technology Assessment. *The Border War on Drugs*. Washington, DC: Supt. of Docs., U.S. Govt. Print. Off., 1987.

U.S. Drug Enforcement Administration. *Intelligence Collection and Analytical Methods*. Washington, DC: Supt. of Docs., U.S. Govt. Print. Off., 1987*a*.

U.S. Drug Enforcement Administration. *Special Report: The Illicit Drug Situation in the U.S. and Canada, 1984–1986*. Washington, DC: Supt. of Docs., U.S. Govt. Print. Off., 1987*b*.

U.S. House Committee on Foreign Affairs. *International Narcotics Control*. Washington, DC: Supt. of Docs., U.S. Govt. Print. Off., 1982.

U.S. House Committee on Foreign Affairs. *Recent Developments in Colombian Narcotics Control*. Washington, DC: Supt. of Docs., U.S. Govt. Print. Off., 1984*a*.

U.S. House Committee on Foreign Affairs. *U.S. Response to Cuban Government Involvement in Narcotics Trafficking and Review of Worldwide Illicit Narcotics Situation*. Washington, DC: Supt. of Docs., U.S. Govt. Print. Off., 1984*b*.

U.S. House Committee on Foreign Affairs. *U.S. Narcotics Control Programs Overseas: An Assessment*. Washington, DC: Supt. of Docs., U.S. Govt. Print. Off., 1985.

U.S. House Committee on Foreign Affairs. *Nicaraguan Government Involvement in Narcotics Trafficking*. Washington, DC: Supt. of Docs., U.S. Govt. Print. Off., 1986*a*.

U.S. House Committee on Foreign Affairs. *Developments in Latin American Narcotics Control*. Washington, DC: Supt. of Docs., U.S. Govt. Print. Off., 1986*b*.

U.S. House Committee on Foreign Affairs. *Annual Review of International Narcotics Control Programs and the Impact of Gramm-Rudman on Overseas Narcotics Control Efforts*. Washington, DC: Supt. of Docs., U.S. Govt. Print. Off., 1986*c*.

U.S. House Committee on Foreign Affairs. *The Role of the U.S. Military in Narcotics Control Overseas*. Washington DC: Supt. of Docs., U.S. Govt. Print. Off., 1986*d*.

U.S. House Committee on Foreign Affairs. *Review of Latin American Narcotics Control Issues*. Washington, DC: Supt. of Docs., U.S. Govt. Print. Off., 1987*a*.

U.S. House Committee on Foreign Affairs. *Status Report on GAO's Worldwide Review of Narcotics Control Programs*. Washington, DC: Supt. of Docs., U.S. Govt. Print. Off., 1987*b*.

U.S. House Committee on Foreign Affairs. *U.S. Narcotics Control Programs Overseas: An Assessment*. Washington, DC: Supt. of Docs., U.S. Govt. Print. Off., 1987*c*.

U.S. House Committee on Foreign Affairs. *Narcotics Issues in the Bahamas and the Caribbean*. Washington, DC: Supt. of Docs., U.S. Govt. Print. Off., 1987*d*.

U.S. House Committee on Foreign Affairs. *U.S. Narcotics Control Efforts in the Caribbean*. Washington, DC: Supt. of Docs., U.S. Govt. Print. Off., 1987*e*.

U.S. House Committee on Government Operations. *Continued Review of the Administration's Drug Interdiction Efforts*. Washington, DC: Supt. of Docs., U.S. Govt. Print. Off., 1985.

U.S. House Committee on the Judiciary. *Drug Production and Trafficking in Latin America and the Caribbean*. Washington, DC: Supt. of Docs., U.S. Govt. Print. Off., 1984.

U.S. House Select Committee on Narcotics Abuse and Control. *Cocaine and Marihuana Trafficking in Southeastern U.S.* Washington, DC: Supt. of Docs., U.S. Govt. Print. Off., 1978*a*.

U.S. House Select Committee on Narcotics Abuse and Control. *Drug Trafficking In and Through Hawaii and Guam*. Washington, DC: Supt. of Docs., U.S. Govt. Print. Off., 1978*b*.

U.S. House Select Committee on Narcotics Abuse and Control. *Cocaine: A Major Drug Issue of the Seventies*. Washington, DC: Supt. of Docs., U.S. Govt. Print. Off., 1980.

U.S. House Select Committee on Narcotics Abuse and Control. *International Narcotics Control Study Mission to Latin America and Jamaica*. Washington, DC: Supt. of Docs., U.S. Govt. Print. Off., 1984.

U.S. House Select Committee on Narcotics Abuse and Control. *The Federal War on Drugs: Past, Present and Future*. Washington, DC: Supt. of Docs., U.S. Govt. Print. Off., 1987.

U.S. Treasury Department Bureau of Narcotics. *Traffic in Opium and Other Dangerous Drugs*. Washington, DC: Supt. of Docs., U.S. Govt. Print. Off., 1943–1961.

Walker, W.O. *Drug Control in the Americas*. Albuquerque, NM: University of New Mexico Press, 1981.

Warner, J. International programs. *Drug Enforcement*. Fall:27–30, 1983.

Wisotsky, S. Exposing the war on cocaine: The futility and destructiveness of prohibition. *Wisconsin Law Review* 1983:1305–1426, 1983.

AUTHOR

Michael Montagne, Ph.D.
College of Pharmacy and Allied Health
Northeastern University
360 Huntington Ave.
Boston MA 02115

Cocaine Price, Purity, and Trafficking Trends

Maurice Rinfret

During Fiscal Year (FY) 1987, the Drug Enforcement Agency (DEA) seized approximately 36,000 kilograms of cocaine hydrochloride, compared to some 200 kilograms of cocaine confiscated in FY1977. Despite this record total, which equates to roughly 60 million retail grams at current street-level purities, cocaine continues to be readily available in multikilogram quantities in all of the larger metropolitan areas throughout the United States and in no less than multiounce quantities in the less populated ones. The primary domestic entry point for much of the Nation's cocaine supply is the Miami/south Florida area. Other domestic areas of significance include New York City and those States adjacent to the Mexican border. Cocaine is trafficked by independent operators and a large variety of groups varying in ethnic composition and size. Colombian nationals are the predominant ethnic group involved in cocaine processing, importation, and distribution.

One means of determining if a drug is increasing or decreasing in availability, provided demand for that drug remains steady, is to monitor trends in its purchase price and purity. Price decreases and purity increases generally reflect larger supplies and greater competition among traffickers to provide the user population with the highest quality product at the lowest possible price. From the early 1980s to the present, cocaine prices have decreased and purities have increased.

In 1982, the national wholesale price for a kilogram of cocaine hydrochloride ranged from $47,000 to $70,000. Currently, the national price ranges from $10,000 to $38,000 per kilogram, the lowest price reported to date. Prices in the major importation and distribution points have also decreased. In Miami, the price of a kilogram declined from a range of $47,000 to $60,000 in 1982 to a current range of $13,000 to $16,000. Prices in New York City over the same period dropped from a range of $50,000 to $65,000 to $14,000 to $25,000. Finally, in Los Angeles, the price of a kilogram decreased from a range of $55,000 to $70,000 in 1982 to $10,000 to $16,000 currently, the lowest price of any area in the country.

While the price at the wholesale kilogram level has decreased, purity has remained very high throughout this period, averaging 90 plus percent according to DEA laboratory analysis, a figure that is considered to be relatively pure cocaine.

At or near the end of the distribution chain, cocaine is increasingly approaching the relatively pure state found at the wholesale level. At the ounce level, purity has increased from an average of 50 to 60 percent in 1982 to roughly 80 percent currently, while purity at the street or gram level has about doubled during this same timeframe from 35 to 70 percent.

As purities increased at this level of the traffic, prices consistently declined. In 1982, the national price for an ounce of cocaine hydrochloride ranged from $2,000 to $3,000. Currently, the national price ranges from $500 to $2,200 per ounce, the lowest price reported to date. In Miami, the price of an ounce declined from $2,000 to $2,400 in 1982 to a current range of $650 to $800. Prices in New York City for the same period dropped from a range of $2,000 to $2,600 to $650 to $1,100. In Los Angeles, the price of an ounce decreased from a range of $2,000 to $3,000 in 1982 to $500 to $800 currently, once again the lowest price of any area in the country. At the street level, the national price for a gram dropped from $100 to $150 in 1982 to a current price of $80 to $120 in most areas.

CRACK

Unlike the pattern for cocaine hydrochloride, the average price and purity of crack has remained basically stable since this form of cocaine first became widely available in late 1985. In most cities, crack sells for $10 to $50 in quantities ranging from one-tenth to one-half of a gram. Most DEA Divisions report purity figures that generally fall within the 50- to 90-percent purity range. The relative stability in crack prices and purity during this timeframe indicates that crack trafficking and use may have stabilized at relatively high levels in a number of cities.

The majority of crack available in most areas is in retail amounts only, manufactured and distributed by numerous street-level distributors. However, crack-cocaine distribution is no longer solely confined to street-level sales and crack houses within a particular city neighborhood, as it was during the latter half of 1985 and early 1986. A number of large, centralized organizations operating in one or more cities or States and capable of manufacturing, trafficking, and distributing wholesale quantities of crack have emerged. Strong law enforcement responses have eliminated some of these organizations, while others continue to operate. Violence and homicides have increased as power struggles over drug territory develop among retail-level groups, inner-city street gangs, and large-scale organizations attempting to expand their distribution areas.

Four major groups dominate the interstate trafficking of crack throughout the United States: Jamaican, Haitian, and Dominican networks and splinter groups of black street gangs based in south central Los Angeles. Jamaican gangs, also known as posses, comprise the largest crack trafficking network uncovered to date. These gangs are actively engaged in the distribution of crack in cities in the eastern and midwestern United States, including Denver, Minneapolis, Miami, New York, Kansas City, Washington, DC, Philadelphia, and Alexandria, Virginia. These posses originally formed in Jamaica, and key members formed their alliances based on neighborhood and political ties with Jamaica. The majority of posse members are convicted felons or illegal aliens. Virtually every geographic area experiencing a Jamaican posse problem has a tremendous increase in violent activity.

Haitian traffickers, consisting primarily of migrant farm workers, are actively engaged in distributing crack along the eastern seaboard of the United States. Principal distribution areas include Florida, Georgia, southern Delaware, eastern Maryland, Baltimore, upstate New York, and Martinsburg, West Virginia. Haitian traffickers process crack in a unique form—small, rectangular strips. These strips, referred to as "French Fry" crack, range in length from 1/2 to 1 inch and usually weigh as much as half a gram. A strip weighing half a gram retails for approximately $50.

Dominican trafficking groups operate primarily in the northeastern United States. Their major crack retail outlets are located in New York City, Providence, Rhode Island, and Stamford, Connecticut. Several large-scale Dominican-run operations, which were distributing several pounds of crack per week, were immobilized in New York City during 1987.

Crack distribution in Los Angeles is mainly controlled by splinter groups of two black street gangs, the "Blood" and the "Crip." These former gang members, ranging in age from the early to mid-twenties, use the gang names to identify their organizations. These subgroups are independent entities, often operating in competition with each other. Although crack operations are not centralized and controlled by one major gang overseeing and coordinating their activities, law enforcement officers warn that these subgroups are highly organized and extremely violent. Crack trafficking has become so competitive in southern California that Crip splinter groups have begun distributing crack in Phoenix, Denver, Salt Lake City, Las Vegas, Seattle, Portland, and New Orleans. Former members of the Blood gang have recently opened distribution networks in Sacramento and Tucson.

CRACK IN THE DEA FIELD DIVISIONS

Atlanta—Crack is available in adequate consumer quantities throughout the area and can be classified as a sporadic, retail-level trafficking situation. Georgia and the Carolinas are primarily transit States for crack originating in Florida and destined for the northeastern United States.

Boston—In the New England region, crack is found predominantly in Connecticut, Rhode Island, and Massachusetts. Connecticut, with its proximity to New York City, is experiencing the most significant crack problem in the Division. New Hampshire, Vermont, and Maine have encountered very little crack use to date. Crack availability has increased in Stamford, Connecticut, and is transported from the Bronx, New York. The availability of crack has risen significantly in Providence, Rhode Island, and is principally controlled by Dominican and Puerto Rican groups.

Chicago—No cases are currently under investigation or being developed in Chicago, as no serious crack problem appears to exist in this city. Sporadic appearances of crack have been reported in North Dakota, Indiana, and Wisconsin. Crack houses have recently appeared in South Bend, Indiana, and Peoria, Illinois. Crack cocaine availability has increased in the Minneapolis-St. Paul area.

Dallas—Crack remains a serious problem in Dallas, Texas, where more than 75 crack houses are currently operating. Distribution is controlled by Jamaican organizations. The Fort Worth Police Department reports that crack and fortified crack houses are becoming more prevalent. Crack has surpassed PCP as the drug of choice among users in Tulsa, Oklahoma, and is readily available in Oklahoma City. California is the main source of supply for Oklahoma.

Denver—Crack availability has increased substantially in the last 6 to 9 months. Crack houses in the city of Denver are run by Jamaicans with the assistance of local recruits. The price of a retail-level dose of crack-cocaine ($25 for one-tenth of a gram) is one of the highest in the Nation.

Suburban dealers convert their own cocaine hydrochloride into crack rather than buying it from Jamaicans in metropolitan Denver.

Detroit—Crack is readily available in the cities of Detroit and Flint. Limited quantities of crack have been reported in Kentucky and Ohio. Although heroin use is still a problem in Detroit, it is overshadowed by the availability of cocaine hydrochloride and crack. An estimated 1,000 crack houses and street corner locations operate in Detroit at any given time.

Houston—The crack problem in the Houston Division has somewhat diminished. Crack is supplied both locally and from sources in Miami and Los Angeles. The Houston Police Department made over 580 arrests for crack sale/possession during the last year. San Antonio is the only other city in the Division that had a crack investigation in the last 3 years. This investigation involved a small crack-house operation.

Los Angeles—Crack distribution and use are widespread in Los Angeles, Riverside, Santa Barbara, and Las Vegas. Crack is available in multikilogram quantities throughout the Los Angeles area. Kilogram quantities can be purchased for $15,500 to $19,500 from the black street gangs, who have distribution networks throughout the northwestern and southwestern United States. Crack has appeared in Hawaii, but is not considered a serious problem.

Miami—Crack is readily available on the streets of Miami, Ft. Lauderdale, Tampa, and several areas in central Florida. Local authorities estimate that Miami has over 700 crack houses. Distributors from southern Florida are expanding operations into the Pensacola and Tallahassee area of northern Florida in an attempt to create new markets or take over existing crack markets. In FY1987, the Tampa office participated in 100 crack investigations, the Metro-Dade Police Department reported 577 arrests, and the Ft. Lauderdale office participated in over 1,500 arrests.

Newark—The crack situation in New Jersey has leveled off or is on the decline, and no city in New Jersey has reported any increase in crack cases or in the use of crack.

New Orleans—Crack continues to increase in popularity among cocain abusers, particularly along the Gulf Coast. In Louisiana, metropolitan New Orleans has the largest crack problem. Abuse levels in New Orleans have increased to the point where suppliers are dealing in kilograms. A black street gang from Los Angeles has emerged as the main source of crack. The Mississippi Bureau of Narcotics reports the greatest increases in central and southeastern Mississippi (Gulfport and Pascagoula). Crack availability is on the rise in Alabama; however, the amounts surfacing there are believed to be for personal use only.

New York—Crack trafficking and abuse continue to be serious problems in New York City and the surrounding suburbs; crack is available on a limited basis in upstate New York. Several large crack organizations whose structure approaches that of mid-level cocaine or heroin dealers have appeared in New York City. Several organizations reportedly are capable of supplying 10,000 vials of crack per week. Primary crack traffickers are of Dominican origin.

Philadelphia—Crack-cocaine houses under control of Jamaican trafficking organizations are beginning to surface in the Philadelphia Field Division. The Wilmington Office reports a crack problem in the southern Delaware area. Fifteen crack-related arrests and 12 pounds of crack were seized during 1987. These investigations centered around a Haitian farm labor community. Neither Harrisburg nor Pittsburgh report having a crack problem at this time.

Phoenix—Crack-cocaine is available in the project areas of Phoenix. Crack is also available in Tucson. Crack-cocaine in Arizona is supplied by the Crip and Blood gangs of Los Angeles.

San Diego—The involvement of black street gangs in crack distribution and related assaults and murders has been considerably reduced. This is the result of 35 Narcotics Task Force cases that targeted these gangs for immobilization. One case resulted in 100 arrests and immobilized the principal crack gang in San Diego. Crack remains a serious problem in minority enclaves of the city and suburban areas.

San Francisco—Crack continues to be a problem in the San Francisco Bay area. Several kilogram-sized seizures have been made in San Francisco and Oakland. The Sacramento area has experienced an increase in crack houses and crack seizures. Gang members from Los Angeles have set up distribution systems in Sacramento, where random shootings among the Crip and Blood street gangs have occurred.

Seattle—Two cities in the Division have measurable crack-cocaine activity: Seattle, Washington, and Portland, Oregon. Two gangs, the Blood and Crip, are attempting to expand their base of operations in these cities. Seattle police estimate the operation of 50 crack houses at any given time and more than 100 gang members in the metropolitan area.

Portland reports widespread availability of crack among all ethnic groups.

St. Louis—Crack does not pose a serious problem in St. Louis. The majority of crack arrests and seizures involve low-level violators and street-level dealers. Crack is a problem in Kansas City, which reports substantial involvement of Jamaican traffickers in the distribution of both crack and cocaine hydrochloride. Their level of crack distribution ranges from several pounds to several kilograms. Crack houses have been identified in the metropolitan area of Omaha, Nebraska. Quantities of ready-made crack have been transported into the area from Los Angeles.

Washington, DC—A growing number of Jamaican distributors have entered the cocaine trade in the Washington, DC, metropolitan area. They have established crack houses in the greater metropolitan area and may also be supplying the Norfolk and Richmond, Virginia, areas. The violence associated with these drug distribution rings is escalating to alarming levels in the Washington, DC, area, with a number of murders attributed to turf battles among rival Jamaican and inner-city black trafficking organizations. Elsewhere in the Division, crack is distributed in the more rural Maryland locations, especially communities with large Haitian and Jamaican migrant worker populations.

AUTHOR

Maurice Rinfret
Office of Intelligence
Drug Enforcement Administration
1405 Eye Street, NW
Room 1223, OIS
Washington, DC 20537

The Dynamic Relationships of the Cocaine System in the United States

Raymond C. Shreckengost

Estimates of the amount of cocaine imported into the United States can be obtained from a dynamic simulation model that replicates the behavior of the cocaine system in the United States. The method used to design and develop the model, system dynamics, has several features that are highly advantageous in this sort of analysis, such as the ability to use expert opinion to identify the critical factors that influence the behavior of the system.

Data supplied by the Office of Intelligence of the Drug Enforcement Administration (DEA) and the National Institute on Drug Abuse (NIDA) were used extensively in the development of the model.

In an earlier paper, it was recognized that the structure of the heroin and cocaine systems had much in common (Gardiner and Shreckengost 1985). This chapter exploits that commonality by adopting the influence structure of the heroin system. However, the heroin model focused on the effects of imports on system behavior, while here we rely initially on the user population, cocaine purity, and consumption pattern to estimate the amount of cocaine imported. Even so, the end product of both the cocaine and heroin models is similar in that the relationship of imports to their street price, purity, and user population are explicitly established in the models.

While their basic system structures are similar, the characteristics of these drugs are strikingly different. For example, heroin acts as a depressant but cocaine is a stimulant; heroin and cocaine overdoses produce different clinical outcomes; in this country, heroin is most commonly injected and cocaine is most commonly taken intranasally; and the major sources of heroin are in the Far East, the Near East, and Mexico, but cocaine comes largely from South America.

The dimensions of the cocaine problem are also strikingly different. According to the 1985 NIDA Household Survey on Drug Abuse (NIDA 1987), nearly 2 million living Americans aged 12 or older had ever used heroin, and slightly more than 10 times as many had ever tried cocaine.

Given the dimensions of the cocaine system, it might be expected that data relating to cocaine would be more readily available than heroin data. Such is not the case. Perhaps because of the heretofore largely unrecognized dangers of cocaine use, fewer data are available to validate a cocaine model. Consequently, the earlier heroin model assists greatly by providing an organizing framework for the data that are available.

THE STRUCTURE OF THE MODEL

The key to the design of the model was the notion that the behavior of the cocaine system in the United States is affected most importantly by how much cocaine is available at any time relative to the 12- to 34-year-old population. This ratio is referred to in the model as the Relative Abundance Measure. This indicates the surplus, adequacy, or shortage of the cocaine supply at any time. This, in turn, directly affects such things as cocaine price, purity, and the number of cocaine users. These influences are depicted in figure 1.

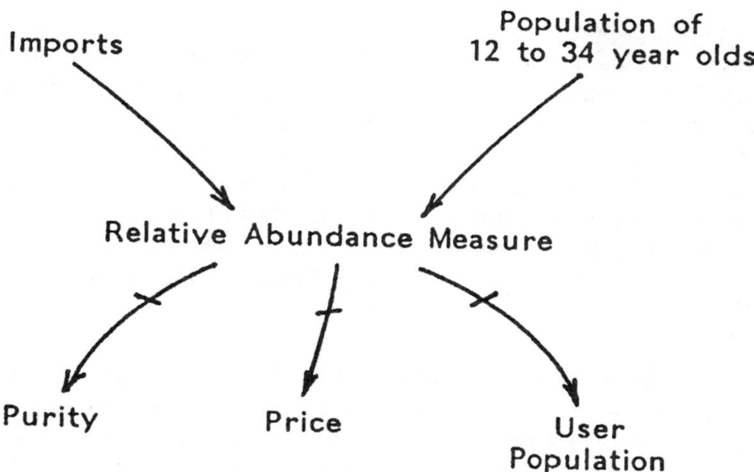

FIGURE 1. *Supply ratio influences in the cocaine system*

A set of invariant relationships among price, purity, and user population and the relative abundance of cocaine was derived iteratively so that the model would generate price, purity, and user population values consistent with observed values when driven by the proper import estimates over the selected period. The bars across the arrows leading to price, purity, and user population indicate that the impact of relative abundance is delayed. The amount of the delay increases with growing abundance, since it takes some time for changes in imports or abundance to propagate through the system.

As is often the case, these relationships appear simplistic and obvious once described, but they are not so apparent beforehand. In addition, some issues, such as the definition of a cocaine user, had to be resolved. Heavy users may use a gram per day; light, sporadic users may use a gram a year; and others fall between these extremes. Some are regular users, others confine their consumption to binges. The heavy users are comparatively few, the occasional users comparatively many. As will be seen later, the purity of the cocaine consumed and the number of users both increase and decrease as the Relative Abundance Measure shifts. Total consumption is thus affected by both the number of users at any time and the purity of the cocaine they buy.

When developing a model, the relationships among the influential factors must be expressed clearly and explicitly—for example, the way the purity of cocaine sold to users varies with the availability of cocaine. Embedding these relationships as references in the model enables a computer to perform the tedious, repetitive processing tasks entailed in producing the data and graphs describing the system's behavior. The factors influencing the behavior of this model of the cocaine system are described in figure 2 and quantitatively defined in the model equations.

The completed model can be used to estimate cocaine Imports, User Population, Purity, and Current Price when any one of these factors and the 12- to 34-year-old population is known. These predictions depend on the model's behavior, and the way the model behaves is determined by the influences, or structure, described above. Whether the model can be used confidently depends largely on how closely the predictions of the model match their real-life counterparts: for example, do the model's predictions for Purity match independently measured national averages for purity for all import levels as the 12- to 34-year-old population changes?

The independently measured values for purity, price, and population are not direct inputs for the model, but they were used as historical data to establish the relationships among the model parameters. Historical data

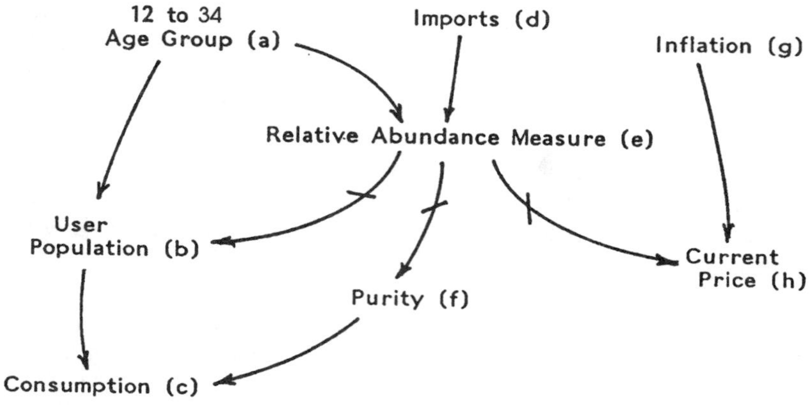

FIGURE 2. *Influence diagram*

a. At the upper left hand corner is the 12- to 34-year-old Age Group, whose population is derived from census data.

b. The User Population, a fraction of the age group, varies with the availability of cocaine—the Relative Abundance Measure. If desired, the User Population could also be shown as responding to Price. As will be explained later, Price is not directly affected as it is in normal marketing systems, and the Relative Abundance Measure was selected as the more appropriate factor to use.

c. The size of the User Population and the Purity of what users buy determines Consumption. The various classes of users and the amounts they normally use per day are not treated separately, but they could be if desired.

d. The sources of cocaine imports for the U.S. cocaine market are aggregated and not treated explicitly in the model.

e. The Relative Abundance Measure provides a simple index relating weekly cocaine imports to the 12- to 34-year-old Age Group. This ratio affects both the cocaine User Population and the Purity of the cocaine it buys. However, effects of a sudden change in imports are delayed depending on the relative abundance when the change occurs. The bar across the arrow showing that Imports influence the Relative Abundance Measure symbolizes the delay.

f. Purity is directly influenced by Relative Abundance and, with the User Population, determines Consumption.

g. The values used to correct for Inflation are taken from the Commodity Price Inflation Index.

h. As distinct from purchases of other things such as bread, beans, or bacon, cocaine is not bought directly at so many dollars per milligram but by the package, in which the amount of pure cocaine is variable. Thus, price per milligram is derived indirectly.

are also used to test how well the estimated cocaine import rates cause model behavior to match real-life behavior. Since the availability of historical data is sporadic (the model predictions are continuous), these comparisons amount to point checks rather than continuous comparisons. Again, the important criterion is whether the model provides good predictions when using only the estimated cocaine imports over the last 10 years as the input to the model. A detailed discussion of system dynamic model tests applied to the heroin model is also relevant to this model (Shreckengost 1985; Gardiner and Shreckengost 1985).

HOW COCAINE ABUNDANCE AFFECTS THE USER POPULATION

Table 1, showing the cocaine User Population and use frequency table, is based on these surveys and Bureau of the Census population data (Miller 1983). The percentages relating to frequency of use refer to the 12- to 34-year-old age group. The 12- to 34-year-old age group users make up 90 percent of the total cocaine users in the United States. The model compensates for this understatement when estimating the total user population, total cocaine consumption, and the value of cocaine sales. The basic data from which table 1 was developed are provided in the appendix.

The growth in the cocaine User Population is shown in figure 3. Note that the percentage of the 12- to 34-year-old population using cocaine in the

TABLE 1. *Cocaine user population and frequency of use (population in thousands)*

Year	12- to 34-year-old population	Ever used No.	Ever used %	Last year No.	Last year %	Last month No.	Last month %
1975	84,141	5,977	7.1	3,393	4.0	1,193	1.4
1976*	85,971	6,454	7.5	3,302	3.8	1,052	1.2
1977*	87,518	8,752	10.0	4,725	5.4	1,657	1.9
1978	88,663	11,818	13.3	6,977	7.9	2,825	3.2
1979*	89,846	14,363	16.0	9,372	10.4	4,263	4.7
1980	90,985	15,979	17.6	9,915	10.9	4,131	4.5
1981	91,810	17,558	19.1	10,407	11.3	3,965	4.3
1982*	91,574	19,154	20.9	10,932	11.9	3,814	4.2

* Household survey years

past month changed little from 1979 through 1982, although the percentage who had ever used cocaine, or used it in the last year, continued to rise. Last Year and Last Month users as a percentage of the Ever Used category peaked in 1979, suggesting a rise in abundance and the introduction of many new users.

In table 1, the Last Year users ranged from 51 to 65 percent of the Ever Used group. However, when Last Month Users were subtracted from Last Year Users, leaving only those who used cocaine in the last year but not in the last month, this group was very stable, varying from about 35 to 37 percent of the Ever Used population. Last Month Users extended from 16 to 30 percent of the Ever Used group, but figure 3 suggests that when there is an influx of cocaine, this group includes a high percentage of new users. Long-term, regular monthly users probably account for 22 percent of Ever Users.

The User Population used in the model is the sum of these long-term trends, which amounts to 58 percent of the Ever Used population. The User Population percentage of the 12- to 34-year-old age group changes with cocaine abundance, as shown in Figure 4.

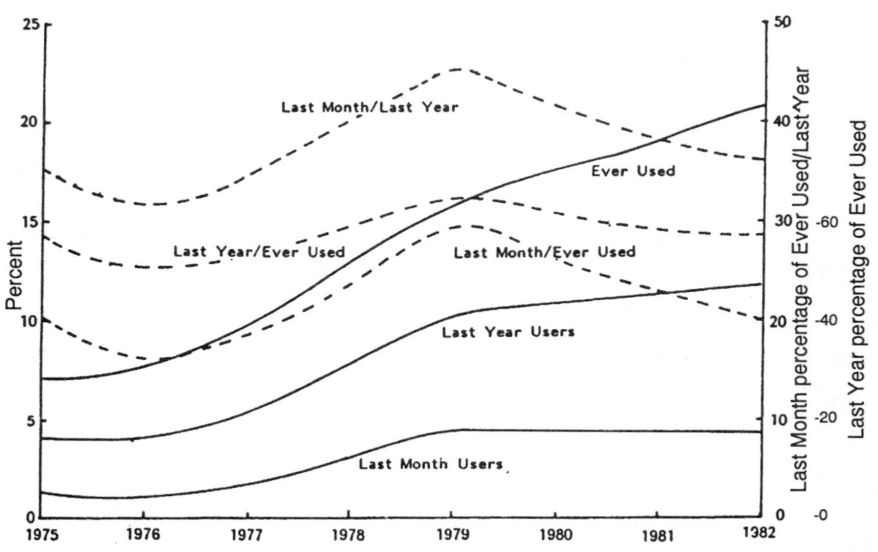

FIGURE 3. *Cocaine user population (as a percentage of the 12- to 34- year-old population)*

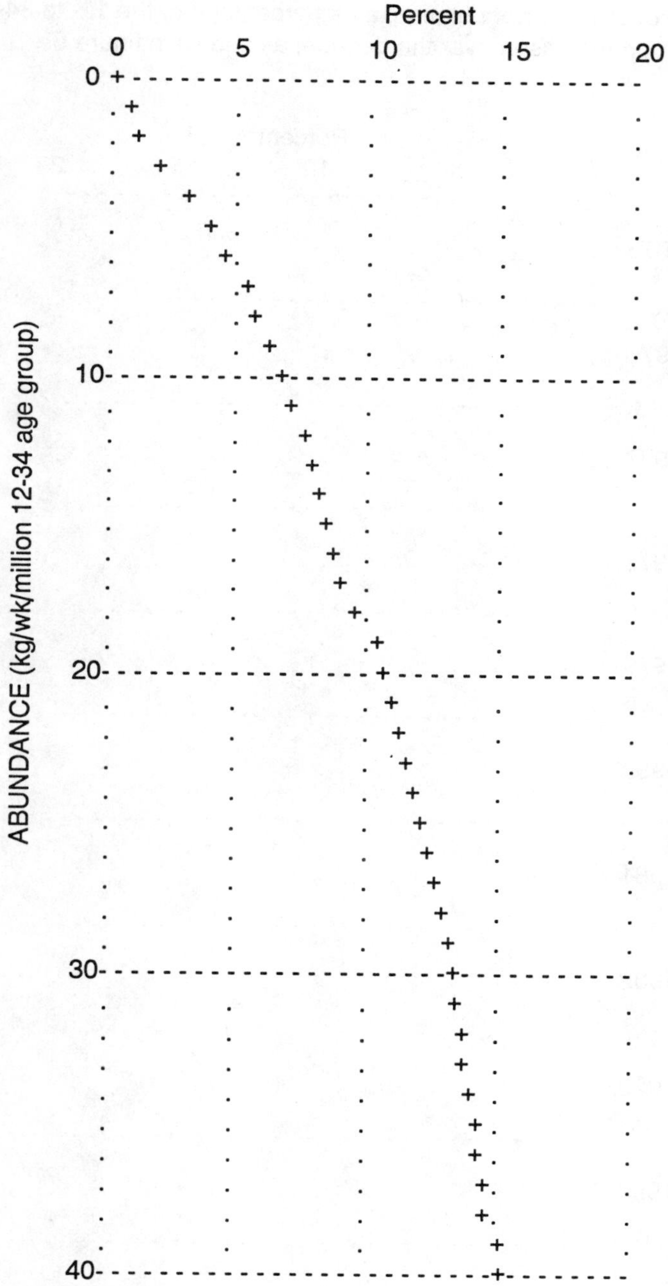

FIGURE 4. *User population fraction change with abundance*

The total cocaine user population, as a percentage of the 12- to 34-year-old age group, has risen over the decade, as shown in figure 5.

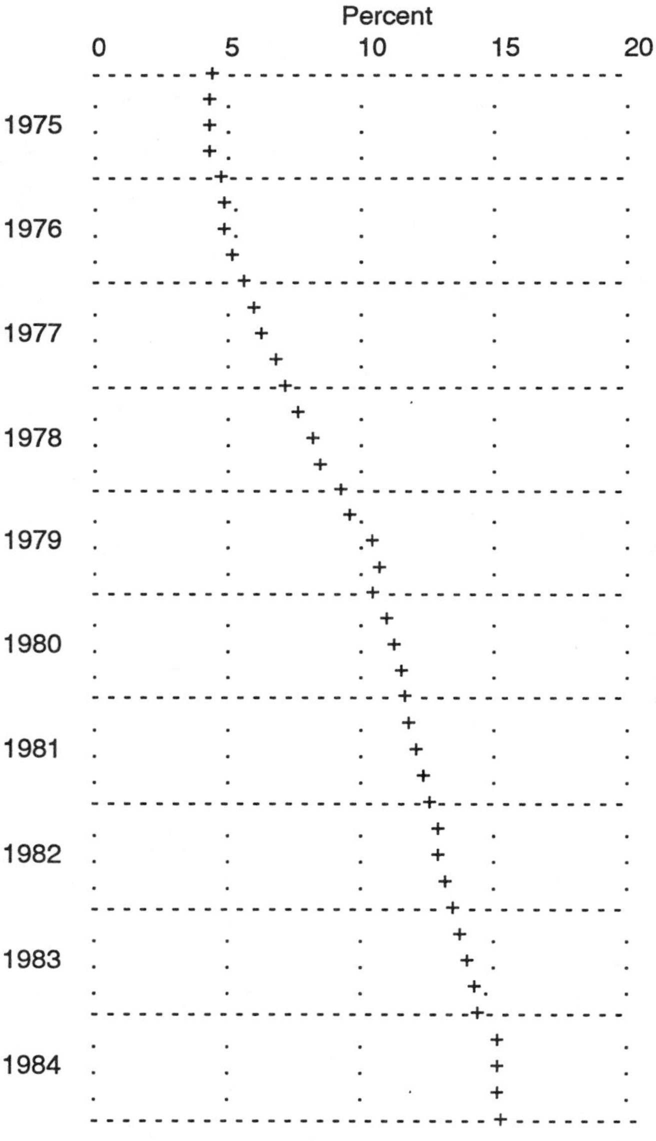

FIGURE 5. *Total cocaine user population as a percentage of the 12-34 age group*

The total cocaine User Population is shown in figure 6. As explained earlier, the 12- to 34-year-old user group is about 90 percent of the total user population shown here.

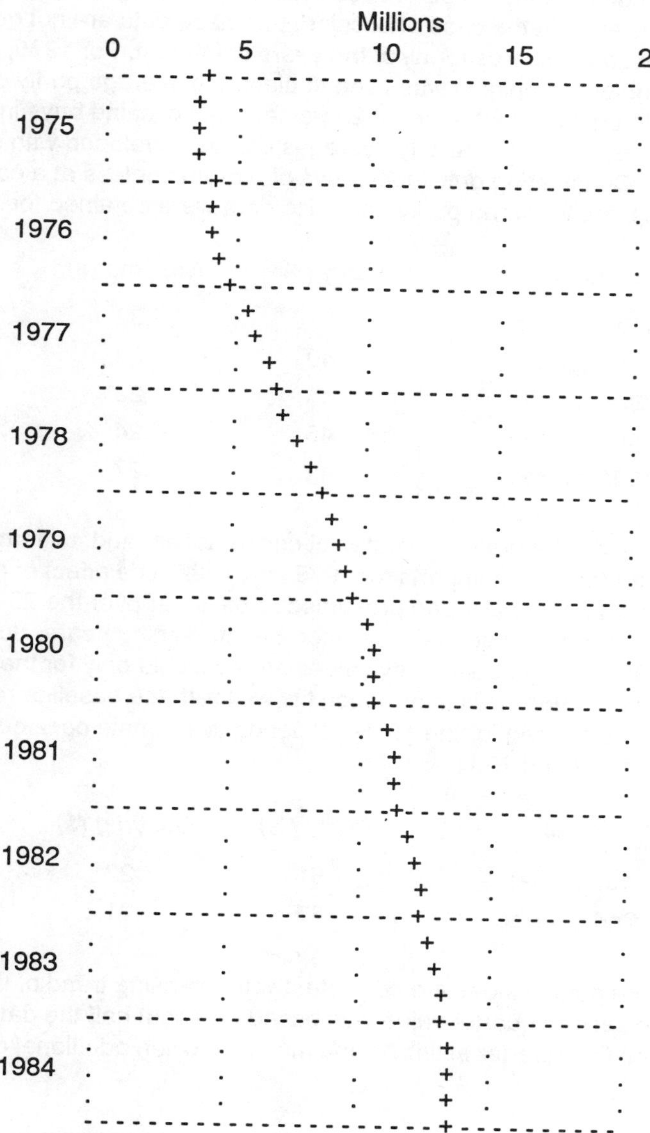

FIGURE 6. *Total cocaine user population*

HOW COCAINE ABUNDANCE AFFECTS COCAINE PURITY

Although the purity of the cocaine sold to users varies throughout the country, averages used in the development of the model were obtained from data acquired through purchases made by the Drug Enforcement Agency. However, in the case of cocaine, purchase data are not generated in adequate volumes for all of the years of interest. For 1975, for instance, subjective opinion was used to place the average purity of cocaine sold on the street at about 25 percent, but cocaine buys in 1982 were so numerous that quarterly averages can be developed with some confidence. Considering only those buys of 6 grams or less at a cost of $600 or less, the following purity and price data were obtained for 1982.

1982	*Purity (%)*	*Cost/mg ($)*
1st quarter	37	.32
2nd quarter	40	.28
3rd quarter	45	.26
4th quarter	45	.24
1982 average	42	.27

These values contribute to estimates of consumption, and, ultimately, the relative abundance and imports for 1975 and 1982. The effect of relative abundance on purity has been presumed to be linear over the 25- to 45-percent range in the absence of data for the intervening years. Subsequent to 1982, comparable purity values are available only for the first two quarters of 1984. This information fits well with the baseline relationship trends developed for the 1975–82 period to estimate cocaine imports for 1983 and 1984.

1984	*Purity (%)*	*Cost/mg ($)*
1st quarter	51	.22
2nd quarter	57	.21

Although the purity values are consistent with the rising trend of the 1980s, the second quarter value was based on about half the data points used for the first quarter estimate and may shift when additional data are available.

Given the ground rules of considering purchases of $600 or less and 6 grams or less, the purity levels may be somewhat conservative, because buys of low purity and high price are included but those of high purity and low price may be excluded. For example, one set of purity analyses processed in April 1984 included one buy in Florida of 4.07 grams for $175 that was 57 percent pure. However, if three additional buys of less than $600 but greater than 6 grams had been included—$500, $370, and $350—then the total amount purchased would have been 34.697 grams with an average purity of 73 percent. The price per milligram for the entire buy would have been $0.06.

The relationship between abundance and purity used in the model is shown in figure 7. The changes in purity from 1975 through 1984 are shown in figure 8.

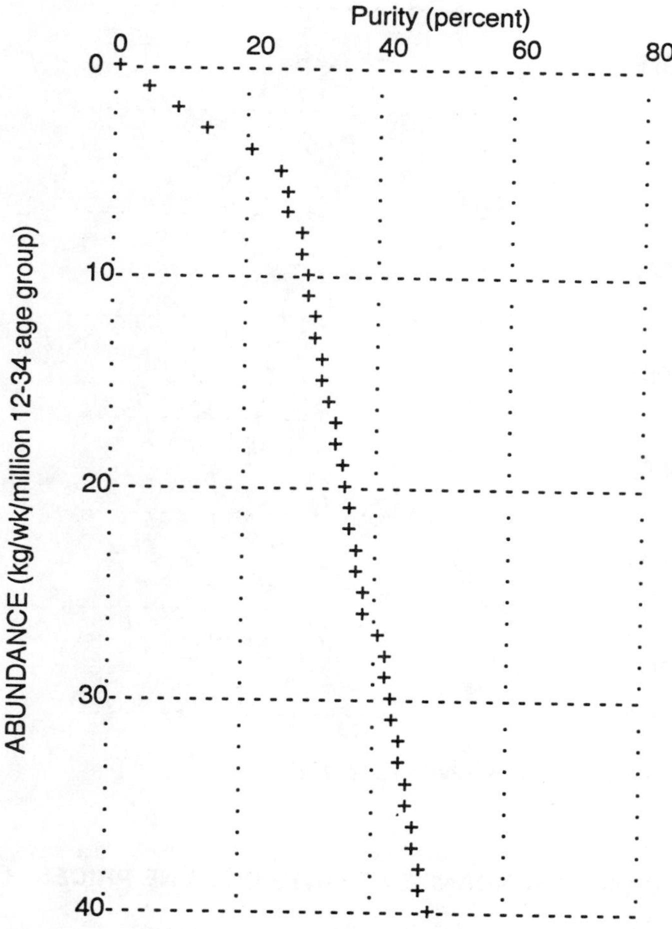

FIGURE 7. *Purity change with abundance*

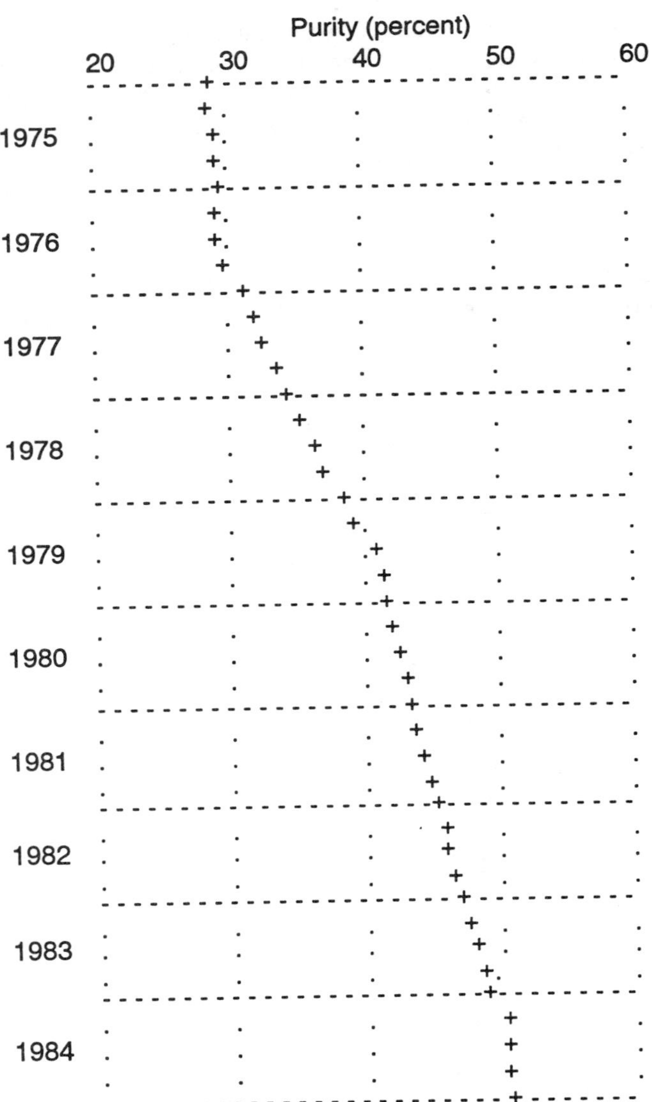

FIGURE 8. *Change in purity 1975 to 1984*

HOW COCAINE ABUNDANCE AFFECTS COCAINE PRICES

Cocaine prices reflect changes in abundance and reached a low of about $.20 per pure milligram in 1984. Allowing for inflation, this equates to about $.10 per pure milligram in 1975 dollars. The change with abundance used in the model, in constant 1975 dollars, is shown in figure 9.

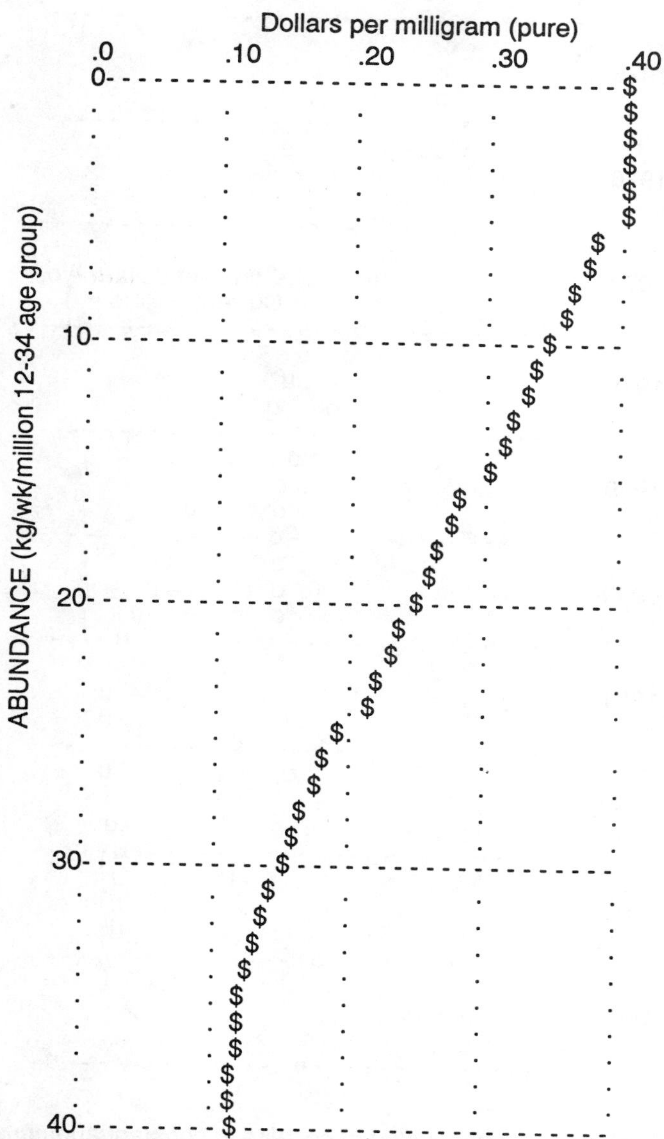

FIGURE 9. *Price change with abundance (constant 1975 dollars)*

The price reductions caused by greater abundance was largely offset by the rising quantity of cocaine sold during the 1975-84 period. This is shown in both constant 1975 dollars and current dollars in figure 10.

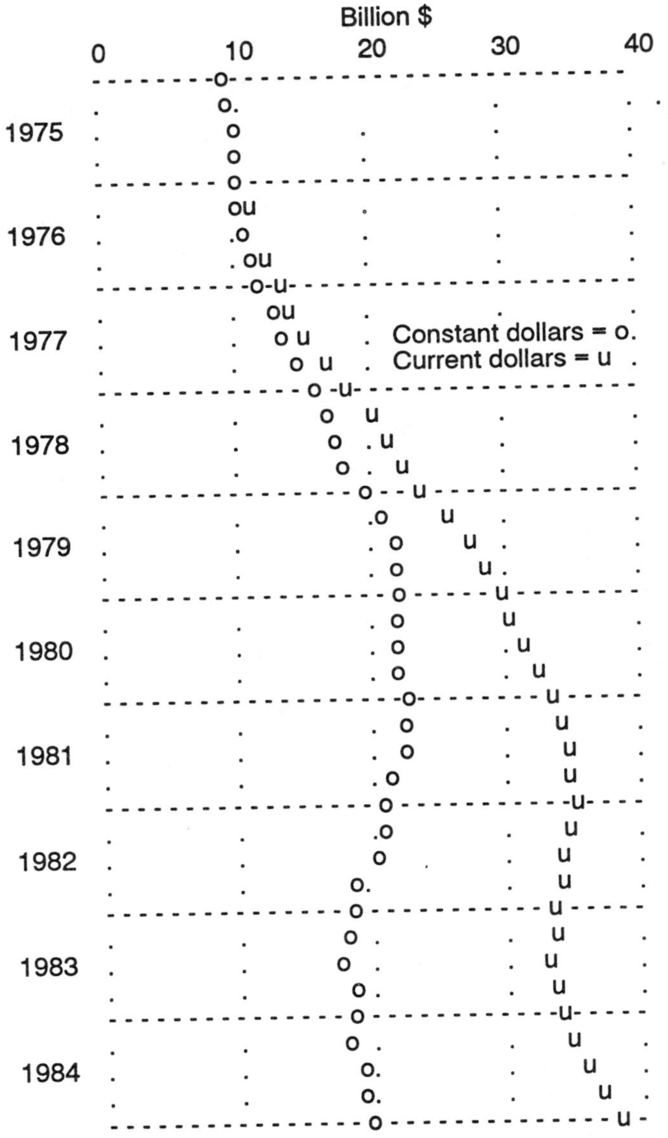

Billion $

0 10 20 30 40

1975

1976

1977

Constant dollars = o.

Current dollars = u

1978

1979

1980

1981

1982

1983

1984

FIGURE 10. *Annual street value of cocaine in constant and current dollars*

COCAINE CONSUMPTION

The amount of cocaine consumed depends on the number of users, their consumption habits, and the purity of the cocaine they use. The definition of users in the model, and their consumption, reflects both the modified User Population data from the NIDA household surveys and the presentations made by clinicians treating cocaine users at the Cocaine Technical Review conducted by NIDA in July 1984.

We assume that 36 percent of the Ever Used population are relatively trivial users who consume about 2 grams per year at the prevailing street purity level. We assume that 22 percent of the Ever Used group are monthly users, with 50 percent of this group using a gram a month, 40 percent a gram a week, and 10 percent a gram a day.

The significance of these assumptions is illustrated in Table 2.

TABLE 2. *Illustrative consumption estimate*

Those who had ever used cocaine in 1982	22 million
Last year users only (36%) number 7.9 million	
At 2 grams/year they use	15.8 tons/year
Last month users (22%) number 4.8 million	
50% of this group is 2.4 million	
At 1 gram/month they use	29.0 tons/year
40% of this group is 1.9 million	
At 1 gram/week they use	100.7 tons/year
10% of this group is .48 million	
At 1 gram/day they use	176.7 tons/year
Total consumption	322.2 tons/year
Total users is 12.7 million	
Average daily consumption is 70 milligrams/day	
At 42% purity, 1982 pure cocaine consumption is . . .	135 tons (pure)

The assumptions and values in table 2 are supported in several ways. The total number of Last Year users determined in table 2 as a percentage of the Ever Used group, 12.7 million, fits well with the Last Year population data for 1982 in table 1 since the truncated value of 10.932 million implies that the total Last Year population would be 12.1 million. The distribution of the consumption is reasonably consistent with a broadly applicable theory developed by the French epidemiologist, Sully Ledermann (1956). A NIDA-sponsored conference on Ledermann's theory, "An Examination of the Distribution of Consumption of Selected Dependence-Producing Drugs," held in 1984, supported the general validity of his notion that a small fraction of the users consume a major fraction of the drug. This is obviously the case here (table 3). The very low users make up a high percentage of the users but account for only about 5 percent of the annual consumption of cocaine. The 4 percent of the population who are big users consume the lion's share, 55 percent, of the cocaine.

TABLE 3. *Distribution of consumption*

User group	Percentage of users	Percentage of consumption
Annual	62	5
Monthly	19	9
Weekly	15	31
Daily	4	55

Because of this distribution, total consumption is quite sensitive to the number of heavy users and the amount they use. Other papers presented at the Cocaine Technical Review support the estimate of about 500,000 heavy cocaine users in the simulation model for 1982 in several ways. For example, Clayton estimated those having "serious problems" with cocaine at 550,000, noting that "The estimate of 550,000 . . . is a conservative one, an 'underestimate' of the 'true' prevalence of the number of problem users of cocaine in this society" (Clayton 1985). Clayton's estimate of 550,000 is just 2.5 percent of the Ever Used population in 1982; the 480,000 gram/day users in table 3 amount to slightly less than 2.2 percent of this Ever Used population. A toll-free hotline established in 1983 to provide information for crisis intervention and treatment referral to cocaine users, their family members, and treatment professionals received more than 450,000 calls in the first 18 months of operation (Gold et al. 1985). Gold reported that interviews with a randomly selected group of 300 callers during the first 3 months of operation of 800-COCAINE revealed that estimates of weekly cocaine use ranged from 1 to 32 grams per week, and the average frequency of use was 5.7 days per week.

Related studies found that upper income callers (over $50,000 per year) used an average of 15 grams per week, and middle-income users averaged 8.2 grams per week. In two separate surveys in the New York tristate area in 1983 and 1984, Gold et al. (1985) found that average weekly consumption rose from 5.5 grams to 6.2 grams per week. Schnoll found that the mean weekly consumption of cocaine by the patients in his Chicago treatment group exceeded 7 grams/week (Schnoll et al. 1985). Slightly over 56 percent of Schnoll's group were daily users, and the mean amount of cocaine used per episode was 2 to 3 grams. A study of 30 consecutive admissions to the Cocaine Abuse Treatment Program at the Drug Dependence Unit of the Yale University School of Medicine found that the mean consumption of cocaine per week was 5.3 grams for intranasal users, 5.6 grams for intravenous users, and 9.1 grams for those smoking cocaine free base (Gawin and Kleber 1985). Cocaine consumption consistent with these data and assumptions is shown in figure 11.

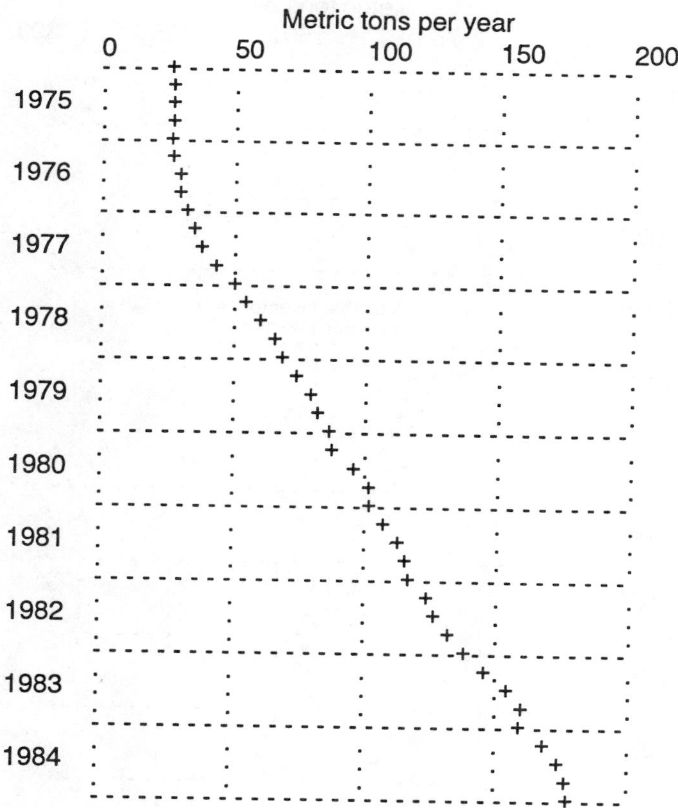

FIGURE 11. *Rate of cocaine consumption*

ESTIMATED COCAINE IMPORTS

The estimated cocaine imports that will result in the model user populations, purities, and prices corresponding to the historical data are shown in figure 12. The import rates are greater than the consumption rates because of the delay between the imports and their impact on the behavior of the system. One import rate is based on the maintenance of a 15-week inventory of cocaine at the present consumption rate. The other rate increases the inventory with abundance, and ends 1984 with a 35-week inventory. The actual imports no doubt lie between these two rates, but no data exist at present against which these inventory levels, and the associated delays, can be assessed. In the heroin model, delays in that system could be as long as 26 weeks. Because of the ready elasticity of

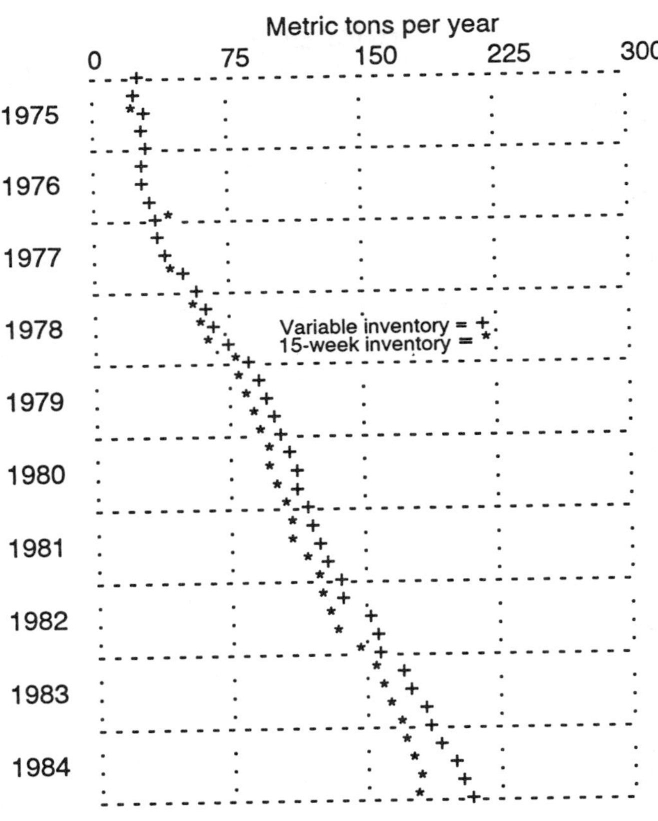

FIGURE 12. *Estimated rates of cocaine imports*

cocaine consumption with abundance, compared to the relative stiffness of heroin consumption, the response of the cocaine system could be faster, but, on the other hand, the cocaine system is much larger.

These estimates may be compared to production-based estimates of imports such as those reported by Montagne (this volume). Production-based estimates are likely to be lower because of active concealment by producers and numerous other factors.

In summary, this model establishes the generic, dynamic relationships among cocaine imports, the user population, price, and purity. These or similar relationships should hold regionally in the United States as well as for countries other than the United States.

REFERENCES

Gardiner, K., and Shreckengost, R.C. Estimating heroin imports into the United States. In: Rouse, B.A.; Kozel, N.J.; and Richards, L.G., eds. *Self-Report Methods of Estimating Drug Use: Current Challenges to Validity*. National Institute on Drug Abuse Research Monograph 57, DHHS Pub. No. (ADM)85–1402. Washington, DC: Supt. of Docs., U.S. Govt. Print. Off., 1985. pp. 141–157.

Gawin, F.H., and Kleber, H.D. Cocaine use in a treatment population: Patterns and diagnostic distinctions. In: Kozel, N.J., and Adams, E.H., eds. *Cocaine Use in America: Epidemiologic and Clinical Perspectives*. National Institute on Drug Abuse Research Monograph 61, DHHS Pub. No. (ADM)85–1414. Washington, DC: Supt. of Docs., U.S. Govt. Print. Off., 1985. pp. 182–192.

Gold, M.S.; Washton, A.M.; and Dakis, C.A. Cocaine abuse: Neurochemistry, phenomenology, and treatment. In: Kozel, N.J., and Adams, E.H., eds. *Cocaine Use in America: Epidemiologic and Clinical Perspectives*. National Institute on Drug Abuse Research Monograph 61, DHHS Pub. No. (ADM)85–1414. Washington, DC: Supt. of Docs., U.S. Govt. Print. Off., 1985. pp. 130–150.

Ledermann, S. *Alcohol, Alcool, Alcoolism, Alcoolisation. Donnees scientifiques de caractere psychologique, economique et social.* (Institut National d'Etudes Demographiques, Travaux et Documents, Cah. No. 29.) Paris: Presses Universitaires de France, 1956.

Miller, J.D.; Cisin, I.H.; Gardner-Keaton, H.; Harrell, A.V.; Wirtz, P.W.; Abelson, H.I.; and Fishburne, P.M. *National Survey on Drug Abuse: Main Findings 1982*. National Institute on Drug Abuse, DHHS Pub. No. (ADM)83–1263. Washington, DC: Supt. of Docs., U.S. Govt. Print. Off., 1983. pp. 16–24.

National Institute on Drug Abuse. *National Household Survey on Drug Abuse: 1985 Population Estimates*. DHHS Pub. No. (ADM)87-1539. Rockville, MD: the Institute, 1987.

Schnoll, S.H.; Karrigan, J.; Kitchen, S.B.; Daghestani, A.; and Hansen, T. Characteristics of cocaine abusers presenting for treatment. In: Kozel, N.J., and Adams, E.H., eds. *Cocaine Use in America: Epidemiologic and Clinical Perspectives*. National Institute on Drug Abuse Research Monograph 61, DHHS

Pub. No. (ADM)85–1414. Washington, DC: Supt. of Docs., U.S. Govt. Print. Off., 1985. pp. 171–181.

Shreckengost, R.C. Dynamic simulation models: How valid are they? In: Rouse, B.A.; Kozel, N.J.; and Richards, L.G., eds. *Self-Report Methods of Estimating Drug Use: Current Challenges to Validity*. National Institute on Drug Abuse Research Monograph 57, DHHS Pub. No. (ADM)85–1402. Washington, DC: Supt. of Docs., U.S. Govt. Print. Off., 1985. pp. 63–70.

Siegel, R.K. New patterns of cocaine use: Changing doses and routes. In: Kozel, N.J., and Adams, E.H., eds. *Cocaine Use in America: Epidemiologic and Clinical Perspectives*. National Institute on Drug Abuse Research Monograph 61, DHHS Pub. No. (ADM)85–1414. Washington, DC: Supt. of Docs., U.S. Govt. Print. Off., 1985. pp. 204–220.

Slayton, R.R. Cocaine in the United States: In a blizzard or just being snowed? In: Kozel, N.J., and Adams, E.H., eds. *Cocaine Use in America: Epidemiologic and Clinical Perspectives*. National Institute on Drug Abuse Research Monograph 61, DHHS Pub. No. (ADM)85–1414, Washington, DC: Supt. of Docs., U.S. Govt. Print. Off., 1985. pp. 8–34.

Social Research Group and the National Institute on Drug Abuse. *Population Projections Based on the National Survey on Drug Abuse, 1982*. National Institute on Drug Abuse, DHHS Pub. No. (ADM)83–1303. Rockville, MD: the Institute, 1983. p. 11.

APPENDIX
COCAINE USER POPULATION

The cocaine user population for the model is derived from national surveys sponsored by NIDA. In these surveys, cocaine users are divided into age groups that are subdivided according to cocaine use frequency. The age groups are 12 to 17, 18 to 25, and 26 and above; frequency of use is classified as those who have ever used cocaine, those who have used cocaine in the past year, and those who have used cocaine in the last month. The surveys are not conducted every year; estimates of the population are used for the years when surveys were not conducted.

The cocaine user population and use frequency table is based on trend data from the 1982 survey and Bureau of the Census data (Miller et al. 1983). The percentages relating to frequency of use refer to the 12- to 34-year-old age group.

Truncating the age group of 26 and above with 34-year-olds means that the populations used in the model are somewhat understated. This understatement is about 10 percent for all frequencies of use for 1982. A table in a supplemental publication gives user age group populations in greater detail (SRG and NIDA 1983). Using the 26- to 34-year-old user population for the three use frequencies, the 12 to 34 totals can be calculated and compared with the totals using the 26 plus age category. For the ever used category, the 12 to 34 population is 19,154,000 versus

21,570,000 for 12 and above; for last year use the values are 10,932,000 versus 11,900,000; for last month use the values are 3,814,000 versus 4,170,000. So, the 12-34 group accounts for 88.8 percent of the ever used population, 91.9 percent of the last year users, and 91 percent of the last month users.

The 26- to 34-year-old populations for various user frequencies for the years prior to 1982 were estimated to be 70 percent of the 26 and over population, based on projected population data (SRG and NIDA 1983). For 1982, the 26- to 34-year-old group who had ever used cocaine amounted to 65 percent of the ever used 26 and over population; for last year users, the 26- to 34-year-old group was 73 percent of the corresponding 26 and over population; for last month users, the 26- to 34-year-old group was 70 percent of those 26 and above.

Table A shows the Household Survey data and the derived values for the years when there was no survey during the period 1975–1982.

TABLE A. *Cocaine user populations by age group and frequency, 1975–82 (population in thousands)*

Age group	Group population	Ever Used No.	Ever Used %	Last Year No.	Last Year %	Last Month No.	Last Month %
			1975				
12–17	24,665	863	*	617	*	247	*
18–25	31,152	4,044		2,365		809	
26+	117,653	1,529		588		196	
26–34	28,324	1,070		411		137	
12–34 total	84,141	5,977		3,393		1,193	
			1976				
12–17	24,567	835	3.4	565	2.3	246	1.0
18–25	31,920	4,277	13.4	2,234	7.0	638	2.0
26+	119,864	1,918	1.6	719	0.6	240	<.5
26–34	29,484	1,342		503		168	
12–34 total	85,971	6,454		3,302		1,052	
			1977				
12–17	24,346	974	4.0	633	2.6	195	0.8
18–25	32,573	6,221	19.1	3,322	10.2	1,205	3.7
26+	122,203	3,177	2.6	1,100	0.9	267	<.5
26–34	30,599	1,557		770		257	
12–34 total	87,518	8,752		4,725		1,657	

TABLE A. *Continued*

Age group	Group population	Ever Used No.	Ever Used %	Last Year No.	Last Year %	Last Month No.	Last Month %
		1978					
12–17	24,078	1,132	*	819	*	265	*
18–25	33,118	7,716		4,935		2,152	
26+	124,772	4,242		1,747		582	
26–34	31,467	2,970		1,223		408	
12–34 total	88,663	11,818		6,977		2,825	
		1979					
12–17	23,596	1,274	5.4	991	4.2	330	1.4
18–25	33,667	9,258	27.5	6,599	19.6	3,131	9.3
26+	127,283	5,473	4.3	2,546	2.0	1,246	0.9
26–34	32,583	3,831		1,782		802	
12–34 total	89,846	14,363		9,372		4,263	
		1980					
12–17	23,045	1,314	*	968	*	323	*
18–25	34,106	9,481		6,582		2,899	
26+	129,923	7,406		3,378		1,299	
26–34	33,834	5,184		2,365		909	
12–34 total	90,985	15,979		9,915		4,131	
		1981					
12–17	22,381	1,365	*	918	*	336	*
18–25	34,344	9,616		6,525		2,610	
26+	132,333	9,396		4,235		1,456	
26–34	35,085	6,577		2,964		1,019	
12–34 total	91,810	17,558		10,407		3,965	
		1982					
12–17	21,725	1,412	6.5	891	4.1	348	1.6
18–25	34,315	9,711	28.3	6,451	18.8	2,333	6.8
26+	134,977	11,473	8.5	5,129	3.8	1,620	1.2
26–34	35,534	8,031		3,590		1,133	
12–34 total	91,574	19,154		10,932		3,814	

Source: Derived from NIDA National Household Surveys, U.S. Census, and Miller et al. 1983.

* Household survey data not available.

NOTES ON MODEL VALIDITY

The data used in the development of the model varied greatly in their statistical properties. For example, the 12- to 34-year-old population in the United States, derived from Census Bureau tables, is based on the national surveys conducted every 10 years. Population estimates for the intervals between surveys are generated by extrapolating the earlier data trends. The population estimates are probably good to within 2 percent.

The NIDA data on the number of cocaine users, and the frequency with which they use cocaine, are based on the National Household Survey taken every 2 or 3 years. Unlike the Census, the NIDA Household Surveys employ sampling techniques that, by their nature, produce values that are subject to increasing error with decreasing sample sizes. For the major categories—ever used cocaine and used it in the last year—the populations are quite large and the 95-percent confidence limits relatively narrow—a few percent. The samples become smaller for the those using cocaine in the last 30 days and last week, and the confidence limits expand accordingly.

The Drug Enforcement Agency conducts the sampling program from which drug purity and price are obtained. Unlike the NIDA program, this sampling program is not readily controlled. Further, purity and price data can vary greatly over short distances—say, between Washington, DC, and Rosslyn, VA—because of customer and marketing practices. Surprisingly, perhaps, the data behave well in the aggregate and can be used confidently to predict system behavior once their overall relationships have been defined. Some analyses presently in process may provide additional insight into the statistical properties of these data.

In system dynamic models, the customary measures for evaluating data and model performance are, for the most part, irrelevant. Simply stated, if the model includes the influences that experts in the field feel are appropriate for the problem being considered, and if the model exhibits behavior that replicates the behavior of the real system under similar circumstances, the model fulfills the objective—behaving like the real system.

BASIC COCAINE MODEL

```
    THE MODEL EXTENDS FROM 1975 THROUGH 84.
    BASIC TIME INTERVAL IS ONE WEEK.
    *** 12 THROUGH 34 AGE GROUP (AG) IS IN MILLIONS ***

AG.K=TABHL(AGT,TIME.K,0,520,26)                                  A,1
AGT=83.7/8.1/8.5/8.0/86.7/8.5/8.3/8.7/8.3/                       T,1.1
    89.8/9.4/9.0/91.4/9.6/9.6/9.6/9.6/9.6/
    91.6/9.6/9.6
        AG        - 12-34 AGE GROUP POPULATION <1>
        AGT       - 12-34 AGE GROUP TABLE <1>

    ********** SUPPLY SECTOR **********
    IMPORTS ARE KILOGRAMS OF PURE COCAINE PER WEEK

IN.K=TABLE(INT,TIME.K,0,520,26)                                  A,2
INT=480/500/525/535/675/840/1105/1385/1590/1820/                 T,2.1
    1940/2125/2220/2430/2600/2850/3100/3350/3600/
    3850/4100
        IN        - IMPORTS <2>
        INT       - IMPORTS TABLE <2>

INA.K=52*IN.K   S,3
        INA       - ANNUAL IMPORT RATE <3>
        IN        - IMPORTS <2>

    **** INVENTORY ****

I.K=I.J+DT*(CIN.JK-CC.JK)                                        L,4
I=II              N,4.1
II=2500           C,4.2
        I         - INVENTORY <4>
        CIN       - INVENTORY INPUT <5>
        CC        - INVENTORY LOSS <6>
        II        - INITIAL INVENTORY <4>

CIN.KL=IN.K                                                      R,5
        CIN       - INVENTORY INPUT <5>
        IN        - IMPORTS <2>

CC.KL=CUC.K                                                      R,6
        CC        - INVENTORY LOSS <6>
        CUC       - COCAINE USER CONSUMPTION <10>

    *** RELATIVE ABUNDANCE ***
```

CSR.K=IN.K/AG.K A,7

CSR - COCAINE ABUNDANCE RATIO <7>
IN - IMPORTS <2>
AG - 12-34 AGE GROUP POPULATION <1>

*** PERCEIVED RELATIVE ABUNDANCE ***

PCSR.K=SMOOTH(CSR.K,PD.K) A,8

PCSR - PERCEIVED ABUNDANCE RATIO <8>
CSR - COCAINE ABUNDANCE RATIO <7>
PD - PERCEPTION DELAY <9>

PD.K=TABHL(PDT,CSR.K,2.5,20,2.5) A,9
PDT=1/1.5/3/5/7.5/1.5/13/13 T, 9.1

PD - PERCEPTION DELAY <9>
PDT - PERCEPTION DELAY TABLE <9>
CSR - COCAINE ABUNDANCE RATIO <7>

*** COCAINE CONSUMPTION ***

CUC.K=MPU.K*CUP.K*CBC*7 A,10
CBC=70 C,10.1

CUC - COCAINE USER CONSUMPTION <10>
MPU - PURITY <23>
CUP - COCAINE USER POPULATION <13>
CBC - AVERAGE DAILY CONSUMPTION <10>

ANNUAL CONSUMPTION RATE

ACR.K=52*(CUC.K/1000) S,11

ACR - ANNUAL CONSUMPTION RATE <11>
CUC - COCAINE USER CONSUMPTION <10>

THE AVERAGE DAILY CONSUMPTION IS 70 MILLIGRAMS (CBC). THE AMOUNT OF PURE COCAINE IN THESE 70 MILLIGRAMS VARIES WITH PURITY—WHICH IS RELATED TO THE ABUNDANCE RATIO. WHEN THIS RATIO FALLS, PURITY FALLS: WHEN THE SUPPLY IS MORE ABUNDANT PURITY RISES.

*** COCAINE USER POPULATION ***

LAST YEAR USERS ARE A FRACTION OF THE 12-34 AGE GROUP (AG). THIS FRACTION IS COMPENSATED FOR THE 10% UNDER-ESTIMATE CAUSED BY TRUNCATING THE 26 AND OVER AGE GROUP AT AGE 34. CUPH POPULATION IS THAT POPULATION (CORRECTED) OF LAST YEAR USERS WHO USE AN AVERAGE OF 70 MILLIGRAMS OF STREET PURITY COCAINE DAILY.

```
CUP.K=FIFZE(CUPH.K,UP.K,US)                                      A,13
US=1                                                             C,13.1
        CUP     - COCAINE USER POPULATION <13>
        CUPH    - USER POPULATION FORM NIDA DATA <14>
        UP      - USER POPULATION BASED ON ABUNDANCE <15>
        US      - USER POPULATION SWITCH <13>

CUPH.K=CF*TABLE(CUPHT,TIME.K,0,520,26)                           A,14
CUPHT=3.4/3.5/3.6/3.7/4.3/5.0/5.9/6.8/7.55/8.3/8.8/              T,14.1
    9.3/9.7/1.2/1.6/1.1/1.1/1.1/1.1/1.1/1.1
    CF=1.1                                                       C,14.2
        CUPH    - USER POPULATION FROM NIDA DATA <14>
        CF      - POPULATION UNDERESTIMATE CORRECTION
                  FACTOR <14>
        CUPHT   - NIDA POPULATION TABLE <14>

    UP IS THE 70 MILLIGRAM USER POPULATION GENERATED
    THROUGH THE ABUNDANCE RATIO AND THE 12-34
    POPULATION

UP.K=CSRPM.K*AG.K                                                A,15
        UP      - USER POPULATION BASED ON ABUNDANCE <15>
        CSRPM   - POPULATION FRACTION BASED ON
                  ABUNDANCE <16>
        AG      - 12-34 AGE GROUP POPULATION <1>

CSRPM.K=TABHL(CSRPMT,PCSR.K,0,40,1)                              A,16
CSRPMT=0/.007/.01/.02/.03/.041/.046/.052/.057/.061/              T,16.1
    .066/.070/.074/.078/.082/.086/.090/.094/.098/
    .102/.105/.108/.111/.115/.118/.121/.124/.126/
    .129/.131/.133/.135/.137/.139/.141/.143/.145/
    .147/.148/.150/.151
        CSRPM   - POPULATION FRACTION BASED ON
                  ABUNDANCE <16>
        CSRPMT- ABUNDANCE-POPULATION FRACTION TABLE <16>
        PCSR    - PERCEIVED ABUNDANCE RATIO <8>

    PERCENT OF 12-34 POPULATION USING COCAINE

CUPP.K=CUP.K/AG.K                                                S,17
        CUPP    - FRACTION OF 12-34 POPULATION USING
                  COCAINE <17>
        CUP     - COCAINE USER POPULATION <13>
        AG      - 12-34 AGE GROUP POPULATION <1>

    THE INFLATION FACTOR IS BASED ON THE CONSUMER PRICE
    INDEX.
```

```
IF.K=TABLE(IFT,TIME.K,0,520,52)                                  A,18
IFT=1.0/1.0/1.06/1.13/1.21/1.35/1.53/1.69/1.79/                  T,18.1
   1.84/1.94
      IF        - INFLATION FACTOR <18>
      IFT       - INFLATION FACTOR TABLE <18>

CO$.K=TABHL(CO$T,PCSR.K,0,40,5)                                  A,19
CO$T=.4/.4/.35/.30/.25/.20/.15/.12/.11                           T,19.1
      CO$       - COST/MG IN CONSTANT DOLLARS <19>
      CO$T      - TABLE RELATING ABUNDANCE TO COST IN
                  CONSTANT $ <19>
      PCSR      - PERCEIVED ABUNDANCE RATIO <8>

CU$.K=IF.K*CO$.K                                                 S,20
      CU$       - COST/MG IN CURRENT DOLLARS <20>
      IF        - INFLATION FACTOR <18>
      CO$       - COST/MG IN CONSTANT DOLLARS <19>

CO$A.K=ACR.K*CO$.K                                               S,21
      CO$A      - ANNUAL CONSTANT DOLLAR RATE <21>
      ACR       - ANNUAL CONSUMPTION RATE <11>
      CO$       - COST/MG IN CONSTANT DOLLARS <19>

CU$A.K=IF.K*CO$A.K                                               S,22
      CU$A      - ANNUAL SALES IN CURRENT DOLLARS <22>
      IF        - INFLATION FACTOR <18>
      CO$A      - ANNUAL CONSTANT DOLLAR RATE <21>
```

MODEL PURITY

```
MPU.K=TABHL(MPUT,PCSR.K,0,50,5)                                  A,23
MPUT=0/.25/.284/.318/.352/.386/.42/.454/.488/.522/               T,23.1
   .556
      MPU       - PURITY <23>
      MPUT      - TABLE RELATING PURITY TO ABUNDANCE <23>
      PCSR      - PERCEIVED ABUNDANCE RATIO <8>

SPEC  DT=1/SAVPER=13/LENGTH=520                                  24
```

```
SAVE  CUPP,CUP,MPU,INA,CO$A,CU$A,ACR,CSR,PCSR,I      25
      CUPP   - FRACTION OF 12-34 POPULATION USING
               COCAINE <17>
      CUP    - COCAINE USER POPULATION <13>
      MPU    - PURITY <23>
      INA    - ANNUAL IMPORT RATE <3>
      CO$A   - ANNUAL CONSTANT DOLLAR RATE <21>
      CU$A   - ANNUAL SALES IN CURRENT DOLLARS <22>
      ACR    - ANNUAL CONSUMPTION RATE <11>
      CSR    - COCAINE ABUNDANCE RATIO <7>
      PCSR   - PERCEIVED ABUNDANCE RATIO <8>
      I      - INVENTORY <4>
```

LIST OF VARIABLES

SYMBOL	*T*	*WHR-CMP*	*DEFINITION*
ACR	S	11	ANNUAL CONSUMPTION RATE <11>
AG	A	1	12-34 AGE GROUP POPULATION <1>
AGT	T	1.1	12-34 AGE GROUP TABLE <1>
CBC	C	10.1	AVERAGE DAILY CONSUMPTION <10>
CC	R	6	INVENTORY LOSS <6>
CF	C	14.2	POPULATION UNDERESTIMATE CORRECTION FACTOR <14>
CIN	R	5	INVENTORY INPUT <5>
CO$	A	19	COST/MG IN CONSTANT DOLLARS <19>
CO$A	S	21	ANNUAL CONSTANT DOLLAR RATE <21>
CO$T	T	19.1	TABLE RELATING ABUNDANCE TO COST IN CONSTANT $ <19>
CSR	A	7	COCAINE ABUNDANCE RATIO <7>
CSRPM	A	16	POPULATION FRACTION BASED ON ABUNDANCE <16>
CSRPMT	T	16.1	ABUNDANCE-POPULATION FRACTION TABLE <16>
CU$	S	20	COST/MG IN CURRENT DOLLARS <20>
CU$A	S	22	ANNUAL SALES IN CURRENT DOLLARS <22>
CUC	A	10	COCAINE USER CONSUMPTION <10>
CUP	A	13	COCAINE USER POPULATION <13>
CUPH	A	14	USER POPULATION FROM NIDA DATA <14>
CUPHT	T	14.1	NIDA POPULATION TABLE <14>
CUPP	S	17	FRACTION OF 12-34 POPULATION USING COCAINE <17>

DT	C	24	
I	L	4	INVENTORY <4>
	N	4.1	
IF	A	18	INFLATION FACTOR <18>
IFT	T	18.1	INFLATION FACTOR TABLE <18>
II	C	4.2	INITIAL INVENTORY <4>
IN	A	2	IMPORTS <2>
INA	S	3	ANNUAL IMPORT RATE <3>
INT	T	2.1	IMPORTS TABLE <2>
LENGTH	C	24	
MPU	A	23	PURITY <23>
MPUT	T	23.1	TABLE RELATING PURITY TO ABUNDANCE <23>
PCSR	A	8	PERCEIVED ABUNDANCE RATIO <8>
PD	A	9	PERCEPTION DELAY <9>
PDT	T	9.1	PERCEPTION DELAY TABLE <9>
SAVPER	C	24	
UP	A	15	USER POPULATION BASED ON ABUNDANCE <15>
US	C	13.1	<13>

WHERE-USED LIST

SYMBOL	*WHERE-USED*
ACR	CO$A,S,21/SAVE,25
AG	CSR,A,7/UP,A,15/CUPP,S,17
AGT	AG,A,1
CBC	CUC,A,10
CC	I,L,4
CF	CUPH,A,14
CIN	I,L,4
CO$	CU$,S,20/CO$A,S,21
CO$A	CU$A,S,22/SAVE,25
CO$T	CO$,A,19
CSR	PCSR,A,8/PD,A,9/SAVE,25
CSRPM	UP,A,15
CSRPMT	CSRPM,A,16
CU$A	SAVE,25
CUC	CC,R,6/ACR,S,11
CUP	CUC,A,10/CUPP,S,17/SAVE,25
CUPH	CUP,A,13
CUPHT	CUPH,A,14
CUPP	SAVE,25

FIFZE	CUP,A,13
I	SAVE,25
IF	CU$,S,20/CU$A,S,22
IFT	IF,A,18
II	I,N,4.1
IN	INA,S,3/CIN,R,5/CSR,A,7
INA	SAVE,25
INT	IN,A,2
MPU	CUC,A,10/SAVE,25
MPUT	MPU,A,23
PCSR	CSRPM,A,16/CO$,A,19/MPU,A,23/SAVE,25
PD	PCSR,A,8
PDT	PD,A,9
SMOOTH	PCSR,A,8
TABHL	AG,A,1/PD,A,9/CSRPM,A,16/CO$,A,19/MPU,A,23
TABLE	IN,A,2/CUPH,A,14/IF,A,18
TIME	AG,A,1/IN,A,2/CUPH,A,14/IF,A,18
UP	CUP,A,13
US	CUP,A,13

SYMBOLS WITHOUT DEFINITIONS

DT
FIFZE
LENGTH
SAVPER
SMOOTH
TABHL
TABLE
TIME

AUTHOR

Raymond C. Shreckengost
RSS Associates, Inc.
2371 S. Queen Street
Arlington, VA 22202

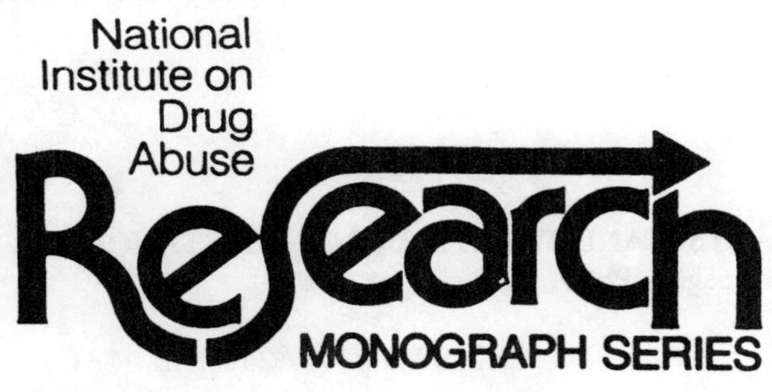

While limited supplies last, single copies of the monographs may be obtained free of charge from the National Clearinghouse for Alcohol and Drug Information (NCADI). Please contact NCADI also for information about availability of coming issues and other publications of the National Institute on Drug Abuse relevant to drug abuse research.

Additional copies may be purchased from the U.S. Government Printing Office (GPO) and/or the National Technical Information Service (NTIS) as indicated. NTIS prices are for paper copy; add $3.00 handling charge for each order. Microfiche copies are also available from NTIS. Prices from either source are subject to change.

Addresses are:

NCADI
National Clearinghouse for Alcohol and Drug Information
P.O. Box 2345
Rockville, MD 20852

GPO
Superintendent of Documents
U.S. Government Printing Office
Washington, D.C. 20402

NTIS
National Technical Information Service
U.S. Department of Commerce
Springfield, VA 22161
(703) 487-4650

For information on availability of NIDA Research Monographs 1-24 (1975-1979) and others not listed, write to NIDA, Community and Professional Education Branch, Room 10A-54, 5600 Fishers Lane, Rockville,

25 BEHAVIORAL ANALYSIS AND TREATMENT OF SUBSTANCE ABUSE. Norman A. Krasnegor, Ph.D., ed.
GPO out of stock
NCADI out of stock NTIS PB #80-112428/AS $31

26 THE BEHAVIORAL ASPECTS OF SMOKING. Norman A. Krasnegor, Ph.D., ed. (Reprint from 1979 Surgeon General's Report on Smoking and Health.)
GPO out of stock NTIS PB #80-118755/AS $23

30 THEORIES ON DRUG ABUSE: SELECTED CONTEMPORARY PERSPECTIVES. Dan J. Lettieri, Ph.D.; Mollie Sayers; and Helen W. Pearson, eds. GPO out of stock
NCADI out of stock Not available from NTIS

31 MARIJUANA RESEARCH FINDINGS: 1980. Robert C. Petersen, Ph.D., ed.
GPO out of Stock NTIS PB #80-215171/AS $31

32 GC/MS ASSAYS FOR ABUSED DRUGS IN BODY FLUIDS. Rodger L. Foltz, Ph.D.; Allison F. Fentiman, Jr., Ph.D.; and Ruth B. Foltz.
GPO out of Stock NCADI out of stock
NTIS PB #81-133746/AS $31

36 NEW APPROACHES TO TREATMENT OF CHRONIC PAIN: A REVIEW OF MULTIDISCIPLINARY PAIN CLINICS AND PAIN CENTERS. Lorenz K.Y. Ng, M.D., ed.
GPO out of Stock NCADI out of stock
NTIS PB #81-240913/AS $31

37 BEHAVIORAL PHARMACOLOGY OF HUMAN DRUG DEPENDENCE. Travis Thompson, Ph.D., and Chris E. Johanson, Ph.D., eds.
GPO out of Stock NCADI out of stock
NTIS PB #82-136961/AS $39

38 DRUG ABUSE AND THE AMERICAN ADOLESCENT. Dan J. Lettieri, Ph.D., and Jacqueline P. Ludford, M.S., eds. A RAUS Review Report. GPO out of Stock NCADI out of stock
NTIS PB #82-148198/AS $23

40 ADOLESCENT MARIJUANA ABUSERS AND THEIR FAMILIES. Herbert Hendin, M.D., Ann Pollinger, Ph.D., Richard Ulman, Ph.D., and Arthur Carr, Ph.D.
GPO out of Stock | NCADI out of stock
NTIS PB #82-133117/AS $23

42 THE ANALYSIS OF CANNABINOIDS IN BIOLOGICAL FLUIDS. Richard L. Hawks, Ph.D., ed.
GPO out of Stock | NTIS PB #83-136044/AS $23

44 MARIJUANA EFFECTS ON THE ENDOCRINE AND REPRODUCTIVE SYSTEMS. Monique C. Braude, Ph.D., and Jacqueline P. Ludford, M.S., eds. A RAUS Review Report.
GPO out of Stock | NCADI out of stock
NTIS PB #85-150563/AS $23

45 CONTEMPORARY RESEARCH IN PAIN AND ANALGESIA, 1983. Roger M. Brown, Ph.D.; Theodore M. Pinkert, M.D., J.D.; and Jacqueline P. Ludford, M.S., eds. A RAUS Review Report.
GPO out of Stock | NCADI out of stock
NTIS PB #84-184670/AS $17

46 BEHAVIORAL INTERVENTION TECHNIQUES IN DRUG ABUSE TREATMENT. John Grabowski, Ph.D.; Maxine L. Stitzer, Ph.D., and Jack E. Henningfield, Ph.D., eds.
GPO out of Stock | NCADI out of stock
NTIS PB #84-184688/AS $23

47 PREVENTING ADOLESCENT DRUG ABUSE: INTERVENTION STRATEGIES. Thomas J. Glynn, Ph.D.; Carl G. Leukefeld, D.S.W.; and Jacqueline P. Ludford, M.S., eds. A RAUS Review Report.
GPO out of stock | NCADI out of stock
NTIS PB #85-159663/AS $31

48 MEASUREMENT IN THE ANALYSIS AND TREATMENT OF SMOKING BEHAVIOR. John Grabowski, Ph.D., and Catherine Bell, M.S., eds.
GPO out of stock | NCADI out of stock
NTIS PB #84-145184/AS $23

50 COCAINE: PHARMACOLOGY, EFFECTS, AND TREATMENT OF ABUSE. John Grabowski, Ph.D., ed.
GPO Stock #017-024-01214-9 $4 NTIS PB #85-150381/AS $23

51 DRUG ABUSE TREATMENT EVALUATION: STRATEGIES, PROGRESS, AND PROSPECTS. Frank M. Tims, Ph.D., ed.
GPO out of stock NTIS PB #85-150365/AS $23

52 TESTING DRUGS FOR PHYSICAL DEPENDENCE POTENTIAL AND ABUSE LIABILITY. Joseph V. Brady, Ph.D., and Scott E. Lukas, Ph.D., eds.
GPO out of stock NTIS PB #85-150373/AS $23

53 PHARMACOLOGICAL ADJUNCTS IN SMOKING CESSATION. John Grabowski, Ph.D., and Sharon M. Hall, Ph.D., eds.
GPO out of stock NCADI out of stock
NTIS PB #89-123186/AS $23

54 MECHANISMS OF TOLERANCE AND DEPENDENCE. Charles Wm. Sharp, Ph.D., ed.
GPO out of Stock NCADI out of stock
NTIS PB #89-103279/AS $39

55 PROBLEMS OF DRUG DEPENDENCE, 1984: PROCEEDINGS OF THE 46TH ANNUAL SCIENTIFIC MEETING, THE COMMITTEE ON PROBLEMS OF DRUG DEPENDENCE, INC. Louis S. Harris, Ph.D., ed.
GPO out of Stock NCADI out of stock
NTIS PB #89-123194/AS $45

56 ETIOLOGY OF DRUG ABUSE: IMPLICATIONS FOR PREVENTION. Coryl LaRue Jones, Ph.D., and Robert J. Battjes, D.S.W., eds.
GPO Stock #017-024-01250-5 $6.50 NTIS PB #89-123160/AS $31

57 SELF-REPORT METHODS OF ESTIMATING DRUG USE: MEETING CURRENT CHALLENGES TO VALIDITY. Beatrice A. Rouse, Ph.D., Nicholas J. Kozel, M.S., and Louise G. Richards, Ph.D., eds.
GPO out of stock NTIS PB #88-248083/AS $23

58 PROGRESS IN THE DEVELOPMENT OF COST-EFFECTIVE TREATMENT FOR DRUG ABUSERS. Rebecca S. Ashery, D.S.W., ed.
GPO out of stock NTIS PB #89-125017/AS $23

59 CURRENT RESEARCH ON THE CONSEQUENCES OF MATERNAL DRUG ABUSE. Theodore M. Pinkert, M.D., J.D., ed.
GPO out of stock NTIS PB #89-125025/AS $23

60 PRENATAL DRUG EXPOSURE: KINETICS AND DYNAMICS. C. Nora Chiang, Ph.D., and Charles C. Lee, Ph.D., eds.
GPO out of stock NTIS PB #89-124564/AS $23

61 COCAINE USE IN AMERICA: EPIDEMIOLOGIC AND CLINICAL PERSPECTIVES. Nicholas J. Kozel, M.S., and Edgar H. Adams, M.S., eds.
GPO out of stock NTIS PB #89-131866/AS $31

62 NEUROSCIENCE METHODS IN DRUG ABUSE RESEARCH. Roger M. Brown, Ph.D., and David P. Friedman, Ph.D., eds.
GPO out of stock NCADI out of stock
NTIS PB #89-130660/AS $23

63 PREVENTION RESEARCH: DETERRING DRUG ABUSE AMONG CHILDREN AND ADOLESCENTS. Catherine S. Bell, M.S., and Robert J. Battjes, D.S.W., eds.
GPO out of stock NTIS PB #89-103287/AS $31

64 PHENCYCLIDINE: AN UPDATE. Doris H. Clouet, Ph.D., ed.
GPO out of stock NTIS PB #89-131858/AS $31

65 WOMEN AND DRUGS: A NEW ERA FOR RESEARCH. Barbara A. Ray, Ph.D., and Monique C. Braude, Ph.D., eds.
GPO Stock #017-024-01283-1 $3.25 NTIS PB #89-130637/AS $23

66 GENETIC AND BIOLOGICAL MARKERS IN DRUG ABUSE AND ALCOHOLISM. Monique C. Braude, Ph.D., and Helen M. Chao, Ph.D. eds.
GPO out of stock NCADI out of stock
NTIS PB #89-134423/AS $23

68 STRATEGIES FOR RESEARCH ON THE INTERACTIONS OF DRUGS OF ABUSE. Monique C. Braude, Ph.D., and Harold M. Ginzburg, M.D.,J.D., eds.
GPO out of stock NCADI out of stock
NTIS PB #89-134936/AS $31

69 OPIOID PEPTIDES: MEDICINAL CHEMISTRY. Rao S. Rapaka, Ph.D.; Gene Barnett, Ph.D.; and Richard L. Hawks, Ph.D., eds.
GPO out of stock NTIS PB #89-158422/AS $39

70 OPIOID PEPTIDES: MOLECULAR PHARMACOLOGY, BIOSYNTHESIS, AND ANALYSIS. Rao S. Rapaka, Ph.D., and Richard L. Hawks, Ph.D., eds.
GPO out of stock NTIS PB #89-158430/AS $45

71 OPIATE RECEPTOR SUBTYPES AND BRAIN FUNCTION. Roger M. Brown, Ph.D.; Doris H. Clouet, Ph.D.; and David P. Friedman, Ph.D., eds.
GPO out of stock NTIS PB #89-151955/AS $31

72 RELAPSE AND RECOVERY IN DRUG ABUSE. Frank M. Tims, Ph.D., and Carl G. Leukefeld, D.S.W., eds.
GPO Stock #017-024-01302-1 $6 NTIS PB #89-151963/AS $31

73 URINE TESTING FOR DRUGS OF ABUSE. Richard L. Hawks, Ph.D., and C. Nora Chiang, Ph.D., eds.
GPO Stock #017-024-01313-7 $3.75 NTIS PB #89-151971/AS $23

74 NEUROBIOLOGY OF BEHAVIORAL CONTROL IN DRUG ABUSE. Stephen I. Szara, M.D., D.Sc., ed.
GPO Stock #017-024-1314-5 $3.75 NTIS PB #89-151989/AS $23

75 PROGRESS IN OPIOID RESEARCH. PROCEEDINGS OF THE 1986 INTER- NATIONAL NARCOTICS RESEARCH CONFERENCE. John W. Holaday, Ph.D.; Ping-Yee Law, Ph.D.; and Albert Herz, M.D., eds.
GPO out of stock NCADI out of stock
Not available from NTIS